M000197794

Death Squads
in Global Perspective

Death Squads
in Global Perspective
Murder with Deniability

Edited by

Bruce B. Campbell
and Arthur D. Brenner

palgrave
macmillan

DEATH SQUADS IN GLOBAL PERSPECTIVE
Copyright © Bruce B. Campbell and Arthur D. Brenner, 2000.
All rights reserved. No part of this book may be used or reproduced
in any manner whatsoever without written permission except in the
case of brief quotations embodied in critical articles or reviews.

First published by PALGRAVE MACMILLAN™ in 2002.
175 Fifth Avenue, New York, N.Y. 10010 and
Houndmills, Basingstoke, Hampshire, England RG21 6XS.
Companies and representatives throughout the world.

PALGRAVE MACMILLAN is the global academic imprint of the
Palgrave Macmillan division of St. Martin's Press, LLC and of
Palgrave Macmillan Ltd. Macmillan® is a registered trademark in
the United States, United Kingdom and other countries. Palgrave is
a registered trademark in the European Union and other countries.

ISBN 0–312–21365–4 hardback
ISBN 1–4039–6094–1 paperback

Library of Congress Cataloging-in-Publication Data
Campbell, Bruce, 1955-
Death squads in global perspective : murder with deniability / Bruce
B. Campbell and Arthur D. Brenner.
        p.   cm.
    Includes bibliographical references and index.
    ISBN 0–312–21365–4 (cl) 1–4039–6094–1 (pbk)
      1. Death Squads.   2. Brenner, Arthur David.   II. Title.

HV6322.C36   2000
303.6'25—dc21   00 - 021797

A catalogue record for this book is available from the British
Library.

Design by Letra Libre, Inc.

First Publishedby Palgrave Macmillian: October 2002
10   9   8   7   6   5   4   3   2   1

CONTENTS

PREFACE

WHILE DOING HIS DOCTORAL RESEARCH IN THE LATE 1980s for a biography of the Weimar German pacifist and professor Emil J. Gumbel, the leading chronicler of political violence in Weimar Germany, Arthur D. Brenner was struck by the parallels between the paramilitary organizations of the 1920s and the Latin American death squads that were much in the U.S. news at the time. Some bibliographic searching, however, revealed no comparative studies of death squads, and by the time he completed his Ph.D. in 1993, he had determined to compile a collection of scholarly essays on death squads around the world. Early the following year, the editors met at an academic conference and discussed the idea, which led shortly thereafter to an agreement to collaborate on this book. Bruce B. Campbell had already been working on German paramilitary groups for some time, and was trying to work out a larger explanation of why paramilitary organizations exist and what purpose they serve. This research proved very useful in looking at death squads in a new way and blended well into the project.

Once we had the basic idea of editing a comparative study of death squads, we began the challenging task of finding likely contributors. This was a long process with many difficulties. We are, after all, both specialists in the history of Germany in the twentieth century. While it was not too difficult to identify scholars working on the well-known death squads of Central and South America, other parts of the world proved more difficult. Some specialists were accustomed to conceptualizing the objects of their study in frameworks that did not include the concept of "death squads." This left us not only trying to find the right people and the right channels of communication in fields well outside our expertise, but also attempting to persuade some colleagues to think about their subjects in new ways. The search was exciting, and the contacts we had with our contributors and a host of others along the way proved very enriching. There were, of course, the usual difficulties involved with bringing a book to press, but some were not so usual. We deeply regret the untimely death of Prof. Gregory Gugel, who was engaged in preparing a chapter for this book on South African death squads in Namibia at the time of his passing. We sorely miss the ebullient personality that shone through his letters and e-mail messages.

If we have other regrets, they are in the nature of "the one that got away." We wanted to include more case studies from Africa and Europe and tried in vain to arrange for a study of the early Ku Klux Klan in the United States. As with historical cases from before the 1950s, a variety of circumstances conspired to negate these plans. Personal and professional commitments prevented several scholars who had expressed an interest in contributing to the book from doing so.

As we began to research death squads more and more, we were rapidly confirmed in our initial belief that death squads are a major problem worldwide. We also discovered that they are not simply a product of the Cold War but have, in fact, been active for much longer than we had at first expected (see the chapter by Bruce B. Campbell, below, for more on the subject of chronology).

The book begins with a theoretical essay (Chapter 1) by Bruce B. Campbell. It prepares the way for the case studies that make up the rest of the book by presenting a working definition of death squads and a review of the literature. Beyond this, it points out several problems in current understanding of how and why death squads exist and proposes a historical framework for considering them that should help resolve some difficulties in how death squads have been defined and conceived to date. He links the appearance of death squads to a crisis of the modern state and considers them as one instance of a much wider process of "subcontracting" that characterizes nearly all states in the twentieth century.

The case studies are divided into four sections. The first covers two historical cases that demonstrate the existence of death squads well before World War II. Michael J. Schroeder's essay, "'To Induce a Sense of Terror': Caudillo Politics and Political Violence in Northern Nicaragua, 1926–34 and 1981–95" (Chapter 2), examines political gang violence and death squad activity in the mountainous Segovias of north-central Nicaragua during two non-contiguous periods of state crisis: the aftermath of the 1926–27 civil war and the Sandino rebellion that followed (1927–34), and the Contra war of the 1980s and its aftermath in the 1990s. He situates the origins and characteristics of the violence within the broader contexts of state formation and crisis, patron-client relations, local-regional *caudillismo,* and imperialist intervention. Schroeder argues that collective action and organized political violence that can be characterized as death squad activity form an integral part of modern Nicaraguan history and that any effort to better understand that history must pay such practices close and abiding attention.

Following this is Arthur D. Brenner's essay, "*Feme* Murder: Paramilitary 'Self-Justice' in Weimar Germany" (Chapter 3). It concerns the murderous "self-justice" practiced by illegal paramilitary units between 1920 and 1923 in order to protect the clandestinity of military activity that contravened the Versailles Peace Treaty. The narrow subculture in which the death squads were active and the limited scope of "crimes" for which they meted out punishment helps account for the relatively low number of victims they claimed. The author argues that a central characteristic of the modern state— its division of vast responsibility horizontally, across many agencies at any given level, and vertically, into national and regional authorities with considerable responsibility and autonomy within their spheres—was a crucial factor in facilitating the emergence of death squads and in giving the state the impunity it desires when it creates or tolerates these forces.

The second section looks at cases in which death squads were used by ostensibly democratic regimes undergoing periods of transition. These chapters suggest conditions that make the appearance of death squads likely in other places in the future. Chapter 4, by Cynthia J. Arnson, discusses one of the best-known and representative appearances of death squads. "Window on the Past: A Declassified History of Death Squads in El Salvador" reexamines the internal conflict in El Salvador from 1979 to 1991 in light of important information recently declassified by the United States government. This new information provides valuable information about the origins, structure, financing, practices, and personnel involved in death squad activity there. The article documents how death squads operated out of officially constituted security bodies, including the police, National Guard, army, and air force, and how privately organized and financed groups maintained close connections to official forces. The article also evaluates the role of the U.S. government in reporting on and attempting to curb death squad activity.

The author of Chapter 5, Eva-Lotta Hedman, examines the Philippines during the Aquino presidency in "State of Siege: Political Violence and Vigilante Mobilization in the Philippines." This chapter focuses on the counterinsurgency campaigns conducted in the Philippines since 1986. After nearly 15 years of de facto martial law, the organizational strength and reach of the Communist Party of the Philippines made it the largest revolutionary movement in Asia by the mid-1980s. The fall of Marcos ushered in the restoration of formally democratic procedures and institutions after February 1986; it also anticipated the stepped-up counterinsurgency campaigns introduced under Aquino. One remarkable aspect of the counterinsurgency campaigns is the spectacular role played by anticommunist vigilantes. Officially designated as "civilian volunteer organizations," such vigilantes have also included de facto paramilitary groups. Their abuses have been portrayed as aberrations in a highly institutionalized and professionalized military counterinsurgency effort. However, closer examination of government policy and military strategy reveals the extent to which the decentralized command structure and deployment of violence allowed this vigilante phenomenon to underpin and to propel this campaign in significant ways.

The third section looks at death squads used for purposes of social control, though they all illustrate fairly complex situations. In Chapter 6, the focus moves to Africa and the bloody regime of Idi Amin, in "State Terrorism and Death Squads in Uganda (1971–79)." Here, Edward Kannyo looks at the three major death squads that were responsible for the killing of thousands of people. The State Research Bureau, the Public Safety Unit, and the Military Police were all formally parts of the security forces, yet all either contained or acted as death squads. The chapter starts with a brief theoretical analysis of the concept of state terrorism that formed the backdrop to these killings. This is followed by a discussion of the political and historical background that led to the emergence of the regime, a description of the nature and modus operandi of the death squads and of the victims of their criminal activities, and a brief analysis of the problem of impunity.

Robert Cribb's piece, "From *Petrus* to Ninja: Death Squads in Indonesia," is Chapter 7. He examines the history of Indonesia, which presents a curious lack of death squad activity, given the great violence that has often been employed there since independence in

1945. He examines two outbreaks of death squads that break with the pattern and seeks an explanation for them. These are the *petrus* killings of criminals by military death squads in the early and mid-1980s and the "ninja" who launched campaigns of kidnapping and assassination against traditional Islamic leaders in the Javanese countryside in the days surrounding the fall of Suharto in 1998. Cribb explains the lack of death squad use in general by the weakness of the rule of law in Indonesia, combined with the very strong influence exercised by the Indonesian military, which refused to compromise its monopoly on the use of violence. The *petrus* killings marked the elimination of criminal elements associated with the losing side in an internal factional dispute within the Indonesian regime, while the ninjas targeted people suspected of using black magic. Cribb concludes his chapter with the prediction that violence in Indonesia is likely to increase, and with it, the potential for the reuse of death squads.

The final chapter in this section is by Martha K. Huggins. Her "Modernity and Devolution: The Making of Police Death Squads in Modern Brazil" (Chapter 8) examines the social and organizational roots of death squads in Brazil from their origins in the military period (1964–85) through their continuation into the redemocratizing era (post-1985). Through several case examples, she illustrates the symbiosis between formal police systems and informal death squads. Her thesis focuses on state devolution and proposes that death squads are a product of state deconstruction, where part of the formal system splits off, debureaucratizes, and increasingly carries out violence clandestinely and extralegally. She proposes six sources of devolution into death squads based on the Brazilian data and suggests that these sources may work not singly, but in tandem.

The fourth section considers three death squad episodes that grew out of national, ethnic, and/or religious conflicts; here again are circumstances that point to the likelihood that death squads will arise to plague other societies in the future. The first essay, Chapter 9, is by Keith Gottschalk and concerns South Africa in the apartheid era. "The Rise and Fall of Apartheid's Death Squads, 1969–93" looks at death squads formed by the Bureau of State Security (BOSS), the Security Police, and the South African Defense Forces. Gottschalk further examines the subcontracting of killing through state support for separate groups of "vigilantes" organized by competing interests within the majority black and "colored" communities. These organizations worked in tandem with "official" death squads to murder opponents of the regime, spread terror, and provide a welcome justification for extreme state measures. Gottschalk's chapter also singles out the important role of South Africa's intervention in Namibia, where many of the techniques and forms of violence later used within South Africa were first tried.

Patricia Gossman approaches the subject of "India's Secret Armies" (Chapter 10) with the tools and methods of a human rights worker. She looks at the use of death squads in counterinsurgency campaigns by the Indian security forces, first in Punjab and then, using the "Punjab solution," in Jammu and Kashmir. She sees their use as symptomatic of a much larger crisis in governance. India, with a long democratic tradition, has been unable to overcome threats to its internal security through legal means, yet is unwilling to tarnish its reputation through too much direct government use of violence. It has thus turned to death squads, often made up of former rebels. The result of this decision is not only thousands of deaths, but also severe damage to democratic institutions and the routinization of extreme and illegal measures.

Finally, in Chapter 11, James Ron examines the recent conflict in Bosnia and the former Yugoslavia in "Territoriality and Plausible Deniability: Serbian Paramilitaries in the Bosnian War." During the first months of the Bosnian war, ethnic Serb paramilitary forces assumed a central role in the fighting, functioning as death squads on behalf of the Bosnian Serb military effort. Some analysts have suggested that paramilitaries are endemic to Serbian or Balkan culture, but Ron argues that the paramilitaries were a rational response by Serbian leaders to a series of external constraints. Although Serbian leaders hoped to send troops to all corners of the Serbian ethnos—including areas of Bosnia and Croatia—its official forces were largely confined to the rump Yugoslav territory of Serbia as a result of pressure by local and international actors. Serbia secretly helped the paramilitaries fight Muslims and Croats in Bosnia, however, hoping to avoid direct responsibility for the violence. Serbian political and military leaders created a web of clandestine connections to the paramilitary death squads, details of which remain hidden until today.

We feel that taken as a whole, the essays in this book advance the state of our understanding about death squads. The collection certainly shows that death squads have a wide—even global—geographic

scope. One of our goals from the beginning has been to bring specialists who work on different regions together to discuss a common problem, and we feel that we have succeeded in at least beginning a wider,
comparative dialogue that should help advance the state of knowledge
about this phenomenon for years to come. We have also demonstrated
that the use of death squads cannot simply be ghettoized as a problem
only of "third world" or of "weak" states, at least in any simplistic
fashion. While they tend to be used mainly in poorer, economically
weaker, and less cohesive states, they appear also in many other societies, and may on occasion even figure in the repertoire of strong, industrialized states. We have not tried to do much here to examine the
kinds of factors that stimulate the use of death squads. There is already
some very useful research on this topic, and we hope that more will
follow, stimulated by our work here to widen the scope of study.

The papers in this collection all illustrate the importance of the
state as an actor in the formation or toleration of death squads. In
every case, states have been actively involved in the killing of their
own citizens or complicit with the killers. But at the same time, all
of the papers here demonstrate the influence and participation of
nonstate forces. With the possible exception of Uganda, each case
also exemplifies the process of "subcontracting" so characteristic of
modern states. This process of subcontracting or devolution of state
authority is a slippery slope; as several papers document (Gossman,
Huggins, Ron), once state security forces embark on a process of
subcontracting killing and intimidation, it begins to snowball,
threatening to get or actually getting out of hand. Use of people
drawn from the criminal underworld, or "turned" opponents, is
often the next step.

The contributions here also demonstrate that death squads may
be used in a wide variety of situations. They are not just products of
the Cold War and proxy wars between superpowers. Certainly, the
Cold War helped produce a characteristic situation for the use of
death squads, and superpower "advice" very likely stimulated their
formation in several cases. Yet we now find ourselves well into the
post–Cold War era, and death squads are still with us. Indeed, there
is every likelihood that they will only grow in prevalence.

While the struggle against a domestic insurgency which was a
part of the context for the best-known Latin American cases is certainly common in cases in which death squads were or are used, it is
by no means the only possible one. Crises of crime control, "ethnic"

conflicts, threats to national security other than an insurgency, certain kinds of bureaucratization, and more can all produce the use of death squads. While economic factors may be important in many of these scenarios, we hope that we have called into question the idea that death squads may be caused simply by a country's position in the world capitalist system. Again, we do not reject the impact of dependency and capitalist exploitation completely, but see its role in the puzzle as no longer determinant. Several of the case studies we present here concern states that are not in conditions of abject dependency and are either developed (Weimar Germany), socialist (Serbia, the former Yugoslavia), well on the way to development (Brazil), or fairly isolated from world markets (Amin's Uganda).

We were also interested from the very beginning in adding more of a historical context to the study of death squads. This was a product of our own training and professional bias—we are both historians—but a study of the literature seemed to point to a lack of consideration of larger historical factors beyond each individual and immediate situation. We have shown that death squads have been around much longer than originally thought and we have advanced some reasons for this state of affairs.

This is not to discount or minimize local and specific factors. If death squads are products of almost universal forces rooted in the shape of the modern state and its particular set of challenges, the exact form they take and their role and function are often the result of highly particular historical contingencies. In this regard, the importance of cultural factors in the expression of violence is of special importance. Modernization, the workings of world capitalism, or sets of international norms may function as nearly universal factors, but they should not blind us to the importance of culture and local history in setting the parameters of each individual case. Our book is a step in this direction, but this is one area where there is considerable room for further research.

Some papers also show the limits of an all too abstract and artificial definition of death squads: any definition such as the one used as a basis here is only a tool, and shouldn't be taken as absolute or "real." Certainly the Bosnian, Ugandan, Philippine, and Nicaraguan cases all challenge our definition in different and important ways. Once again, there is much yet to understand, and we hope and expect that the process of investigating death squads will not stop with this volume.

In putting together this book, we have benefited from the support and assistance, large and small, of many people who submitted proposals that for one reason or another could not be included in the anthology; shared with us their expertise on the subject; or put us in contact with other interested parties, some of whose contributions are included in the present work. These individuals deserve our thanks for this help: Richard Abel, Gary Abramson, Olutayo Charles Adesina, M. Cherif Bassiouni, Russell A. Berman, Perry Biddiscombe, Jim Bill, Ruth Bettina Birn, Lizie Brock, Christopher Browning, Carl Boyd, Agnes Callamard, David Chandler, Robert Corbett, E. Valentine Daniel, Patricia Dorval, Allen Feldman, Michael Fisher, Eric Goldstein, Jeannine Guthrie, Elaine Hagopian, A. D. Harvey, Joost Hiltermann, Robert Holden, Oscar Jaime-Jimenez, Suzanne Jonas, George Klay Kieh, Jr., Robert Koehl, Tom Lansford, Zunetta Liddell, Susan Linnée, George Lopez, John Lynch, Bronwen Manby, Ron May, Tom McKenna, Al McCoy, Richard Millet, José Ramon Montero, Negin Nabavi, Paula Newberg, Ronald C. Newton, Augustus Richard Norton, Stanislao G. Pugliese, Fernando Reinares, Tony Robben, Sara Roy, Rosanne Rutten, Madeleine Sann, Andrew Selth, Goldie Shabad, Steve Shalom, John Sidel, Ivanka Sket, Geoffrey Sluka, Frank Smyth, Doris Somer, Robert Springborg, Eric Strahorn, Anthony Vital, Eric Wakin, Walter Weiker, and Bill Wiley.

Several people merit special thanks for their special contributions to the development and fruition of this project. They are István Deák, Renate Bridenthal, Fritz Stern, and Martha K. Huggins. Our gratitude is also due to Sue Kuebler, of Faculty Support Services at Siena College, who helped prepare the manuscript for publication. Finally, we have been most fortunate to have worked with our editor, Michael Flamini of St. Martin's Press.

Arthur D. Brenner would like to thank the Committee on Teaching of the Siena College Faculty Committee for providing a series of summer grants and stipends. He would also like to thank Siena College and Mrs. Betsy Harvey for the award of a Harvey Fellowship in the summer of 1997. This grant, together with those by the Committee on Teaching, enabled him to hire Kristine Hoffman, Greg Lewis, and Greg Jackson, who helped with research for the Appendix. Thanks, too, to his colleagues in the Department of History for their moral support and (along with Dean Lois Daly and Vice President for Academic Affairs Tim Lederman) for enabling him to take a year's leave of absence to complete this project. Arthur deeply appreciates the warmth and interest in his work exuded by many other Siena colleagues. The wonderful librarians at Siena College—particularly Pat Markley—also had an important hand in facilitating his work. Among the many friends in and outside the academy who deserve thanks, Michael Brenner, Ruth Moghtader, Soheil Moghtader and Laurence Plateau, and Brian Ladd deserve special mention for their hospitality, friendship, and company during two research trips to Germany. Finally, and most important of all, Arthur thanks to his wife, Nanette, and children, Lianna, Misha, Camille and Ravi, whose joy and love energize his (and whose energy exhausts him!) and who inspired him to try to help make the world a safer and more harmonious place.

Bruce B. Campbell would like to thank the library staffs at the College of William and Mary and Old Dominion University for their support. Thanks are also due to Dean Geoffrey Feiss and Chairperson of the Department of Modern Languages and Literatures Katherine Kulick of the College of William and Mary, for their support; and to Ann-Marie Stock and Craig Canning of the Reves Center for International Studies at the College of William and Mary, for making possible a public presentation of our ideas about death squads. In France, Bruce would like to thank Daniel and Michèle Som and Martine Pulver for their help. He also owes thanks to Prof. Maurin and the students in his doctoral seminar at Université Paul Valéry. Most special thanks go to Bruce's long-suffering partner, Maryse Fauvel. She deserves great credit for her patience, forbearance, and advice. Without her he could not have finished this project, and his part in it would have been paler without her ideas and counsel.

We must finish our list of acknowledgments with very heartfelt thanks to our contributors, whose scholarship is impressive. But hidden behind the words and layout of this book are their great patience with lengthy editorial comments, short deadlines, and "editing by committee." They were all professional and generous with their time beyond the strict demands of the book, and it has been a pleasant and rewarding experience to work with them. Thank you one and all.

As we finish this book, killers—in Colombia, Turkey, Sri Lanka, Indonesia, and elsewhere—are hard at work delivering the raw material for further research on death squads. This prospect saddens us; as human beings and as historians, we hope to see them become a piece of the past. We dedicate this book to the victims of death squads, and to all those around the world who work to stop the killing.

Bruce B. Campbell
Williamsburg, Va.
September 1999

Arthur D. Brenner
Albany, N.Y.

CHAPTER 1

Death Squads: Definition, Problems, and Historical Context

Bruce B. Campbell

DEATH SQUADS ARE FOUND ALL OVER THE WORLD TODAY, and in just the last 30 years have been responsible for hundreds of thousands, perhaps millions, of deaths.[1] They did not disappear with the end of the Cold War, and they are certainly not a uniquely Latin American or even a "third world" problem. At the same time, they differ from other tools of repression in a number of significant aspects, notably in the way they mix state and private interests and in the way they call into question the very legitimacy and substance of the state. Their prevalence, destructive capacity, and unique nature all combine to make them an important object of study.

The purpose of this chapter is threefold. First, it will provide a working definition of death squads, review the literature on them, and set the stage for the case studies which follow. Second, it will call attention to several problems in our understanding of the phenomenon. Third, it will propose a historical framework for examining the issue that promises to resolve many of these difficulties.[2]

Definition

Death squads are clandestine and usually irregular organizations, often paramilitary in nature, which carry out extrajudicial executions and other violent acts (torture, rape, arson, bombing, etc.)

against clearly defined individuals or groups of people. Murder is their primary or even sole activity. Except in the rare case where an insurgent group forms them, death squads operate with the overt support, complicity, or acquiescence of government, or at least some parts of it.[3] In many cases, government security forces have participated directly in the killing. Yet at the same time, death squads may be privately constituted, almost always involve the support and participation of elements outside of government, and develop considerable independence from their backers.[4] Except in unusual circumstances, organizations or units involved in killings of combatants in the context of war between sovereign states, even where irregular resistance forces are involved, do not fall under this definition, although the killing of noncombatants may indeed do so.[5]

Death squads must be distinguished from three other distinct but closely related phenomena: assassination, vigilantism, and terrorism. Death squad activity and assassination lie on a continuum, and it is both difficult and of limited utility to try to identify the exact point where the transition occurs. One major difference lies in scale: assassination typically targets a single individual, or at most a small handful of individuals. Death squads operate on a much larger scale, and their victims typically number in the thousands.[6] Assassination usually targets prominent members of an elite or political leaders. Death squads may also target these elites, but their scope of victims is likely to be much wider. Moreover, aside from targeting individuals, death squads usually also attempt to spread terror among the general population through various means. Assassination may be the work of a single individual and rarely involves more than a small number of actual killers organized for a single killing. Death squads have a more permanent (if still ad hoc) organization and are set up to conduct ongoing operations on a fairly large scale.

Death squads are often treated or discussed as an aspect of vigilantism.[7] Vigilantism may be defined as the temporary usurpation of the state's powers of law and monopoly on violence by groups of ordinary citizens, usually to control crime or enforce social norms.[8] Vigilantes most often claim to be the enforcers of a kind of popular justice. The differences between death squads and vigilantism lie in the fact that death squads directly involve the state in addition to other actors, while vigilantism comes primarily at the initiative of private (civil) interests and therefore involves a greater degree of spontaneity.[9] Death squads tend to punish political acts and to be

concerned with issues that are wider than purely local ones. They
also operate on a larger geographic scale and with more coordination and planning; vigilantism tends to be more locally based and
grassroots in origin.

In reality, though, there is considerable overlap between the two
categories. Some death squads do act to combat crime or enforce social norms. Similarly, vigilantism often involves state or elite influence and participation, even instigation, and is generally both covert
in nature and murderous in outcome, all features that make a clear
distinction between it and death squad activity difficult. The members of death squads may even see themselves as vigilantes working
to enforce justice. To further muddy the waters, death squad activity
is also frequently portrayed or disguised as spontaneous acts of vigilantism in order to hide its true sponsorship.[10] One good example is
the government-sponsored and -encouraged "vigilante" groups
formed in apartheid-era South Africa, which not only committed
murder themselves but were consciously and deliberately used to
supplement and cover the activities of government death squads; another would be government claims in El Salvador that the acts of
death squads were "simply" the spontaneous vigilante acts of patriotic citizens.[11] Yet, the proximity of the two concepts is due to more
than the problem of translating practice into theory or to conscious
manipulation and actually points to something characteristic of
death squads. Even in death squads that are well disciplined and
closely tied to legitimate state structures there is still an element of
spontaneity that makes them resemble vigilantism. This comes because of the inevitable insinuation of private interests into the actions
of death squads, be it in the form of individual abuse of power or of
direct involvement of organized private interest groups. This public-
private mix is in fact one of the most important characteristics of
death squads.

Terrorism is also closely related to death squad activity, but
again should be distinguished from it. Terrorism is the commission
of acts of murder and extreme, exceptional brutality and destruction
in order to influence groups of people to act or refrain from acting
in certain ways. The people terrorism seeks to influence are generally different from its targets, which gives it a somewhat random,
unpredictable quality. The violence is rarely committed for its own
sake, at least when it begins, but serves rather to send a message.
This only heightens the terror, and terrorism works through extreme

fear. Death squads may well be a part of a government strategy of state terrorism, and they very often attempt to use terror themselves, for example when they publicly announce their killings, use torture prior to murdering their victims, or leave the bodies of their victims in conspicuous places. Clearly, the two concepts easily exist simultaneously. And yet, there is an important distinction between these concepts. Terrorism differs from death squad activity in that its targets are largely instrumental or symbolic and the main effect is intended to be felt elsewhere. To put it another way, in terrorism, murder and other dreadful acts are committed to send a message, while for death squads, murder is the main point.[12] Once again, in practice, the two concepts are difficult to separate: terrorists may intend to send a message, but they usually pick targets as painful for their enemies as possible, so that the infliction of damage can quickly overshadow the sending of a message. In a similar way, death squads nearly always include a terrorist component, for their killings are usually very public and particularly gruesome. The distinction between the two remains an academic one; in practice it is often much less clear.

Conceptual distinctions such as the ones made above matter, but in actual situations of state violence, they may be much less clear than they seem on paper. The three taxonomic categories "death squad," "vigilantism," and "terrorism" are clearly distinct in the abstract, but much less so in actual practice. Death squads nearly always show aspects of both terrorism and vigilantism in their operations, so it is prudent not to draw too fine a point about the differences between the three concepts. Conceptually, such distinctions are useful, but seem puny when compared to the realities of modern violence, and do not matter much to the victims.

Special Factors

Death squads have several key, distinguishing characteristics that make them either unique or unusual within the panoply of possible ways of organizing violence. First of all, they are *covert*, without necessarily, however, being *secret*. The solution to this apparent paradox lies in distinguishing organization from actions. What makes death squads different from the murderous use of regular police and military forces is that death squads give no visible indication that they exercise *legitimate* use of force and they make no acknowledgment of whose orders they follow. Regular military forces and most police wear uniforms, which shows that they act in the name of the state and that the power they exercise is therefore legitimate. Even plainclothes police are required to carry and display identification marking them as legitimate representatives of state power. Regular security forces also have a formal organizational structure and clear chain of command which allows responsibility for their actions to be determined. Death squads have neither. This makes it possible for the state (and/or any other backers they may have) to claim no knowledge of or influence over death squads, and therefore to deny any responsibility for their actions.[13] On the other hand, if the work of death squads is intended to spread terror, then their acts cannot be kept completely secret, for then they would lose much of their intended effect on their targets. For this reason, most death squads (though by no means all) make sure that their actions are very public: they leave their victims to be found in public places, they torture and mutilate them in memorable and horrific ways, and they sometimes even leave notes or visible signs that they were victims of a particular unit. In some case, lists of intended victims are even published in advance in public media.[14] Nor is state complicity or support a real secret for long: death squads may visibly be made up of members of the security forces, and the sheer lack of state success in stopping them is generally enough to raise the reasonable assumption that the state therefore does not want them to stop.[15] Hence, death squads generally involve the paradox of being secretive and covert organizations that nevertheless often act in particularly public and gruesome fashion.

But this is not the most significant paradox involving death squads. One of the central, defining characteristics of states is that they maintain a monopoly over the use of violence. In a sense, the prime task of modern states is to organize and control violence.[16] And yet in tolerating or using death squads, states inevitably compromise their defining monopoly, often putting their very legitimacy into question. Given this paradox, the central question regarding death squads is why states would choose to use them at all, given that other, ostensibly equally effective means are at their disposal in the form of regular military and police forces. The answer is quite complex, and not completely clear.

It is easy to see why states (and/or other backers) lose control over death squads: their irregular, informal organization and the

demands of covert action make the exercise of control very difficult. Moreover, death squads exist to act outside of the law: by definition, their "job" is to commit extrajudicial murder. Once the
decision is made to cross the line of legality, where are they to stop?
The smooth action of death squads practically requires that their
members be granted the widest possible exemption from prosecution and interference. That this often leads to personal abuses for
private gain is easily understood. But the independence of death
squads may also mean that they develop their own political agendas separate from their backers, while as appendages of a bureaucratic system (no matter how informal their organization), they
often act according to organizational imperatives of competition
with other agencies.[17]

One element enhancing the independence and uncontrollability
of death squads is the curious fact that most of them arise out of a
peculiar symbiosis between the state and nonstate interests. For example, death squads in El Salvador involved the considerable support and influence of large landowners and were often directed by a
political movement (the ARENA party), even though some arose or-
ganizationally within state agencies like the National Guard and all
worked in some form of cooperation with state forces to stamp out
an internal insurgency. The influence of these nonstate forces may
possibly arise because of the inability of states to prevent powerful
social groups from killing their opponents, though even then, states
may indeed welcome such "help." Much more likely, though, is the
fact that the need to maintain plausible deniability of state involvement often forces the creators of death squads to seek aid from private groups and individuals.[18] After all, one way to establish
deniability is to have the killing organized and done by people who
are not formally or officially associated with the state. The desire to
make death squads seem like a spontaneous expression of the public will also leads to the involvement of nonstate actors.

There are a number of contributing factors to the insinuation of
private interests into death squads. Since death squads are not part
of the formal organizational structure of the security forces and
state support for them must remain covert, they are difficult for
states to finance. Private interests may be asked to provide covert
funding. This was the case in El Salvador, for example, where
wealthy exiles financed many death squads.[19] Another factor may
sometimes lie in a sense of professionalism within the security

forces, which can lead to a desire to stay apart from death squads for a variety of reasons,[20] and in the difficulty in general of pushing humans to commit murder without a strong normative justification.[21] Another contributing factor lies in the modern concept of citizenship itself. What distinguishes a citizen from a subject, after all, is that the citizen feels a personal responsibility for the well-being of the state. This sense of personal responsibility for the state may lead individuals or groups to act according to what they perceive is required, even if this means breaking other norms of behavior such as the law.[22] Ironically, death squads may be partially motivated by the very sense of social responsibility that is a cornerstone of both nationalism and democracy, and they may be encouraged by the very professionalism in the armed forces that many see as a barrier to state terrorism.

Literature Review

There is surprisingly little research that deals specifically with death squads. Much of what does exist is concerned with case studies of death squad activity, and very little takes a synthetic or theoretical approach.

The largest body of work dealing specifically with death squads comes from either the human rights and development community[23] or the media.[24] This research, often conducted at great risk, has provided much of the basic information now available on the subject. It has mainly been interested in exposing the problem and trying to stop the killing and has almost always focused on specific case studies.

In the scholarly literature, death squads fall under the larger category of "state violence" or "state terrorism" and are sometimes also treated as a kind of vigilantism, and so a discussion of the literature on these broader categories of violence must come first. There is now a fairly large body of literature on state violence and state terrorism.[25] Among the most important of these are a number of works, which came from George Lopez, Raymond Duvall, and especially Michael Stohl in a series of publications in the 1980s.[26] In 1983 Duvall and Stohl developed an "expected utility" model for the employment of terror by states: terror is used because it appears either more effective or less ineffective than alternative means.[27] They specify that weak states tend to use it when it is perceived as

better (or at least less bad) than the alternatives, whereas strong
states use it only when highly isolated from the international community or when they are either militaristic states or feel they have a
special ideological mission, as in the National Socialist "mission" to
cleanse the world of Jews.[28] Also in 1986, Stohl identified three additional variables that can constrain or promote state terrorism:

- the cultural value of violence in a given place
- the social distance between killers and victims, or the ease
  with which the targets can be denied human attributes
- the routinization of violence within a context of bureaucratic irresponsibility.[29]

A further development and synthesis of the work by Stohl,
Lopez, and Duvall was done by Ted Robert Gurr in the same year.[30]
He also defined state terror as a rational, intentional choice. He
listed a range of factors likely to lead to the employment of state violence, even terror, against domestic populations. Gurr postulates,
as a necessary precondition for the use of state terror, the existence
of a class, group, or party that the ruling elite sees as a threat to its
continued rule. The greater this threat, the greater the likelihood of
violence. Similarly, the greater the latent support for this challenger
group within the population, the greater the likelihood of violence.
Challengers to the system who use violence are more likely to be met
with terror than those who don't. Furthermore, state terror is more
likely to be used against marginal groups rather than against groups
with close ties to ruling elites. According to Gurr, weak regimes are
more likely to use terror than strong ones, and elites that come to
power through violence are more likely to use it to stay in power
than those that didn't. The successful situational uses of terror are
likely to lead to its permanent use, whereas the initial decision to use
terror is usually modeled on outside or earlier examples: states tend
to imitate each other. Gurr states that democratic values and traditions are likely to inhibit the use of violence by states against their
own citizens, while the greater the racial, class or religious hetero-
geneity of a society and the greater its social stratification, the
greater the likelihood of state violence. He argues that ethnic or religious minority elites in highly stratified societies are very likely to
use terror against their populations. In fact, Gurr maintains that the
greater the degree of stratification, the greater the likelihood of vio-

lence. Naturally, external threats are likely to cause force to be used against internal opponents, and regimes involved in the proxy conflicts of major powers are highly likely to use the most extreme forms of terror. Regimes peripheral to world capitalism, especially when they are autarchic and less vulnerable to international sanctions, are also more likely to use violence. For Gurr, the biggest predictor of all for state terror is the existence of units or institutions specialized in combating terrorism.

Other approaches to explaining state violence and terror include the cultural school of anthropologists, who see violence as learned or as the result of socialization[31]; those who see it as a fundamental part of totalitarianism[32]; dependency and social structure theorists, who see it as resulting from the imbalanced character of existing North-South economic relations[33]; and imperialism theorists, who use a paradigm of global structural violence resulting from capitalist imperialism.[34] Finally, some theorists simply blame the United States for most, if not all, state terror.[35]

Another common way of explaining some forms of state terror is to discuss it in terms of vigilantism, and the relationship between the two concepts has already been discussed above.[36] Peter C. Sederberg, in particular, provides valuable insights. He sees vigilantism as being "often the reaction to a widening range of officially tolerated innovation and [even] the existence of state-sponsored innovation."[37] Vigilante groups are then organized either privately or by the state against those seen as real or symbolic threats to existing order. According to his research, vigilante groups tend to recruit those whose status is insecure or who have authoritarian personalities.

This relatively recent work on state violence has greatly increased our understanding of the circumstances under which states opt to exercise extreme violence against their own people. Unfortunately, none of it really explains why certain forms of violence such as death squads are used in any particular case and not other forms. It also rarely even mentions death squads at all, and if so, only in passing as one of many possible forms of state violence.

There is a fairly small body of scholarly literature that deals with death squads directly and specifically instead of subsuming them under the larger category of state terrorism. Most of it, like the work of journalists and human rights workers, is in the form of case studies focusing on a single country or at most a limited geographic area.[38] While all of these are important and supply crucial information, they generally do not attempt to develop a comprehensive idea of why death squads are used or to draw broader conclusions about their nature. A few works do take a more synthetic and comprehensive approach, however. One of the most important is a short article by David Mason and Dale Krane.[39] Much like more general work on state terrorism, they see the use of death squads as a rational choice for comprador regimes. Once countries adopt an agro-export growth model that ties them closely to the world capitalist system, they lack the resources to alleviate mass unrest provoked by concomitant economic changes (unemployment, expropriation, depressed wages, etc.). Their easiest response to this dissatisfaction is violence. This, in turn, leads to popular violence in response, and a process of mutual escalation follows. Governments in this kind of situation often resort to the use of death squads. State terror is unable to resolve the conflict, however, so that after a period of great brutality and destruction, the result is ultimately mutual exhaustion and stalemate. In effect, the weakness of the state precludes less violent alternatives to death squads and terror. The problem with Mason and Krane's approach is that it is narrowly focused on economics and state weakness and does not explain the use of death squads by states that have significant resources. Their theory also does not explain why death squads are used in preference to other means of repression, other than citing the need for reasonable denial.

Perhaps the best of the handful of studies specifically on death squads is in the work of Miles Wolpin.[40] He places the responsibility for their existence squarely on states and their leaders, citing only a handful of cases in which they might have been formed simply because states were too weak to prevent them.[41] He says that death squads are particularly likely to be employed against strong, urban-based opposition groups and where deniability is considered necessary for domestic and/or international reasons. He sees states using them mainly where an opposition movement is both growing and a major threat to a highly stratified exploitative system. He holds that their use is also likely if success in mobilizing public bias against popular, left-wing, or ethnic opposition movements is problematic; in this case, death squads are employed to compensate for a lack of sufficient electoral mobilization against the perceived internal threat, especially in low-income countries. He also raises the important proposition that death squads may be used in weak states simply because they may turn out to be more "efficient" than other state sectors.

Wolpin stresses the importance of deniability in choosing to use death squads, but doesn't really say why, other than to serve as a fig leaf for those elements among a ruling coalition who do not want to acknowledge the state's use of violence. This is not a sufficient explanation, but it is a start. Wolpin is actually best in discussing why states may resort to violence,[42] and he also does well to include acknowledgment of cultural factors and specifically local context in his analysis. Nevertheless, he doesn't really add much to our knowledge of why some states use death squads instead of other forms of violence. He still regards death squads mainly as a function of the degree of a state's economic stratification and exploitation; he sometimes conflates vigilantism and death squads; and though he formally rejects it, he still implies that death squads are the recourse of "weak" states.

Wolpin himself acknowledges the limits of our understanding of death squads and calls for more research, particularly the need to look further at the impact of child-rearing practices and other cultural factors on the willingness to use violence, the need for measures of the thresholds and degrees of socioeconomic oppression leading to death squads, and the need for more study of elite group cohesion, quality, and values.

One new study that sheds light on many of these issues is a collection of work by a group of anthropologists edited by Jeffrey Sluka.[43] This new work adds valuable new perspectives to the study of death squads and state violence. Current research on state violence seems to be growing more and more open to a consideration of cultural factors specific to a given society, precisely the sort of question anthropology as a discipline is able to answer.[44] Future research, freed from a Cold War context and an overemphasis on economic factors as the ultimate origin of all evil, will certainly advance our understanding of death squads greatly.

Problem Areas

The question of why some states use death squads instead of other means of violent repression is a central one for human rights practitioners and academics alike, and neither group has yet found a definitive answer. An answer can be approached only by citing a number of contributing elements simultaneously.

The thesis that death squads may exist because a given state is simply too weak to prevent powerful social interests from engaging in murder can be rejected in all but a handful of cases. It sounds plausible, yet in practice, the state, rather than being a "victim," actually either initiates the formation of death squads or cooperates with them. The "weak state" thesis has additional problems. To begin with, the concept of a "weak" state is seldom defined in any rigorous manner, and all too often it amounts to the expression of an ideological bias: "weak" states are those that are simply not as "democratic" as "we" are. It also implies a strict dichotomy between "weak" and "strong" states that usually does not reflect reality. Modern states, even "weak" ones, are complex, and given the multitude of functions even relatively feeble states have to fulfill today, it is quite possible for a state to be strong in some areas and weak in others. Finally, even keeping the previous point in mind, the sheer number of deaths caused by some death squads makes it perverse to attribute them to any form of state weakness.

The kind of economic argument advanced by Mason and Krane, that states dependent on an agro-export economy lack the resources to satisfy domestic demands and are therefore forced to rely on extreme violence, has certainly been shown to apply to numerous situations in which death squads have been used.[45] Much the same may be said of the "expected utility" argument of Duvall, Stohl, Gurr, and others. Yet both may explain the recourse to state terror, but not which type, and are therefore only parts of the puzzle.

One major factor for the use of death squads lies in the need of states to deny that they are breaking established norms of behavior. The modern state is bound by a whole range of internal and external norms that place strict limits on a state's range of options—if respected. Only death squads and other covert means provide plausible deniability of state involvement in violent acts. Domestically, citizens expect the rule of law, adherence to certain norms of behavior, or at least predictable behavior from their governments. States may engage in covert violence in order to protect the sensibilities of domestic populations and thus preserve state legitimacy.[46] This is, however, a fairly weak explanation, given that death squads often make their acts public to sow terror, and given the fact that plausible deniability of state complicity in death squad violence can hardly be maintained domestically for long, if it ever works at all.

The rise in interest in human rights and legal norms for state behavior internationally since at least the late nineteenth century also plays a role.[47] Today states find themselves under scrutiny from foreign governments, both allied and enemy; semigovernmental agencies such as the World Bank; and a multitude of nongovernmental organizations (NGOs), such as Amnesty International, Human Rights Watch, and Greenpeace, not to mention the international media.[48] Failure to meet international norms of behavior can have all sorts of serious repercussions today, including loss of foreign loans and investment, diminution or loss of foreign aid, loss of tourist revenue, trade boycotts, etc. States wishing to use extreme forms of extralegal violence thus have every reason to appear uninvolved. Though the charade doesn't usually last very long, it is difficult to prove government complicity in death squad actions—such proof usually comes at great cost to local human rights organizations and monitors, who are themselves often among the prime targets of the death squads.[49] This is one of the many cruel ironies that crop up in connection with state violence, for it is quite likely that the increased concern for human rights has itself inadvertently been a contributing factor in the use of covert violence by governments, and in particular, in the use of death squads.[50]

Wolpin provides other elements of an answer. His prediction that death squads are more likely to be employed against successful, urban-based insurgencies and in electoral systems where it is impossible to mobilize sufficient electoral potential against popular left-wing and/or ethnically based opposition movements does at least address the question of when death squads are likely to be used rather than other forms of violence, though he still doesn't go very far in saying why this is the case. He also underscores the importance of deniability and mentions the probable importance of cultural factors. Most important of all, his notion that death squads may be used because they are perceived as being more efficient than other state agents is a useful way of getting at relative areas of state weakness, without falling into a weak-state, strong-state dichotomy.[51] Still, while this provides a number of important pieces of the answer, it is not complete.

The influence of ideological and cultural factors coming from both internal and external actors bears future research, as numerous authors have already concluded.[52] Several authors have explored the influence of national security doctrine that became popular among noncommunist state leaders during the Cold War and may perhaps have included at least a regional exchange of information on tactics, including death squads.[53] Yet once again, neither of these is able to explain why the choice of death squads over other forms of violence is made.

Finally, one other reason for the decision to use death squads may be the simple calculation that the state faces an extraordinarily dangerous situation that requires extraordinary methods. An inclination to see the threat of even moderate change in the status quo, particularly when the challenge is ideologically based, as being profoundly threatening and justifying the most extreme measures imaginable is nothing new in human history, yet provides a powerful explanation for the panic of established elites in the face of even modest change. This again begs the question of why states support or tolerate death squads and not some other, equally violent approach to solve their most intractable and existential political or social challenges.

Historical Interpretation

What may be needed to advance the understanding of death squads, and in particular to begin to better answer the question of why states resort to death squads as opposed to other means of repression, is a more historically based explanation.

The process begins by locating death squads in time. How far back does it make sense to speak about them? Though the use of violence by rulers against their own people goes as far back as recorded history, it makes no sense to label every instance of this type as a death squad.[54] One key is that by definition, death squads carry out "extrajudicial murder" and other extrajudicial acts. The operant phrase here is "extrajudicial"; death squads as such could not have existed before the establishment of the principle that even rulers or states must respect the rule of law, or before the establishment of a state monopoly on the use of force (in Western Europe, roughly in the seventeenth and eighteenth centuries).[55]

But there is good reason to set the temporal limit for the existence of death squads even later: one of the most interesting characteristics of death squads is the fact that they are not always simply the tools of the state. As already mentioned, they often draw support, motivation, and resources from outside official circles, and they usually develop their own agendas and exercise some amount of independence from their sponsors. What this means is that death squads cannot exist without a strong degree of social plurality and without the historical development of the notion that private individuals can and should play a role in the political process. In short, death squads cannot exist before the concept of citizenship does.[56]

Another important clue for situating death squads historically lies in the clandestine nature of death squad activity. By both definition and practice, death squads operate in the shadows and margins of society. The secretive nature of death squads has some "tactical" purpose to heighten the terror produced by their activities, but this is clearly not the main reason for it. Instead, death squads operate in a clandestine manner so that their backers (usually governments) may plausibly deny to both a domestic and a foreign audience that they are connected to the death squads. Domestically, this makes no sense before the existence of the concept that governments derive their legitimacy from the consent of the governed, and that this consent is based, among other things, on holding to the rule of law. Externally, it makes no sense without the idea that the opinion of foreign states and their citizens is also an important aspect of a state's legitimacy. Thus, we can't speak of the existence of death squads before the development of states that have a monopoly on the use of force and are expected to abide by laws. Only after this time do the things death squads do become unusual or extraordinary. Similarly, the creation of the autonomous citizen as a political actor, the invention of mass politics, and the development of a "world court of public opinion" are all crucial prerequisites for the existence of what we call death squads. Therefore death squads cannot reasonably be said to exist before the French Revolution and the early nineteenth century, which means before the creation of the modern state.

One of the first proto–death squads was the early Ku Klux Klan, a secret society originally created by former Confederate soldiers in the American South just after the end of the American Civil War. It conducted death-squad-like killings and other terrorist acts against recently freed black slaves, "carpetbaggers," and those thought to collaborate too closely with the agents of the victorious federal government engaged in "reconstructing" the recently rebellious South. Though it was formed in opposition to the legitimate state government, unlike most modern death squads, it acted in the name of a former, defeated Confederate one, and in the name of a system of racially based social stratification and economic exploitation. Otherwise, in its murderous intent, links to private elite interests, and covert nature, it very closely resembles modern death squads.[57] Note that it originated in what is not commonly referred to as a weak state, nor one that was uniformly in the thrall of an export-oriented agricultural policy geared to the capitalist world market.[58]

The Crisis of the Modern State and "Subcontracting"

One potentially fruitful approach is to consider death squads as one—albeit extreme—manifestation of what may be called the crisis of the twentieth-century state.

The modern state is conceived in terms of force. In his classic definition of the state, the nineteenth-century German scholar Max Weber defined the state as "that human community, which, within a given territory, claims for itself the legitimate monopoly of physical violence."[59] Developing out of the medieval kingdoms of Western Europe, the history of the modern state is linked to violence from its very beginning.[60]

Only in the nineteenth century did the western state take the form that has become the model and norm today for all modern states. At that time, and under the impact of classical liberalism, the role of the state was defined in fairly narrow terms, and thus so were the means that the state had at its disposal to fulfill that role.[61] The continuing industrial revolution, the growing complexity of society, and the impact of world war—in short, ongoing modernization— have all served to widen the role of the state. The means at the disposal of states have not always kept up with this expansion, so that in the twentieth century, states have increasingly felt it necessary to reach outside themselves—that is, to reach outside that normative liberal-legal framework established in the nineteenth century—in order to find the tools or helpers necessary to perform all the tasks at hand. This has led to the widespread use of semistate or semipublic entities by modern states to "subcontract" important political, social, and economic tasks. Because of this, the modern state bleeds sovereignty, which is one of its defining characteristics.

This process may be initiated either by the state or by private interest groups or both. Benign examples of the process include such diverse organizations as the Boy Scouts[62] and regulated monopolies such as the former Bell Telephone System. Yet in crisis situations or situations in which the legitimacy of states is called into question, this "subcontracting" can assume more malevolent forms, such as the formation or toleration of paramilitary auxiliaries or, in extreme cases, death squads. This way of looking at death squads certainly fits within a rational choice model, and it has the advantage of placing death squads in a larger context that is common to all modern states, "weak" or "strong," and irrespective of their position in the world capitalist system. Further, it is consistent with scholarship that sees an increased danger of extreme violence in situations in which states or elites are in the process of rapid modernization.[63] Thus, cases such as the early KKK in the mid-to-late-nineteenth-century United States or Spain in the 1980s, neither involving a state that was a weak state or was in a dependent position within the world capitalist system at the time, do not appear to be such anomalies. Moreover, it overcomes the pejorative connotations associated with the weak-state hypothesis. The point is not to discount state weakness or economic factors in making the use of death squads more likely, but rather to escape the danger of failing to see the universal possibility that any state may choose to use death squads.

Modern states have a habit of subcontracting. In certain crisis situations (and here the literature on state violence in general is still very useful), this subcontracting can occur even at the risk of diminishing the states' legitimacy by violating the law, or by compromising its monopoly on the use of violence.[64] This would then place death squads at the outer limits of a much larger continuum that would encompass all sorts of state and semistate organizations, from "quasi-autonomous, nongovernmental organizations" ("quangos")[65] to paramilitary groups, but still, unfortunately, within a spectrum of normal state behavior.

The advantage of this framework is that it allows us to locate death squads as a part of a larger historical trend, while still allowing for the specifics of each individual instance of their use. At the same time, it permits the inclusion of nonstate or nongovernmental actors, for whether states instigate death squad violence or merely tolerate it, such violence is symptomatic of the same crisis. This is important, for the extent of nonstate initiative in death squads is often underestimated. Finally, this explanation leaves room for state weakness or lack of legitimacy to be considered as contributing factors.

Conclusion

It may be that the trend toward subcontracting that characterizes modern states signals enough of a blurring of the traditional definition of a state that we will need to develop a new one, or perhaps that we will need to begin speaking of a "postmodern" state that can be and not be at the same time.[66] In any case, we can now see one of the roots of death squad use in more conventional forms of state behavior and stop trying to measure how a state's weakness or its condition of dependency made it turn to death squads. Sadly, the historical context introduced here does not provide any grounds for optimism that the use of death squads is likely to end soon. Quite the contrary: they are likely to become a more frequent phenomenon.[67] The end of the Cold War has brought an increase in small wars, domestic revolts, and ethnically or nationally based conflicts. Meanwhile, the demands placed on states by the sheer complexity of modern life continue to grow, and therefore the habit of subcontracting, which contributes to the formation of death squads in already violent situations, is likely only to grow stronger. It is ironic, in a world of nearly endemic "ethnic" and nationalist conflict, that the strong, unitary state, the very agent that should (theoretically) support and defend these essentialist identities, is in such decline.[68] This is not to say that the death squads themselves will not change to fit new contexts or will not react to moves designed to stop them. There is already evidence, for example, that state-sponsored killers are working harder to hide evidence of their acts, in order to escape punishment from international courts.[69] It is also likely that continued and better domestic and international scrutiny of violence will cause direct government involvement in death squads to decline. The likely result will unfortunately be a greater degree of private involvement and thus even less control and discipline of the killers than ever before. And yet international scrutiny, the dedication of countless human rights workers, and, not least, the resistance of the victims themselves have had a positive effect in reducing the use of death squads and bringing their members to justice. This, too, will continue.[70] Death squads will likely never go away completely, but they can be opposed, exposed, limited, and stigmatized until their use by states becomes unacceptably costly.

Notes

1. One superficial measure of the scale of the problem is the frequency with which the topic appears in the media. For example, a search of the Lexis-Nexis electronic database of major U.S. and international newspapers turned up 147 references to the term "death squad" for the short period from January 1 to September 1, 1999, alone.

2. Death squads are not an easy topic. In a subject so extreme, some disagreement is inevitable. While the other participants in this book have seen the definition this chapter sets out, they do not necessarily agree either with it or with the rest of the analysis that follows. Nor is this meant to be the last word on the subject, not least because all of the papers in this volume, in one way or another, push out the limits of our understanding of the subject and prepare the way for further research.

3. The vast majority of notorious death squad cases have involved the complicity of sovereign states. There are very few cases where insurgent groups have created true death squads. Examples might include special groups alleged to have been set up by the Irish Republican Army (IRA) or the Palestine Liberation Organization (PLO). Even here, however, the insurgent groups in question have aspired or claimed to represent a not as yet recognized state in the making, and have claimed state powers and legitimacy.

4. The literature from human rights organizations takes particular pains to stress government control over death squads in order to emphasize accountability, yet in the end even it must admit that death squads often enjoy considerable independence in practice and that they often follow their own agendas. See, for example, Amnesty International, *El Salvador: "Death Squads"—a Government Strategy* (London: Amnesty International, 1988), 1, 3 (note 1), 15–18, 44–45.

5. The definition is the author's, but draws on earlier definitions provided by Amnesty International, *El Salvador,* 1; T. David Mason and Dale A. Krane, "The Political Economy of Death Squads: Toward a Theory of the Impact of State-Sanctioned Terror," *International Studies Quarterly* 33 (1989): 175–98 (here, 178); and the Library of Congress, Bibliographic Category Definition of "death squads," obtained on-line from the Library of Congress electronic catalog, 1995. Further help on the definition has come from Arthur D. Brenner, Cynthia Arnson, Jeffrey Sluka, James Ron, and Allen Feldman.

6. Assassination is defined as the "premeditated murder of a political figure for reasons of the victim's prominence, [or] political perspective." Joel Krieger, *The Oxford Companion to Politics of the World* (New York: Oxford University Press, 1993), 55–56. On the subject, see Thomas H. Snitch, "Terrorism and Political Assassinations: A Transnational Assessment 1968–80," *Annals of the American Academy of Political and Social Sciences,* no. 463 (September 1982): 54–66; Franklin L. Ford, *Political Murder: From Tyrannicide to Terrorism* (Cambridge: Harvard University Press, 1985).

7. See Ray Abrahams, *Vigilant Citizens: Vigilantism and the State* (Cambridge: Polity Press, 1998); H. Jon Rosenbaum and Peter C. Sederberg, eds., *Vigilante Politics* (Philadelphia: University of Pennsylvania Press, 1976); Martha K. Huggins, "Vigilantism and the State: A Look South and North," in *Vigilantism and the State in Modern Latin America: Essays on Extralegal Violence,* ed. Martha K. Huggins (New York: Praeger, 1991); or David Kowalewski, "Countermovement Vigilantism and Human Rights, A Propositional Inventory," *Crime, Law and Social Change* 25 (1996): 63–81. In the present volume, see Chapter 5.

8. The definition of vigilantism is a contentious issue; the one offered here is loosely based on material offered in Abrahams, *Vigilant Citizens,* 7–9.

9. This is not to imply that all vigilante groups are completely spontaneous, for many are highly organized and usually involve the active participation of at least local elites, and they may even enjoy the support of the national government.

10. This discussion takes up in modified form the division of vigilantism into three types as outlined in H. Jon Rosenbaum and Peter C. Sederberg, "Vigilantism, an Analysis of Establishment Violence," in Rosenbaum and Sederberg, *Vigilante Politics,* 9–19. Their third category, "regime-control vigilantism," includes the type of activity denoted here as death squads. Also highly useful in drawing the differences between death squads and vigilantism is Abrahams, *Vigilant Citizens.* See also Huggins, *Vigilantism and the State.*

11. On South Africa, see Chapter 9 in this volume; also Peter Harris, "The Role of Right-Wing Vigilantes in South Africa," and Mark Phillips, "Divide and Repress: Vigilantes and State Objectives in Crossroads," both in *States of Terror: Death Squads or Development?* ed. Mike Kirkwood (London: Catholic Institute for International Relations, 1989). On El Salvador, see Chapter 4 in this volume.

12. This distinction is drawn from a highly instrumental reading of the following works: Raymond D. Duvall and Michael Stohl, "Gover-

nance by Terror," in *The Politics of Terrorism*, 3rd. ed., ed. Michael
Stohl (New York: Marcel Dekker, 1988), 231–71; Michael Stohl,
"Demystifying Terrorism: The Myths and Realities of Contemporary
Political Terrorism," in Stohl, *The Politics of Terrorism*, 1–27; Alex
P. Schmid and Albert J. Jongman, *Political Terrorism. A New Guide
to Actors, Authors, Concepts, Data Bases, Theories and Literature*,
2nd. ed. (Amsterdam: North-Holland Publishing Company, 1988),
esp. 1–59. Note that the literature on terrorism is particularly voluminous, and there are literally hundreds of definitions. See Schmid
and Jongman, *Political Terrorism*, 239–482, for a good bibliography.

13.   States often claim that death squads are spontaneous acts of an aggrieved public, or that they are actually agents of an insurgent group,
but this is simply to conceal the true state of affairs and is irrelevant
to our definition. (See Chapter 10 in this volume for examples of
both.) Note that the covert nature of death squads may also serve the
secondary purpose of enhancing the terror they generate, since an
unnamed threat can be extremely frightening.

14.   See Abram de Swaan, "Terror as a Government Service," in *Repression and Repressive Violence*, ed. Mario Hoefnagels (Amsterdam:
Swets and Zeitlinger, 1977), 44–45, on the "twilight nature" of
knowledge about acts of terror under terrorist regimes. While the
publication of the names of potential victims or of target lists may
well be considered terrorism, without their subsequent murder by
organized groups, it cannot be considered an instance of death squad
activity.

15.   Examples of this abound. See, for example, Chapter 4 below.

16.   See, for example, Charles Tilly, *Coercion, Capital, and European
States, AD 990–1990* (Oxford: Basil Blackwell, 1990), 67–70.

17.   The Brazilian death squads examined by Martha Huggins in Chapter 8 of this volume are a perfect example.

18.   For example, this is well documented in the case of Serbian paramilitary groups that functioned as death squads in Bosnia and Croatia.
See below, Chapter 11.

19.   See Chapter 4 below.

20.   In some cases, the conventional armed forces may be put off by the
illegality of death squads (even if they do not step in to stop them),
or they may simply be repelled by the ad hoc nature of death squads
or their perceived lack of discipline. As an example, the Yugoslav
Federal Army preferred to leave "ethnic cleansing" and other brutal
acts in Bosnia to the privately organized paramilitary groups. In a
similar fashion, the conventional military often felt rivalry with private death squads in El Salvador, yet cooperated with them and even
formed their own. Clearly, though, this varies from case to case, and

many professional armies or police forces have no difficulty working with, or even acting as, death squads.

21. See Lt. Col. Dave Grossman, *On Killing: The Psychological Cost of Learning to Kill in War and Society* (Boston: Little, Brown, 1995).

22. See, for example, the Weimar German case in Chapter 3, below.

23. For example, Amnesty International, *Political Killings by Governments* (London: Amnesty International, 1983); Amnesty International, *El Salvador;* and Ben Penglase, *Final Justice: Police and Death Squad Homicides of Adolescents in Brazil* (New York: Human Rights Watch, 1994). See also Kirkwood, *States of Terror,* which lies at the border of human rights and academic studies.

24. For example, "El Salvador's Reborn Death Squads," *Economist,* 13 November 1993, 52; "Chronicle of a Death Foretold," *Economist,* 9 September 1995, 50–51; "A Chilling Tale," *Economist,* 9 December 1995, 45–46; Tony Stark, "Masked Gunmen and Death Squads in Drag," *New Statesman and Society* 5, no. 218 (4 September 1992): 18–20; Anne Nelson and Cynthia Arnson, "Death Squads, D'Aubuisson and 'Democracy,'" *Nation,* 28 January 1984, 88–90; Lucia Annunziata, "The Death Squads," *Nation,* 31 March 1984, 372–73; and Christopher Dickey, "Behind the Death Squads: Who They Are, How They Work, and Why No One Can Stop Them," *New Republic* 189, no. 26 (1983): 16–21.

25. A good, if by now somewhat dated, summary may be found in Schmid and Jongman, *Political Terrorism,* 72–79 and 259–69. A similar, more up-to-date one may be found in Miles D. Wolpin, "State Terrorism and Death Squads in the New World Order," in *The Culture of Violence,* eds. Kumar Rupesinghe and Marcial Rubio C. (Tokyo: United Nations University Press, 1994), 200–216. The following draws heavily on Wolpin in its topology of the literature.

26. Aside from those discussed below, see George A. Lopez and Michael Stohl, eds., *Dependence, Development, and State Repression* (New York: Greenwood Press, 1989); Michael Stohl and George A. Lopez, *Terrible Beyond Endurance? The Foreign Policy of State Terrorism* (New York, Greenwood Press, 1988); George A. Lopez, *Terrorism and World Order,* The Whole Earth Papers, no. 18 (New York: Global Education Associates, 1983); Michael Stohl and George A. Lopez, *The State as Terrorist: The Dynamics of Governmental Violence and Repression* (Westport, CT: Greenwood Press, 1984).

27. Duvall and Stohl, "Governance by Terror," 231–71 (quotation from 255).

28. Duvall and Stohl, "Governance by Terror," 256–62.

29. Michael Stohl, "The Superpowers and International Terrorism," in *Government Violence and Repression: An Agenda for Research,* eds.

Michael Stohl and George A. Lopez (Westport, Conn.: Greenwood Press, 1986), 207–34, esp. 212.

30. Ted Robert Gurr, "The Political Origins of State Violence and Terror: A Theoretical Analysis," in Stohl and Lopez, *Government Violence and Repression,* 46–48.

31. Johan Galtung, "Cultural Violence," *Journal of Peace Research* 27, no. 3 (1990): 291–305; Carolyn Nordstrom and JoAnn Martin, eds., *The Paths to Domination, Resistance, and Terror* (Berkeley: University of California Press, 1992).

32. Alexander Dallin and George W. Breslauer, *Political Terror in Communist Systems* (Stanford: Stanford University Press, 1970); Hannah Arendt, *The Origins of Totalitarianism* (New York: Harcourt Brace Jovanovich, 1973), 440.

33. Conway W. Henderson, "Conditions Affecting the Use of Political Repression," *Journal of Conflict Resolution* 35, no. 1 (1991): 120–42; Gernot Kohler, "Global Apartheid," in *Toward a Just World Order,* eds. Richard Falk, Samuel S. Kin, and Saul H. Mendlovitz (Boulder, Colo.: Westview Press, 1982), 1: 315–25. See also Mason and Krane, "Political Economy of Death Squads."

34. Johan Galtung, "Self-Reliance: An Overdue Strategy for Transition," in Falk et al., 602–622.

35. Richard E. Rubenstein, *Alchemists of Revolution: Terrorism in the Modern World* (New York: Basic Books, 1987); Harry E. Vanden, "Terrorism, Law, and State Policy in Central America: The Eighties," *New Political Science* 18/19 (Fall/Winter 1990). See also the literature on the activities of the CIA, for example, John Stockwell, *Praetorian Guard: The U.S. Role in the New World Order* (Boston: South End Press, 1991); Philip Agee, *Inside the Company: CIA Diary* (New York: Bantam Books, 1975); and Edward Herman, *The Real Terror Network* (Boston: South End Press, 1982).

36. Among the best scholars on vigilantism are Sederberg and Abrahams.

37. Peter C. Sederberg, "The Phenomenology of Vigilantism in Contemporary America: An Interpretation," in Rosenbaum and Sederberg, *Terrorism,* 287–305 (here, 297).

38. One reason for this is that the academy still organizes specialization mainly along national lines. Good examples of the literature include Martin van Bruinessen, "Turkey's Death Squads," *Middle East Report* 26, no.2 (April-June 1996): 20–23; and Justus M. Van der Kroef, "Terrorism by Authority: The Case of the Death Squads of Indonesia and the Philippines," *Current Research on Peace and Violence* 10, no. 4 (1987): 143–58. Several of the contributors to this present volume have also published important academic case studies.

39. Mason and Krane, "The Political Economy of Death Squads," 175–98. See also William Anthony Lavelle, "State Terrorism and the Death Squad: A Study of the Phenomenon" (M.A. thesis, California State University, Sacramento, 1992), reprinted as unclassified Technical Information Report by the Defense Information Agency, Alexandria, VA, 1993. This is largely a summary of existing research.

40. Miles D. Wolpin, *State Terrorism and Death Squads in the New World Order,* Peace Research Reviews 12, no. 3 (Dundas, Canada: Peace Research Institute, 1992); Wolpin, "State Terrorism and Death Squads in the New World Order," 200–16.

41. He includes Lebanon in 1970s and '80s, Colombia in the 1940s, and possibly even Sri Lanka in the 1990s. Wolpin, *State Terrorism,* 38.

42. See Wolpin, *State Terrorism,* 42–44. Many of his arguments in this context are very similar to the work of Ted Robert Gurr, cited above.

43. Jeffrey Sluka, ed., *Death Squad: The Anthropology of State Terror* (Philadelphia: University of Pennsylvania Press, 1999).

44. Other books that don't deal directly with death squads but sometimes discuss them peripherally and that are particularly useful in understanding the subject include Allen Feldman, *Formations of Violence: The Narrative of the Body and Political Terror in Northern Ireland* (Chicago: University of Chicago Press, 1991); María José Moyano, *Argentina's Lost Patrol: Armed Struggle 1969–1978* (New Haven: Yale University Press, 1995); Hans Werner Tobler and Peter Waldmann, eds., *Staatliche und parastaatliche Gewalt in Lateinamerika* (Frankfurt am Main: Vervuert Verlag, 1991).

45. T. David Mason and Dale A. Krane, "The Political Economy of Death Squads: Toward a Theory of the Impact of State-Sanctioned Terror," *International Studies Quarterly* 33 (1989): 175–98. See also Steven Jackson et al., "Conflict and Coercion," *Conflict Resolution* 22, no. 4 (December 1978): 627–57.

46. This was a factor in the use of death squads in El Salvador, for example. See Chapter 4 below.

47. See, for example, Michael Ignatieff, "Human Rights: The Midlife Crisis," *New York Review of Books,* 20 May 1999, 58–62. See also Geoffrey Best, *War and Law Since 1945* (Oxford: Clarendon Press, 1994); and Michael Howard, George J. Andreopoulos and Mark R. Shulman, eds., *The Laws of War: Constraints on Warfare in the Western World* (New Haven: Yale University Press, 1994).

48. Indeed, most of the scholarly work on state violence would be impossible without this scrutiny.

49. Death squad members who talk or are suspected of being liable to talk are also themselves prime candidates for murder. See, for example, chapters 8, 9, and 10 in this volume.

50. This should not be taken as license to blame human rights activists or the media, however; the responsibility for the use of all state violence, covert or open, lies with states and their ruling elites alone.

51. Wolpin, "State Terrorism," 222–23. This idea bears further research.

52. Wolpin, "State Terrorism"; Galtung, "Self-Reliance"; Sluka, *Death Squad*; Nicholas Werz, "Die Ideologische Wurzeln der 'Doktrin der nationale Sicherheit' in Lateinamerika," in Tobler and Waldmann, 163–92; and Moyano, *Argentina's Lost Patrol*.

53. Werz, "Die Ideologische Wurzeln"; George A. Lopez, "National Security Ideology as an Impetus to State Violence and State Terror," in Stohl and Lopez, *Government Violence and Repression*, 73–95; David Pion-Berlin, "The Ideological Governance of Perception in the Use of State Terror in Latin America: The Case of Argentina," in *State Organized Terror: The Case of Violent Internal Repression*, eds. P. Timothy Bushnell et al. (Boulder, Co.: Westview Press, 1991), 135–52.

54. Lavelle, "State Terrorism," 15–23, for example, conflates death squads and all other forms of state terrorism and therefore argues that death squads existed far back in recorded history.

55. The paradox here is precisely that death squads represent a violation of the state's monopoly over the use of violence, but that is part of what makes them worthy of scholarly analysis.

56. Even where death squads are simply the tools of governments, they are usually used against insurgent or protest movements that themselves have a notion of citizenship as a precondition.

57. See, for example, Wyn Craig Wade, *The Fiery Cross: The Ku Klux Klan in America* (New York: Simon & Schuster, 1987); David M. Chambers, *Hooded Americanism: The History of the Ku Klux Klan* (Durham: Duke University Press, 1989); Scott Nelson, *Iron Confederacies: Southern Railways, Klan Violence, and Reconstruction* (Chapel Hill and London: University of North Carolina Press, 1999).

58. Note, too, that the proto–death squads investigated by Michael Schroeder in Chapter 2 of this volume also existed during a period of modernization.

59. *From Max Weber: Essays in Sociology*, eds. H. H. Gerth and C. Wright Mills (New York: Oxford University Press, 1946), 78.

60. Tilly, *Coercion*, esp. 1–33.

61. Hagen Schulze, *Staat und Nation in der Europäischen Geschichte*, 2nd ed. (Munich: C. H. Beck, 1995); Tilly, *Coercion*; Dieter Grimm, ed., *Staatsaufgaben* (Suhrkamp: Frankfurt am Main, 1996).

62. In most countries today, local Scout organizations are nominally private but enjoy a high degree of government support while serving as an adjunct to government in many ways. For example, scouting teaches patriotism and other citizenship skills, and, at least at its origin, served to prepare adolescents for military service.

63. For example, see Mustafa O. Attir, Burkart Holzner, and Zdenek Suda, eds., *Directions of Change: Modernization Theory, Research, and Realities* (Boulder, Colo.: Westview Press, 1981); Ronald Inglehart, *Modernization and Postmodernization: Cultural, Economic, and Political Change in 43 Societies* (Princeton, N.J.: Princeton University Press, 1997); Meredith W. Watts, *Xenophobia in United Germany: Generations, Modernization, and Ideology* (New York: St. Martin's Press, 1997); Hans-Ulrich Wehler, *Modernisierungstheorie und Geschichte* (Göttingen: Vandenhoek & Ruprecht, 1975).

64. Of course, states using death squads do so as part of a calculated risk. They are usually not meant to be permanent institutions, only temporary tools whose expiration should coincide with the end of the state of crisis. Thus the state doesn't consider itself to be risking its sovereignty any more than it believes it is actually risking its security and existence when it goes to war.

65. An example of a quango is the mixed private and public Training and Enterprise Councils in England. See "How to Control Quangos," *Economist,* 6 August 1994, 45–47.

66. See, variously, Hans-Georg Betz, *Postmodern Politics in Germany: The Politics of Resentment* (New York: St. Martin's Press, 1991); J. Peter Burgess, ed., *Cultural Politics and Political Culture in Postmodern Europe* (Amsterdam and Atlanta, Ga.: Rodopi, 1997); Leslie Paul Thiele, *Thinking Politics: Perspectives in Ancient, Modern, and Postmodern Political Theory* (Chatham, N.J.: Chatham House Publishers, 1997); Stephen K. White, *Political Theory and Postmodernism* (Cambridge: Cambridge University Press, 1991).

67. For a more extended discussion of the factors likely to lead to the continued use of death squads, see Wolpin, "State Terrorism," 198–99, 224–26; and Wolpin, *State Terrorism,* 1, 45–46.

68. Of course, the rise of competing essentialist identities within formerly quiet states, such as newly militant ethnic minorities, for example, may indeed be one source of state decline.

69. On the concealment of evidence, see John Daniszewski, "Evidence Details Systematic Plan of Killings in Kosovo . . . ," *Los Angeles Times,* 8 August 1999, 1.

70. For example, domestic human rights organizations seem to be multiplying, growing in sophistication, and building useful links to foreign counterparts in many violent states. See Ignatieff, "Human Rights."

PART I

Historical Cases

CHAPTER 2

"To Induce a Sense of Terror": Caudillo Politics and Political Violence in Northern Nicaragua, 1926–34 and 1981–95[1]

Michael J. Schroeder

"I'M GOING TO NARRATE A CASE TO YOU," the young Nicaraguan merchant began.

> One day I was going past the mountain of Pipián, in the jurisdiction of Somoto [in northern Nicaragua], accompanied by four other men, on a business trip. In one of the houses along the road lived a woman, and I asked her if she could serve us lunch. While she was preparing it, she told me the following:
> One day Anastacio Hernández, a bandit chief, arrived in a neighboring village with five of his followers. He dismounted at one of the houses and pulled twelve human heads from his saddlebags. He put them on a table and later began to dance around them, a savage dance, leaping around. Later he invited a young woman from the house to dance the same macabre dance. The young woman, afraid of losing her life, began to dance with the

bandit Hernández. But he told her, "Your head will remain with these others here." And he killed her with a gunblast, whose bullet also happened to kill one of the soldiers accompanying him. Hernández coldly, ferociously cut off the head of the young woman and the soldier, tossed them in his saddlebags, and marched off with the four men who remained.

Under the headline "The Dance of the Decapitated Heads," this bizarre news item, relating a tale told by José Anastacio Castellón, merchant and resident of El Ocotal in the mountainous north, appeared in the Managua daily *La Noticia* on April 19, 1928. This story about a story about a very strange story surely seems too fantastic and too far removed from the events it describes to be credible. Yet José Castellón's tale corresponds closely with a substantial body of evidence. More than half a century later, Pedro Antonio Arauz, brother-in-law of the famed Nicaraguan patriot Augusto C. Sandino, described this scene:

> Anastacio Hernández ... with an overflowing barbarity used to cut off the heads of those humble peasants who refused to serve him and stuff them in his saddlebags. His group had three guitars and an accordion, and he found the greatest pleasure in arriving in the valleys and meeting with the pretty women to dance all night long. He would remove the heads he had cut that day from his saddlebags and put them on a table, in plain view of the owners of the house, in order to induce a sense of terror. He would threaten the women who refused to go to the dance, telling them, pointing to the table full of heads, "That's where you're going to end up."[2]

Fusing terror, sexuality, culture, and politics, such "dances" were one way the notorious Conservative gang leader Anastacio Hernández worked "to induce a sense of terror" in this place and time. Fortuitously for historians, in a country where most political deals have left no paper trail, and where archives have suffered destruction and neglect, the Hernández case became one of the best-documented instances of local-regional political violence in Nicaraguan history before World War II. Much additional evidence, including Hernández's prison declaration and twenty eyewitness depositions, produced and compiled by the United States Marine Corps and Nicaraguan National Guard in early 1928, amply confirm these two macabre tales. For example, nineteen-year-old Benita López, illiterate peasant and resident of Hernández's natal district of Mosonte, describes a second Hernández tactic (one that explains how he acquired the heads he later stuffed into his saddlebags)—murderous gang assaults on people's homes:

> I . . . declare that on September 9, 1927, Anastacio Hernández and his gang came to my house about noon, killing my [two] brothers and taking away my [other] brother as their prisoner. Anastacio personally killed [one of] my brothers, cutting his head off, while David and Antonio Cárdenas killed [another brother] with machetes and rifles. [My other brother] was hung by his hands. . . . They killed him at El Zapote, where they killed four others. . . . Those accompanying Hernández were [22 first and last names], and others more whose names I do not recall. . . . X her mark.[3]

Especially remarkable in this terse narrative are the 22 first and last names: López (and presumably her brothers) knew the members of this murderous gang. Unlike many of the death squad activities described in this volume, this violence was personal and public as well as political. Anastacio Hernández, the faithful client of a small cabal of beleaguered Conservative power-holders, led a group of murderers that killed dozens of people in northern Nicaragua during a particularly volatile moment in that country's history.[4] The violence he and his followers produced was deeply rooted in local social relations and was at once political and personal, public and ritualized, gendered and sexualized, and based on intersecting relations of family, community, party, ethnicity, and class. Such grisly episodes illuminate key social and political dynamics underlying much of modern Nicaraguan history and illustrate the extent to which such violence was woven into the social and cultural fabric of the country—in this place and time and beyond.

This essay examines political gang violence and death squad activity in the mountainous region of Las Segovias in north-central Nicaragua during two noncontiguous periods of state crisis: (1) the 1926–27 civil war and the Sandino rebellion that followed (1927–34), and, more briefly, (2) the U.S.-supported Contra war against the Sandinista state and revolution in the 1980s and its aftermath in the early 1990s. The first section sketches the region of Las Segovias, focusing on historical geography, political economy, political culture, and the historic organization of violence (see map). The second section returns to the case of Anastacio Hernández before surveying less well documented instances of Conservative political violence during the turbulent 1926–28 period. The third section examines extrajudicial violence and murders committed against noncombatant civilians by rebels operating under Augusto C. Sandino's Defending Army of Nicaraguan National Sovereignty from 1927 to1933. The fourth section, surveying the Contra war, seeks to identify the principal continuities with and departures from earlier episodes of political unrest and violence.[5]

Las Segovias:
History, Caudillo Politics, Violence-Making

Like most nation-states around the world, Central America's were cobbled together from a number of distinct regions. Among the least studied but most important of these in postcolonial Nicaraguan history is Las Segovias, a frontier region bordering southwestern Honduras. Varying in elevation from one to 5,000 feet above sea level, the region was (and is) characterized by a bewilderingly variegated physical and human geography: steep mountains and volcanoes, some rising several thousand feet above the surrounding terrain; numberless hills, ridges, and escarpments separating myriad ravines and valleys; vast expanses of nearly impenetrable tropical forest and jungle merging into large rolling plains and semiarid savannas—all interspersed with fields of corn, beans, and sugarcane, cattle pastures, groves of banana and fruit trees, and coffee farms (from the 1890s), and crisscrossed by countless bull-cart paths and trails. The region supported a relatively dense indigenous population in the pre-Columbian period, and by the 1920s and 1930s, perhaps as many as a third of its 100,000 inhabitants self-identified as Indians. Mestizos, those of mixed Spanish and Indian ancestry, composed the remainder, along with a tiny "Spanish" or white minority. From 85 to 90 percent of the region's inhabitants could be described as campesinos; most were smallholders, living and cultivating crops in scattered hamlets and villages and working for wages seasonally on nearby commercial estates. Perhaps 5 percent of the population were the region's powerholders—white-skinned, propertied, politically connected. Segovian society thus mirrored the extreme class, ethnic, and social divisions and inequalities of the country as a whole.[6]

Political authority across the Segovias remained highly fragmented and hotly contested well into the twentieth century, making it a kind of Nicaraguan "wild west," where the rule of law routinely succumbed to the dictates of personal ambition and collective violence. Historically beyond the reach of the central state, the Segovias had long served as a haven for smugglers, outlaws, and bandits, as a crucible for rebellions against the national state, and as a conduit for revolutionary armies and movements crossing to and from Honduras and Nicaragua. While independent brigands were not uncommon, contending networks of local and regional caudillos generated most collective violence. Such caudillos had long dominated violence-making capacities in the region. From independence from Spain in the early 1820s until the late 1920s, the central state proved unable or unwilling to challenge this system of fragmented sovereignties, patrimonialism, and indirect rule.

Local-regional caudillos wielded and reproduced political power through patronage networks and alliances with other notables, victory in periodic elections, and sporadically mobilized private armies.[7] Coercive capacities frequently determined electoral outcomes, and across the Segovias and western Nicaragua, political violence surged during electoral periods. According to a succession of constitutions, national elections were held every four years, with only propertied adult males enfranchised as "citizens"; local elections were held more frequently. In 1928, the McCoy electoral law extended the franchise to all adult males.[8]

Historically, electoral periods generated widespread political violence across western Nicaragua and the Segovias.[9] During such periods, politically powerful patrons mobilized their clients into bands of armed men, ranging from five to 50 or more, who intimidated, harassed, and sometimes killed their political foes and their foes' family members, clients, and allies. Called "armies" by the men who organized and constituted them, such armed groups are more usefully conceived as bands or gangs. Occasionally the patron led his subordinates into battle, though more commonly, favored clients, or those skilled in the arts of war, served as gang leaders. The mobilization of such armed bands by local caudillos was the most important form of collective action in the region. The period of "Chamorrismo" from 1911 to 1928, when the Conservative caudillo Emiliano Chamorro dominated national political life, saw the continuation of these longstanding patterns: a weak state, indirect or caudillo rule, the fragmentation of political authority, and frequent tactical use of violence.[10]

As is well known, the early twentieth century also saw intensified United States interest in the circum-Caribbean region, a result of U.S. commercial and geostrategic concerns centering on the Panama Canal. From 1898, as the United States rapidly acquired its overseas empire, the political instability of Nicaragua came to represent a serious obstacle to U.S. imperial ambitions. The U.S. executive branch thus worked diligently to forge something unprecedented out of the maelstrom of traditional Nicaraguan politics: a stable polity, free of faction fighting and civil war, governed by uniform liberal-capitalist law under a genuinely national state. Importantly, by the 1910s and '20s, these goals corresponded with the aspirations of a growing segment of the Nicaraguan liberal elite who wished to transcend the destructive political anarchy of the previous century.[11]

By the early 1920s, the Conservative Party, dominated by Chamorro, was the principal obstacle confronting the U.S. executive branch and Nicaragua's leading Liberals. Chamorro and his allies were determined to retain the fragmented authority structure and indirect rule. While Chamorrista Conservatives had served as more or less pliant U.S. allies from 1910 to 1924, Chamorro's coup d'état of October 1925 represented a serious throwback to an earlier era. As Liberals clamored for revolution, the United States worked unsuccessfully to end Chamorro's rule. Liberals revolted, and civil war raged from May 1926 to May 1927. On May 4, 1927, with the victorious Liberal army on the outskirts of Managua, the U.S. special envoy and Liberal general José María Moncada signed the Espino Negro Accord. The accord called for U.S.-supervised elections in November 1928, for the establishment of a Guardia Nacional, and, until the 1928 elections, for Chamorro's ally Adolfo Díaz to serve as president.[12]

The Espino Negro Accord officially ended the war but did little to defuse the explosive political situation. Unpopular Chamorristas had every reason to expect defeat in the upcoming elections, and many worked feverishly to disrupt the electoral process by fostering violent, anarchic conditions under which "free and fair" elections could not be held. From the resultant political turmoil emerged one of the most notorious mass murderers in modern Nicaraguan history.

"A War of Parties": Caudillo Politics and Gang Violence in the Segovias after the Civil War

Anastacio Hernández headed up a Segovian-style death squad that, according to eyewitnesses, killed 49 people from May to November 1927, though he and his gangs probably murdered several hundred more.[13] His overarching objective, as expressed especially in the nature and structure of his violence, was to defend and augment the power of his patrons and their favored clients, particularly himself. In the post–Espino Negro political landscape, which virtually guaranteed a transfer of power to the Liberal opposition, he and his Conservative patrons pursued their objectives by mobilizing their followers into armed bands charged with killing some political enemies while generating a paralyzing sense of danger and fear among anyone challenging their power. Relatedly, since the November 1928 elections were to be governed by universal adult male suffrage, Conservative powerholders sought to diminish the voting power of the Liberal Party. This aim they pursued by murdering prospective Liberal voters and by sending thousands fleeing into Honduras (since Nicaraguans exiled in Honduras could not vote in Nicaraguan elections). Indeed, only two months before the elections, the estimated 5,000 mostly Liberal Nicaraguans who had sought refuge in Honduras were encountering major obstacles blocking their return.[14]

Hernández's principal patrons included three of the leading caudillos of Nueva Segovia: Gustavo Paguaga, Abraham Gutiérrez Lobo, and Pedro Lobo. Firmly ensconced in the Chamorrista wing of the Conservative Party, they nonetheless exercised considerable autonomy from the "big man" himself. For at least two decades, all had been major players in the Byzantine world of local-regional politics, accruing lucrative political posts, tax breaks, and other favors from a succession of Chamorrista regimes. Since at least 1921, Hernández had stood among their most favored henchmen and clients. Notably, despite a mountain of evidence against them, none of Ocotal's Chamorrista gang patrons suffered legal prosecution for their crimes, thanks to a corrupt judiciary beholden to Conservative interests.

As the eyewitness depositions make clear, the violence produced by the Hernández gangs exhibited a range of common features. Gang leaders made every effort to ensure that their actions would become publicly known and collectively remembered. Gangs commonly announced their assaults with shouts and gunblasts. Surprising their victims in their homes and wounding them with machete blows or gunshots, gang members bound their victims' hands with rope, raped and/or beat their loved ones, and robbed and destroyed household property. Slashing, bludgeoning, and otherwise torturing their bound and bleeding victims as they paraded noisily through adjacent hamlets or villages, gangs selected a nearby site of execution, where they performed various rituals of death and dismemberment—all to the raucous sounds of gunfire, shouts, music, songs, laughter, dancing, and drinking, punctuated by the anguished cries of the victims. In the final act of this macabre drama, the gang displayed the mutilated corpses along heavily trafficked roads. They also always left behind surviving eyewitnesses to tell the tale—usually women, children, and the elderly. These acts, then, were terrifying public spectacles, intended to dehumanize ritually and utterly their murdered victims and their families, and thereby to generate among survivors a densely packed field of social memories of terror, pain, fear, and death.

Of the gang members little is known, other than their names, that all were men, that most were members of local families and communities, and that most were related to other gang members by marriage or blood. Gang rosters shifted constantly. On September 9, 1927, according to eyewitnesses, Hernández took to the field with more than 34 men who killed and mutilated seven people; the next day he led at least 15 men—none from the previous day's roster—who killed and mutilated at least six others. Thus, in a single day the gang was entirely reconstituted, or nearly so. Such fluidity suggests both the dynamism of gang mobilization and the rootedness of gang leaders and members in local families and communities. Similar dynamics obtained between gang leaders and their patrons. If most gang leaders served as their patrons' faithful clients most of the time, they also exercised considerable independence—killing personal enemies as well as their patrons', choosing precisely how and when they would engage in certain actions, cutting new deals if circumstances merited. Rivalries and conflicts between gang leaders were common. Like their followers, gang leaders acted not only as tools of the powerful to be wielded at critical moments but as autonomous agents, selecting whom they would serve and how.

Importantly, victims and assailants were usually well acquainted; most eyewitnesses could identify a dozen or more gang members by face and by name. This points to one of the most striking aspects of this violence: its locally rooted, locally generated qualities. Gang patrons hailed from the region's most prominent families. Gang leaders, members, and victims were all born and raised in neighboring hamlets, villages, and towns; all trod, as children, on interlacing sets of footpaths in the same set of mountains. These were neighbors butchering neighbors.

Of the victims little is known, beyond their names, where they lived, that all were middling or poor campesinos, and that all were acquainted with many of their attackers. None, it appears, were important political actors. With the single exception of the murdered woman in José Castellón's newspaper story, all of the murdered victims were adult men; most were married and fathers. Gangs targeted entire families, beating and raping the women, brutalizing children and the elderly. While it would greatly enhance understanding of this violence to know more about the victims—particularly their political affiliations and previous relations with their assailants—the investigators did not pursue these questions. Still, since most rural folk knew who was affiliated with whom, it seems likely that targets were carefully selected. Most of those targeted by Hernández were probably clients of Liberal or non-Chamorrista Conservative patrons, who in turn were opposed by the patrons of the Chamorrista gangs.

Yet if patrons and gangs usually selected their targets carefully, gangs' actions often displayed a strong element of caprice and improvisation. On the evening of September 16, 1927, Tómas González had just returned from a day's labor in his fields when the Hernández gang descended on his home and macheted him to death. They also murdered three laborers he had hired—apparently nothing more than a stroke of catastrophic misfortune for the three. Surprise and unpredictability appear as key weapons in the gang's arsenal. Hernández, it seems, endeavored to nurture a deeply felt sense of paralysis, fatalism, and resignation, a sense that people inhabited an inherently irrational and dangerous world—a world lacking chains of causality and reason, where *fortuna*, luck, and not hard work or stubborn commitment to a goal were the driving forces of fate.[15] That this cultural sensibility ran directly counter to the Enlightenment project of reason and rationality undergirding liberalism suggests that clashes between Liberal and Conservative gangs were also clashes between profoundly opposed worldviews.

From May 1927 until the November 1928 elections, in short, political gang violence exploded across the region. At one level, this pattern replicated the region's and country's traditions of electoral violence.[16] And if Hernández could lay claim to be the period's most notorious Conservative Segovian gang leader, dozens more like him perpetrated similar crimes. Altogether more than 30 Conservative gang leaders were active in the western Segovias during this period; some were Hernández's allies, others competitors.[17] Extant documentary evidence in these cases is slight, limited to cursory reports on murders and atrocities committed by armed groups, with victims and perpetrators often remaining nameless. Shadowy "Conservative clubs" organized many such gangs—small groups of politically powerful Conservatives who met, strategized, and mobilized client gang leaders to kill and terrorize political enemies in the locales under their domination.[18] All such gangs appear similar in origin and structure to Hernández's, deploying the same basic organizational forms, tactics, and strategies.

A close examination of the Hernández violence, in short, can provide an enriched understanding of long-standing cultural and historical patterns that became especially manifest during times of elections, political instability, and state crisis—conditions obtaining throughout much of the previous century. The elimination of political foes and rivals formed the principal raison d'être of the Hernández gangs and one of the principal activities of Segovian gangs generally. Other episodes of violence during this same period reveal a differently textured landscape of violence, while providing further evidence that the death squad activities of political gangs were integral to the region's political culture and social fabric.

One such case unfolded a day's ride southeast of Ocotal, in the mountains northeast of La Trinidad and San Isidro, which saw a series of running battles between Liberal, Conservative, and Sandinista gangs during this period (see map). In the spring of 1928, as the marines began settling into the area, marine intelligence began tracking the activities of two opposing networks of gangs. Leaders of the Conservative gangs included La Trinidad's police chief, the mayor, a local judge, at least one prominent local landowner, and a number of local "bad men"; other Conservative patrons remained in the shadows.[19] A number of Estelí's municipal officials, including the tax inspector and police chief, were reportedly in league with them. "The [Conservative] group," according to one report, "are very cruel and kill their victims."[20] In response, prominent local Liberals mobilized their own gang.[21] Each group, usually composed of some 30 men, threatened, robbed, and murdered their opponents.[22]

Throughout March and April the Liberal and Conservative gangs fought bitterly for supremacy, while smaller groups of Sandinista rebels battled and allied with factions of both sides, and all groups tried to avoid the marines. According to one captured Conservative gang member, "The [Conservative] gang was in the field robbing and killing personal enemies, chiefly against the [Liberal] gang. These two gangs were fighting each other all the time." The captured gang member explained why he had killed one La Trinidad resident: "[The man I killed] was a member of Tiburcio Vargas's gang of bandits. Vargas was a Liberal and I am a Conservative."[23] This kind of plainspoken Manichaeism suggests something of the depth of the hatred and divisions separating the two major political parties.

In early April, the Conservative gang blundered into a firefight with a marine patrol; soon after, a León newspaper reported that a group of Conservatives had murdered a Liberal landowner.[24] After an investigation, the Conservative gang leader was arrested and jailed, while the gang remained active under another Conservative.[25] Around the same time, the main Liberal gang leader entered into nominal alliances with two Sandinista generals. By the end of May, weary of eluding relentless and well-armed marine-guardia patrols, surviving gang leaders and most of their followers accepted amnesties offered by the guardia. By June, gang activity had decreased substantially, though robberies and murders continued sporadically through the rainy summer months.[26] In September, Sandinista general Pedro Altamirano killed the leader of the main Liberal gang as a traitor to the revolution, while the principal remaining Conservative gang leader switched allegiances and fought with the Sandinistas until he was killed by the marines-guardia in June 1930.[27]

As the November 1928 elections approached, political gang violence in this subregion subsided while reaching a crescendo across much of the rest of the Segovias. As one Liberal wrote at the bottom of a lengthy list of reported murders and outrages around Jinotega, "All of the above delinquencies have been committed by conservative bandits, and per the general opinion to put fear into the Liberals and handicap the [voting] registrations."[28] *Para infundir terror*—"to put fear into": this was the fundamental objective for all political groups, from machete-wielding gangs of campesinos to well-heeled members of brandy- and tobacco-soaked Conservative clubs. Taken together, the extant sources paint a gruesome portrait and provide a grisly documentary record of gang violence and death squad activity in the region. Many blamed the Sandinistas for these crimes, but in fact Chamorrista Conservatives committed most of them.[29] At the same time, personal grudges, family feuds, and other struggles often intersected with more purely political goals, generating in any given case a complex field of motivating forces.

In November 1928, the Liberal José María Moncada was elected as president, and modern Nicaraguan political history entered a new era—and ousted Chamorristas knew it. While a handful of Liberal and Conservative gangs in the Segovias remained active, from this point the central dynamics of violence-making shifted to the triangular conflict characteristic of guerrilla wars: the state (the invading marines and newly formed guardia), the guerrillas (Sandino's Defending Army), and the Segovian civilian populace.

Death Squad Activity in Sandino's Rebellion

The civil war of 1926–27 provided a rare opportunity for the campesinos of Las Segovias to mobilize, organize, and press claims of their own. And, as in the Mexican Revolution a decade before, once the popular mobilizations had begun, they proved exceedingly difficult for the central state to suppress. After June 1927, Segovian campesinos, initially motivated by the desire for vengeance against popularly despised local-regional Chamorrista powerholders, suddenly confronted a new and even deadlier enemy: the invading marines and the newly formed Guardia Nacional. In a complex political dynamic, the popular war against the Conservatives continued while simultaneously transforming into a popular-nationalist crusade to expel a foreign invader. The relative thinness of patronage networks in the region (compared to the more densely populated zones farther south) and the extreme violence of the invading and occupying forces spurred the rapid growth of Sandino's Defending Army: the first made possible, and the second impelled powerfully, the formation of dense and deeply felt horizontal allegiances—a "fraternity" or "brotherhood"—in place of relatively weak vertical ones.[30]

Following a pattern characteristic of most guerrilla wars of the nineteenth and twentieth centuries, as the conflict grew into a genuinely popular war of national liberation, the lines dividing rebel soldiers from noncombatant civilians became increasingly blurred.[31] In everyday practice, across the Segovias from 1927 to 1934, such distinctions meant little. The marines and guardia had no practical way to distinguish between rebel sympathizers, supporters, and soldiers and "peaceful civilians." Facing these uncertainties, they opted to wage a brutally violent offensive against Segovian campesinos generally.[32]

The rebels, occupying a very different moral and political terrain, confronted a similar conundrum: distinguishing between "traitorous collaborators" and "neutral civilians" was next to impossible, while the exigencies of guerrilla war against a technologically superior and resource-rich foe worked strongly to render meaningless the category "neutral civilian." Rebel violence against what latter-day historians might call "noncombatant civilians" (a category that as a practical matter hardly existed in this time and place) was thus integral to Sandino's rebellion against the invading marines.

Despite fundamental differences, discussed below, the violence of Sandino's rebels against "noncombatant civilians" exhibited very close parallels with the Liberal-Conservative gang violence that preceded and coexisted with it. In all cases, gangs led by charismatic chiefs deployed spectacular public violence against select targets in order to eliminate some foes and "to induce a sense of terror" among others, and thereby augment their own power vis-à-vis their enemies. Altogether more than 100 small rebel groups, each headed by its own chief, emerged over the course of five years of rebellion. While a handful of larger groups, designated "expeditionary columns," roved far and wide across northern and eastern Nicaragua, scores of smaller groups remained rooted in specific and exclusively Segovian locales. All were composed of ever-shifting groups of men sporadically mobilized through personalistic webs of kin and community relations. All had to rob to remain in the field (or, in their words, to levy "forced contributions"), and virtually all acted, at one time or another, as death squads, killing known enemies (most of whom one might categorize as "noncombatant civilians") and instilling an acute sense of fear and terror among all actual and potential "traitors"—a category that came to include just about everyone.[33]

The most infamous episode of such rebel violence, the "San Marcos Massacre," came on the eve of the November 1928 elections, when forces under Sandinista general Pedro Altamirano killed and mutilated four Liberal propagandists in the village of San Marcos near Jinotega. In this instance, as in most others, Sandinista methods of murder and mutilation closely resembled the attacks perpetrated by Anastacio Hernández and his gangs. On October 2, Altamirano's gang assaulted the designated house with shouts and gunshots; dragging the four Liberals from their beds, the gang marched their captives a short distance from the house and killed and mutilated them with guns and machetes. Altamirano purposely left the mutilated cadavers on the main road through San Marcos, while seizing some local residents to warn them that "a similar fate awaited the other leaders of the liberal party." The rebel chieftain made known "the political nature of this brutal crime," stating it was "intended as an example [to] the Liberals, especially the leaders, . . . only 'a beginning' of what was to follow."[34] Here as in most cases, the rebels attacked civilians, and their families, known to have supported or assisted the invading forces.[35]

Pedro Altamirano, the most infamous of all the rebel chieftains, led what was surely the deadliest and longest-lived functionally autonomous rebel group engaged in periodic death squad activity in Nicaraguan history up to that time, active and in the field from at least 1926 until his death more than a decade later, and responsible for hundreds of killings.[36] Much of his notoriety derived from his frequent use of the "vest cut," in which victims were decapitated, their arms cut off at the shoulders, and their abdomens sliced open, the corpses thus resembling a waistcoat or vest. The documentary record brims with such episodes.[37]

In short, Sandinista rebels frequently killed and mutilated noncombatant civilian enemies and "traitors." For a range of personal and political reasons, a broad cross section of Segovian civilians either allied with the invading forces or refused to assist Sandino's.

The threadbare rebels were thus constantly on guard against not only hunger and destitution but "treason" and "traitors," some of whom were wealthy, and many more of whom were middling or poor. In this vastly unequal battle against a foreign invader, the tactical use of fear quickly emerged as one of the rebels' most important weapons against internal opposition.

As the war grew in ferocity, even the refusal to lend assistance became punishable by death. In October 1931, in one such instance that also speaks to the politics of Segovian gender relations, Sandinista general Juan Santos Morales reported to his supreme chief that some women at El Cuje near Telpaneca were refusing to provide his forces with tortillas, and that, in consequence, "I have ordered [my men] to organize a commission and pass through El Cuje, in order to give the 'vest cut' (*chalequear*) to everyone they encounter who belongs to the families that are impeding the forward march of our cause."[38] At the same time, the rebels' frequent recourse to such violence must be seen within the broader context of even more extreme marine and guardia violence against the Segovian civilian populace.

At least three fundamental features distinguished Sandinista violence from traditional Segovian political gang violence: (1) the social origins of its patrons, in this case a substantial proportion of Segovian campesinos; (2) the nature of the relationship between its patrons and practitioners and the legally constituted state, i.e., one of absolute opposition; and (3) the popular-patriotic ideals and aspirations motivating the rebels' use of violence. Seizing on a range of political tools long used by dominant groups—gang organization, ritual terror, property destruction and appropriation, bureaucratic and state forms, revenue-generating mechanisms such as forced loans and contributions—Sandino's rebels succeeded in "democratizing" or "popularizing" these tools in order to pursue an agenda entirely at odds with the agenda animating Anastacio Hernández and his patrons. The wide gulf separating these sources of violence are illustrated in the rebels' strong moral and legal sanctions against rape, which the evidence indicates were strictly enforced and widely adhered to. Such sanctions were part and parcel of the gendered qualities of Sandino's nationalist discourse and project. Sandino constructed "the nation" as female, a mother figure being brutally raped and degraded by the invading marines. Not to impose severe sanctions against rape by rebel soldiers would be to undermine the very premise of the rebellion. This is but one of the many ways that Sandinista, marine-guardia, Liberal, and Conservative gang violence and death squad activity need to be carefully distinguished from one another. Springing from a different source, in many respects Sandinista violence was fundamentally unlike the violence of Liberal and Conservative gangs.

In addition to bona-fide rebels, many brigands and common criminals seized on the opportunities created by Sandino's rebellion to continue their old practices under a new banner. Juan Heriberto Rodríguez, for instance, aka Juan Butón ("John Booty"), a notorious rapist and murderer at one time allied with Matagalpa's Conservative elite, was released from prison in February 1929 and resumed his criminal career. Briefly allied with two Sandinista generals (who evidently overlooked his propensity to rape), Butón counted among his troops a number of local criminals and brigands who robbed, raped, and murdered before the marines-guardia finally tracked him down and killed him in the spring of 1930.[39] Among the dozens of criminals and gang leaders exploiting the opportunities opened up by the Sandinista rebellion were Juan Castillo, a gang chief responsible for numerous murders and atrocities in the mountains around Limay and El Sauce, and Rubén Barreto, a gang leader in the early 1920s who was arrested by the marines-guardia in 1928 and subsequently served as their scout and guide.[40]

In short, for nearly six years, scores of small bands of ragtag rebels waged a war without quarter against hundreds of small bands of heavily armed soldiers of the state. If the murder of non-combatant civilians was but one of the many activities undertaken by these rebel bands, such murders were common, and integral to the process of war. Bands on both sides exhibited, in different ways, many of the classic characteristics of Segovian death squads as exemplified by the Anastacio Hernández gangs. And yet in each case, the origins, character, and consequences of the violence exhibited notable differences.

In February 1934, Somoza's National Guard assassinated Sandino, and in the weeks to follow it crushed the rebellion utterly. For the first time in Nicaraguan history, the central state effectively monopolized all substantial means of organized coercion. Political stability of a sort reigned across the country for more than four decades under the Somoza dictatorship and dynasty (1936–79)—a stability marked by the state's systematic cooptation and/or brutal repression of opposition, strong United States support for a series of nondemocratic Somocista regimes, and the transition to a dependent capitalism that enriched a few while miring the vast majority more deeply in poverty and social misery. But with the end of World War II came the Cold War, a global wave of decolonization and anticolonial nationalism, the Cuban Revolution, and soon after, a new group of Nicaraguan rebels, the Sandinista National Liberation Front (FSLN). After nearly two decades of struggle, in 1979 these self-proclaimed "children of Sandino" toppled the Somoza regime, ushering in a new era in Nicaraguan history. From the dynamics of revolution and counterrevolution that followed in the wake of the Sandinista triumph there emerged across the country, and especially in the Segovias, a new and even deadlier round of political gang violence and death squad activity that continued for most of the next two decades.

The Contra War and Its Aftermath

"[A] calamity beyond reckoning, probably the worst thing that had happened to those regions since the Spanish Conquest."[41] This is how the freelance journalist Paul Berman describes the impact of the Sandinista revolution and counterrevolution in the Nicaraguan countryside. And by any measure, he is right: in duration, scope, intensity, and number of civilians terrorized, displaced, maimed, and killed, the Contra war is a much bigger story than everything just described—a war involving the highest levels of the U.S. national security state in a high-profile Cold War battle, embroiling the U.S. presidency in a major scandal (the Iran-Contra affair), spilling over into neighboring Costa Rica, Honduras, El Salvador, and beyond, and transforming the United States into Nicaragua's leading patron of gang violence and death squad activity. Beginning within months of the Sandinista victory in July 1979, the Contra war raged through most the decade of Sandinista rule (1979–90), formally ending with the peace accords of 1987—though as we have seen, "official" endings to wars in Nicaragua do not necessarily bring an end to the killing. The 1987 peace accords resulted in the demobilization of thousands of Contra combatants. They also marked the onset of a fresh round of political battles no less complex or deadly than those that had come before.

A staggering array of mostly U.S.-supplied advanced military technologies made this a far deadlier conflict and a fundamentally different kind of war. The partisan and rebel gangs of the 1920s and 1930s depended mainly on machetes, single- and double-barrel rifles, and, very rarely, Lewis and Thompson machine guns. Killing was widespread but on a relatively small scale. The Contras, in contrast, depended on a host of sophisticated military technologies, all procured through millions of dollars in aid funneled from Argentina, Israel, South Africa, and the world's leading superpower in the waning years of the Cold War, and as a result were able to kill a far greater number of noncombatant civilians.

Sandino's rebellion was limited mainly to the Segovias, and directly touched the lives of perhaps one-seventh of Nicaragua's total population of 700,000. The Contra war also was centered in the Segovias; an estimated 83 percent of the Contra foot soldiers were poor peasants and wage laborers from Nicaragua's northern and central regions.[42] But the conflict also raged across large parts of the country that in Sandino's time had remained relatively quiescent—especially Chontales, Matagalpa, and the entire Atlantic coast region—and directly touched the lives of virtually all of the country's more than three million inhabitants. Reliable estimates place the number of persons uprooted as a result of the war at more than 600,000 and the number of combatant and civilian deaths at some 30,000—in other words, an estimated 1 percent of Nicaragua's total population was killed in the war, and one-fifth displaced.[43]

At the same time, the Contra war resembled in many ways the smaller conflicts of half a century earlier. "To induce a sense of terror" was also the Contras' principal aim, as much evidence testifies. As *New York Times* correspondent Steven Kinzer observed, "Some armies seek to control and channel the violence of their soldiers, but Contra soldiers were taught quite differently. The form of warfare they adopted in their first years was straightforward terror."[44] Beginning in the mid-1980s, a stream of reports and eyewitness accounts documented a policy of deliberate and widespread Contra terror and death squad activity against the rural civilian populace, particularly in the Segovias.[45]

Corroborated Contra atrocity stories abound. On October 28, 1982, in a representative episode, five armed and uniformed Contras assaulted the home of María Bustillo of El Jícaro. "The intruders ordered everyone to the floor, face down, and warned that whoever moved would be killed. . . . When María went out the next morning to look for her family, she found her five children dead, about 50 yards from the house. They were left all cut up. Their ears were pulled off, their noses and other parts were cut off." Nearby, María found the mutilated bodies of her husband and another man.[46] Such episodes reveal that the self-imposed boundaries of the Hernández gangs—who rarely killed children or women—had been replaced by an even less discriminating form of terror. Contra bands and death squads killed thousands of noncombatant civilians—children, women, and men.

The Contras aimed to destroy the Sandinista revolution by inflicting as much material, ideological, and human damage as possible. In the countryside they especially targeted teachers, communications, health care, and government workers, and members of Sandinista agricultural cooperatives. They combined kidnapping, torture, rape, and murder with the systematic destruction of key installations and institutions of the revolutionary government: health clinics, schools, agricultural cooperatives, grain storage facilities, bridges, and power stations. After eight months of firsthand observation, Bob Barnes, a plainspoken Friend and Witness for Peace volunteer from California, summarized his view of the Contra war in the Segovias. "This is what the war is here—attacks on civilians and their homes, goods and food, attacks on health centers, nutrition centers, and schools. I cannot recall an attack on a military base as such."[47] Barnes described events he witnessed in August 1986 in the mountains northeast of Estelí:

That morning the Contra came down a road/path roughly from Chicopipe to La Caracao, hauling men from their homes and forcing them to accompany them. All in all, they kidnapped twenty-two. Two they left dead on the road. Nine they simply walked away from; they returned to their homes or fled to safer areas nearby. Eleven were forced to go with their captors. A week later two campesinos were working in remote fields far from their homes and were stimulated by an obnoxious smell. It came from the bodies of the eleven who had been killed at the end of a box canyon. They had been tortured in various ways. . . . One of the campesinos had been looking for his son. He found him there.[48]

It is something of a paradox that despite their campaigns of terror and the emergence of widespread popular opposition against them, Contra rebels in the Segovias and elsewhere came to enjoy considerable support among substantial segments of the populace. Many campesinos bitterly opposed the Sandinista regime, despite the Sandinista ideological commitment to advancing the material well-being and political power of the country's majority, the workers and campesinos. In keeping with a long tradition, most campesinos harbored strong suspicions against state intrusions, and many quickly came to resent an often heavy-handed Sandinista bureaucracy and administration in the countryside—including price controls, compulsory marketing boards, and systematic credit discrimination against autonomous campesinos in favor of cooperatives and collective producers.[49] The anticommunist teachings and propaganda of the Roman Catholic Church also found deep resonance among many Segovianos, as did the vociferous complaints of landowners, cattle ranchers, coffee growers, and businessmen in anti-Sandinista newspapers, radio stations, and the popular culture generally. Popular mobilizations in the Segovias and elsewhere against the Sandinistas emerged as early as mid-1980, around the same time as the first invasions of the main Contra forces from bases in southern Honduras—forces composed overwhelmingly of former national guardsmen exiled in Honduras and funded, organized, trained, and equipped by the CIA and the Reagan administration.

Once the U.S.-supported invasions had begun, popular mobilizations against the Sandinistas mushroomed across the Segovias and beyond. According to Ariel Armony, a leading analyst of the Contra war, "The rich and middle peasantry, who were among the first to organize anti-Sandinista armed bands following the triumph of the revolution, played a major role in the recruitment of rank-and-file troops for the Contra forces." Thousands of propertyless campesinos joined the counterrevolution. Armony's study concludes: "Only 25 percent of the Contra combatants owned any form of property, 60 percent were under twenty-five years old, and 90 percent were illiterate or semi-literate."[50]

Contra terror reached its peak in the mid-1980s. By this time, the Reagan administration had become a new kind of patron for Segovian and Nicaraguan private armies, gangs, and rebel groups, providing millions of dollars' worth of aid and supplies to the many individuals and groups composing the counterrevolution. During the same period, other groups of campesinos were organizing to pressure the Sandinista state for land, credits, subsidies, and other resources.

But the state had few resources to dispense and was making many demands of its own. Gang mobilization and violence once more became weapons of the popular classes in their struggle against the state, the powerful, and each other, though on a much larger scale. While the political and rebel gangs of the 1920s and '30s comprised at most 1,000 or 2,000 people, by 1990 the Nicaraguan resistance claimed to represent more than 170,000 people in rural areas, including over 22,000 officially demobilized Contras and their families.[51] From the mid-1980s, the "democratization" or "popularization" of gang violence in the Segovias and elsewhere had reached a crescendo, with catastrophic results.

After the Sandinista electoral defeat of February 1990, the Contra war entered a new and even more volatile phase. A decade of war had devastated much of the country, especially the northern and central regions, while the central government reeled under a mountain of debt. As the Contra and Sandinista (EPS) armies demobilized, thousands of young men were left without any means of earning a living; for many ex-soldiers on both sides, life in the bush had become the only life they knew. By the early 1990s, then, a bewildering array of armed groups ranged at will across northern and central Nicaragua—ex-Contras and EPS soldiers (re-Contras and re-compas, who sometimes joined forces despite ideological and political differences), independent bandits and brigands, bands of thugs and criminals hired by large landlords, and militant groups of armed campesinos making claims on the state for land, credits, and other resources. In 1992, an estimated 23,000 armed insurgents remained active in the Nicaraguan countryside.[52] In a replay writ large of the post–1926–27 civil war period, once the genie of popular mobilization had been let out of the bottle, it proved mightily difficult for the central state to force it back in again.

Journalistic accounts of the war, like Christopher Dickey's *With the Contras* (1985), Steven Kinzer's *Blood of Brothers* (1991), and Sam Dillon's *Commandos* (1991), paint vivid portraits of the counterrevolution in the countryside, filled with dozens of colorful and ruthless Contra leaders like Suicida, Comandante Bravo, Bull's Eye, Krill, Cancer, the Jackal, 3–80—men whose visceral hatred of the Sandinista revolution manifested as systematic terror against all Segovianos sympathetic to the regime. These accounts also make clear that externally imposed and locally rooted death squad activities were both integral to the war. Paul Berman, in an extended "search for Ben Linder's killers" through the Segovian mountains in the mid-1990s, conveys much of the localism and personalism of the war in the northern countryside in the 1980s and 1990s.[53] Beginning his search near El Chipote, famous as Sandino's "mountain fortress" against the invading marines in the 1920s and '30s, Berman discovered that locally prominent families, some with ties to the police, had organized the counterrevolution in the area. "Within a year or two of the Sandinista People's Revolution," writes Berman, "some twenty armed groups were running around the countryside, most of them in the north, others in the Indian zones to the east, where regionalist sentiments were strong." After the 1987 peace accords and subsequent demobilization, the killings continued—"People were killed over personal grudges, over land, and, above all, over politics."[54] As Shirley Christian noted in the *New York Times* in early 1993, "unsolved murders with political overtones [continue to] occur almost daily."[55] Only with the election of Arnoldo Alemán in 1996, followed in late 1998 by the extraordinary devastation wrought by Hurricane Mitch, has political gang violence in the Segovias substantially diminished.

Conclusion

Writing at the dawn of the twentieth century, Salvador Mendieta, the founder and leader of the Central American Unionist Party and self-proclaimed crusader against fracture, hate, ignorance, and foolishness, decried what he called "the disease of Central America" (*la enfermedad de Centro-América*). Much of his insightful and broadranging critique of Central American society and politics focused on the centrality of violence in the political culture of his homeland of Nicaragua and Central America—a political universe in which the "agents of the government" and their allies systematically "robbed, raped, tortured, murdered by applying the 'law of fire,' and committed every excess of a party of thugs and criminals."[56]

As the twentieth century draws to a close, much of Mendieta's stinging critique still resonates forcefully. On the one hand, fundamental differences separated the periods and episodes of death squad activity described in this chapter: differences in gang patrons, leaders, and members and their social origins, aspirations, ideologies, and relationship to the state; differences in world-historical

time and in the magnitude of the conflicts. Yet the Segovian gang violence and death squad activities surveyed above share many features and themes. Historically, locally rooted political gang violence
and death squad activity in Nicaragua and the Segovias have
erupted during periods of state crisis and political instability, as
local authorities and would-be power-holders have struggled to fill
the power vacuum created by the waning of state power. The fundamental purposes of such gang violence and death squad activity—
to eliminate some enemies and "to induce a sense of terror" among
all actual and potential opposition—have remained largely unchanged. Family, community, gender, patron-client, and party-fac-
tional relations in the Segovias and Nicaragua all changed in various
ways from the 1920s to the 1990s. What did not change is that these
fundamental social glues, whatever the precise nature of their transformation, continued to spawn gang violence and death squad activity. The major change came mainly in the extent of the killing, a
consequence of an abundance of advanced weaponry, an exceedingly pernicious form of imperialist intervention, and a much larger
universe of political risks and opportunities.

The foregoing suggests that political gang violence and death
squad activity form an integral part of modern Nicaraguan political,
social, and cultural history. It would seem to follow that any effort
to eliminate such extrajudicial violence would require, at the level of
the state, the institutionalization of genuine political democracy and
compromise, an independent judiciary, accountable executive and
legislative branches, and a truly participatory political system that re-
sponds effectively to the claims of all social sectors, especially the
popular classes. Essential for this, in turn, is genuine economic development that advances the material interests of the country's majority—a possibility that, at the current writing, appears to be
extremely remote, at least within the next two to three decades. An
end to the violence would also seem to require the conscious aban-
donment of some long-standing political-cultural traditions and
practices, combined with the florescence of an alternative political
ethos—one based more on compromise, power-sharing, and media-
tion than on hatred, fracture, demonization, and vengeance. Quality
universal public education, a popular and searingly honest reap-
praisal of Nicaraguan history,[57] and equality in gender relations
would also appear to constitute *sine qua non* for an end to the violence. Until the state proves able to monopolize violence-making not

only through a national army but through the systematic nurturing of a democratic and educated civil society, and unless and until neoliberalism proves more enriching than impoverishing for Central America's laboring poor, political gang violence and death squad activity will likely continue.

In an essay on his journey through Sandinista Nicaragua in the mid-1980s, the writer and novelist Salman Rushdie wrote: "To understand the living in Nicaragua, I found, it was necessary to begin with the dead. The country was full of ghosts."[58] As the millennium draws to a close, the ghosts of the past in Nicaragua continue to haunt and elude as well as inspire. Paradoxically hiding in the shadows of the popular culture and national memory while also readily apparent most everywhere, the culture and legacy of violence symbolized in an anonymous countrywoman's tale about "the dance of the decapitated heads" has yet to be fully acknowledged and confronted, much less transcended.

Notes

1. I am indebted to David C. Brooks, Nora Faires, Robert H. Holden, Rosario Montoya, John Peters, and the editors of this volume for their incisive commentaries on previous drafts of this essay. Research and writing were supported by the Office of Research at the University of Michigan-Flint.

2. Pedro Antonio Arauz, "Después de la terminación de la guerra constitucionlista," unpublished ms., Instituto de Estudio del Sandinismo, Managua (currently Instituto de Historia de Nicaragua, hereafter IES), c. 1980. Unless otherwise noted, all translations from the Spanish are mine.

3. Deposition of Benita López, United States National Archives, Record Group 127, Entry 127, Box 5, File: Hernandez, Anastacio; hereafter cited as NA[Record Group]/[Entry]/[Box]/[File].

4. Michael J. Schroeder, "Horse Thieves to Rebels to Dogs: Political Gang Violence and the State in the Western Segovias, Nicaragua, in the Time of Sandino, 1926–1934," *Journal of Latin American Studies* 28 (May 1996): 383–434. Unless otherwise indicated, see this source for all evidence and arguments relating to the Hernández case.

5. I might note that I reserve a modicum of skepticism about applying the term "death squad" to the Segovian gangs described in this essay. The efforts of the volume's editors to refine the term's definition and

thereby craft a specialized sociological vocabulary are potentially both enabling and constraining, sharpening one analytic focus—on a specific type of collective action defined by a specific outcome—while potentially effacing another—the social, cultural, and historical contexts out of which those actions and outcomes arose and the meanings contemporaries attached to them. My hesitancies about the term are partly suppressed here because the activities described conform to the editors' rigorous and precise definition, because these are fascinating cases that reveal a great deal about this type of activity, and because of a periodic desire to transcend what is perhaps a historian's inherent skepticism toward overgeneralization. The literature on death squads in 1970s and 1980s El Salvador and Guatemala is enormous; see esp. the works of Patricia Alvarenga, Thomas Anderson, Sewall H. Menzel, Americas Watch, and Amnesty International in the general bibliography to this volume.

6. See Michael J. Schroeder, "To Defend Our Nation's Honor: Toward a Social and Cultural History of the Sandino Rebellion in Nicaragua, 1927–1934" (Ph.D. diss., University of Michigan, 1993), chap. 3.

7. From a voluminous literature on patron-client relations, S. N. Eisenstadt, *Patrons, Clients, and Friends: Interpersonal Relations and the Structure of Trust in Society* (New York: Cambridge University Press, 1984), remains useful; on patrons and clients in Nicaragua see E. Bradford Burns, *Patriarch and Folk: The Emergence of Nicaragua, 1798–1858* (Cambridge: Cambridge University Press, 1991); José Coronel Urtecho, *Reflexiones sobre la historia de Nicaragua*, 3 vols. (Managua, 1962); Salvador Mendieta, *La enfermedad de Centro-América*, 3 vols. (Barcelona, 1932), esp. vol. 1.

8. Burns, *Patriarch and Folk*, 45, 79–80; United States Department of State, *The United States and Nicaragua: A Survey of Relations from 1909–1932* (Washington, D.C.: Government Printing Office, 1932).

9. On the Conservative interregnum see Harold N. Denny, *Dollars for Bullets* (New York: Dial Press, 1929); and United States Department of State, *United States and Nicaragua*.

10. On Segovian armies and gangs see Michael J. Schroeder, "The Sandino Rebellion Revisited: Civil War, Imperialism, Popular Nationalism, and State Formation Muddied Up Together in the Segovias of Nicaragua, 1926–1934," in Gilbert Joseph, Catherine LeGrand, and Ricardo Salvatore, eds., *Close Encounters of Empire: Writing the Cultural History of U.S.–Latin American Relations* (Durham: Duke University Press, 1998). On the personalism, brutality, and violence that were integral to Chamorrista rule, in addition to sources cited above, see Salvador Mendieta, *Alrededor del problema unionista de Centro-América*, 2 vols. (Barcelona: 1934), esp. 1: 61–100.

11. See Denny, *Dollars for Bullets;* United States Department of State, *United States and Nicaragua.*

12. On the terms of the treaty see United States Department of State, *The United States in Nicaragua.*

13. On the Hernández case see Schroeder, "Horse Thieves to Rebels to Dogs."

14. See the two very revealing reports by Lt. Col. J. A. Rossell, "Repatriation of Destitute Nicaraguans in Honduras," 18 Aug. 1928, and "Conditions in Honduras," 19 Aug. 1928, NA127/220/2. Nicaraguan women did not gain suffrage until the mid-1950s.

15. For a reminder of the antiquity of this process, see Benjamin Farrington, *Science and Politics in the Ancient World* (London: G. Allen & Unwin, 1939).

16. Glimpses of this history occasionally surface in marine-guardia reports, e.g., "It has been reported that the police forces [in the north] and throughout Nicaragua are being recruited from among a lower element known as cirujuanos [surgeons] because of their skill with machetes and knives. This is said to be a custom of the authorities preceeding every election." R-2 Periodic Report, Managua, 6 May 1928, NA127/209/2. ("R-2" refers to the intelligence section of the Guardia Nacional.) The Records of the United States Department of State (Record Group 59, Records of the Department of State Relating to the Internal Affairs of Nicaragua, 1910–1929) provide a detailed documentary record of this violence.

17. José Torres, for instance, arrested and imprisoned along with Hernández, headed up his own gang that sometimes merged with Hernández's, as did Teodoro Polanco, Timoteo Blanco, the Cárdenas brothers, and others; Medardo Vallejos's Conservative gang, on the other hand, was in frequent conflict with Hernández's. See Schroeder, "Horse Thieves to Rebels to Dogs."

18. Marine-guardia archives contain occasional references to such "Conservative clubs," e.g., letters from Feliciano Gutiérrez to Emiliano Chamorro, c. 2 June 1928, NA127/43A/3; R-2 Report, 14 Oct. 1928, p. 6, NA127/209/1.

19. J. Barcenonal M [?] to Sr. Oficial de Relaciones Civiles, telegram, Managua, 28 May 1928, NA127/220/5; "Conservative citizens," La Trinidad, to Ministry of Police, Managua, 18 March 1928, NA127/209/12.

20. R-2 Intelligence Report, Ocotal, 27 May 1928, NA127/209/2.

21. J. N. Frisbie, Memorandum for District Commander, Matagalpa, 31 May 1928, NA127/220/11.

22. In a typical report, Chief of Police Carmen Vilchez in early April reported to the marines that "in a place called Santa Ana [near La

Trinidad] appeared a group of outlaws murdering a Conservative, whom they cut off an ear, and has many wounds." R-2 Periodic Report, Matagalpa, 8 April 1928, and R-2 Report, Ocotal, 15 April 1928, in NA127/209/1 and /2.

23. Investigation of Juan Davila Torres, V. F. Bleasdale, Managua, 22 Sept. 1928, NA127/209/3.

24. Report of Patrol to Trinidad-San Isidro, B. W. Atkinson, 5 April 1928, NA127/212/1, and Report of Patrol, H. C. Pierce, 6 April 1928, NA127/43A/33; *Diario de Occidente*, León, 8 May 1928; see also Andres Jirón in *Diario de Occidente*, 28 May 1928 (English trans. only), NA127/220/5.

25. Vilchez was arrested on April 14 and imprisoned in Matagalpa; Bn–2 Report, 15 April 1928, NA127/209/2.

26. J. N. Frisbie to District Commander, 30 May 1928, E. R. Beadle to Commanding General, 4 June 1928, NA127/220/5 and /11; Bn–2 Report, Jinotega, 10 June 1928, NA127/209/2; Surrender of Certain Bandits, F. S. Kieren, 10 June 1928, NA127/220/5. Despite the amnesties, depredations by Conservative gangs were reported as late as November 1928; intelligence reports, June-November, NA127/209/1 and /2 and NA127/43A/4.

27. Anastacio Somoza, *El verdadero Sandino, o el Calvario de las Segovias* (Managua, 1936), 95; "List of assassinations committed by bandits, Department of Jinotega, during the registration," Major Parker, Managua, 4 Nov. 1928, NA127/220/7; Jefe Político Alvarez to Ministerio de Gobernación, 16 April 1928, NA127/220/5; *La Noticia*, 20 April 1928; Fidel Vilchez to Gertrudis Mairena and Carmen Vilchez, 4 April 1928, NA127/220/5 and /209/1; R-2 Period Report, A. C. Larsen, Managua, 21 May 1928; B. S. Berry, Communication to Jose Leon Diaz, 3 June 1928, NA127/220/5; Patrol Report, J. M. Cobb, Estelí, 9 June 1930, NA127/202/10/52.

28. Telegram from Juan Carlos Mendieta, Jinotega, to General José María Moncada, Managua, 30 Sept. 1928, NA127/220/7. Sandinista rebels killed Mendieta the very next day in the San Marcos murders; see below.

29. See Schroeder, "Horse Thieves to Rebels to Dogs."

30. Following Benedict Anderson, *Imagined Communities* (London: Verso, 1985), the Defending Army might be characterized as a limited, horizontal, sovereign, fraternal political community composed overwhelmingly of (self-described) "Indohispanic" Segovian campesinos. See Schroeder, "Sandino Rebellion Revisited"; cf. Richard Grossman, "'Hermanos en la patria': Nationalism, Honor, and Rebellion: Augusto Sandino and the Army in Defense of the National Sovereignty of Nicaragua, 1927–1934" (Ph.D. diss., University of Chicago, 1996).

31. From a voluminous literature, excellent studies include Michael Fellman, *Inside War: The Guerrilla Conflict in Missouri During the American Civil War* (New York: Oxford University Press, 1989); Bruce J. Calder, *The Impact of Intervention: The Dominican Republic During the U.S. Occupation of 1916–1924* (Austin: University of Texas Press, 1984); Walter Lacqueur, *Guerrilla: A Historical and Critical Study* (Boston: Little, Brown, 1977); Francis FitzGerald, *Fire in the Lake: The Vietnamese and the Americans in Vietnam* (Boston: Little, Brown, 1972); Mao Tse Tung, *On Revolution and War* (Garden City, N.Y.: Doubleday, 1969); Franklin M. Osanka, *Modern Guerrilla Warfare* (New York: Free Press of Glencoe, 1962); Peter Paret and John Shy, *Guerrillas in the 1960s* (New York: Praeger, 1962).

32. While an exploration of the violence produced by the marines, the guardia, and their auxiliaries (including several bands of *voluntarios* [volunteers]) lies beyond the scope of this essay, any comprehensive account of death squad activity in the Segovias would have to consider this issue. For one treatment see Schroeder, "To Defend Our Nation's Honor," chaps. 5, 9–10; cf. Grossman, "Hermanos en la patria," chaps. 5–6.

33. See Schroeder, "To Defend Our Nation's Honor," chaps. 8 and 11.

34. "Statement of José Santos Rivera on the events occurring from the 1st to the 2nd of October, 1928," 10 Oct. 1928, NA127/220/7; cf. Somoza, *El verdadero Sandino,* 98–100; Volker Wünderich, *Sandino, una biografía política* (Managua: Nueva Nicaragua, 1995), 165–66.

35. As one marine lieutenant explained it, "In bandit infested areas all natives are very wary of being known as friends of the Yankees or Guardia. They cannot be blamed for this as cases are all too prevalent of suspected informers being found beheaded on the trail. Through the area covered at least a dozen instances of houses being destroyed by bandits were reported. Generally the owners were known or suspected to have assisted the Guardia or marine authorities." Patrol Report, J. D. O'Leary, Condega, 5 July 1930, NA127/202/13/56.

36. The figure cited above represents an estimate derived from published and archival sources, though of course the exact number will never be known. On A Hamirano's death in 1937 see Miguel Jesús Blandón, *Entre Sandino y Fonseca Amador* (Managua: Departamento de Propaganda y Educación Política del FSLN, 1981), 10–13.

37. See Somoza, *El verdadero Sandino,* and the marine-guardia archives.

38. Letter from Juan Santos Morales to Sandino, 23 Oct. 1931, in Somoza, *El verdadero Sandino,* 272; cf. 286–87. The authenticity of

this letter, allegedly taken from the body of Sandinista soldier Felicito Prado, killed on 10 Nov. 1931 at El Cuje, is attested to by related correspondence taken from Prado and later deposited in the National Archives; e.g., the original of a letter from J. S. Morales to F. Prado of 10 Oct. 1931 (quoted, with a key paragraph omitted, in Somoza, 286–87) can be found in NA127/209/8.

39. On Juan Butón, see Records of Prisoners, Casefiles and Special Orders, National Penitentiary, Managua, NA127/202/16/76; Prisoners confined in this Penitentiary on orders other than Judges, A. A. Gladden, Division de Penitenciaria Nacional, Managua, 13 Feb. 1929, and Data on Juan H. Rodríguez, n.d., c. July 1928, NA127/209/8. On his death see Contact Report, G. C. Smith, 8 Aug. 1930, Esteli, and First Endorsement to Smith Contact Report, D. McDonald, 8 Aug. 1930, NA127/202/10/52.

40. On Juan Castillo see R-2 Report, 29 July 1928, NA127/209/1; GN-2 Report, 1 June 1931, NA127/43A/29: Patrol and contact report, W. W. Stevens, Leon, 29 July 1931, NA127/202/11; GN-2 Report, 1 Sept. 1931, NA127/43A/29. On Rubén Barreto, see El Centroamericano, 7 Dec. 1923; B-2 Report, 11 March 1928, NA127/43A/3; R-2 Report, 17 Dec. 1929, and 18 Jan. 1930, NA127/209/1 and /2.

41. Paul Berman, "In Search of Ben Linder's Killers," New Yorker, 23 Sept. 1996, 69.

42. Ariel C. Armony, "The Former Contras," in Thomas W. Walker, ed., Nicaragua Without Illusions (Wilmington, Del.: Scholarly Resources, 1997), 207. See also the excellent study of Orlando Núñez et al., La guerra y el campesinado en Nicaragua, 3rd ed. (Managua: CIPRES, 1998), 310–30ff.

43. Armony, "Former Contras," p. 205. Comparable figures for the contemporary United States would be some 2.6 million deaths and 50 million refugees.

44. Steven Kinzer, Blood of Brothers: Life and War in Nicaragua (New York: Anchor Books, 1991), 147.

45. See Marlene Dixon, ed., On Trial: Reagan's War Against Nicaragua (San Francisco: Synthesis Publications, 1985); Americas Watch, Violations of the Laws of War by Both Sides in Nicaragua, 1981–1985 (New York: Americas Watch Committee, 1985), and Human Rights in Nicaragua: Rhetoric and Reality (New York: Americas Watch Committee, 1985); Witness for Peace, What We Have Seen and Heard: The Effect of Contra Attacks Against Nicaragua (Washington, D.C., 1985); Reed Brody, Contra Terror in Nicaragua: Report of a Fact-Finding Mission: September 1984-January 1985 (Boston: South End Press, 1985); Teofilo Cabestrero, Blood of the Innocent: Victims of the Contras' War in Nicaragua (New York: Orbis Books,

1985); Richard Garfield and David Siegel, *Health and the War Against Nicaragua, 1981–1984* (New York: Central America Health Rights Network/LINKS, 1985); E. Bradford Burns, *At War in Nicaragua: The Reagan Doctrine and the Politics of Nostalgia* (New York: Harper & Row, 1987); Catholic Institute for International Relations, *Right to Survive: Human Rights in Nicaragua* (London: CIIR, 1987); Holly Sklar, *Washington's War on Nicaragua* (Boston: South End Press, 1988); Jaime Morales Carazo, *La Contra* (Mexico City: Grupo Editorial Planeta, 1989); Alejandro Bendaña, *La tragedia campesina* (Managua: Ediart-CEI, 1991).

46. Brody, *Contra Terror in Nicaragua,* 63.
47. Bob Barnes, *NicaNotes* (Nevada City, Calif.: Friendsview Press, 1987), 65.
48. Ibid., 72.
49. See Laura Enríquez, *Harvesting Change: Labor and Agrarian Reform in Nicaragua, 1979–1990* (Chapel Hill: University of North Carolina Press, 1991); Paul Rubén and Jan P. de Groot, eds., *El debate sobre la reforma agraria en Nicaragua* (Managua: INIES, 1989); Núñez et al., *La guerra y el campesinado.*
50. Armony, "The Former Contras," 207.
51. Barnes, *NicaNotes,* 72.
52. Armony, "The Former Contras," 208–9.
53. Benjamin Linder was a North American mechanical engineer working to produce small rural hydroelectric stations until he was killed by the Contras in April 1987. Berman, "In Search of Ben Linder's Killers."
54. Berman, "In Search of Ben Linder's Killers," 68, 70.
55. *New York Times,* 16 Feb. 1993.
56. Mendieta, *La enfermedad de Centro-América,* 1: 162, 241.
57. Important recent contributions to this effort include *Historia y violencia en Nicaragua* (Managua: Instituto de Investigaciones y Acción Social "Martin Luther King," Universidad Politecnica de Nicaragua, 1987); and Jeffrey Gould, *To Die in This Way: Nicaraguan Indians and the Myth of Mestizaje, 1880–1965* (Durham, N.C.: Duke University Press, 1998).
58. Salman Rushdie, *The Jaguar Smile* (New York: Viking, 1987), 16.

CHAPTER 3

Feme *Murder:*
Paramilitary "Self-Justice"
in Weimar Germany

Arthur D. Brenner

ERNST RÖHM, THE HEAD OF THE NAZI Storm Troops (SA), wrote in his memoir of a curious incident that had taken place in the early 1920s. One day, he wrote, "an alarmed statesman" approached Bavarian Police president Ernst Pöhner and whispered in his ear, "'Herr President, political murder organizations exist in this country!' Pöhner replied, 'I know—but there are too few of them!'"[1] This remark provides an apt introduction to the subject of death squads in Weimar Germany: first, because of the tolerant, if not to say favorable, attitude toward them among many government officials; second, because of the prominent role played in this story by local and regional governments and their functionaries; and third, because the scope of the violence perpetrated by death squads was limited to a few dozen victims in the time period 1920–23.

The extensive political violence that helped undermine the Weimar Republic in Germany (1919–33) has tended to be over-shadowed by the overwhelming scale of murder committed by the Third Reich. To the extent that nonspecialists are familiar with Weimar violence, it is mostly associated with spectacular public acts such as the assassinations of a handful of leading political figures—most prominently, Foreign Minister Walther Rathenau in July 1922—and failed coups like the Beer Hall Putsch of November 1923. Yet what can be termed death squad murders, which are known mostly under the rubric of *Feme* cases, involved numerous crosscurrents that were critical to the tenuous life of the Republic, despite the fact that the murders themselves were few in number and involved, as perpetrators and victims, no one who could be termed "prominent" or "dangerous" in any normal set of circumstances. Nevertheless, during the second half of the 1920s the revelation of this episode in courts, parliamentary hearings, and the press constituted a national sensation. Moreover, the resolution of these cases was a key step in legitimizing extralegal murder in Germany, which in turn was an important precondition for the Nazi Blood Purge of 1934 (which claimed Ernst Röhm among its victims), the *Einsatzgruppen* of 1941, and the Nazi death camps.

Background

Between its establishment in November 1918 and the end of 1923, the Weimar Republic was beset by conditions tantamount to civil war. Neither extreme right nor extreme left accepted the legitimacy of the regime; on the contrary, "they were opposed in principle to the system of parliamentary democracy and did their best to destroy it."[2] Both sides tried and failed several times to overthrow the government and establish a dictatorship, and nearly every attempt set off a violent reaction by the other side. In between these more dramatic spasms of terror, quotidian violence—mostly the handiwork of the extreme right—grew in magnitude. Thousands of people were killed or wounded in street fighting, isolated attacks, lynchings, assassinations, and executions. Strong governmental action might have quelled the violence, but this was unlikely at a time when no party held an outright majority and a kind of parliamentary gridlock—which saw ten different governing coalitions between early 1919 and the end of 1923—paralleled the instability in the streets.

A further hindrance to a strong state response to the violence was the complex matrix of Germany's international situation and the status of its security forces after the conclusion of World War I. The shock of sudden defeat after the arduous and bitter war, combined with the collapse of the old regime, led to the disintegration of the German armed forces after the armistice of November 11, 1918. Yet that same armistice authorized the German military to continue fighting in the Baltic region, whereby, in effect, German forces acted as the military instrument of the victorious powers in their attempt to contain the Soviet Union. However, the German government was itself poorly positioned to provide these soldiers, as its own army, the Reichswehr, was in an embryonic state. In order to fight this border war and to protect itself against political threats at home, the government subcontracted the provision of state security to a wide variety of voluntary public, private, and mixed public-private paramilitary organizations, most notably the Free Corps. These were mobile, heavily armed units composed mainly of demobilized younger officers, NCOs, and enlisted men who were unable or unwilling to return to civilian life, and they were the bulwark of state defense of Germany's eastern borders and of its suppression of left-wing insurrection. In emergencies they were aided by auxiliary volunteer forces (*Zeitfreiwilligenverbände*), which were reserve troops formed and trained by government forces in Berlin. Throughout Germany, too, the Free Corps and auxiliary units were complemented by civil guards (*Einwohnerwehren*), locally recruited, armed organizations created with government consent by conservative interests to protect private property and maintain municipal order against the specter of proletarian depredations. In ruthlessly suppressing the left and fighting off the Soviets in the Baltic region in 1919, these paramilitary forces "evolved into independent power factors" bound only indirectly by the command of the provisional Reichswehr.[3]

The seriousness this problem posed to the regime was compounded by the fact that the paramilitary bands were violently opposed to the parliamentary republic as a form of government, and to the particular foreign policy conducted by the Berlin government. The leaders and members of the paramilitary organizations longed for the neater, superficially more harmonious, and recent authoritarian past. Not only were they instinctively distrustful of democracy, but they were particularly angered by the fact that this democracy had been established on the rubble of the Hohenzollern dynasty, in their view, by socialists, pacifists, and Jews, whom they blamed for having betrayed the wartime army while it was still effective in the field—the famous "Stab in the Back" legend.

This militantly nationalistic and antirepublican spirit was given further impetus when the Weimar government accepted the terms of the Versailles Peace Treaty in the spring of 1919. Few Germans found any redeeming features in the document: it removed substantial territories from German control, blamed the entire war on Germany and compelled it to pay enormous reparations, excluded Germany from the new League of Nations, and plundered Germany's colonial empire. The treaty also limited Germany to an army of 100,000 men, with no armor and no aircraft and bearing only defensive weapons, while simultaneously decreeing the dissolution of the General Staff, the war academy, and cadet schools. The military provisions struck the paramilitaries like a thunderbolt: of the roughly half million men still at arms in mid-1919, fewer than 20 percent could expect induction into the truncated army. This was a devastating prospect for thousands of men for whom a career as an officer was the highest ambition, and for the mostly young soldiers who formed the cadres, a return to civilian life seemed out of the question. They had gone directly from school to the front at age 16 or 17 and knew nothing about work, only the camaraderie of the corps and the excitement of battle. Moreover, the men at arms were furious with the abject response of the government to the treaty terms, which they regarded contemptuously as a dictated peace. Behind the soldiers stood an array of conservative and nationalistic interests that were spooked by the specter of Bolshevism. Thus the paramilitary forces held in contempt the very state that engaged and sanctioned their services, and they were supported morally and materially by a vast right-wing movement that was determined to keep the so-called "national" forces armed and ready. Collectively, this movement was determined to rearm Germany, to suppress the left, and forcefully to revise the Versailles Peace Treaty.

During the first half of 1919, these forces carried out the first two elements of this mission successfully and brutally. They stemmed the westward surge by the Red Army and stamped out the domestic rebellions throughout Germany. Given carte blanche by Defense Minister Gustav Noske, the irregulars used overwhelming force to subdue armed opposition and frequently carried out murderous reprisals. Political violence, mostly directed against the left, flourished as it became increasingly clear that the government was neither able nor inclined to stop it. Moreover, it was also evident that the criminal justice system sympathized with the rightist causes. From police and investigating magistrates to prosecutors and judges, the legal system generally looked the other way when faced with right-wing political crimes. Murderers were acquitted when they claimed that prisoners were shot while trying to escape. Prosecutors argued that defendants had been acting from the best patriotic motives and should be treated leniently. Judges, using a nineteenth-century penal code that permitted them to weigh a defendant's motives, sentenced perpetrators of violent crimes to shockingly mild sentences, if they convicted at all.[4] Between the consent of the Weimar government and the leeway given by the criminal justice system, the right-wing forces concluded that they could act with impunity if they could plausibly claim that they were acting to defend the national interest.

This comfortable arrangement continued as long as the Entente powers averted their gaze from the proliferation of armed units throughout Germany, and that lasted only as long as doing so suited the aims of the victors. The success of German forces in the Baltic region and in securing the Republic against the domestic threat from the left seemed to spell the end of their existence, as the Entente began in June 1919 to demand that German government meet the force limits established by the Versailles Treaty. Most of the soldiers and their officers grumbled but complied with orders and returned to civilian life, but a minority went underground into a flourishing panoply of secret armed units. A few of the larger Free Corps resisted dissolution, first by noncompliance and finally, in March 1920, by attempting a coup (the Kapp Putsch) in order to install a dictatorial government that would resist foreign pressure, abrogate the treaty, and restore the German army to greatness. A general strike by workers in Berlin and elsewhere forced the collapse of the coup but, paradoxically, also ensured that the paramilitary organizations would live on in some form. The successful general strike reawakened communist hopes for revolution and touched off an insurrection in the industrial Ruhr region. To meet the threat, the government called on the head of the revived, if truncated, Reichswehr—who just days before had declined to order his rump forces to squash the coup—to lead Germany's armed forces (regular and irregular) to put down the rebellion, and he in turn engaged the temporary assistance of some of the same Free Corps units that had been the backbone of the Kapp Putsch.[5] The lesson was clear: in certain circumstances, the state wanted and needed the paramilitary forces to continue to exist. The difficulty was that this could no longer take place with the degree of openness that had marked state-paramilitary relations since the beginning of 1919, because of the likelihood that the Entente powers, particularly the French, would take a harder line on implementing other provisions of the treaty and possibly even invade Germany in order to enforce it. The solution to this dilemma was equally transparent: the paramilitary forces would have to continue to exist, but in forms that were suffi-ciently altered to make their functions—primarily maintaining mili-tary preparedness through organization, recruitment and training, and the stashing of illegal weapons—and their relations to the state opaque.

Officially disarmed and disbanded, the remaining paramilitary organizations recast themselves as labor associations, security firms, sporting societies, or other fictitious entities whose real purpose was to keep units together, ready for the next battle for the borders or for control of the German state. In this semiclandestine existence they sustained military command structures and arms caches and conducted military training exercises while the central and regional governments looked the other way. Many officials—particularly in the Reichswehr—sympathized with the organizations' goals, felt their existence offered a greater measure of security, or were simply afraid to enforce orders for these groups to disband, thereby en-abling the secret military organizations to continue their shadowy existence throughout the early 1920s.

Thus there existed in Germany several conditions conducive to the formation of death squads: autonomous paramilitary organiza-tions of dubious legality whose existence was nevertheless tacitly condoned by the state, a climate of violence that was reinforced by the leniency granted by the criminal justice system to right-wing po-litical criminality, and foreign threats that made publicity about these enterprises a danger to state security and the national interest in the view of many participants, supporters, and observers. Fur-thermore, the irregulars faced serious problems with their internal order. A substantial proportion of the ranks were composed of young men who had been socialized not by civilian mores but by the crudity and brutality of the German side in the last two years of World War I; often they were poorly paid, which created motives for petty thievery, black marketeering, and the like; and, deprived of the action they craved during periods of relative calm, they drank and quarreled among themselves. Since the illegal organizations were not part of the army, and since they could not risk blowing their cover by taking disciplinary issues to the criminal justice system, they imposed discipline internally, and it was based on brutality, not on a military code of conduct and punishment. Severe beatings were the usual punishment for even minor offenses like complaining about conditions or command, petty theft, and dereliction of duty.

The most serious offense was betrayal: of the secrets of the organization, of its illegal activities, of weapons. If any of this information was made public, it could fall into the wrong hands (namely, the Entente powers and their military inspectors), and that spelled the dissolution of the organization, since the government could not openly tolerate the existence of the illegal organizations. From the earliest days the paramilitary bands included in their regulations an oath of loyalty to the organization that concluded with the sentence "Traitors will fall to the *Feme!*" (*Verräter verfallen der Feme*). This was a euphemism for murder.[6]

The term *Feme* or *Femgerichte* (sometimes rendered in English as Vehmic courts) originally referred to a kind of frontier justice practiced in medieval Germany. These vigilante courts, which were especially numerous in Westphalia, "tried and executed common criminals in areas where an ordered judicial system was lacking."[7] Princes extracted fees as the price for legitimizing *Feme* verdicts passed in their territories. The modern version used by the Weimar paramilitary organizations was actually closer in form to military field justice, except that the military units involved were illegal and therefore their proceedings lacked legitimacy.

The death squad murders constitute a subset of the *Feme* murders committed in the Weimar years. The motivating factors were essentially the same: a group or organization determined that someone—usually a renegade or suspect member, more rarely a civilian nonmember—had to be eliminated because of the danger this person posed to the illegal enterprises undertaken by a secret society. The fundamental difference gets to the nub of the definition of a death squad. In several instances, a few members of a paramilitary group carried out only a single *Feme* murder; whereas in those considered death squad cases, distinct subunits of larger organizations were responsible for a handful or more of *Feme* murders.

The Death Squads Murders[8]

The Business Affairs Division of the Bavarian Civil Guard (Einwohnerwehr)

As indicated earlier in this chapter, the right-wing paramilitary organizations of Weimar Germany considered it their patriotic duty to play cat-and-mouse games with Entente military inspectors, and hiding illegal weapons was the primary motivating factor for the death squad murders (and one alleged attempted murder) that were committed in Bavaria in late 1920. In these cases, state organs played a central role.

The dominant paramilitary organization in Bavaria in the period from 1919 to 1921 was the civil guard (Einwohnerwehr) that was established by the energetic forestry director and avid hunter Georg Escherich. Its membership peaked at about 250,000 in February 1920, and it remained a potent and well-organized operation until it was dissolved in May 1921. Within the organization, the Business Affairs Division, headed by Otto Braun, took responsibility for hiding weapons and moving caches that the organization suspected were at risk of being seized by Entente inspectors based on tips from the men who had transported or unloaded the weapons in the first place, or from private citizens who had gained knowledge of the hidden munitions. These informants were the targets of an Einwohnerwehr death squad that operated out of the Business Affairs Division.

The right-wing government that ruled Bavaria beginning in March 1920 made the state a haven for anti-Republican, anti-Semitic, and anti-Versailles organizations, as well as a busy center for arms smuggling. A sleazy underworld of gunrunners, arms dealers, and informants thrived in the midst of postwar economic hardship, which provided many people with the incentive to sell knowledge of hidden weapons to Entente agents and officers, or to extort money from the Entente's foes by offering to sell the same knowledge to those who wanted to keep the caches clandestine.[9]

An attempt to win a reward for revealing hidden arms cost the life of the only female victim of the German death squads. Marie Sandmayr was a young domestic worker who in late 1919 was dismissed from the service of one Bavarian aristocrat, but not before she had learned that illegal weapons were being concealed on his estate. The following September she saw a poster from the German disarmament commissioner advertising a reward for information about secret armaments, but since the poster included no address to which she could take this information, she went to the print shop that had produced the poster and whose address appeared on the bottom. There she told her story to a young man, who happened to be a member of the Bavarian Civil Guard. He sent her not to the disarmament authorities but to his employer, Alfred Zeller, an important Einwohnerwehr figure. Zeller did not disclose his true identity, leading Sandmayr to believe she was speaking to the appropriate authorities, and told her he would be back in touch with her in a few days. A few days later, on October 5, 1920, a young man came to her new place of employment, spoke privately with her, and departed. Sandmayr left there alone that evening, and her body was found the next morning in a nearby park. She had been strangled, and attached to her was a note that read, "You slut [*Schandweib*], you have betrayed your fatherland, the Black Hand murdered you."[10]

This was the first of a handful of murders and attempted murders of putative "traitors" carried out over the next year by a group of men associated in one capacity or another with the Business Affairs Division of the Bavarian Civil Guard, which led to the unsubstantiated but highly likely conclusion that the killings were ordered or inspired by its chief, Otto Braun. In several instances, vehicles traced to the Business Affairs Division were seen at times and in places where shots were heard or bodies were found. A passerby found the body of Hans Hartung in a stream between the Bavarian cities of Augsburg and Ulm in March 1921; a vehicle belonging to the Business Affairs Division had been seen in the immediate vicinity at the time of the murder.[11]

Most significant for the present study is the evidence of connivance by some Bavarian public officials with the circle of instigators and perpetrators. Shortly after the Sandmayr murder, a man later revealed to have been involved in her disappearance sought and received on demand a passport issued by Bavarian police, even though the immediate issuance of such documents was extraordinary. Following another attempted murder in which Braun's unit was implicated, the head of the political division of the Munich police testified before a Bavarian parliamentary investigation that he had been informing the Einwohnerwehr about alleged betrayals of weapons caches so the Business Affairs Division could move any arms that were at risk of falling into Entente hands.[12] The same parliamentary inquest turned up evidence that the police had conspired to release several suspects from custody, probably in order to intimidate a key witness. In the Hartung case, an attorney working for the Civil Guard met with the Augsburg prosecutors handling the investigation and persuaded them to ride with him back to Munich. He took them straight to the Bavarian Ministry of Justice, where they were instructed to suspend arrest warrants for several suspects, who fled and escaped justice until four years later, when they were acquitted.[13] Furthermore, the man who had been Bavarian minister of justice at the time of the incident testified in 1926 that there was nothing unusual about the fact that the attorney from the Civil Guard, rather than an official of the ministry, had summoned the prosecutors from Augsburg.[14] Critics of Bavarian justice charged that this conduct was part of a pattern of complicity between leading figures of the Bavarian criminal justice system and the campaign to undermine compliance with the Versailles military provisions in Bavaria.[15]

Unlike other places where regional governments have undertaken the formation of death squads at the behest of the central government—as in the Indian cases discussed in this volume by Patricia Gossman—in Bavaria, organs of the state government, acting on their own initiative, and often with the encouragement or connivance of the Reichswehr, tolerated or encouraged the application of death squads to promote a practice they supported. Moreover, in this case it was done without encouragement from civilian officials in Berlin; relations between the central government and Bavaria were prickly at best and frequently tended toward open antagonism.

Upper Silesian Self-Defense

By agreement of June 30, 1921, Germany and Poland agreed to amnesty all violent political crimes on either side that had been committed during a struggle for control of Upper Silesia, a region inhabited by both Polish and German nationals. This amnesty ensured that the question of the existence and extent of *Feme* murders in the region would never be answered definitively. There is sufficient evidence to substantiate the claim that such homicides took place, but there is also reason to believe that the most extensive estimate, which asserted that a German "Special Police" in the region was responsible for roughly 200 murders, was a gross exaggeration.

One provision of the Versailles Peace Treaty stipulated that in March 1921, the inhabitants of Upper Silesia were to vote to determine whether the territory would remain part of Germany or be annexed to the new Polish state. A pair of Polish uprisings in 1920 were intended to preempt the plebiscite, and although Allied forces, acting on a League of Nations mandate, occupied the region in late

1920 to help preserve order in advance of the election, interethnic violence rose throughout the period. Neither Poland nor Germany sent troops to the region, but both supported with financial and material aid the formation of supposedly local forces to defend what each perceived to be their embattled brethren. With the support of the German and Prussian governments (Upper Silesia was administratively part of Prussia), the local German militia were supplemented in the three months before the vote by increasing numbers of volunteers recruited from throughout Germany, many of whom remained in the territory for months after they were ordered by the German government to leave. These units, collectively operating under the rubric "Upper Silesian Self-Defense" (SSOS), were composed of a mixture of old Free Corps, which assumed leadership of the SSOS operations, and new recruits—mostly university students who had been too young to serve in the Great War and were eager to earn their patriotic stripes.

These paramilitary groups operated with the approval of the German state. Most of their resources came from the Weimar government; Chancellor Joseph Wirth, who was also finance minister at the time, used state funds to finance the activities of SSOS and was reputed to have made the last gold reserves in the Reichsbank available to purchase weapons from Russia to arm them.[16] The central and Prussian state governments sent representatives to Breslau, the region's largest city, to establish an office ostensibly to serve as the eyes and ears of the German state, in reality to help oversee the German effort to win the election and to defend the German population there against Polish "terrorism." It was headed by Prussian state commissioner Carl Spiecker, and it was assigned, according to one ominous document, to carry out "certain tasks" with "strict secrecy."[17] Among its responsibilities was the elimination of "traitors"; in this case, that could mean Germans working on behalf of Polish interests, Poles working for Poland, or SSOS members who revealed to the occupying forces compromising information about German operations in the region. For this purpose, the Spiecker Organization financed and maintained a liaison with a "Special Police" force of 160 men under the command of Heinz Oskar Hauenstein, a former Free Corps officer.[18]

In 1928, Hauenstein caused an uproar by estimating that his "Special Police" had murdered about 200 "traitors" and by claiming that he had been acting on orders from Spiecker. The former commissioner denied only that he had ordered such acts and challenged the characterization of these homicides as murder; he freely acknowledged that Hauenstein's figure might be accurate. Their confrontation over this matter took place at an unrelated *Feme* murder trial in which the defendants had hoped, by calling Hauenstein and Spiecker, to prove that many *Feme* murders had been committed under direct or indirect orders from German state officials, but after a consultation among the prosecution, defense, and judges, the tribunal announced that it would no longer accept testimony about the Upper Silesian issue. With that, the opportunity to penetrate the matter further was lost.[19]

One recent historian of the German attempt to influence the outcome of the Upper Silesian plebiscite argues persuasively—and against the common public perception of the time—that Hauenstein's claim of 200 *Feme* victims in the territory was an exaggeration. It came long after the fact and was intended to enhance its author's credentials within the right-wing circles in Germany for whom a reputation for patriotic action in Upper Silesia had become a kind of litmus test.[20] Still, an unknown number of people were killed in *Fememorde* in Upper Silesia in 1921, and some of these were the handiwork of Hauenstein's "Special Police" and the Free Corps active in the region.[21]

The Black Reichswehr

In 1926, the German commissioner for the observation of public order (*Reichskommissar für die Überwachung der öffentlichen Ordnung*), who headed a department responsible for the collection of public affairs information for the benefit of other government agencies, wrote that the procedures of murderous "self-justice," which had been developed by the Free Corps in 1919, subsequently became an ingrained custom of right-wing paramilitary organizations. This was due to the fact that many of the same individuals who served in the Free Corps in 1919 also participated in the Kapp Putsch in 1920 and the defense of Upper Silesia in 1921. Moreover, the German government was never willing to cut its ties to these men altogether. Political leaders knew from the Kapp Putsch that the paramilitary bands posed a serious danger to the state and that the right-wing forces remained unreconciled to the republic.[22] Periodically they issued and enforced orders for paramilitary groups to disband, but the effect was mitigated by the continued existence of other armed organizations that dismissed soldiers could join. Generally, this was how the army wanted it: the head of the Reichswehr, General Hans von Seeckt, considered them soldiers and sought by various measures to bring these units under army control; he wanted to expand the forces available at his disposal, and he, too, disliked the danger they posed to the state's monopoly on the use of force. Co-opting them by turning them into auxiliary or reserve units was thus the preferred solution, and in the multiple crises of 1923, the product was a rapid expansion of the secret force known as the Black Reichswehr (Schwarze Reichswehr, SR).

One of the many points of conflict in German political life in the early 1920s was the question of compliance with the Versailles Peace Treaty. The policy of fulfillment that was followed by Wirth and his foreign minister, Walther Rathenau, was shattered by Rathenau's assassination in the summer of 1922. Franco-German relations deteriorated rapidly thereafter, as did the value of the German currency. When the German government defaulted on a reparations payment in January 1923, the French army moved into the industrial Ruhr region, determined to exact by compulsion what the Germans would not provide willingly. The German government responded by calling on the citizens and workers of the occupied territory passively to resist the invader and resorted to the printing press to pay the idle workers. Ten months of passive resistance, with no resolution in sight, sent inflation soaring to unimaginable heights and severely impaired the credibility of the German government; it also engendered increasing calls from the German right to turn passive resistance into bold action to redeem the honor and independence of Germany. The ultraconservative and ultranationalist camps also asserted that the weakened state was vulnerable to other presumed enemies, namely the Poles and the proletariat.

The various goals identified above—of the state, to co-opt the paramilitary forces; of the Reichswehr, to make them into disciplined auxiliaries of the armed forces; and of the paramilitaries themselves, to protect the nation against internal and external threats, and possibly, to install a government more to their liking—found their confluence in the growth of so-called "labor troops" *(Arbeitskommandos,* or AKs). These were civilian battalions initially formed by the Reichswehr in 1921 whose stated purpose was to collect, sort, and decommission or destroy weapons that exceeded the Versailles limits. AKs were usually commanded by former Reichswehr officers, and the ranks were composed mostly of old Free Corps and Upper Silesian veterans. They were housed in army barracks at active Reichswehr bases and wore regular army uniforms; they also received training in the use of weapons, participated in military exercises, and in some cases performed guard duty at various locales near Berlin and in eastern Germany. Most tellingly, they were issued regular Reichswehr identification that included a system of ranks that corresponded exactly to that of the regular troops.[23] They also stockpiled the useful weapons they collected and turned over to Allied military officials mostly material that was useless anyway. In short, the AKs were a shadow force being trained to supplement the army in an emergency.

Like the Free Corps and the Upper Silesian Self-Defense forces before them, the labor troops practiced a brutal form of internal justice to deal with the considerable difficulties they had with discipline. These units were recruited from some of the roughest and most untamed elements of German right-wing young men, and the rapid expansion of these forces in the course of 1923, to a total of some 50,000 to 80,000 men,[24] only compounded the problem. Once again, theft, dereliction of duty, and drunkenness were common, and most units had their own *Rollkommando,* a special internal police whose main tools were fists, rubber truncheons, and rifle butts.[25] Though it would appear that the *Rollkommandos* could easily have become death squads, they generally limited themselves to handling relatively minor disciplinary matters. More serious was treason; as defined by the Black Reichswehr, that meant betrayal of the secret nature of the enterprise to the public or to the Entente, or redirecting illegal weapons for sales on the side—allegedly to communists—in order to line one's own pockets. The man charged with handling cases of betrayal in the SR was also the person responsible for managing its acquisition, transport, and secreting of illegal weapons, Paul Schulz, who headed the Schwarze Reichswehr death squad.

As far as Schulz and his superior officers were concerned, the stockpiling and concealment of arms were vital to the national interest, which would be seriously endangered if knowledge of these activities was made public or otherwise transmitted to the Entente. Since the AKs were civilian irregulars, they could not be subject to the military penal code; and because secrecy was so urgent, treason (as the SR defined it) could not be reported to the civilian criminal justice system, lest the illicit military activity be revealed to presumed enemies.[26] It was therefore imperative to have a tool to punish traitors, and Schulz, who had served in the Reichswehr and participated in various other paramilitary enterprises from 1919 until his engagement by the SR in early 1922, naturally looked to the practice that had by then become the norm among Germany's right-wing paramilitaries.

He set up a special detail that between March and December 1923 was responsible for the deaths of at least eight alleged traitors to the SR.[27] There was a pattern to these *Feme* murders. The victim aroused suspicion or anger by remarks complaining of treatment or low pay, or by stealing and selling SR weapons on the black market. When word of such a "traitor" made its way to Schulz in Berlin, he would ensure that the soldier was repeatedly reassigned from one AK to another, in order to separate the man farther and farther from those who knew him, and ultimately the putative traitor ended up in service at a base where hardly anyone was even aware of his presence. At this point, Schulz sent out his minions: a group usually consisting of three to five of his most trusted subordinates would simultaneously converge at or near the base to which the prospective victim was assigned and involve him in what was supposed to be a secret weapons transport, or get him drunk. Either way, the group would convene at night, take the victim by car or truck to an isolated location, shoot him (usually in the back of the head), and dispose of the body by burial or by dropping it, leaden with weights, into a nearby body of water. The disappearance was usually explained as the result of the victim's desertion or his fatal encounter with communists during a failed arms transaction that had turned violent.[28]

Exposition, Judgment, and Amnesty of the Black Reichswehr Death Squad Murders

The history of the exposition of the SR *Feme* murders reveals much about what motivated the state's relationship to the crimes and the paramilitary groups that perpetrated them and highlights the difficulty of using a monolithic definition of "the state" when discussing death squads.

For two years after the crimes, government and criminal justice officials declined to investigate and prosecute the Schulz death squad. The army was not eager to see its secret activities dragged into the open, and the central government, which was locked in delicate negotiations with France, wanted nothing revealed that could upset the talks on reparations and security issues. The Prussian state government, which had jurisdiction for most of the SR cases, went along with the national government on this issue.

This conspiracy of silence was pierced by the aggressive assaults of pacifist journalists, who throughout the mid-1920s published reams of revelations of the continued existence of the SR.[29] This was a huge embarrassment for the German government and army, which repeatedly denied that the German armed forces exceeded the 100,000-man limit mandated by the treaty. The revelations threatened to upset the negotiations by damaging or destroying the credibility of the German side. At the same time, human rights activists—often the same writers and journals that published the revelations about the SR—were engaged in a campaign against the class justice they believed was being practiced in Germany.[30] By 1925 these dual campaigns, and the facts they uncovered, converged to create pressure on the criminal justice system to prosecute the *Feme* murders.

The product of this confluence of factors was a series of sensational trials and, partly coterminously, investigations of the *Feme* murders by subcommittees of the Reichstag and the Prussian state parliament.[31] The daily press reported extensively on the proceedings, and the cases were analyzed in pacifist and left-wing weeklies that also uncovered new information about the *Fememorde*.[32] The fact that some trials were closed to the public because the courts—often at the urging of the Reichswehr—were concerned that state secrets might be made public caused an uproar; so did the testimony and counter-testimony of various high-ranking army officers (retired or active), who were called upon to explain the circumstances surrounding the murders or to elaborate on the atmosphere of paranoia that had prevailed in military circles when the SR death squad was active.

Amid all the testimony, the plausible deniability commonly associated with the state relationship to death squads crossed with the devolution evident in the formation of many death squads. The perpetrators, their attorneys, and friendly witnesses argued that Schulz

and his operatives not only had regarded themselves as regular soldiers, but had believed that in committing murder they were acting
on implicit government orders to take care of the business of building up clandestine units and stockpiling illegal weapons using all
necessary means. According to many sources, including Hans von
Seeckt, who had been chief of the army at the time of the events in
question, the men of the SR also believed that since the government
had tolerated *Feme* murder by the Free Corps in Upper Silesia in
1921, it surely wanted the same defense of its interests in the crisis
of 1923.[33] As to the question of whether government or army officials ever ordered a murder, Schulz himself was inexact: among
higher-ranking officers, he stated, "responsibility was always denied
if anything came of a treasonous act. Everything was loaded onto
the poor chaps below. We stood under colossal pressure. That which
you call *Feme* murder was known and left uninvestigated by officials for two years' time."[34] As Schulz acknowledged, his unit had
devolved far enough from official sources of power and command
that his actions could reasonably be interpreted as the autonomous
efforts of an overzealous former officer.

For several years, officials of the German government and Reichswehr continually denied that illegal units had been allowed to
exist with the knowledge of the state. Their whipping boy was SR
head Major Bruno Buchrucker, Schulz's immediate boss, who in
September 1923 was arrested to forestall a coup he was planning to
mount using AKs and regular units. This act, together with the fact
that in 1923 several AKs had been dissolved once their existence
had been made public,[35] permitted the army to claim that any *illegal* forces were promptly shut down when they were found out. As
far as the army was concerned, this "proved" that Schulz had been
acting on his own initiative. The Reichswehr position was abetted
by the absence of a paper trail regarding the SR; to avoid the creation of documents that could be seized and examined by Entente
military inspectors, the army eschewed the use of written commands
in all matters regarding troop strength, training, and movement, and
the Reichswehr leadership had destroyed related materials in late
1923 or early 1924.[36]

In courts of law, the government arguments held sway. Prosecutors were reluctant to challenge the testimony of the respectable officers of the Reichswehr and the official denials they presented, and
they often avoided pursuing lines of questioning that would have led

to examinations of the links between the Schulz death squad and the Reichswehr. There was no smoking gun here, though: state's attorneys in a particular district in some cases may have acted on their own initiative, but typically their work was followed closely by regional state's attorneys, who answered to the state's minister of justice. The Prussian government, in turn, was faced with competing pressures: from its left flank, pressure to act vigorously, in order to sustain the loyalty of its leftist constituency and to keep working-class voters from turning to the Communist Party, which agitated for aggressive investigation and prosecution of the *Feme* cases; and from the central government, to delay, silence, or altogether squash the prosecutions. Professional judges (most cases were tried in courts with a kind of jury composed of professional and lay judges), too, whose collective ethos was notoriously anti-Republican and deferential to the military, often agreed to avert sensitive questioning, as the example of the Hauenstein-Spiecker confrontation over Upper Silesia demonstrates. By early 1928, Schulz and several dozen codefendants in a handful of cases had been unable to prove that they had been acting on orders from higher authorities and were convicted of ordering, planning, and executing several *Feme* verdicts.

Though high government and Reichswehr officials were not identified as legally culpable, the court of public opinion found their denials implausible, and during the course of *Feme* trials and the subsequent appeals there was a perceptible rise in popular sympathy for Schulz and his fellow convicts. This sentiment was encouraged by an aggressive publicity campaign on their behalf by private right-wing interests, which had helped fund the legal defense of Schulz and his codefendants in various trials (and which were also implicated in having financed attempted escapes by several of the accused) and which insisted that these men had performed meritorious patriotic service and were being hung out to dry by an ungrateful and self-interested government. *Die Weltbühne,* an influential left-wing weekly magazine, also took up Schulz's cause: just days before a death sentence was handed down for Schulz's role in the 1923 murder of the SR soldier Walter Wilms, it published a remarkable article by the pacifist journalist Berthold Jacob. Jacob insisted on justice for Schulz, who, the author argued, had simply been acting on orders originating at the highest levels of the army.[37] Jacob hoped to see these other officials brought to trial, but that never happened. Nor did the two parliamentary investigations, which between them held roughly 100 meetings over a period lasting from early 1926 to mid-1928, do much to expose the background to the *Feme* murders. Their work was severely hampered by a procession of uncooperative and at times hostile witnesses, by the lack of Reichswehr documentation, and by partisan conflict that both hindered the progress of the committees and led to attempts from the outside to influence the course of the investigations.[38]

By the end of 1928, trials in a few SR *Feme* cases had been completed and ended in convictions for many defendants, but several more had not yet begun, and two main participants in the crimes were still fugitives. Throughout these trials, the Reichswehr and the Foreign Office consistently argued in the cabinet and in other venues for the government to pressure Prussia to stop the trials or to ensure that the proceedings would be closed to the public, lest "state secrets" be revealed.[39] This was a well-grounded concern, since the defense attorneys in the remaining *Feme* cases promised to put the army and other state organs on trial along with their clients.

Despite the Reichswehr and Foreign Office entreaties, the wheels of Prussian justice ground on, and only the successful conclusion of the amnesty campaign in late 1930 saved the central government from further embarrassment. The campaign gained momentum throughout the late 1920s, bolstered by a series of other amnesties issued by the President Paul von Hindenburg and by various state governments during the period. These acts were designed to wipe away the bad taste left over from the turmoil of the early part of the decade, and they included reductions in the sentences and changes in the incarceration (from penitentiary to less severe jails) for the *Feme* convicts. The argument for amnesty was pushed on two fronts: by private supporters with the argument that it was unfair for these "heroes" to rot in jail while political criminals of the left walked free; and by some in the Reichstag and government who believed this step was necessary to help calm the increasing agitation over the issue. The Reichswehr was only too happy to jump on the bandwagon, for it had its own reasons to see the issue go away. Amnesty meant that there would be no further trials, and no further means to put its relationship with its covert auxiliaries under the microscope. This extra-parliamentary support was to no avail, because a majority in the Reichstag opposed amnesty for the *Feme* murderers. As a result, repeated attempts to pass the bill failed. Only after the parliamentary elections of September 1930, which saw a decisive shift in electoral

strength to the extremes, did the supporters win enough seats to ensure passage of the amnesty bill, which became law in October
1930.[40]

Conclusion

From beginning to end, government officials, particularly in the
Reichswehr, pursued a policy of outright denial of their personal
or institutional involvement in aiding or condoning the acts of the
Weimar death squads. Like a compass, though, the dial kept pointing in their direction no matter how insistently they tried to cover
their tracks. The Business Affairs Division of the Bavarian Civil
Guard, the Upper Silesian Self-Defense organizations, and especially Schulz's special unit within the Schwarze Reichswehr all operated in a gray zone. There is no proof that state officials
commanded them to murder, but at the same time, there is ample
evidence to conclude that the paramilitary forces had acted with
the consent or complicity of government organs, often at the highest levels. In the SR episode, the perpetrators were not alone in
benefiting from the amnesties that ultimately wiped away their
culpability; the government officials who had to answer questions
about their own or their department's trafficking with the death
squads also found relief in the whitewash, which put a halt to the
inquiries that made them squirm.[41]

The use of death squads to maintain the clandestinity of illicit
activity is not unique to the Weimar German case: other authors in
this volume explain that similar things have happened in Brazil,
India, and South Africa. Death squads swallowing their own is not
far removed from intimidation or murder by organized crime gangs
of former members who turn state's evidence against the group, or
against other witnesses to their criminal activity. The exceptional
feature of the Weimar death squads—which, it must be added, were
part of a larger milieu in which political violence, including assassination, was not uncommon—is that they used extrajudicial executions exclusively to protect illicit activity that was condoned or
encouraged by the state but that was not itself lethal.

The narrowly defined scope of activity that the death squads
were meant to protect worked together with several other factors to
limit the number of victims claimed by the Weimar *Feme*. First, the

death squads operated largely within subgroups of society that numbered at most in the tens of thousands, and they punished particular acts, rather than targeting entire categories of people, which limited the scope of the violence. Second, the vast majority of members of these paramilitary organizations were volunteers or politically sympathetic mercenaries; as the head of the Schwarze Reichswehr, Bruno Buchrucker, noted, the most effective tool for minimizing the risk of betrayal had been careful screening of recruits.[42] This meant that there were relatively few cases of "treason" among the troops. It is also possible that AK officers who learned of acts of betrayal handled some of them locally, lest the integrity of their command be called into question at SR headquarters in Berlin. The sparing use of *Feme* murder among the paramilitary organizations also served to intimidate potential renegades while simultaneously not reaching a scale that would have provoked unrest, defections, or mutiny. Paradoxically, too, although brutal discipline was the rule within illegal troop formations, there was a kind of rough respect for legal norms that dictated that only the most extreme transgression against the group—betrayal, which constituted an existential threat to an enterprise deemed vital to the national interest—merited a death penalty. Finally, the fact that in most *Feme* murders the perpetrators attempted to hide the bodies of their victims (and in some instances fled when their involvement was alleged) was an acknowledgment of respect for the effectiveness and integrity of the German criminal justice system, and of fear that political pressures (at least in Prussia) would ensure prosecution of such crimes. As Robert Cribb notes elsewhere in this book, the absence of such factors in Indonesia helps account for the death squad murders there; the lack of fear of punishment must also account at least in part for the enormous numbers of death squad murders in some extreme instances, such as Colombia, Guatemala, and Sri Lanka.

Historically, the Weimar case took place at a time when moral constraints on extrajudicial executions and the killing of civilians still existed. These German death squads, after all, were active before the Holocaust and the Stalinist terror, before the mass attacks on civilian populations during World War II, and before the Cold War provided the rationale for some states to take lethal action against their own citizens. If debased standards of morality account for genocide and the breadth of death squad activity in the late twentieth century, it stands to reason that the public values extant in Weimar Germany still included a solid, if eroding, respect for the sanctity of life.[43] In fact, the amnesty of most violent political crimes in Germany in the late 1920s and early 1930s helped hasten the decay of those values and pave the way for legalized murder in the Third Reich.

While numerous factors may have contributed to the relatively low number of victims claimed by death squads in Weimar Germany, several more made them possible. Some were historically conditioned, such as the German domestic, military, and international positions after World War I, or the eroding morality of the time. Yet one more factor—one that is not peculiar to Germany, and that has ominous implications for the future appearance of death squads— also stands out: the decentralization of authority within the German state. One premise postulated by the editors of this book is that death squads are by definition appurtenances of modern states. Among the characteristics of modern states is that they are multi-faceted entities in which authority is divided both horizontally, across many ministries and agencies at a national level, and vertically, with significant responsibility given to regional governments. This multifariousness was itself a factor in facilitating the establishment and activities of the German death squads and ultimately was a vital feature in the landscape that permitted most of their members to escape or face only abbreviated punishment for their crimes and allowed the state to shield itself altogether from responsibility for its complicity in the murders. Bureaucratic complexity was a double-edged sword, though, because it also meant that Germany had other, independent loci of authority—the state governments, the state's prosecutors, the Reichstag and state parliaments—that were able to expose, investigate, and prosecute the death squad crimes. Since the distribution of authority among many layers of government is characteristic of most modern states, it suggests that, like a shell game, states and their security forces will continue to find opportunities to erect the foundations of plausible deniability on which all death squads depend.

Notes

1. Ernst Röhm, *Geschichte eines Hochverräters*, 7th ed. (Munich: F. Eher Nachf., 1934), 131, quoted in Robert G. L. Waite, *Vanguard of Nazism: The Free Corps Movement in Postwar Germany,*

1918–1923, reprint (Cambridge: Harvard University Press, 1970), 213.

2. Eberhard Kolb, *The Weimar Republic*, trans. P.S. Falla (London: Unwin Hyman, 1988), 34.

3. James M. Diehl, *Paramilitary Politics in the Weimar Republic* (Bloomington: Indiana University Press, 1977), 24–30 (direct quotation from p. 28); Waite, *Vanguard;* Hagen Schulze, *Freikorps und Republik, 1918–1920* (Boppard: H. Boldt, 1969); and Harold J. Gordon, *The Reichswehr and the German Republic, 1919–1926* (Princeton, N.J.: Princeton University Press, 1957). All organizations, including these paramilitary forces, were required by German law to register with government authorities.

4. E. J. Gumbel, *Vier Jahre politischer Morde* (Berlin: Verlag der neuen Gesellschaft, 1922); Heinrich Hannover and Elisabeth Hannover-Drück, *Politische Justiz 1918–1933,* 2nd ed. (Bornheim-Merten: Lamuv, 1987).

5. Gordon Craig, *Germany, 1866–1945*, paperback ed. (New York: Oxford University Press, 1980), 426–32.

6. Kuenzer, Reichskommissar für die Überwachung der öffentlichen Ordnung (Commissioner for the Observation of Public Order), report to the Reichsminister des Innern, 20 February 1926, in Bundesarchiv Deutschland, Abteilung Koblenz (BA-K), Akten der Reichskanzlei, R43I/2732, pp. 98–115, esp. 100 (reel 557, 79–97).

7. Howard Stern, "The *Organisation Consul,*" *Journal of Modern History* 35, no. 1 (March 1963): 24.

8. Contemporary left-wing analysts asserted in 1922 that another group, the Organization Consul (OC), was a "murder central," i.e., a death squad. This was because OC members were involved in the assassinations of two leading political figures, the former finance minister and head of the Catholic Center Party Matthias Erzberger in September 1921 and of Finance Minister Walther Rathenau in June 1922; and the attempted murders of a leading Social Democratic politician, Philipp Scheidemann, and a prominent pro-Republican magazine editor, Maximilian Harden, both also in June 1922. I have excluded the OC from consideration in this chapter because evidence of the charge is inconclusive. See Stern, 20–32; and Martin Sabrow, *Der Rathenaumord: Rekonstruktion einer Verschwörung gegen die Republik von Weimar* (Munich: R. Oldenbourg Verlag, 1994), esp. p. 8.

9. This is evident particularly from the testimony of numerous witnesses before the investigating committee of the Bavarian *Landtag,* 28 October–5 November 1920, a typed transcript of which is available in Staatsarchiv München, Staatsanwaltschaft/3123 (hereafter, BFA).

10. Gumbel, *"Verräter verfallen der Feme."* *Opfer/Möder/Richter 1919–1929* (Berlin: Malik-Verlag, 1929), 102–106; Irmela Nagel, *Fememorde und Fememordprozesse in der Weimarer Republik* (Cologne: Böhlau, 1991), 53–54; Reichstag, III. Wahlperiode 1924/28, 27. Ausschuß, (Untersuchungsausschuß) Feme-Organisationen und Feme-Morde (hereafter, RFA); reports and testimony on the Sandmayr case in sessions 17, 18, 21, and 23, passim. Because this investigating committee never issued a report, its transcripts were not made part of the bound Reichstag proceedings; instead they are housed archivally in Bundesarchiv Deutschland, Abteilungen Berlin-Lichterfelde (BA-B), Reichstag, R101/1645–1648.

11. RFA, 18th session, 17–20; Gumbel, *Verräter,* 112–13; Nagel, 54–55.

12. Testimony of Police Commissioner Friedrich Glaser on 29 October 1920, BFA, 282.

13. RFA, 20th session, 18–21; 21st session, 3–5; 22nd session, 13ff.; 25th session, 11–13.

14. Gumbel, *Verräter,* 113–14.

15. Gumbel, *Verräter,* 81–131; also, E.J. Gumbel, *Verschwörer. Zur Geschichte und Soziologie der deutschen nationalistischen Geheimbünde seit 1918* (Vienna: Malik-Verlag, 1924). See also Paul Levi's article in the 12 August 1926 issue of *Vorwärts,* no. 352, and the acrimonious discussions it touched off within the RFA (sessions 17–19) and between Bavarian officials and the RFA, in BA-B, R101/1645, pp. 439–43, and BA-K, R43I/2732 (reel 557, 179–85).

16. Akten der Reichskanzlei, Kabinett Wirth, "Erkärung" of 1 December 1921, BA-K, Finanzministerium, R2/24686, cited in T. Hunt Tooley, *National Identity and Weimar Germany: Upper Silesia and the Eastern Border, 1918–1922* (Lincoln: University of Nebraska Press, 1997), 298, note 60. Further: Otto Geßler, *Reichswehrpolitik in der Weimarer Zeit* (Stuttgart: Deutsche Verlags-Anstalt, 1958), 221, cited in Nagel, 34.

17. Kalle, Prussian Staatskommissar der öffentlichen Ordnung, letter to Reichsminister des Innern, 21 July 1921, BA-B, Reichsministerium des Innern, R1501/13306, p. 135.

18. *Vorwärts,* 24 April 1928; *Berliner Tageblatt,* 24 April 1928. See also Gumbel, *Verräter,* 168–72; Tooley, 299–30; and Nagel, 33–35.

19. This episode is recounted at length in Gumbel, *Verräter,* 164–72, esp. 165; Gumbel quoted testimony recorded and reported by the Association of German Newspaper Publishers.

20. Tooley, 231–34.

21. See especially Gumbel, *Verräter,* 155–97.

22. Reichskommissar für die Überwachung der öffentlichen Ordnung, report of 28 September 1921, BA-K, R43I/2707, pp. 132–45 (reel 552, 268–81).

23. Kuenzer, Reichskommissar, report of 20 February 1926, 102–5 (reel 557, 84–87); Reichswehrminister [Otto] Geßler, report to RFA, 2 March 1926, RFA Proceedings, Nr. 5, in BA-B, R101/1645, p. 53.

24. Gordon Craig, *The Politics of the Prussian Army, 1640–1945,* paperback ed. (New York: Oxford University Press, 1964), 402.

25. Kuenzer, Reichskommissar, report of 20 February 1926, 101 (reel 557, 83).

26. [Bruno Ernst] Buchrucker, "Schwarze Reichswehr. Gessler und seine 'Arbeiter,'" typescript, undated (ca. 1928/29), BA-K, Nachlaß Walter Luetgebrüne, N1150/152, pp. 6–7.

27. "Denkschrift über die Notwendigkeit einer Befriedigungsamnestie. Verfaßt im Auftrage des Ausschusses zur Förderung der Amnestiebestrebungen aus Anlaß der Rheinlandräumung von Rechtsanwalt Professor Dr. Grimm, Essen/Münster," printed manuscript, 20 January 1930, Bundesarchiv, Abteilung Militärarchiv (Freiburg) (BA-F), Nachlass Hans von Seeckt, N247/128, p. 90. The figure provided here should be taken as a minimum: these are the cases that went through the criminal justice system. There may have been additional murders that were never found or processed through the criminal justice system. Gumbel, *Verräter,* 279–81, identifies an additional three failed *Feme* murders attempted by Schulz's squad, while Nagel, 66–69, counts two failed *Fememorde.*

28. See Nagel, 63–79, and Gumbel, *Verräter,* 265–330. For the exposition of a single case, see, e.g., the indictment in the death of Walter Wilms: Oberstaatsanwalt bei dem Landgericht III, Berlin, "Strafsache gegen Stantien u. Gen. (Mord an Wilms)," 28 January 1927, BA-K, N1150/65.

29. Deutsche Liga für Menschenrechte (DLM), ed., *Weißbuch über die Schwarze Reichswehr: "Deutschlands Geheime Rüstungen?"* (Berlin: Verlag der Neuen Gesellschaft, 1925); J. H. Morgan, "The Disarmament of Germany and After," *Quarterly Review* 242, no. 481 (October 1924): 415–57. After Morgan estimated the strength of the SR at 500,000 men, the DLM distributed a translation of Morgan's article in Germany. See Reinhold Lütgemeier-Davin, *Pazifismus zwischen Kooperation und Konfrontation. Das Deutsche Friedenskartell in der Weimarer Republik* (Cologne: Pahl-Rugenstein, 1982), 174–91; Otto Lehmann-Russbüldt, *Der Kampf der Deutschen Liga für Menschenrechte vormals Bund Neues Vaterland für den Weltfrieden 1914–1927* (Berlin: Hensel & Co., 1927), 116; and Michael Salewsky, *Entwaffnung und Militärkontrolle in Deutschland 1919–1927* (Munich: Oldenbourg, 1966), 280–315.

30. The most influential works on this were Gumbel, *Vier Jahre politischer Morde;* and E. J. Gumbel, ed., *Denkschrift des Reichsjustizministers zu "Vier Jahre politischer Morde"* (Berlin: Malik-Verlag, 1924). Also,

Robert Kuhn, *Die Vertrauenskrise der Justiz (1926–1928). Der Kampf um die "Republikanisierung" der Rechtspflege in der Weimarer Republik* (Cologne: Bundesanzeiger, 1983).

31. RFA proceedings in BA-B, R101/1645–1648; Prussian Landtag investigation proceedings in Preußischer Landtag, *Sitzungsberichte,* Wahlperiode 1924/28, Drucksache Nr. 8924–28. See also Nagel, 285–324.

32. For a sample, see the newspaper clippings files in Geheimes Staatsarchiv Preußischer Kulturbesitz, Rep. 84a/14408–14413; also Nagel, 102–18.

33. [Hans von Seeckt], "Einige Hinweise für ein militärisches Gutachten zu dem Rechtsgutachten des Herrn Professor Dr. Grimm," typescript, undated (ca. 1928), BA-F, N247/126, pp. 6–7.

34. Extract from Schulz's testimony as a witness in a libel suit against two journalists who accused the army of having sanctioned the Schulz death squad murders, from *Berliner Tageblatt,* 17 December 1927, cited in Nagel, 241.

35. [Seeckt], "Einige Hinweise," 6.

36. See the correspondence between the RFA and the Reichswehr and transcripts of the RFA, 42nd session, in BA-B, R101/1647, pp. 80–121.

37. Berthold Jacob, "Plädoyer für Schulz," *Die Weltbühne* 23 (1927): 446–50.

38. Nagel, 298–323.

39. This trail is too long and complex to be recounted in detail. Some examples: transcript of the cabinet discussion of 30 January 1926, BA-K, R431/2732, p. 88 (reel 557, 69–70); Staatssekretär in der Reichskanzlei, note ("Vermerk") of 18 May 1927, BA-K, R431/2733, p. 39 (reel 557, 481); Martius, Auswärtiges Amt, letter to Friedrich Grimm, 7 September 1928, BA-K, R431/2733, p. 103 (reel 557, 548); Staatssekretär in der Reichskanzlei, note of [n.d.] June 1929, BA-K, R431/2733, p. 208 (reel 557, 653); and Staatssekretär in der Reichskanzlei, note of 2 October 1930, BA-K, R431/2733, p. 246 (reel 557, 691).

40. The history of this amnesty campaign is chronicled in Jürgen Christoph, *Die politischen Reichsamnestien 1918–1933* (Frankfurt a.M.: Peter Lang, 1988), 219–321. See also Klaus Petersen, *Literatur und Justiz in der Weimarer Republik* (Stuttgart: Metzler, 1988), 71–72 and 153–59; and Nagel, 325–48.

41. This had been one of the factors complicating Spiecker's testimony in Stettin in 1928. The German-Polish agreement of 1921 amnestied only the perpetrators of violent crime in Upper Silesia in the plebiscite period; it did not cover illegal acts by government officials.

Thus Spiecker and others were liable to prosecution as accessories to violent crimes if there was sufficient evidence that they had ordered murders in Upper Silesia.

42. Buchrucker, "Schwarze Reichswehr. Gessler und seine 'Arbeiter,'" 2.
43. Hagen Schulze, *Weimar. Deutschland 1917–1933*, 2nd ed. (Berlin: Siedler Verlag, 1982), 240.

PART II

Democratic Regime Transitions

CHAPTER 4

Window on the Past: A Declassified History of Death Squads in El Salvador

Cynthia J. Arnson

DURING A BRUTAL CIVIL CONFLICT BETWEEN 1979 and 1991, the small Central American country of El Salvador, with a population of about five million people and a territory approximately the size of the state of Massachusetts, became virtually synonymous with human rights abuse and political terror. It is not difficult to understand why. World attention was riveted on El Salvador beginning in 1980 when a string of prominent assassinations speeded the country's descent into full-scale civil war. In March 1980, Archbishop Oscar Arnulfo Romero, a champion of the poor who had antagonized the right by calling for an end to state-sponsored repression, was gunned down while saying mass in a hospital chapel. In November of that year, the entire leadership of the leftist political opposition was kidnapped from a press conference and then murdered, their mutilated bodies strewn about the outskirts of the capital. In December, three U.S. nuns and a Catholic lay worker were abducted, raped, and murdered, their bodies dumped in a shallow

grave. In January 1981, two U.S. labor advisers and the head of the
Salvadoran land reform agency were gunned down in the coffee
shop of a luxurious San Salvador hotel. Over the next decade, tens
of thousands of less prominent Salvadorans—university professors,
trade unionists, opposition political figures, rural laborers, journalists, and church and humanitarian workers—lost their lives in acts
of targeted or indiscriminate terror.

Despite the multiplicity of actors in El Salvador's carnage in the
1980s, perhaps nothing so epitomized the violence in the eyes of the
public as the actions of death squads. With numbing regularity, tortured, mutilated bodies appeared by the roadside or in notorious
body dumps. At times the squads took overt credit for their work,
carving the initials EM (Escuadrón de la Muerte, Death Squad) into
the chest of a corpse or tucking a piece of paper into the victim's
pocket indicating the work of the Brigada Anticomunista General
Maximiliano Hernández Martínez (Gen. Maximiliano Hernández
Martínez Anti-Communist Brigade), named for one of the country's
former dictators. Multiple testimonies delivered to human rights organizations such as the archdiocesan human rights office Tutela
Legal identified captors or executioners as "heavily armed men in
civilian dress," acting alone or in the company of uniformed troops.
The style and brazenness of operation suggested either state complicity or, at a minimum, because of the frequency of killings and the
squads' freedom of operation, state acquiescence. The objective of
death squad terror seemed not only the elimination of opponents or
suspected opponents but also, through torture and the gruesome
disfiguration of bodies, the terrorization of the population.

A brief sketch of recent Salvadoran history helps to place the
death squad phenomenon in a political context.[1] A series of military
governments ruled El Salvador almost without interruption beginning in 1932, maintaining their hold on political power through
electoral fraud and selective repression of political opponents. A
tiny elite held economic power, such that in a country where 60 percent of the population was engaged in agriculture, the top 10 percent of landowners held 78 percent of arable land, while the lowest
10 percent of the population held a mere 0.4 percent.[2]

Opposition to the military regime grew in the 1970s, a period
that witnessed increased mobilization by rural and urban workers,
students, and a burgeoning middle class demanding an end to the
military's monopoly on political power and greater economic jus-

tice. These efforts were supported by progressive Catholic clergy spurred by the mandate of the 1968 bishops' conference in Medellín, Colombia, to work on behalf of the poor. Several guerrilla groups advocating the violent overthrow of the regime were also formed during this period, engaging in targeted assassinations and kidnappings for ransom. Their actions and following remained limited. Official repression by the army and security forces soared after massive electoral fraud in 1977, as unprecedented numbers of Salvadorans protested the military's violation of the democratic process. At the same time, as challenges to the military's hold on power multiplied in the late 1970s, duly constituted death squads with names like the Unión Guerrera Blanca (White Warrior's Union, UGB) and FALANGE emerged, killing or threatening those considered subversive.[3] Unlike the organized thuggery on behalf of the state that had characterized rural El Salvador for much of the twentieth century, the emergence of death squads linked to the security forces and to far-right landowners' associations appeared more purposeful and selective, aiming, through terror, to neutralize and suppress opposition to the status quo. By the end of the decade, El Salvador was a polarized, fragmented society. "Violations of rights of . . . opponents of the government," said the International Commission of Jurists in 1978, "are not isolated incidents due to an excess of zeal on the part of members of the security forces, but form part of a deliberate campaign to preserve the privileged position of the ruling minority."[4]

To stave off violent revolution of the sort that had erupted in neighboring Nicaragua, a group of reformist military officers staged a coup in El Salvador on October 15, 1979. They invited progressive civilians to form a junta and announced sweeping political and economic reforms. Over succeeding months, however, El Salvador's social and political transformation was blocked by an orgy of violence. Waves of civilians in the junta and cabinet resigned from the government, protesting their inability to control the military or curb violent excesses of the army and security forces. Grassroots organizations, some with direct or indirect links to the guerrillas, stepped up their demands, overwhelming a fragile period of opening and transition with decades of accumulated grievances. Death squads based in the security forces and bankrolled by wealthy landowners launched a bloody war to counter the perceived threat of subversion from within (the governing junta) and without (the mass mobilization of civil society). The civilian death toll in 1980 alone was between 9,000 and 10,000, according to the State Department and the Salvadoran Catholic Church, up from about 1,000 in all of 1979. By 1981, the death toll for the first six months equaled the total of the entire previous year. Government forces were responsible for the vast majority of deaths.[5] As the repression escalated, guerrilla groups coalesced to form the Farabundo Martí National Liberation Front (FMLN) in late 1980. They staged an ill-fated "final offensive" in January 1981 that came far short of its goal of toppling the regime, but effectively launched El Salvador into a full-scale civil war that lasted for the rest of the decade.

The United States became deeply involved in the Salvadoran conflict, committing itself to "draw the line" against communism and ultimately spending some $6 billion to counter what President Ronald Reagan considered a "textbook case" of Soviet, Cuban, and Nicaraguan aggression in the hemisphere.[6] Throughout the decade, and particularly during the years 1980–1983 when the killing was at its height, assigning responsibility for the violence and human rights abuses was a product of the intense ideological polarization in the United States. The Reagan administration downplayed the scale of the abuse as well as the involvement of state actors.[7] Because of the level of denial, as well as the extent of U.S. involvement with the Salvadoran military and security forces, the U.S. role in El Salvador—what was known about death squads, when it was known, and what actions the United States did or did not take to curb their abuses—becomes an important part of El Salvador's death squad story.[8]

The end of the Cold War permitted a negotiated settlement to the Salvadoran conflict in January 1992. The settlement, in turn, created an official mechanism for investigating past violence and assessing responsibility for major crimes. A United Nations–sponsored Commission on the Truth for El Salvador, created by the peace accords, began in July 1992 to investigate "serious acts of violence . . . whose impact on society urgently demands that the public should know the truth." In March 1993, the commission concluded that almost 85 percent of cases of extrajudicial executions, disappearances, and torture were attributable to "agents of the State, paramilitary groups allied to them, and the death squads." Guerrillas of the FMLN were named in approximately 5 percent of cases.

The Truth Commission found the death squads' share of abuses to be relatively small, amounting to just over 10 percent of documented cases. But, according to the Truth Commission, they played a unique role in the 1980–83 period, when "[o]rganized terrorism, in the form of the so-called 'death squads,' became the most aberrant manifestation of the escalation of violence."[9]

> The death squads, in which members of State structures were actively involved or to which they turned a blind eye, gained such control that they ceased to be an isolated or marginal phenomenon and became an instrument of terror used systematically for the physical elimination of political opponents. Many of the civilian and military authorities in power during the 1980s participated in, encouraged and tolerated the activities of these groups.... Frequently, death squads operated in coordination with the armed forces and acted as a support structure for their activities. The clandestine nature of these activities made it possible to conceal the State's responsibility for them and created an atmosphere of complete impunity for the murderers who worked in the squads.[10]

The function of death squad terror, rather than its proportionate claim of lives, underscores a central point related to the understanding of political violence in El Salvador: numerically speaking, the overwhelming number of abuses were committed by the military and security forces themselves. While the cases of Archbishop Romero and the land reform advisers cited above were, according to the Truth Commission, classic death squad operations, other targeted killings, including the case of the four U.S. churchwomen, were committed by units of the army or security forces. Similarly, large-scale massacres of civilians were committed in the early part of the decade during regular army operations.[11] As the Central Intelligence Agency (CIA) noted in October 1983, "human rights abuses committed in the course of military operations, no matter how abhorrent, are not 'death squad activities.'"[12]

If overall numbers of murders were proportionally not large, the principal importance of the death squads lay in their place in the repressive machinery of the state and the guarantee of clandestinity, terror, and impunity such activities conferred on operatives.

Much of what can be officially documented about death squads owes a large debt not only to the Truth Commission but also to the reaction its findings spawned in the United States. The gap between the commission's conclusions and the portrayals of successive U.S. administrations prompted members of Congress to ask President Bill Clinton to declassify U.S. government documentary material relevant to the 32 human rights cases investigated by the Truth Commission. By the end of 1993, over 12,000 documents from the Department of State, Department of Defense, and Central Intelligence Agency were released.[13] Although focusing primarily on cases covered by the Truth Commission, the documents contain a wealth of information on the origins, structure, financing, practices, and personnel involved in death squads.

The documents make it possible to reassess the U.S. role in El Salvador with respect to death squads, illustrating, as was claimed by policy critics throughout the 1980s, that the U.S. government knew far more about right-wing violence than it was willing to admit publicly. More significant, however, is what the documents reveal about a systematic lapse in U.S. intelligence-gathering and priorities: not until mid to late 1983—several years into the death squad rampage—did the U.S. government began the systematic collection of information on death squad operations, sources of financing, personnel, and connections to official units. Even though the toll of civilian victims was at its height between 1980 and 1983, U.S. reporting during this period focused on left-wing, not right-wing or state, terrorism. According to a House Intelligence Committee report, "It did not appear that collection tasking for information on right-wing terrorism was a high priority until late 1982 . . . at policy levels no firm priority was established for such collection during the period 1979 to 1982. Rather, U.S. intelligence concentrated in that earlier period on left-wing terrorism and Salvadoran insurgent activities."[14]

The documents also make it possible to reinterpret U.S. policy initiatives with respect to death squads, particularly the December 1983 visit by Vice President George Bush to San Salvador to demand a crackdown on death squads and the removal or transfer of personnel involved in their operations. In addition, they reflect the lack of comprehensive reporting on death squads until 1985, long after the Bush visit, a lapse decried by senior U.S. diplomats.[15]

This chapter draws primarily on information in the declassified U.S. documents to trace the evolution of the death squad phenomenon in El Salvador throughout the 1980s, but most particularly in the early part of the decade when the violence was at its worst. The declassified documents constitute an official record of the individuals and institutions that U.S. intelligence and diplomatic sources reported to be engaged in death squad activity. Given the nature of the declassification process, that record is necessarily incomplete: Congress asked the administration to declassify documents relevant to the cases investigated by the Truth Commission, not documents on death squads per se. Nonetheless, the documents available describe in unflinching candor and detail a phenomenon that U.S. officials publicly described as unknowable. Many of the documents released were designated secret or top secret. That they were never intended to see the light of day accounts, in some measure, for their startling nature.

Origins

The ultra-right in El Salvador has a long history of using violence as a political tool, perhaps marked most vividly by the widespread repression and murder of campesinos following the failed peasant rebellion in 1932.

—United States Central Intelligence Agency, March 18, 1981[16]

State-sanctioned violence as a mechanism of social control had its origin in the economic transformation of El Salvador in the late nineteenth century. To make way for the rapidly expanding cultivation of coffee in the 1880s, indigenous tribal lands and large municipal landholdings were abolished by presidential decrees in 1881–82.[17] To evict peasants from communal lands, El Salvador's leaders created rural police forces between 1884 and 1889, centered in the coffee-growing areas in the western part of the country. These rural militias subsequently were reorganized into the national guard in 1912.[18] For almost a century, El Salvador's security forces and agricultural elites found common purpose in the desire to control, and suppress if necessary, the rural population.

Worldwide depression and the plunge in coffee prices set the stage for the military's formal entry into politics. Minister of War General Maximiliano Hernández Martínez seized power in a coup in December 1931. Poorly armed and poorly organized peasants staged an uprising in western El Salvador, led by socialist organizer

Farabundo Martí, from whom the latter-day guerrillas took their name. To put down the rebellion, Hernández Martínez and his troops massacred between 10,000 and 30,000 people in a matter of weeks.[19] According to the CIA,

> The resulting endemic national paranoia over the Communist threat reinforced authoritarian rule by the armed forces and its affluent civilian backers for the next half century. The chain of military regimes provided order and stability, and largely gave the plantation owners and monopolist businessmen a free hand over the economy. . . . Control over society was handled by the military government and civilian elites largely through paramilitary constabulary forces, regular Army units, and numerous official and private vigilante organizations. The historical record shows that, given the inherent weaknesses of the formal judicial process, these security bodies would often function at the local level as judge, jury, and executioner of individuals perceived to be criminals or subversives.[20]

Among the "numerous official and private vigilante organizations" that operated in El Salvador was the Nationalist Democratic Organization (Organización Democrática Nacionalista, or ORDEN, Spanish for "order"), a rural paramilitary force created in the mid-1960s by intelligence service chief José Alberto "Chele" Medrano. Described by the CIA as a "notorious and powerful figure in military and rightwing civilian circles," Medrano and his protégés focused on "counterintelligence and rural security."[21] ORDEN served to illustrate the way that organizations created for intelligence purposes and linked to official security bodies "effectively institutionalized vigilanteism" in the countryside.[22] As the CIA put it, ORDEN was "comprised of tens of thousands of conservative rural peasants and served as a tool of the landed elites . . . [it] served principally as an intelligence gathering organization—identifying and taking direct action against real and suspected enemies of the regime."[23] According to another U.S. government agency, ORDEN was "responsible for the intimidation, murder, and disappearance of Salvadorans suspected of involvement with the extreme left."[24]

Throughout the 1960s, when Medrano served successively at the helm of the intelligence service and National Guard, the United States government was deeply involved in bolstering El Salvador's capacity to fight internal subversion.[25] Some of the assistance went to the same units—ORDEN, the National Police, the Treasury Police, and the National Guard—that subsequently became loci of death squad activity. Trainees of the Agency for International Development's Office of Public Safety (OPS) included top officials in the intelligence division of the National Police, the Treasury Police, the Customs Police, and the Immigration Service. An "investigations adviser" worked with the intelligence units of the National Police, National Guard, and Immigration Service, as well as with the Salvadoran Intelligence Agency. This same investigations adviser was "lending aid to an intelligence unit of 15 persons headed by Col. Medrano directly responsible to the Presidential Palace." In a reference to ORDEN, AID reported that "Col. Medrano claims to have a 30,000-man military reservist informant network that channels intelligence to his group. . . ."[26]

ORDEN was officially disbanded in October 1979, following the reformist military coup aimed at stopping El Salvador's slide toward full-scale civil war. But, in a pattern that would repeat itself throughout the next decade, ORDEN's structure remained intact and its personnel integrated into other units at the service of the state. Many of its former members joined the Territorial Service and civil defense force, described by the CIA as "Army-run militias that provide local security in outlying villages and tactical intelligence to the military."[27] According to other U.S. documents, some of the cadre for "right-wing terrorist groups" were "probably drawn from the ranks of ORDEN," and "many former associates of Medrano's were subsequently linked to death squad activities in the early 1980s."[28] These associates included Medrano protégé and National Guard officer Roberto D'Aubuisson, who through the 1980s played a central role in the organization and direction of death squad activity.[29]

Medrano is also credited with founding the national intelligence agency that eventually became known as ANSESAL (Agencia Nacional de Seguridad de El Salvador, National Security Agency of El Salvador), which operated out of the presidency until the 1979 coup.[30] ANSESAL's importance lies in the extensive data base it compiled on opposition political activists. Some of ANSESAL's files were stolen following the coup by its number three operative, Roberto D'Aubuisson, who was cashiered in a purge of right-wing military officers.[31] Over the next several years, D'Aubuisson spearheaded a terror campaign directed against not only actual and suspected leftists but also centrist Christian Democrats and others engaged in promoting political and socioeconomic reforms. In a mirror image of leftist political tactics,[32] he founded first a political front and then a political party, the Alianza Republicana Nacionalista (Nationalist Republican Alliance, ARENA), to complement military actions by his terrorist network. D'Aubuisson was not the only but certainly the most prominent individual identified to date as associated with death squads in El Salvador. Because of his catalyzing role, the next section describes in considerable detail his personal trajectory, the workings of the death squad operating out of ARENA, and the links between the latter and other groups run out of the security forces.

The Role of Roberto D'Aubuisson and ARENA

. . . behind ARENA's legitimate exterior lies a terrorist network led by D'Aubuisson henchmen and funded by wealthy Salvadoran expatriates residing in Guatemala and the United States.

—Central Intelligence Agency, February 1985[33]

In March 1981, the Central Intelligence Agency scathingly described Roberto D'Aubuisson as the "principal henchman for wealthy landowners and as a coordinator of the right-wing death squads that have murdered several thousand suspected leftists and leftist sympathizers during the past year." They described him as "egocentric and reckless" (an earlier draft called him "perhaps mentally unstable")[34] and as favoring the "physical elimination" of leftists that he defined as "anyone not supportive of the traditional status quo." According to the CIA, D'Aubuisson was funded by members of the "extreme right-wing Salvadoran elite" who mostly lived abroad in the United States and Guatemala. "These wealthy expatriates have reportedly spent millions of dollars to support D'Aubuisson and his few followers in their effort to overthrow the present junta and return the country to right-wing military rule."[35]

D'Aubuisson maintained close contact with the intelligence sections (S-II) of the security forces following his dismissal from the armed forces, combining what the Truth Commission called "two elements in a strategic relationship": money (and weapons, vehicles, and safe houses) provided by the extreme right, and ideology, "the definition of a political line," for the intelligence units of the security forces. The objective, according to the U.S. Embassy in San Salvador, was to "terrorize those who are still working for a moderate outcome, in or out of the government, and to impose a right-ist dictatorship."[36]

Numerous documents describe the political rationale for death squad activity and the objectives of D'Aubuisson and his wealthy backers. "Rightwing extremists have viewed government reformers as national security threats equal to those posed by the guerrilla movement," reported the CIA, fighting what they considered a "legitimate clandestine war against the left."[37]

One of the earliest documents chronicling right-wing terror surfaced in 1980 in El Salvador, some seven months after the military coup that ushered in a period of attempted reforms and intensified political violence. D'Aubuisson, along with about two dozen active-duty and retired military personnel and civilians, was arrested in May 1980 for plotting a coup against the new government. Among the documents seized with the plotters was the "General Framework for the Organization of the Anti-Marxist Struggle in El Salvador." It detailed a political goal—to seize power—as well as a plan for "direct action," "combat networks," and "attacks on selected individuals."[38]

Among other captured documents was a notebook belonging to former captain Alvaro Saravia, which carried details of Operación Piña (Operation Pineapple), listing a night vision device, driver, sharpshooter, security, and a specialized rifle. Former ambassador to El Salvador Robert White testified publicly in April 1981 that Operación Piña was, in fact, the plan for the March 1980 murder of Archbishop Romero. According to other information gathered by the embassy, D'Aubuisson presided over the drawing of lots for the "privilege" of killing the archbishop.[39]

D'Aubuisson was jailed briefly for his involvement in the coup plot and then released following protests by powerful supporters in the military. He fled to Guatemala, using his period of "exile" to establish links to far-right individuals and anticommunist networks and continuing to plan and direct death squad attacks in El Salvador.[40] From abroad D'Aubuisson organized the Broad National Front (Frente Amplio Nacional, FAN), described by the CIA as "a semi-clandestine political organization bent on overthrowing the reformist regime in San Salvador." With funding from right-wing exiles living abroad, the FAN "used black market contacts to arm a small paramilitary organization in El Salvador that included both civilians and military personnel...."[41] D'Aubuisson traveled to Washington in July 1980, holding a press conference hosted by the

American Legion and the American Security Council. He denounced United States Ambassador to El Salvador Robert White for imposing "socialist measures" on El Salvador and described the main purpose of the FAN as "to oppose communist penetration."[42]

By October 1981, D'Aubuisson had reorganized the FAN into a bona fide political party, the Nationalist Republican Alliance (ARENA). In search of greater legitimacy, he sought to attract the support of other conservative businessmen and professionals. ARENA drew on extensive support in rural areas provided in part by former members of ORDEN. D'Aubuisson was elected to El Salvador's Constituent Assembly in 1982, and only intense jockeying by the United States government prevented him from being named provisional president of the country.[43] He became, however, president of the Constituent Assembly. From that post, and using ARENA as cover, he continued to direct a team that engaged in "political intimidation, including abduction, torture, and murder."[44]

D'Aubuisson's right-hand man in directing death squads out of the Constituent Assembly was Héctor Antonio Regalado, a former dentist and longtime D'Aubuisson associate who served as the assembly's security chief. In the 1970s, Regalado had organized a group of young men posing as a Boy Scout troop to carry out murders of suspected leftists; then, out of fear that the youths knew too much, Regalado had them killed in 1980.[45] Under the guise of providing protection for ARENA functionaries and party headquarters, Regalado headed a paramilitary unit described by the CIA as "the group from which death squad members are principally drawn."[46] According to the CIA, the ARENA death squad headed by Regalado consisted of 10 to 20 individuals drawn from the military, National Police, and Treasury Police, as well as selected civilians. It had as its principal targets members of the revolutionary left and the Christian Democratic Party. Between 1982 and 1983 the ARENA death squad was credited with the assassination of Christian Democratic mayors and party workers prior to the March 1982 elections, the machine-gunning of PDC headquarters, the torture and murder of guerrillas, including one whose body was dumped in the parking lot of the Camino Real hotel frequented by foreign journalists, and the bombing of a printshop, the car of a labor leader, and the homes of Jesuit priests and a professor at the prominent Central American University (UCA).[47]

Notably, the CIA identified the notorious and highly visible Secret Anticommunist Army (Ejército Secreto Anticomunista, ESA) as being the public face of the ARENA death squad; according to U.S. intelligence, the ESA was ARENA's "primary instrument for clandestine operations."[48] In contrast to death squads that attempted to conceal their responsibility for specific acts, the ARENA squad was "publicity seeking," using the ESA name in order to have a "public front for issuing communiqués and threatening people while covering the true source of the violence." To conceal its origins, the ESA even issued a communiqué attacking D'Aubuisson.[49]

Death Squads Operating out of the Military and Security Forces

The U.S. government has information which corroborates public claims that death squad activities, as well as other abuses provoked by extreme rightwing officers or their associates, have originated in the Salvadoran security services, including the National Police, National Guard, and Treasury Police.

—United States Senate, Select Committee on Intelligence[50]

The National Guard (Guardia Nacional, GN)

D'Aubuisson's central vehicle for violence—the paramilitary unit of the ARENA party—was but part of a multifaceted, overlapping network of terrorists based in and out of the security forces and financed by wealthy civilians. As the CIA noted in October 1983, rank-and-file membership in death squads was "fluid and sometimes interchangeable, while leadership positions are more permanent. Leaders of one group are likely to know the leaders of others operating in the same area or against common targets and and [sic] distinct groups occasionally conduct joint operations."[51]

Prominent among the squads operating alongside D'Aubuisson in the early 1980s was one organized out of the intelligence section (G-II) of the National Guard, the security force to which D'Aubuisson had previously belonged.[52] In 1981, the CIA ascribed "the majority of bank bombings that have taken place in recent months" in the capital to the National Guard unit, noting that it also had carried out the "assassinations of many individuals thought to support leftist causes."[53] The G-II unit was headed by Major Mario Denis Morán, identified in a CIA bibliographic profile as the director of the White Warrior's Union (Unión Guerrera Blanca), a death squad active in the 1970s that was described elsewhere as specializing in the murder of Catholic priests.[54]

The National Guard death squad was financed by a "cabal" of right-wing civilian backers who freely visited G-II headquarters "bearing briefcases full of money, guns, and other recompense" and, according to the U.S. Embassy, defined the work agenda of the intelligence unit. Argentine advisers also frequented the unit and, according to a trusted embassy source, "assisted on 'certain jobs.'"[55]

Perhaps the most notorious killing ascribed to the National Guard death squad was the January 3, 1981, murder of Rodolfo Viera, peasant leader and director of the land reform agency ISTA (Instituto Salvadoreño de Transformación Agraria), and two U.S. advisers from the American Institute for Free Labor Development (AIFLD), Michael Hammer and Mark Pearlman. According to the U.S. Embassy, the plot to kill Viera was launched at a meeting at G-II headquarters between Major Morán and two rightist civilians. The most prominent of them was Ricardo Sol Meza, described in other U.S. documents as a "longtime loyalist of Roberto D'Aubuisson," an "oligarchic family member," and the former owner of the disco at the Sheraton Hotel. The rationale for murdering Viera was a complaint by Sol Meza and an associate that the government's land reform programs "were putting them in the street."[56] The group designated Morán's second-in-command, Lieutenant Rodolfo Isidro López Sibrián, to kill Viera.

After two botched attempts to assassinate Viera, López Sibrian and G-II members succeeded. On the night of January 3, 1981, Viera was spotted in the restaurant of the Sheraton Hotel while dining with Hammer and Pearlman. López Sibrián and death squad member Captain Eduardo Alfonso Avila ordered two National Guard agents to kill all three men. Following the murders, Sol Meza and others who had organized and carried out the plot celebrated at National Guard headquarters, bringing Morán an attaché case stuffed with money.[57] The two national guardsmen who pulled the trigger on Viera, Hammer, and Pearlman were convicted of murder in 1986, only to be released a year later in a government-sponsored amnesty. Morán's role was never probed; he was promoted to colonel and served as military attaché in Guatemala and later headed the Engineer Instruction Center. López Sibrián and Avila eluded justice in the case (Avila's uncle was a Supreme Court justice), although López Sibrián was arrested in 1986 for his role in an army-led kidnapping ring that, posing as guerrillas, had seized wealthy Salvadorans and held them for ransom.[58]

The National Police (Policía Nacional, PN)

In contrast to the "publicity-seeking" death squad operating out of ARENA, the death squad operating out of the National Police tended "to avoid high profile operations," using no name, and other than the evidence of torture, left "no indication of its responsibility" for specific acts. In 1983, the CIA reported that the National Police death squad had been in operation since at least late 1979, although it probably functioned much earlier. Most members of the paramilitary group were drawn from three sections of the police: the Criminal Investigation section, the Special Political Investigation section, and the Narcotics Control section. The squad was headed by Lieutenant Colonel Arístides Márquez, the chief of the intelligence department.[59]

The National Police death squad maintained several links to D'Aubuisson and his ARENA unit, and death squad members themselves believed that D'Aubuisson was responsible for selecting leftists to be "interrogated or executed" by the National Police group.[60] A detective named Edgar Sigifredo Pérez Linares was one of Márquez's key liaisons to D'Aubuisson and Regalado; Pérez Linares's name surfaces repeatedly throughout the decade as a key figure in death squad and other criminal operations, including the March 1980 assassination of Archbishop Romero and a kidnapping-for-profit ring run by death squad operatives between 1982 and 1986.[61] An unnamed and unsourced U.S. document describes Pérez as an "intermediary" between Márquez and Regalado on death squad matters.[62] Another link to ARENA was through Lieutenant Colonel René Emilio Ponce, identified by the CIA in 1983 as a "National Police death squad member" and director of the police Traffic Department.[63] Ponce became Salvadoran minister of defense in 1990, and was by then viewed as a moderate and enjoying strong U.S. backing. In 1993, the Truth Commission named him as one of the senior officers who ordered the 1989 murders of six Jesuit priests and two women on the campus of the Central American University, a human rights case which transformed the public debate in the United States over El Salvador policy and was a turning point toward a negotiated settlement of the war.[64]

The National Police and ARENA death squads jointly operated a clandestine prison in the wealthy Escalón neighborhood of San Salvador. Another clandestine prison was maintained separately by the National Police in La Libertad department and used for "detention, interrogation, and execution of suspected leftists and leftist sympathizers." The La Libertad prison was run by the chief of the National Police political section, a Márquez deputy.[65]

The Treasury Police (Policía de Hacienda, PH)

Although uniformed troops of the Treasury Police were among the most brutal of El Salvador's established security forces, the declassified U.S. documents contain far less about death squads operating out of the Treasury Police. The relative lack of information may be attributable to the focus of the declassification effort—the cases investigated by the Truth Commission—or to the fact that Colonel Nicolás Carranza, Treasury Police director from 1983 to 1984, was a key CIA informant, paid some $90,000 a year until the relationship was exposed in the U.S. press.[66] That the CIA's landmark 1983 report on death squads contains not a word on the involvement of the Treasury Police suggests that Carranza himself may have been a principal source.[67]

The sketchy information that is available includes an intelligence profile of 1980–82 Treasury Police director Francisco Antonio Morán, which noted that he was "reportedly active in death squad activities." Because of his alleged involvement in "various rightwing terror activities," in late 1983 he was placed on a State Department "watchlist" intended to prevent known criminals from entering the United States. Later, as director of the electric utility known as CEL (the Lempa River Hydroelectric Commission), Morán was still reportedly "very active in death squad activities" and had recruited two leftist guerrillas "to commit assassinations and other terrorist acts."[68]

Other fragmentary evidence points to the murderous animosities that sometimes existed between death squads. The Treasury Police death squad, unlike its counterparts in the National Police and National Guard, had sour relations with ARENA's paramilitary unit. "Animosity between the ARENA squad and the Treasury Police has included kidnappings and executions," reported the CIA in 1983. "There appears to be rivalry" among some of the groups involved in death squad terror.[69]

The Armed Forces

If the security forces and ARENA harbored many of the key death squad operatives of the early 1980s, the army itself also played a role in death squad activities. "Rightist terrorist cells . . . use both active-duty and retired military personnel in their campaigns," according to a 1985 assessment by the CIA: " . . . death squads in the armed forces operate out of both urban military headquarters and rural outposts. They are led by senior enlisted personnel and junior officers, and they may function with or without the knowledge of immediate superiors." The armed forces field and staff commands were controlled by a "younger generation of ambitious officers" who were motivated and talented on the battlefield. "Unfortunately," reported the CIA, they were former military academy classmates and colleagues of D'Aubuisson "who share his ultrarightist views" and were "alleged to have associations with rightwing terrorist organizations and, in some cases, to have been leaders of death squads within the Army and security forces."[70] The CIA went on to list a number of the "regular military units implicated, [deleted] in abductions and death squad activities." These included the San Salvador–based First Brigade, the Air Force,[71] and Army Signal Corps, the Second Brigade in Santa Ana, and cavalry, artillery, engineer, and infantry detachments throughout the country. That these units were led by commanders with "strong political sway" within the military underscored the difficulty facing "efforts to improve the human rights record of the armed forces."[72]

The Crackdown

The administration's attempt to curb death squad violence had several origins, although all had a common denominator: the growing perception that U.S. efforts to defeat the insurgency, build a democratic government, and maintain a congressional majority in favor of aid were becoming unsustainable in the face of ongoing high-profile death squad killings.[73] A wave of murders and kidnappings in the third quarter of 1983, which targeted centrist peasant and labor leaders supportive of government reforms and officials of the incumbent Christian Democratic Party, threatened to undermine the credibility of El Salvador's presidential elections scheduled for early

1984 and stoke the ongoing defection of Republican moderates in Congress previously supportive of aid. Among those kidnapped, for example, was the third-ranking official of the Salvadoran Foreign Ministry. In November, the tortured bodies of nine people, including three members of a peasant cooperative and two pregnant women, were found stuffed into grain sacks in the town of Zaragoza. Bomb attacks and death threats multiplied against the ever-beleaguered Catholic Church.[74] The father of auxiliary bishop Gregorio Rosa Chávez was kidnapped. Church officials privately blamed death squads operating out of the military and the National Police.[75]

Ambassador Pickering sent cables to Washington detailing what he called the "terrorist activities" by the extreme right,[76] and, in a widely quoted speech before a conservative group of Salvadoran businessmen, he lambasted the private sector for the "self-deluding belief that nothing is really known about the shadowy world of these individuals." He mentioned the Zaragoza incident by name, asking rhetorically, "Is there anyone in this room who can find any pretext, any excuse, to justify this?"[77] Meanwhile, in early November, the U.S. Embassy began leaking to the press the names of those it believed most responsible for the death squad networks, a preemptive move, perhaps, given that reporters were independently gathering and publishing extensive information on death squad violence.[78]

On December 11, 1983, Vice President George Bush visited El Salvador on his way to a presidential inauguration in Argentina.[79] Underscoring that he spoke for President Reagan, Bush held a series of meetings with senior military and government officials. These included a private meeting with President Magaña, a meeting with the minister and vice-minister of defense and the army chief of staff, a session with an expanded group of senior military commanders, and a meeting with the country's three vice presidents, representing the principal political parties. According to a lengthy report on the meetings sent to Washington under Pickering's signature, Bush drove home a central message: the "death squads are undermining the credibility and work of the government." Bush demanded that military officers and civilians linked to death squads and to the murders of U.S. citizens be transferred abroad, arrested, or prosecuted. According to Pickering's report, Bush insisted that "the main point is the death squad issue. The President has asked me to come to express that point to all here. This no smoke screen, this is a reality . . . all who support us know we cannot get done what must be done to increase our support for you if you are not able to help yourselves in this way." Bush indicated that Ambassador Pickering would separately deliver a list of participants in death squad activity, including officials, ex-officials, and civilians, who were to be out of the country before January 10, 1984, shortly before Congress was due to reconvene.[80] He insisted on progress in the murder investigations involving U.S. citizens and demanded that orders be issued, also by January 10, outlawing the torture of prisoners, arrests in plainclothes, or the holding of prisoners in anything other than official places of detention. The private messages were reiterated during a public state dinner, during which Bush declared: "These cowardly death squad terrorists are just as repugnant to me, to President Reagan, to the U.S. Congress, and to the American people as the terrorists of the left. . . . If these death squad murders continue, you will lose the support of the American people."[81]

The extensive notes of Bush's meetings indicate that Bush also offered significant inducements to the Salvadoran military in exchange for the steps requested regarding death squads. In his meeting with the most influential commanders of the armed forces, a group that included the heads of the three security forces as well as the army chief of intelligence and key brigade commanders, Bush described at length the administration's willingness "to consider seeking from our Congress an immediate increase in funding for the war effort in El Salvador. . . . We now face a stalemate with no victory in sight," he said. "We need to change this outlook. We need to begin to win and sustain the winning effort." He described a two-year plan of augmented aid that would allow the Salvadoran military to "field 39 newly-organized, fully-equipped countersubversion battalions," as well as two rapid reaction battalions, an engineering battalion, and a battery of new equipment: A-37 counterinsurgency aircraft, helicopters, artillery, naval patrol boats, and medical evacuation aircraft. Bush detailed battlefield and operational reforms that, according to General Paul Gorman of the U.S. Southern Command, needed to be implemented to "greatly aid in prosecuting the war." Bush offered the assistance as an explicit quid pro quo: "If you do your part, we will do ours." He stressed the Salvadoran military's "very important endeavor: the defeat of communist insurgency in your country and elsewhere in the region."[82]

The Bush visit to El Salvador, long touted as a turning point in U.S. policy, thus emerges in a different light. For all its public and private emphasis on curbing death squad terror, the trip also stands out for its emphasis on the security dimensions of the conflict, the offers of vastly expanded military aid, and the shared U.S. and Salvadoran interest in defeating the insurgency. Subsequent events bore out that the hierarchy of U.S. security interests remained unchanged: aid would flow and reach unprecedented levels despite the lack of progress on the concrete steps Bush outlined with such clarity.

Reports of death squad killings did decline following the Bush visit, and the decline was acknowledged not only by human rights groups at the time but also by the UN Truth Commission.[83] But private assessments by the U.S. government of Salvadoran steps in the wake of the Bush visit were scathing. According to information requested by Vice President Bush and prepared by the CIA, "deaths attributed to political violence have not declined significantly, only notorious high-level death squad *claims* of violence" (emphasis added). On January 20, 1984, ten days after the deadline Bush gave the Salvadorans for resolute actions against the death squads, the CIA made the following assessments:

> ... Efforts by the civilian government and the military high command to crack down on rightwing violence have made little progress and have been aimed almost exclusively at placating Washington. ... Since December, the response of the government and military leaders to the problem of rightwing violence has been mainly verbal. ... Two mid-level police intelligence officers have been transferred to diplomatic posts overseas. This gesture is offset, however, by their replacement with ultrarightist officers, one of whom is a [deleted] leader of a police death squad. Moreover, in the course of recent general orders, several other notorious rightwing extremists have been assigned to prestigious commands. These include Lieutenant Colonels Moran, Zepeda, Zacapa, Ponce, and Staben—all close associates of ultrarightist standard-bearer Roberto D'Aubuisson and his Nationalist Republican Alliance.[84]

In one of its more disturbing findings, the CIA reported that Defense Minister Vides Casanova—described as appearing "personally disinclined and professionally unable to effect a major cleanup within the armed forces any time soon"—had appointed an investigative team within the armed forces to oversee reports of abuses. It was headed by a Captain Arango of the National Guard, identified by the CIA as a "cohort of former Major D'Aubuisson" and a "leader of the notorious White Warriors Union—a death squad that specialized in eliminating members of the Catholic clergy."[85] A separate CIA assessment prepared in advance of El Salvador's 1984 elections noted that "the far right's growing influence in the military . . . is making Vides's position increasingly difficult. . . . Mindful of the fate of his moderate predecessor, General Garcia [who was forced out by rightist officers in 1983], Vides probably is unwilling to risk his own position by forcing a halt to extralegal activities."[86]

Despite the failure of the Salvadoran government or military to take more than limited action against the death squads, U.S. aid to El Salvador dramatically expanded in the months following the Bush visit. This expansion was due primarily to a shift in congressional attitudes toward the Salvadoran government following the May 1984 election of Christian Democrat José Napoleón Duarte as president. The CIA channeled covert aid to Duarte in order to keep his opponent, Roberto D'Aubuisson, from office. The U.S. government correctly perceived that the battle for the hearts and minds of Congress would be lost if D'Aubuisson were to be elected. The covert funding became public when Senator Jesse Helms (R-NC), a longtime D'Aubuisson supporter, complained about the partisan interference in Salvadoran affairs.[87] Subsequently, D'Aubuisson and others of the ARENA party plotted to kill Ambassador Pickering. The plot generated yet another high-level visit to San Salvador, this time by retired general Vernon Walters, to impress on D'Aubuisson and his associates that "any such attempts against the Ambassador would unquestionably terminate U.S. assistance programs."[88] The assassination plot failed to materialize, and El Salvador retreated from the front pages of U.S. newspapers for the next several years.

The Resurgence of Death Squad Activities

Beginning in mid-1987, the human rights situation in El Salvador began to take a sharp turn for the worse. The reductions in claims of death squad killings that had been attributed to the Bush visit and the political backlash that had forced groups to lower their profile or lie dormant gave way to reports that death squads were reactivating in response to perceived deterioration in the political and security situation in the country. In mid-1988, Benjamin Cestoni, the head of the Salvadoran government's own human rights commission, told the U.S. Embassy that the situation marked "the beginning of the return to the appalling human rights situation of the early 1980s," with victims abducted from their houses and subsequently murdered and more bodies appearing with signs of torture.[89] In his state of the union address in that same year, President Duarte himself decried the "'extremist death squads that seem to be coming back to life.'"[90] These fears were echoed by the U.S. Embassy. "One thing is clear," said a June 1988 report. "For the first time in years blindfolded bodies are again beginning to appear in San Salvador with their hands tied behind their backs. . . . While finding a body like this is not ipso facto evidence of death squad activity, it sure is a pretty strong indicator of the same."[91]

U.S. government explanations for the deterioration and assessments by nongovernmental human rights groups focused on several factors: (1) the expiration of state-of-siege legislation in January 1987, which effectively reduced the period of incommunicado detention from 15 days to the constitutional limit of 72 hours; (2) an October 1987 amnesty that released over 400 leftists as well as a handful of members of the armed forces accused of crimes; (3) a political opening fostered by the Central American peace process known as Esquipulas II, which prompted a return of exiled political leaders representing the Frente Democrático Revolucionario (FDR), formally allied with the FMLN guerrillas; (4) the return of thousands of Salvadoran refugees from Honduras to their homes in conflictive zones, a resettlement viewed by the military as helping to reestablish civilian support networks for the guerrillas; and (5) the declining leadership of President Duarte, who was suffering from terminal cancer.[92]

It should be noted that urban terrorism by the guerrillas was also on the increase, as part of a deliberate effort beginning in mid-decade to take the war to the cities. Guerrillas openly attacked the March 1988 elections, using kidnappings, car bombs, and murders to undermine what they viewed as the political side of a governmental counterinsurgency strategy. "If rightists are indeed involved" in increased death squad activity, reported the CIA in November 1988, "we believe they have been acting primarily out of frustration with the slow rate of progress against the insurgents on the battlefield and out of fear that the insurgents are participating in the political process solely to expand their urban support networks for terrorism and subversion."[93]

Several United States government documents refer to the role of the ARENA party and D'Aubuisson, its founder, in the death squad resurgence. According to the CIA, there was no "definitive proof" that hardliners in the ARENA party were involved in crimes, but D'Aubuisson continued to "maintain close ties with Dr. Hector Antonio Regalado, the former chief of a notorious death squad active in the early 1980s, though the two avoid appearing together in public."[94] A series of *Washington Post* articles in August 1988 on the death squad resurgence, based on interviews with two former operatives, also named Regalado as a key figure in the effort to rebuild death squad networks. As in the early 1980s, they were to be based in the ARENA-controlled Legislative Assembly and a party-influenced 5,000-member Municipal Police.[95] The CIA did link ARENA's 1988 electoral triumph to the killings, noting that it "may have inspired lower-ranking party members or independent rightists to act without the official knowledge or sanction of the party."[96]

In August 1990, more than a year after Alfredo Cristiani took office as president, deep divisions within ARENA between the Cristiani and the D'Aubuisson wings of the party threatened to erupt into violence. D'Aubuisson supporters within ARENA "were discussing ways to assassinate President Alfredo Cristiani, his closest personal advisors and selected cabinet ministers." The CIA took the threats seriously, noting that "many of D'Aubuisson's loyalists are politically unsophisticated and quick to resort to violence to remedy their problems, which makes them all the more dangerous."[97] Information reported to the CIA also indicated that "rightwing elements plan to [deleted] kill leftist labor leaders, students, and politicians." D'Aubuisson, ARENA hard-liner Vice President Francisco Merino, "and other wealthy Salvadorans will pay squad members and cover expenses."[98]

The reactivation of terrorist networks within ARENA constituted but one facet of the upsurge in death squad killings. Information gathered by the U.S. Embassy in San Salvador and the CIA indicated that, as in the early 1980s, units of the military and security forces were also involved:[99]

- A series of four cables on murders, disappearances, torture, and helicopter disappearances compiled by the human rights officer of the U.S. Embassy in San Salvador in 1989 blamed the National Guard intelligence section (S-II) for numerous death squad killings. According to an embassy informant, "hardly a night goes by during which the GN S-2 section is not torturing someone." The National Guard used a safe house on a Pacific coast beach "as a cooling-off place when the search for a prisoner in San Salvador was becoming too intense" and as a "holding place for prisoners whose bodies would be dumped at sea to 'disappear' them." The cable entitled "Murders" detailed the capture, torture (and, in the case of women, rape), and execution of over a dozen people by death squad units of the National Guard and Treasury Police between 1987 and 1988.[100]

- In 1991, the Defense Intelligence Agency (DIA) detailed death squad activities carried out by the Salvadoran air force intelligence unit, A-II, saying that prior to September 1989, "gross human rights abuses were common at the FAES [Fuerza Aerea de El Salvador]" and that such abuses had been "deliberate and sanctioned." The head of A-II, Roberto Leiva, had taken a leave of absence from the air force in the early 1980s "to serve as Roberto D'Aubuisson's personal pilot and serve in D'Aubuisson's death squads." According to the DIA, Leiva "believed in extreme measures (even by Salvadoran standards) against insurgents operating clandestinely in urban areas." His "aggressive and radical" approach included ordering that prisoners be thrown "bound but alive from an FAES C-47 at night over the Pacific Ocean. . . . The practice of dropping prisoners from FAES helicopters and airplanes was called 'night free fall training' and was common during Leiva's term as A-II and A-III [Operations]." Leiva also had authorized the execution of suspected criminals by "shooting them in the head and disposing of the bodies by helicopter over Guazapa Volcano," a guerrilla stronghold.[101]

- In October 1990, the U.S. Embassy reported that the commander of the army's First Brigade, Colonel Francisco Elena Fuentes, was "permitting the use of his brigade's civil defense training program as cover for the recruitment, training, and possible dispatch of paramilitary civilian death squads."[102] The group called itself Los Patrióticos (the Patriotic Ones) and consisted of 50–60 ARENA-affiliated professionals described elsewhere by the Defense Department as "rich momma's boys and pot-bellied patriots."[103] According to Ambassador William Walker, the First Brigade and Elena Fuentes were also "providing phantom slots and other support to D'Aubuisson and his death squad contingency planning." Perhaps most disturbing to Walker was the fact that Los Patrióticos were being trained by the U.S. Military Group based in San Salvador and that the U.S. commander there argued to continue the training, given that "we are already 'a little pregnant.'" Walker ordered that the training be stopped, citing intelligence that the unit was being used as a "cover for death squad activity."[104]

Heightening Walker's concerns for the potentially explosive implications of the training were prior allegations by a First Brigade death squad defector, César Vielman Joya Martínez, who had provided testimony in 1989 about a death squad operating out of the First Brigade intelligence unit in which he said he participated. He also alleged that U.S. advisers stationed at the First Brigade funded the unit's operations, while insulating themselves from its dirty work. The human rights group Americas Watch independently investigated several cases of death squad executions in which Joya Martínez said he participated, finding them to have taken place as he described.[105]

- In December 1990, Deputy Secretary of State Lawrence Eagleburger instructed Ambassador Walker to press President Cristiani "about efforts to revive death squads and to engage in other abuses of human rights." Among those alleged to participate were D'Aubuisson, First Brigade head Elena Fuentes, and head of the air force Juan Orlando Bustillo. Eagleburger referred to "serious human rights violations" at the Comalapa and Ilopango air force bases and to "reports that the ultra-right is considering creation of its own intelligence service to infiltrate and carry out possible violent activities against labor unions and political parties. The Air Force, First Brigade and Treasury Police allegedly support the plan."[106]

The Peace Accord and Beyond

The persistence of death squads as a feature of El Salvador's violent landscape throughout the 1980s lends itself to several generalizations. First, unlike several of the cases discussed in this book, death squads in El Salvador were deeply rooted in official security bodies, particularly the intelligence sections of the Treasury Police, National Police, and National Guard, but also the army and air force. Privately constituted groups, especially the one headed by Roberto D'Aubuisson, distinguished themselves less for their independence from than for their degree of contact, and, at times, coordination with state security bodies. Death squads in the military and security forces and the civilian sector shared a common far-right ideology that viewed measures taken by the government to contain the insurgency—however repressive—as insufficient. Only extreme terror would suffice to eliminate subversives and the threat they posed to the political and socioeconomic order. Thus, death squad activity appeared to wax and wane in proportion to the degree of threat perceived by the extreme right in and outside the government, always occurring against a backdrop of far greater repression by state forces. Second, death squads organized primarily outside the government enjoyed the financial, ideological, and logistical backing of members of the wealthy elite, who saw their interests affected by the insurgency as well as by reformers in the government. Third, widespread impunity—the failure to prosecute members of the military or death squads for abuses, and the declaration of successive amnesties—served as an incentive to continue death squad killing. Fourth, external political considerations—the existence or lack of pressure from the United States, and the degree of dependence of the Salvadoran military on U.S. aid—could have an impact on the level of death squad activity, indicating a level of rationality (however limited) in its execution. Finally, death squad members demonstrated a remarkable resilience, disappearing and resurfacing throughout the decade, ultimately combining their political crimes with those of a purely economic nature.[107]

This latter point is important inasmuch as it casts light on death squad activities following the signing of a peace agreement in 1992 between the Salvadoran government and FMLN. In the period leading up to El Salvador's first postwar elections, in which a fully demobilized guerrilla force was to participate openly for the first time, death threats as well as a spate of high-level assassinations of FMLN leaders raised fears that "illegal groups" were continuing to operate in peacetime.[108] The Salvadoran government created a Joint Group for the Investigation of Politically Motivated Illegal Armed Groups (Grupo Conjunto) in late 1993. It found that although the death squads of the 1980s "answered to the political and social situation prevailing at the time, which is unquestionably not the same today," politically motivated violence was linked to "the broad network of organized crime" assaulting Salvadoran society. The Joint Group raised "important questions . . . concerning the present ties of persons earlier identified with the activities of the 'death squads' to highly organized criminal structures that devote themselves in particular to bank robberies, car theft, and traffic in arms and drugs, among other illicit activities." The transition from war to peace in El Salvador "has left no operating room for persons who participated in the armed conflict and members of the 'death squads,' who have had to seek other structures and *modi vivendi* to which to transfer the methods and procedures used in the recent past." The metamorphosis of the death squads, concluded the Grupo Conjunto, had led to a "fragmentation of earlier structures" and acts of common crime "characterized by a high degree of organization, logistics, and the support, in certain cases, of State agents." [109]

What, finally, do the documents examined in this study reveal about the U.S. role in El Salvador? The most important aspect is not that U.S. officials developed over the decade significant information about the death squads, or that, at times, efforts were made to curb death squad abuses. An equal case can be made that efforts to crack down on death squads were partial and ultimately unsuccessful because they were made in the context of an overriding policy goal: the defeat of the insurgency. Rather, the documents underscore the lack of priority accorded to the collection and analysis of information on the death squads at the height of the killing and during a period of rapidly expanding U.S. involvement in El Salvador. This lapse in intelligence gathering and the fixation on leftist and not rightist threats to the survival of the Salvadoran regime constitute, in retrospect, one of the war's most bitter legacies.

Notes

1. Early English-language histories of the conflict include Robert Armstrong and Janet Shenk, *El Salvador: The Face of Revolution* (Boston: South End Press, 1982); Cynthia Arnson, *El Salvador: A Revolution Confronts the United States* (Washington, D.C.: Institute for Policy Studies, 1982); Enrique Baloyra, *El Salvador in Transition* (Chapel Hill: University of North Carolina Press, 1982); Raymond Bonner, *Weakness and Deceit: U.S. Policy and El Salvador* (New York: Times Books, 1984); Michael McClintock, *The American Connection: State Terror and Popular Resistance in El Salvador* (London: Zed Books, 1985); and Tommie Sue Montgomery, *Revolution in El Salvador*, 2nd ed. (Boulder, Colo.: Westview, 1995). Recent comprehensive accounts include Hugh Byrne, *El Salvador's Civil War: A Study of Revolution* (Boulder, Colo.: Lynne Rienner, 1996); William Leogrande, *Our Own Backyard: The United States in Central America 1977–1992* (Chapel Hill: University of North Carolina Press, 1998); William Stanley, *The Protection Racket State: Elite Politics, Military Extortion, and Civil War in El Salvador* (Philadelphia: Temple University Press, 1996); Teresa Whitfield, *Paying the Price: Ignacio Ellacuría and the Murdered Jesuits of El Salvador* (Philadelphia: Temple University Press, 1995); and Philip J. Williams and Knut Walter, *Militarization and Demilitarization in El Salvador's Transition to Democracy* (Pittsburgh: University of Pittsburgh Press, 1997).
2. International Commission of Jurists, *Review,* "El Salvador," June 1978, 2; Organization of American States, Inter-American Commission on Human Rights, *Report on the Situation in El Salvador,* OEA/Ser.L/V/II.46, doc. 23 rev. 1, 17 November 1978, 164.
3. The UGB announced its formation in May 1978, when Salvadoran guerrillas kidnapped Salvadoran foreign minister Mauricio Borgonovo, who was subsequently murdered. In June 1978, the UGB issued a threat to all Jesuits to leave the country or be executed. A flyer that circulated at the time urged Salvadorans, "Be a Patriot! Kill a Priest!" See Penny Lernoux, *Cry of the People* (New York: Doubleday, 1980), 76.
4. International Commission of Jurists, 2.

5. Americas Watch and American Civil Liberties Union, *Report on Human Rights in El Salvador* (New York: Vintage Books, 1982), 37.

6. Quoted in Cynthia J. Arnson, *Crossroads: Congress, the President, and Central America 1976–1993*, 2nd ed. (University Park, Pa.: Penn State Press, 1993), 54, 56.

7. Americas Watch and American Civil Liberties Union, *Report on Human Rights in El Salvador;* Americas Watch, *El Salvador's Decade of Terror: Human Rights Abuses Since the Assassination of Archbishop Romero* (New Haven, Conn.: Yale University Press, 1991); and Arnson, *Crossroads.*

8. Concerning death squads, for example, senior administration officials stated in the early 1980s that they were a "spontaneous phenomenon," that there was "not a structure that has a headquarters that gives commands," that death squads represented a "phenomenon that was without a center," and that "there is no campaign directed out of a headquarters somewhere, or several headquarters somewhere, in the government, associated with the government, to eliminate the following numbers of people." Another claimed that "the assumption that the death squads are active security forces remains to be proved. It might be right, though I suspect it isn't right." See testimony of Assistant Secretary of State for Inter-American Affairs Thomas Enders in United States Congress, Senate, Committee on Foreign Relations, *Presidential Certification on Progress in El Salvador,* Hearing, 2 February 1983, 98th Cong., 1st Sess. (Washington, D.C.: U.S. Government Printing Office, 1983), 143, 544; and United States Congress, House, Committee on Foreign Affairs, Subcommittees on Human Rights and International Organizations and Western Hemisphere Affairs, *U.S. Policy in El Salvador,* Hearings, 98th Cong., 1st Sess. (Washington, D.C.: U.S. Government Printing Office, 1983), 18, 31, 16, and 42. The latter statement is by Assistant Secretary of State for Human Rights and Humanitarian Affairs Elliott Abrams, quoted in *Christian Science Monitor,* 3 August 1983, cited in Cynthia Arnson, Aryeh Neier, and Susan Benda, *As Bad As Ever: A Report on Human Rights in El Salvador, Fourth Supplement* (New York: Americas Watch, 1984), 52.

9. United Nations Commission on the Truth for El Salvador, *From Madness to Hope: The 12-Year War in El Salvador,* UN Doc. S/25500, 1 April 1993 (hereafter cited as Truth Commission Report), 11 ("serious acts of violence"), 43 (percentages), 27 ("escalation of violence").

10. Truth Commision Report, 132, 134.

11. The most famous of these is El Mozote in Morazán province, where the army's elite Atlacatl Battalion killed hundreds of civilians in December

1981. The massacre was first reported by Alma Guillermoprieto of the *Washington Post* and Raymond Bonner of the *New York Times,* on 27 January 1982. At the time, the reports were heavily disputed by the State Department. A book-length account of the massacre can be found in Mark Danner, *The Massacre at El Mozote* (New York: Vintage Books, 1994).

12. CIA, "Briefing Paper on Right-Wing Terrorism in El Salvador," 1706Z, 27 October 1983, 2.

13. The State Department released 10,400 documents to the CIA's 939 and DOD's 916. The releasing agencies identified over 3,000 documents responsive to the congressional request that would remain classified, principally in order to protect intelligence sources and methods. Unpublished correspondence, Secretary of State Warren Christopher to Representative Lee H. Hamilton, Chairman, Committee on Foreign Affairs, undated; Director of Central Intelligence R. James Woolsey to Representative Lee H. Hamilton, Chairman, Committee on Foreign Affairs, 31 October 1993; and Secretary of Defense Les Aspin to Congressman George Miller, 2 November 1993. State Department documents referred to in this paper were available for consultation in the Office of Freedom of Information and Privacy and subsequently deposited at the National Archives. CIA and Defense Department documents were available in the periodicals reading room of the Library of Congress, Madison Building. The National Security Archive, a private, non-profit research group in Washington, D.C., also has a collection of most of the documents.

All documents cited in this paper were declassified and released publicly by the agencies responsible; some had extensive parts excised prior to release.

14. United States Congress, House, Permanent Select Committee on Intelligence, *Report* 98–1196, 98th Cong., 2d Sess. (Washington, D.C.: U.S. Government Printing Office, 1985), 19. The same committee issued a scathing report in 1982 on intelligence collection and analysis in Central America, which stated that "intelligence has provided little firm information about the subject of violence by the right and the security forces. The entire subject of political killings—whether by the right or the left—is often described as unknowable. . . . Nevertheless, relatively more is known about the organization and whereabouts of the insurgents in their conduct of both guerrilla operations and of terrorist killings, than about the circumstances or lines of authority resulting in abductions of alleged leftist sympathizers or in the depositing of bodies along Salvadoran highways during curfew hours." United States Congress, House, Permanent Select Committee on Intelligence, *U.S. Intelligence Performance on*

Central America: Achievements and Selected Instances of Concern, 97th Cong., 2d Sess. (Washington, D.C.: U.S. Government Printing Office, 1982), 10. In one revealing cable written in 1982, for example, then Secretary of State Alexander Haig treated reports of human rights abuse by government forces as mostly a problem of public relations. SecState WashDC to AmEmbassy San Salvador, "Public Affairs and Handling of Press," 3 March 1982, 1–2.

15.   U.S. Ambassador to El Salvador Thomas Pickering complained to Washington as late as April 1984 about "the lack of any systematic study" of the problem of the violence in El Salvador. "We rely on Washington agencies," he said, "to integrate [embassy] data with what is available from other U.S. sources and to put it into historical perspective." Such a comprehensive report was not produced by the CIA until February 1985. AmEmbassy San Salvador to SecState Wash DC, "Special Project to Analyze Salvadoran Violence," 03831, 7 April 1984, 1.

16.   CIA, National Foreign Assessment Center, "El Salvador: The Right Wing," 18 March 1981.

17.   This displaced subsistence farmers and created a landless rural work force. See David Browning, *El Salvador: La Tierra y El Hombre* (San Salvador: Dirección de Publicaciones, Ministerio de Educación, 1975), 337–57; Arnson, *El Salvador,* 11–13.

18.   Browning, *El Salvador,* 357; Howard Blutstein, ed., *Area Handbook on El Salvador* (Washington, D.C.: U.S. Government Printing Office, 1971), 195.

19.   The most authoritative account of the massacre, known as the *matanza,* appears in Thomas Anderson, *Matanza: El Salvador's Communist Revolt of 1932* (Lincoln: University of Nebraska Press, 1971).

20.   CIA, "El Salvador: Controlling Rightwing Terrorism," February 1985, 3.

21.   CIA, Directorate of Intelligence, "El Salvador: D'Aubuisson's Terrorist Activities," 2 March 1984, 2.

22.   CIA, "Briefing Paper on Right-Wing Terrorism in El Salvador," 7.

23.   CIA, "El Salvador: The Right Wing," 3.

24.   The memorandum is entitled "El Salvador: The Assassination of the Father of Rightwing Violence," May 1985. No author or originating agency is specified. It was written following Medrano's assassination by the FMLN in March 1985.

25.   Through the Agency for International Development's Office of Public Safety (OPS), the United States spent millions of dollars to train and equip the National Police, National Guard, and Treasury Police, as part of a global effort to bolster internal security forces' ability to

combat communist-inspired revolutionary movements. By 1967, an AID consultant concluded that U.S. public safety advisers had successfully trained the National Guard and National Police to handle political demonstrations. Richard R. Martinez, "Termination Phase-Out Study, Public Safety Project: El Salvador," mimeograph, United States Agency for International Development, Office of Public Safety, May 1974, 5; C. Allen Stewart, "Report on Visit to Central America and Panama to Study AID Public Safety Programs," mimeograph, Agency for International Development, Office of Public Safety, 1967, 25, 23; Cynthia Arnson, "Background Information on the Security Forces in El Salvador and U.S. Military Assistance," Institute for Policy Studies, mimeograph, March 1980, 7–9; Americas Watch and American Civil Liberties Union, *Report on Human Rights in El Salvador,* 179–80.

26. Stewart, "Report on Visit to Central America and Panama," 8, 4, 5, and 24.

27. CIA, "El Salvador: Controlling Rightwing Terrorism," 6.

28. CIA, "Briefing Paper on Right-Wing Terrorism," 7; "El Salvador: The Assassination of the Father of Rightwing Violence."

29. CIA, "El Salvador: The Right Wing," 2.

30. Truth Commission Report, 133; AmEmbassy San Salvador to SecState WashDC, "Bio on Apparent Source for NYT Death Squad Article," 02653, 12 March 1984, 2.

31. According to a report by the CIA, D'Aubuisson, along with ANSESAL chief Colonel Roberto Santiváñez, stole the files "for use in organizing D'Aubuisson's anti-subversive campaign." CIA, title deleted, 1429Z, 10 March 1984, 2. See also Truth Commission Report, 134. D'Aubuisson admitted to the theft of files in an interview with the *Washington Post* in 1988, in order, he said, "to have a base of information and know what was going on. . . . If the war was coming, as it was, the best thing was to know a little about who is and who is not the enemy, and besides, I suspected the information could land in bad hands." See Douglas Farah, "Rightist Denies Past, Present Role in Squads," *Washington Post,* 28 August 1988, A26.

32. Craig Pyes, "Right Built Itself in Mirror Image of Left for Civil War," *Albuquerque Journal,* 18 December 1983, reprinted in *Salvadoran Rightists: The Deadly Patriots* (Albuquerque: Albuquerque Journal, 1983), 5–9.

33. CIA, "El Salvador: Controlling Rightwing Terrorism," 4.

34. CIA, National Foreign Assessment Center, "El Salvador: The Role of Roberto D'Aubuisson," 4 March 1981, 1.

35. CIA, "El Salvador: The Right Wing," 2. This document went through several drafts, dated 25 March and 17 April 1981. The

characterization of D'Aubuisson did not change, although details of extreme right wing activities were more extensive in the later versions.

In January 1981, the U.S. Embassy in San Salvador reported that "a group of six Salvadoran millionaire emigres in Miami have directed and financed rightwing death squads here for nearly a year," through "their agent, Roberto D'Aubuisson." The embassy called for immediate steps to investigate, calling it "unacceptable that such an operation is guided from a major American city." For over three years, the State Department failed to act on this information and other cables containing the names of specific individuals involved in organizing and financing death squad activities from abroad. AmEmbassy San Salvador to SecState WashDC, "Millionaires' Murder Inc.?" 00096, January 6, 1981; memorandum, Robert Millspaugh to J. Mark Dion, Deputy Chief of Mission, U.S. Embassy San Salvador, "Possible Leads on Rightist Terrorist Activities," 11 December 1980.

In one of its few statements criticizing the U.S. role in El Salvador, the Truth Commission stated that "the United States Government tolerated, and apparently paid little official heed to the activities of Salvadorian exiles living in Miami, especially between 1979 and 1983." Truth Commission Report, 137.

36. Truth Commission Report, 135; AmEmbassy San Salvador to SecState WashDC, "Millionaires' Murder Inc.?" 2.

37. CIA, "El Salvador: Controlling Right Wing Terrorism," 3.

38. Truth Commission Report, 129.

39. A transcribed and partially translated version of the Saravia notebook was produced by the Senate Foreign Relations Committee in 1981. Page 17 of the mimeograph contains the entry for Operación Piña. The Saravia notebook constitutes a virtual "who's who" of death squad operatives and financiers whose names resurfaced throughout the decade in connection with prominent murders or criminal enterprises, including the assassination of Archbishop Romero, the kidnapping for profit case, and the operation of death squads out of the Constituent Assembly. Regarding White's testimony, see Cynthia Arnson, "White's Paper," Nation, 9 May 1981, 557; regarding lots, AmEmbassy San Salvador to SecState WashDC, "Assassination of Archbishop Romero," 09718, 21 December 1981, 1–2. The cable indicated that the information had been reported to an embassy political officer in November 1980.

40. Truth Commission Report, 135.

41. CIA, Directorate of Intelligence, "El Salvador: D'Aubuisson's Terrorist Activities," 2.

42. Author's notes of the press conference, Rayburn House Office Building, Washington, D.C., 2 July 1980.

43. Arnson, *Crossroads*, 95–99.

44. CIA, Directorate of Intelligence, "El Salvador: D'Aubuisson's Terrorist Activities," 3.

45. Douglas Farah, "Death Squad Began as Scout Troop," *Washington Post*, 29 August 1988, A1.

46. CIA, title deleted, 2317Z, 17 April 1984, 1. Using his dentist's tools, Regalado was alleged to have manufactured the explosive bullet used to assassinate Archbishop Romero. CIA, title deleted, 0122Z, 22 April 1983.

47. CIA, "Briefing Paper on Right-Wing Terrorism in El Salvador," 4.

48. CIA, "El Salvador: Controlling Rightwing Terrorism," 6.

49. CIA, "Briefing Paper on Right-Wing Terrorism in El Salvador," 3, 4.

50. United States Congress, Senate, Select Committee on Intelligence, *Recent Political Violence in El Salvador*, 98–659, 98th Cong., 2d Sess. (Washington, D.C.: U.S. Government Printing Office, 1984), 11.

51. CIA, "Briefing Paper on Right-Wing Terrorism," 2.

52. As evidence of the overlap between various squads, the CIA noted that the head of the National Guard unit provided military credentials to the Constituent Assembly death squad directed by Héctor Regalado. CIA, "Mario Denis Morán Echeverría," 0031Z, 2 May 1990, 3.

53. CIA, title deleted, 2020Z, 30 May 1981.

54. CIA, Directorate of Intelligence, "El Salvador: Dealing with Death Squads," 20 January 1984, 3.

55. AmEmbassy San Salvador to SecState WashDC, "Avila Case," 03720, 26 March 1985, 3; AmEmbassy San Salvador to SecState WashDC, "Sheraton Case," 03681, 25 March 1985, 1.

56. CIA, "Mario Denis Morán," 2; "Briefing Paper on Right-Wing Terrorism in El Salvador," 6; CIA, "File Summary Ricardo Sol Meza," 1303Z, 4 May 1985, 1; and "Sheraton Case," 1.

57. "Sheraton Case," 2; Truth Commission Report, 144–47. The Truth Commission was unable to establish Morán's central role in ordering the killings, ascribing to him complicity in the cover-up.

58. On Morán, see CIA, "Reluctance of the Salvadoran Minister of Defense to Prosecute Military Officers for Alleged Human Rights Violations," 20 July 1983, 1–2; on López Sibrían, see Americas Watch, *El Salvador's Decade of Terror*, 96–99.

59. CIA, "Briefing Paper on Right-Wing Terrorism in El Salvador," 2. Nongovernmental human rights groups in El Salvador frequently mentioned a National Police unit known as CAIN, the Center for Analysis and Investigations, as responsible for torture and murder of detainees. At least one ARENA member who was a CIA informant

also referred to the National Police death squad unit as CAIN. See CIA, title deleted, "Members and Collaborators of the Nationalist Republican Alliance (ARENA) Paramilitary Unit Headed by Hector Regalado," 1649Z, 13 July 1984, 2.

60. CIA, title deleted, "Existence of Rightist Death Squad Within the Salvadoran National Police; Location of Clandestine Prison Used by the Death Squad," 2023Z, 19 March 1983, 3.

61. An ARENA member who provided information to the CIA in 1984 about ARENA's paramilitary unit described Pérez Linares as "among Regalado's closest collaborators in the Salvadoran military and security services." CIA "Members and Collaborators of the Nationalist Republican Alliance (ARENA) Paramilitary Unit," 2.

62. CIA, "Existence of Rightist Death Squad Within the Salvadoran National Police; Location of Clandestine Prison Used by the Death Squad," 2. The document indicates that in March 1981, Pérez was reported to "be a member of the Archbishop Romero assassination team," and that in May and June 1983, Pérez "directed assassinations from his position in the National Police." A March 1983 CIA document on the National Police also names Pérez Linares as a member of the "Romero assassination squad" consisting of National Police members.

63. CIA, "Briefing Paper on Right-Wing Terrorism in El Salvador," 7, 6.

64. Whitfield, *Paying the Price.*

65. CIA, "Briefing Paper on Right-Wing Terrorism in El Salvador," 6; CIA, "Existence of Rightist Death Squad Within the Salvadoran National Police; Location of Clandestine Prison Used by the Death Squad," 1–2.

66. See Philip Taubman, "Top Salvadoran Police Official Said to be a CIA Informant," *New York Times,* 22 March 1984. The accusation was made by former ANSESAL director Colonel Roberto Santiváñez, who in 1984 accused numerous military officials of being involved in death squads and political murder. See Fenton Communications, "Short Circuit: Inside the Death Squads," News Release, New York and Washington, D.C., 21 March 1985, 1–14.

67. Despite the silence regarding Treasury Police death squad activities, it is worth noting that one of the officers identified for dismissal or transfer by Vice President Bush in December 1983 was head of the Treasury Police intelligence section.

68. CIA, "Francisco A. Moran," 2230Z, 10 April 1992, 1–2.

69. CIA, "Briefing Paper on Right-Wing Terrorism in El Salvador," 7.

70. CIA, "El Salvador: Controlling Rightwing Terrorism," 7.

71. A March 1984 CIA document described Air Force captain Roberto Leiva as "allegedly the most active and most dangerous

military officer involved in death squad activity." CIA, title and subject line deleted, 1429Z, 10 March 1994, 2.

72. CIA, "El Salvador: Controlling Rightwing Terrorism," 8. Complicating efforts to press the air force on human rights was its role in supporting the Contra war in Nicaragua. Ilopango Air Base was used regularly as a staging ground for Contra resupply missions, something exposed by the press when the Nicaraguan government shot down a CIA contract pilot in 1986.

73. See Arnson, *Crossroads,* 136–41.

74. According to Cristóbal Alemán Alas, a leader of the centrist Unión Comunal Salvadoreña (UCS) and member of the governmental Human Rights Commission, the cooperativists "died for attending UCS meetings." Cristóbal Alemán Alas, interview by the author, El Salvador, 10 January 1983, quoted in Arnson, Neier, and Benda, *As Bad As Ever,* 11, 30–37.

75. AmEmbassy San Salvador to SecState WashDC, "Bishop Rosa Chavez Discusses Salvadoran Death Squads with Asst. Secy Abrams," 10417, 10 November 1983, 1.

76. AmEmbassy San Salvador to SecState WashDC, "Private Sector Attitudes Toward Resurgence of Violence," 09398, 13 October 1983, 1.

77. Arnson, Neier, and Benda, *As Bad As Ever,* 11.

78. See, for example, AmEmbassy San Salvador to SecState WashDC, "U.S. Journalist Investing [*sic*] Death Squads Threatened," 10022, 28 October 1983.

79. Accompanying Bush, according to records of the meetings he held, were Enders's successor as assistant secretary of state for inter-American affairs, Langhorne ("Tony") Motley, National Security Council aide Oliver North, Ambassador to El Salvador Thomas Pickering, and Admiral Daniel Murphy.

80. AmEmbassy San Salvador to SecState WashDC, "Vice President Bush's Meetings with Salvadoran Officials," 11567, 14 December 1983, 3 ("credibility"), 1–2 ("main point"), 5 (list of participants). According to press reports, those on the list included National Police intelligence chief Arístides Márquez and Treasury Police intelligence chief José Ricardo Pozo. U.S. cables drafted after the Bush visit indicate that Héctor Antonio Regalado and Ramón González Suvillaga, both involved with the ARENA death squad operating out of the Constituent Assembly, were also included. González Suvillaga had also been implicated in threats against U.S. congressman George Miller.

81. Toast of Vice President Bush at a dinner hosted by Salvadoran president Alvaro Magaña in San Salvador, El Salvador, United States Department of State, Bureau of Public Affairs, Current Policy No. 533, 11 December 1983, 1–2.

82. AmEmbassy San Salvador to SecState WashDC, "Vice President Bush's Meetings with Salvadoran Officials," 11, 4, 3.

83. Truth Commission Report, 33.

84. CIA, Directorate of Intelligence, "El Salvador: Dealing with Death Squads," 20 January 1984, 1–2. The assessment appears in a "Comments" section. A separate addendum notes that although the efforts at crackdown had been mostly verbal, they had had a "positive effect" in El Salvador. "Rightwing violence has been greatly reduced in the past month, and the death squads have generally toned down their public threats and propaganda efforts." On p. 3, the report indicates that "D'Aubuisson's civilian henchmen" on the Bush list (presumably Héctor Regalado and Ramón González Suvillaga) had "made clear that they intend to remain in El Salvador."

85. CIA, Directorate of Intelligence, "El Salvador: Dealing with Death Squads," 1, 3.

86. CIA, "Special Analysis: El Salvador: Threat from the Right," undated, 2–3. The document's reference to approaching elections indicates that it was prepared following the Bush visit but before the May 1984 presidential elections.

87. Arnson, *Crossroads*, 157–58.

88. AmEmbassy San Salvador to SecState WashDC, "General Walters' Talk with D'Aubuisson," 05682, 19 May 1984, 2. Pickering and Walters met privately with D'Aubuisson and ARENA member Francisco Guirola. Walters told D'Aubuisson that "President Reagan was greatly disturbed by what he believed to be absolutely reliable information that ARENA people are plotting to assassinate Ambassador Pickering and others. He ordered me here immediately to express his concern and to seek reassurance that no such plots are underway." D'Aubuisson stated that the reports were "part of a slander campaign against him" and insisted that the accusations were false.

89. AmEmbassy San Salvador to SecState WashDC, "Human Rights in El Salvador," 08711, 29 June 1988, 7. The statement is particularly notable in that nongovernmental human rights groups, including Americas Watch, were generally critical of Cestoni and the Comisión de Derechos Humanos (CDH) for their lackluster performance.

90. Anne Manuel with Jemera Rone, *Nightmare Revisited 1987–88* (New York and Washington, D.C.: Americas Watch, September 1988), 1.

91. AmEmbassy San Salvador to SecState, WashDC, "Human Rights in El Salvador," 1, 8.

92. AmEmbassy San Salvador to SecState, WashDC, "Human Rights in El Salvador," 2; CIA, Directorate of Intelligence, "The FMLN in El

Salvador: Insurgent Negotiations Strategy and Human Rights Abuses," 22 November 1988, 3; and Manuel with Rone, *Nightmare Revisited*, 6–8.

93. CIA, Directorate of Intelligence, "The FMLN in El Salvador," 3.
94. CIA, Directorate of Intelligence, "The FMLN in El Salvador," 4.
95. According to the *Post*, Regalado had spent much of his time in Guatemala following the 1983 Bush visit, but had been hired by the Drug Enforcement Administration in January 1987 as a shooting instructor for an antidrug unit of the National Police. Douglas Farah, "Salvadoran Death Squads Threaten Resurgence," *Washington Post*, 28 August 1988, A1. ARENA's influence over the San Salvador Municipal Police derived from its having captured the mayor's office in the March 1988 elections.
96. CIA, Directorate of Intelligence, "The FMLN in El Salvador: Insurgent Negotiations Strategy and Human Rights Abuses," 4. The death squad resurgence highlighted a long-simmering rift within ARENA between party moderates, led by businessman Alfredo Cristiani, and the D'Aubuisson wing. According to the CIA, D'Aubuisson had allowed moderates such as Cristiani "to assume a wider public role" during the 1989 presidential campaign in order to enhance the party's electoral appeal, but "D'Aubuisson's public deference to Cristiani is largely cosmetic in our view, calculated to put a better face" on ARENA. See CIA, Directorate of Intelligence, "El Salvador: Rightist ARENA Party Election Frontrunner," 14 March 1989, 2, 3–4.
97. CIA, title deleted, subject line reads "Discussion Among Supporters of Roberto D'Aubuisson of Plans to Assassinate President Cristiani and Other Political Figures," 2323Z, 10 August 1990, 2.
98. CIA, "El Salvador: New Rightist Plots," 28 June 1990, 1.
99. United States policy in El Salvador was coming under increased scrutiny in the late 1980s. This was a product of the November 1989 murders of six Jesuit priests and two women by members of an elite army unit, during a major guerrilla offensive in San Salvador. A congressional investigation, led by Rep. Joe Moakley (D-MA), implicated senior military leaders and the army high command for their role in covering up or planning the murders. For the first time in years, aid requests were coming under attack as the Cold War was drawing to an end. George Bush was elected president in 1988, taking office with a more pragmatic and less ideological vision of Central America's wars. These developments altered the tone and focus of reporting, as officials in Washington came to fear not only what might be happening on the ground in El Salvador, but also the impact of its disclosure in Washington.

100. AmEmbassy San Salvador to SecState WashDC, "Security Force Human Rights Abuses, Part Three: Torture," 05535, 3 May 1989, 2; AmEmbassy San Salvador to SecState WashDC, "Security Force Human Rights Abuses, Part Two: Disappearances," 05534, 2 May 1989, 2; AmEmbassy San Salvador to SecState Wash DC, "Security Force Human Rights Abuses, Part One: Murders," 05553, 2 May 1989, 2–4. Ambassador William Walker issued an unusual disclaimer at the end of each of the four cables, calling into question the reliability of one source who was known to have extorted the family of a disappeared youth in exchange for information, and tasked "all elements of the mission" to investigate security forces' involvement in human rights abuses (cable on "Murders," 4).

101. DIA, "Improvement of Human Rights Abuses by Salvadoran Airforce," 1706Z, 18 March 1991, 1–3. The DIA cable confirms what the embassy human rights officer had reported in 1989 regarding the dropping of bodies from aircraft over dry land, a report whose reliability had been questioned by Ambassador Walker.

102. AmEmbassy San Salvador to SecState Wash DC, "US MILGP Involvement with Questionable Civil Defense Training at First Brigade," 14634, 29 October 1990, 1; Tim Weiner, "Documents Assert U.S. Trained Salvadorans Tied to Death Squads," *New York Times,* 14 December 1993, A1.

103. Memorandum, USMC Brigadier General M.J. Byron, Acting Deputy Assistant Secretary of Defense (Inter-American Affairs), to ASD Rowen, "Civil Defense Training in El Salvador," date illegible, 1.

104. AmEmbassy San Salvador to SecState Wash DC, "US MILGP Involvement with Questionable Civil Defense Training at First Brigade," 1–2. In response to Walker's complaint, the Defense Department terminated training of Los Patrióticos and ordered a review of U.S. involvement with the civil defense program. See Memorandum, Henry S. Rowen, Under Secretary of Defense for Policy, to Secretary of Defense and Deputy Secretary of Defense, "MilGP Training and Support to Salvadoran Civil Defense Units," 5 November 1990, 1–2.

105. See Americas Watch, "El Salvador: Extradition Sought for Alleged Death Squad Participant," 14 August 1991, 3.

106. SecState WashDC to AmEmbassy San Salvador, "Resurgence of Death Squad Activity," 430734, 22 December 1990, 1–6.

107. According to Ambassador Walker, for example, individuals involved in efforts to obstruct justice in the Archbishop Romero case included "an entire realm of coup plotters, death squad chiefs, kidnappers, baby robbers, mad bombers, car thieves, and other assorted criminals." AmEmbassy San Salvador to SecState WashDC, "The Saravia

Extradition and the D'Aubuisson [illegible]," 13183, 3 October 1988, 8.

108. The term was the UN's, whose political mission, ONUSAL, was overseeing the implementation of the peace accords. United Nations, *Further Report of the Secretary General on the United Nations Observer Mission in El Salvador,* S/26790, 23 November 1993, paragraphs 43–44.

109. United Nations, *The United Nations in El Salvador 1990–1995* (New York: United Nations Department of Public Information, 1995) 570–71; Grupo Conjunto para la Investigación de Grupos Armados Ilegales Con Motivación Política en El Salvador, *Informe,* mimeograph, San Salvador, 28 July 1994, 61–62.

CHAPTER 5

State of Siege:
Political Violence and Vigilante
Mobilization in the Philippines[1]

Eva-Lotta Hedman

Kill for Peace! Kill for Democracy!
                    —Alsa Masa Checkpoint Slogan, Davao, 1987

Due to the spontaneous proliferation of these volunteer organiza-
tions for community self-defense all over the country, it is neces-
sary to define the police guidelines and limitations for such
organizations in order that respect for the law and human rights
is observed.

—Armed Forces of the Philippines (AFP) "Guidelines for Civilian
        Volunteer Self-Defense Organizations," April 1, 1987

THUS SOUNDED POWERFUL VOICES DURING THE transition from authoritarian rule in the Philippines of the late 1980s. On the one
hand, the most notorious manifestation of uncivil society, the so-
called vigilante volunteers of the Alsa Masa ("Masses Arise"), reverberating with widely reported anticommunist fanaticism and
extrajudicial violence. On the other hand, the highest-ranking official of coercive state apparatuses, AFP chief of staff Fidel V. Ramos,
reasserting with formal authority *raison d'état* and rule of law.
While seeking to distance itself from widespread military and paramilitary abuses under the long authoritarian reign of Ferdinand E.
Marcos (1972–86), the AFP oversaw a reinvigorated counterinsurgency drive, deploying new men and methods against the enduring

presence, activities, and appeal of guerrilla units and popular fronts associated with the Communist Party of the Philippines/New People's Army (CPP/NPA). Thus, the Alsa Masa, which first emerged in the southern frontier and guerrilla stronghold of Davao City at a time when the much-celebrated "People Power" revolt in Manila ushered in a new national government under Corazon C. Aquino in February 1986, gained renewed momentum a year later in the aftermath of the failed cease-fire and peace talks between representatives of the new regime and the guerrilla movement. Viewed alternately as sinister experiment or model success in adopting—and adapting—Reagan-era "low-intensity conflict" doctrine[2] to the Philippines, the Alsa Masa mobilized armed neighborhood patrols and checkpoints, anticommunist radio broadcasts, and mass rallies in its campaigns of sustained intimidation and spectacular violence.

Beyond the seeming dissonance between the shrill calls to summary execution and the perfunctory appeals to proper procedure, such public proclamations worked in tacit, mutually reinforcing ways. First of all, they redrew the imaginary map of the national battlefield in such ways as to identify the key combatants as vigilantes defending the good people of the Philippines from communist threats to peace and democracy rather than the old lineup of Marcos-era abusive military and paramilitary forces against its most sustained opposition, the New People's Army (NPA, known, in places, as "Nice People Around"). Moreover, they subsumed under the broader rubric of democratization and "People Power" the phenomenon of vigilante mobilization by underscoring its local origins and spontaneous irruptions, thus in a sense substituting the redistribution of violence for more far-reaching structural reforms of Philippine state and society. This emphasis on the populist nature of demands for such mobilization also signaled a departure from the coercive formations and political violence associated with politicians' "private armies" and state auxiliary paramilitaries. Finally, these loud voices of the early post-Marcos years relegated the state to an essentially regulatory and reactive role in relation to the forces of (un)civil society. In combination, they thus anchored the origins and dynamics of anticommunism and counterinsurgency in the late 1980s and early 1990s within a political discourse of "vigilantism" that seemed to recall, however faintly, historical legacies of popular mobilization and pacification in the Philippine Islands.

Drawing in part on the discrepant histories collected by human rights organizations, investigative journalists, and other concerned chroniclers, this essay reexamines critically not merely the claims laid out above but, significantly, the nature and direction of political violence and vigilante mobilization in the transition period between exhausted dictatorship and consolidated democracy. To that end, this essay investigates the overt manifestations and underlying dynamics of anticommunism and counterinsurgency in the Philippines during this period. Of course, extrajudicial killings have long played a role in Philippine politics, whether in local political rivalries or in the suppression of land and labor disputes, as documented in existing scholarship.[3] The formal lifting of martial law in 1981, moreover, spurred a marked increase in unsolved "salvagings" and "disappearances" at the hands of military units, paramilitary forces, covert intelligence operatives, and even so-called "lost commands" stalking the twilight years of the Marcos era. While there were thus important precursors to the morbid symptoms of the Aquino presidency, the dynamics and legacies of which demand further scrutiny, the expanding scope and spectacle of such violence in the early post-Marcos years hold particular significance for shaping in decisive ways the nature and direction of Philippine politics during this regime transition. In terms of the broader project of mapping death squads and their significance for shaping politics and society, this essay thus invites a perhaps often neglected comparative perspective upon regime democratization through its illumination of the peculiarly morbid symptoms that accompanied and, to a marked extent, circumscribed the transition from authoritarian rule in the Philippine context.

After nearly a decade and a half of de facto martial law in the Philippines, the CPP had emerged as the largest revolutionary movement in Asia by the mid-1980s, with its NPA commanding strongholds especially in sugar, coconut, and logging areas in many provinces,[4] and with its above-ground affiliates organizing among squatter communities, student leagues and labor unions in the cities. As the fall of Marcos ushered in the restoration of formally democratic procedures and institutions after February 1986, however, it also anticipated the intensified counterinsurgency campaigns introduced under Aquino's embattled transitional regime (1986–1992). These Philippine campaigns also emerged during a period when the Reagan rollback and "low-intensity conflict" doctrines signaled both renewed commitment and strategic innovation behind U.S.-supported "contra"-revolutionary warfare.[5]

Perhaps the most remarkable aspect of the recent counterinsurgency campaigns in the Philippines was the peculiarly spectacular role played therein by so-called anticommunist vigilantes.[6] Officially designated "civilian volunteer organizations," such vigilantes also included paramilitary groups of reportedly ill-trained, machete-equipped, and sometimes even ex-convict recruits. As a result, some of the most notorious human rights abuses reported from this recent campaign have been linked to vigilante groups. Based on statistics compiled from local and national coverage of vigilante groups in the print media, for example, one study showed that "[t]he most serious violation, killing, was also the most frequently recorded" in the period between June 1987 and March 1988.[7] Moreover, carefully documented reports by human rights organizations underscore the extent to which vigilantism revolved around terrifying violence such as dismemberment and, especially, beheading.[8]

> On June 27, 1987, 27-year-old Emilio Morales was shot and beheaded by members of Alsa Masa in Barangay Palale, MacArthur [in Leyte]. According to witnesses, Morales, a member of BAYAN (Bagon Alyansang Makabayan, or New Nationalist Alliance, the above-ground left's umbrella organization), was arrested by Alsa Masa members . . . and was taken to Palale Auditorium, where he was handcuffed and questioned. Summarily deciding that Morales was a member of the NPA, the men shot and beheaded him. The victim's head was then displayed in the MacArthur Town Hall.[9]

In this context, government officials in Manila typically portrayed such abuses as unfortunate aberrations to otherwise highly institutionalized and professionalized military counterinsurgency operations. However, this vigilante phenomenon not only emerged against the backdrop of civilian government support and military "holistic" strategy—in part inspired by the NPA's own methods[10]—but also, official disclaimers to the contrary, served to underpin and to propel in significant ways the overall counterinsurgency campaign. In this regard, it is no coincidence that the considerable—instrumental as well as symbolic—powers realized in this form of decentralized and irregular violence accompanied the regime transition in the Philippines of the late 1980s.

In descriptive terms, vigilante formations in the Philippines, not unlike the other death squads discussed in this volume, were irregular, paramilitary groups that carried out extrajudicial killings and other violent acts such as torture and rape. That said, it would be mistaken to view them as primarily tasked with bringing "death" or as operating in clandestine "squads," although, as noted below, they did both of these as well. Rather than simply incorporating the vigilante phenomenon as a subcategory under the broader rubric of "death squads" as they are typically defined, however, this chapter seeks to illuminate the peculiar manifestation and dynamic of the irregular, paramilitary groups that emerged against the backdrop of a particular regime transition from authoritarian rule. That is, while the vigilantes examined here did serve as death squads at times, their significance lay precisely in the public demonstrations of "spontaneous voluntarism" (e.g., mass rallies) and the often spectacular displays of grotesque violence (e.g., severed heads). In analytical terms, this chapter thus anchors the extrajudicial killings carried out by paramilitary groups in the Philippines of the late 1980s within a specific context of regime transition and against the historical backdrop of (American colonial) state formation and a distinctive pattern of subcontracted political violence.

The Rise of Vigilantism

If paramilitary mobilization and counterinsurgency campaigns trace a long lineage in Philippine history, the (re)emergence of vigilantes signaled an especially sinister turn in the aftermath of the collapsed cease-fire negotiations between the Aquino government and the insurgent forces (i.e., the CPP/NPA and the so-called National Democratic Front) in early 1987. Leaving aside for the moment the contested relations between such so-called civilian volunteer organizations and official agents of coercive state apparatuses, this chapter focuses attention on the significance of vigilante violence in the transition from authoritarian rule in the Philippines. While the symbolic powers of such real and rumored violence merit further scrutiny, the pages below seek to recover traces of the peculiar instrumentalities of vigilantism during this period.

Inasmuch as the rise of the vigilantes seemed to defy democratization itself, in theory as well as in practice, it is perhaps unsurprising

that, with a few exceptions,[11] neither scholarly studies nor government authorities have yet shed much light on this murky phenomenon. Instead, nongovernmental human rights organizations have led
the way in systematic and vigorous pursuit of vigilantes amid the unpredictable rip tides and strong cross-currents of Philippine politics
and society at the time. As a result, the carefully documented "fact-
finding" reports issued by such organizations provide the obvious
starting point for purposes of examining the instrumentalities of vigilante violence. In the process of seeking to establish the identity of
vigilantes and their victims, these reports also contribute to the fixing
of the violence to a particular time and place in Philippine history and
society.

As indicated above, the rise of vigilantism peaked with the official return to armed struggle of government and insurgent forces in
February 1987. In many parts of the country, moreover, the May
1987 congressional elections lent additional impetus to the surge of
violence, as evidenced by the attacks upon supporters of the new
legal left party, the Partido ng Bayan (PnB), and its Alliance for New
Politics (ANP).[12] Against the backdrop of the 1987 constitution,
which stipulated that the notoriously abusive martial-law-era paramilitary Civilian Home Defense Forces (CHDF) "shall be dissolved
or, where appropriate, converted," vigilante groups also seemed to
proliferate locally as the proposed official CHDF successor, the Citizen Armed Force Geographical Unit (CAFGU), met with public
criticism in the national media and, eventually, the Philippine Congress.[13] By late 1987, more than 200 vigilante groups were thought
to operate across the Philippines. By early 1989, moreover, the
United States State Department put the figure of such "Citizens Voluntary Organizations" at 640.[14]

While this wave of vigilantism first crashed upon the southern
shores of Mindanao with the reported mobilization of the notorious
Alsa Masa, it eventually reached not merely the Visayas and parts of
Luzon, but even Metro Manila itself.[15] In particular, vigilantes appeared to gravitate toward rural and to a lesser extent urban poor,
areas identified as actual or potential CPP/NPA strongholds such as
Davao, Samar, and Negros Occidental. As for actual sites for vigilante violence, these ranged from street abductions and "safe house"
tortures to bolo (a machetelike large, single-edged knife) attacks
against peasants working in the fields and so-called "strafing" with
automatic weapons fire of entire families in their homes.

Lauded by civilian and military government officials alike for their overall "effectiveness" in the counterinsurgency, vigilantes were implicated by national as well as international human rights organizations in "a widespread pattern of extrajudicial execution, torture and illegal arrest throughout the Philippines."[16] The Senate Committee on Justice and Human Rights also reported on vigilantes regularly performing "police and military activities such as armed patrols, manning of checkpoints, and search and seizure operations."[17] During this period, vigilantism thus appeared to span the entire spectrum of coercion, ranging from the routinized threats of force on behalf of rational law to the spectacular deployments of violence well beyond the pale of law. Significantly, extrajudicial killings and violence by vigilantes remained endemic to this phenomenon and, as argued elsewhere, offer justification for the appellation "death squads."[18] As for the spectacular nature of much vigilante violence, which arguably sets it apart from the terror associated with the death squads of masked men operating under the cover of darkness elsewhere, it would be mistaken to infer that this resulted somehow inevitably—and/or unfortunately—from the lack of proper government regulation and training of so-called "civilian volunteer organizations." Instead, the proclivity for capturing heads and headlines rather than the usual "hearts and minds" underscores the extent to which this modern military-backed "counterinsurgency" campaign involved a chilling recognition of the power of severed heads and dismembered, rotting corpses "not only to frighten and humiliate an adversarial community, but also to stir dread and awe. . . ."[19] In this vein, the spectacle of decapitated rebel guerrillas or alleged guerrillas posed an unmistakable challenge to the NPA's strongest source of power and legitimacy—the comparatively compelling claims to its own sovereignty and violence in the course of mobilizing (armed) opposition to and protection from abusive military and paramilitary forces long associated with an authoritarian regime. As Kenneth M. George argues in a recent ethnography of violence, "The violent deformation of the victim's body also should be read as the disintegration and debasement of an oppositional or adversarial community."[20]

Despite difficulties due to lack of cooperation from civil and military authorities, as well as from witnesses fearful of reprisals, Philippine and international human rights organizations identified the following pattern of vulnerability to vigilante violence:

Victims ranged from suspected NPA supporters and their families
to persons who opposed the formation of vigilante groups in their
area. Frequently harassed and attacked were members of social activist groups labeled as NPA sympathizers, including labor and
peasant organizers, human rights monitors and church workers.[21]

As often noted in such reports, the practice of so-called "red-label-
ing" was not merely widespread at the time but, significantly, integral to vigilantism itself. As a result, the "identification" of victims
as "suspected NPA supporters" became something of a foregone
conclusion. Under the PC provincial command of Lieutenant
Colonel Miguel Coronel, for example, local chapters of labor, religious, and human rights organizations such as the Negros Federation of Sugar Workers (NFSW), the Basic Christian Communities
(BCC), and the Task Force Detainees (TFD) were openly and indis-
criminately targeted as "leading communist fronts."[22] At the national level, the Aquino government publicly declared stepped-up
measures against many legal and aboveground left organizations in
an intensified effort "toward the dislodging of these legal fronts."[23]
In addition to targeting actual or alleged communist guerrillas and
sympathizers, vigilantes also unleashed their violence against "sur-
rogate victims" of unarmed civilians and family relatives, typically
in retaliation for frustrated combat or search efforts.[24]

While the very nature of vigilantism necessarily renders highly
problematic the issue of establishing culpability, let alone accountability (see further below), certain patterns may nonetheless be dis-
cerned behind this phenomenon. In addition to stepped-up PC/AFP
efforts to counter and copy CPP/NPA strategies and tactics, the anticipated demobilization and eventual reorganization of the paramilitary CHDF under the new regime in Manila also contributed to
the growth of vigilante groups around the Philippines. Contradictory government signals of initial public censure and eventual tacit
support vis-à-vis other peculiar predatory formations encouraged
under conditions of martial law—private armies, lost commands,
and so-called fanatical religious cults—also seemed to propel in significant ways the further spread of vigilantism in the late 1980s.
With the introduction of so-called "mass surrenders" as part of military counterinsurgency strategy in the late 1980s and early 1990s,
moreover, current or former NPA supporters or local activists also
emerged as new recruits for mobilization into such "community-

based self-defense organizations."[25] Even as the mobilizational dynamic of vigilantism must be situated within this broader political context, the sociological profile of recruits seemed decidedly lumpen. Not unlike the "cult" followings that tended to rise and fall in tandem with local counterinsurgency operations in the later Marcos years, "poor peasants, particularly rural immigrant settlers and tribal minorities in remote areas,"[26] once again found themselves especially vulnerable to the intensifying pressures of local PC/AFP commanders to "choose sides" and, this time around, to the peculiar mobilizational dynamics that drew them into the orbit of the vigilantes. Not uncommonly led by notorious criminals, including "police characters with criminal records,"[27] vigilante groups also prominently featured youths and, in the words of some residents interviewed in one heavily afflicted provincial barrio, "predominantly illiterate local bullies."[28]

While vigilantism surely presented welcome opportunities for protection and revenge against, in particular, CPP/NPA activists and supporters in some cases, it thus also served to perpetuate a vicious circle that, by force of dull compulsion or acute terror, locked (career) predators and (would-be) victims alike into a macabre embrace of violence and death. This is not to argue that vigilantes only inspired opportunism and/or fear among those who encountered or even joined these formations. As suggested by this example of Davaoeño gallows humor, for example, a rather more playful irreverence can also be found in popular references to the Alsa Masa as "Alsa Drama" to signify the feigning of support by people intimidated into joining or backing the vigilantes.[29]

Vigilantism and Philippine Government Officials

As suggested above, the incidence of vigilantism remained intimately linked to that of counterinsurgency. That is, the timing, location, and activities of vigilante mobilization, as much as its victims and "volunteers," showed notable affinities with the nature and direction of state-backed counterinsurgency efforts. To explore the significance of such affinities, the pages below focus more explicit analytical attention on the relations between official agents of the state and "vigilante volunteers." In view of the previous discussion, the following questions merit especially careful consideration: To what extent did the Aquino government express public support toward vigilantism and extrajudicial killings? What other informal practices characterized the treatment of this phenomenon by government officials serving under the Aquino administration(s)?

Reflective of theoretical as well as empirical concerns, the first question emphasizes public manifestations of government support for vigilantism rather than official policy per se. On the one hand, the search for evidence of government backing beyond policy formulation and implementation highlights the import of signals of support other than duly legislated policy, which, unsurprisingly, remained in virtual limbo on the issue of vigilantism and extrajudicial killings. On the other hand, it underscores the wider resonance of public political discourse rather than secret military strategy, which, of course, spilled into bloody excess with the rise of vigilantism.

Public pronouncements by high-ranking Philippine Constabulary/Armed Forces of the Philippines (PC/AFP) officers on vigilantism must be situated against the backdrop of military and intelligence counterinsurgency operations.[30] Indeed, such statements took on added significance in the wider context of intensifying police and military action that, with the massacre of thirteen peasant demonstrators by government security forces at the foot of the Mendiola Bridge near the presidential palace in Manila in January 1987, supplanted the 60-day cease-fire. Within another month, the government declared "Total War."[31]

In this environment, vigilantism received prominent military endorsements from local field commanders and national top brass alike. Upon his posting to Davao City as local commander of the PC Metrodiscom (Metropolitan District Command) in mid-July 1986, for example, Lieutenant Colonel Franco Calida lent increasingly public support to the mobilization of anticommunist vigilantes, notably the notorious Alsa Masa.[32] Self-professed "God/Father of Alsa Masa," Calida also acknowledged the practice of recruiting children as young as eight to serve as lookouts *(pasabilis)* against rebel guerrillas.[33] As early as April 1987, moreover, AFP chief of staff General Fidel V. Ramos singled out the Alsa Masa as deserving "full support and encouragement in dismantling communism" in Davao and elsewhere.[34] Echoing this sentiment, PC chief Major General Ramon Montano reassured a rally of Fuerza Masa ("Power of the Masses") vigilante supporters in Leyte province with the following words: "[Y]ou all deserve the support and protection of your government and the military."[35]

While predating the reopening of the Philippine Congress in July 1987 and thus lacking the authority conferred by due legislative process, the so-called "Guidelines for Civilian Self-Defense Organizations" were issued by AFP chief of staff General Ramos in a "memo" dated April 1, 1987.[36] Arguably the single most comprehensive effort at formulating "public policy" on vigilantism thus originated with the military rather than the civilian leadership of the Aquino administration. Moreover, these AFP guidelines followed within two weeks of a presidential directive to Defense Secretary Rafael Ileto and Local Government Secretary Jaime Ferrer to disband not merely the CHDF and so-called "private armies" but also, reportedly, vigilante groups such as the Alsa Masa.[37] Finally, these guidelines seemed to authorize the much-contested arming of vigilante groups while also insisting upon the essentially reactive and regulatory role of military and police forces.

A caveat is perhaps in order here. It would be mistaken to infer that the military somehow prevailed over the civilian government on the issue of vigilantism during this period. Granted, even as "the Philippine armed forces were deeply divided, they were largely united in their support for vigilantes."[38] Meanwhile, vigilantism provoked more evident contradictions and criticism within the ranks of the civilian branches of government. However, if electoral and human rights concerns at times served to circumscribe public support for vigilantism from among Philippine politicians, the Aquino administration also accommodated the most virulent of vigilante proponents at cabinet level, significantly in the departments of National Defense and Local Government. Exercising special presidential powers, moreover, Aquino herself issued the executive order dated July 25, 1987, providing for a citizens' armed force "subject to mobilization as the need arises."

Apart from high-profile public praise, what position did government officials in the Aquino administration(s) adopt vis-à-vis vigilantism? While typically less well advertised and more difficult to document, what might be referred to as "informal practices of governance" by civilian and military officials provided encouragement to the mobilization of vigilantes during this period. Such practices ranged in their scope and impact from national-level efforts at allocating resources, partly through presidential discretionary funds, to localized arrangements under provincial military and police, as well as local politicians and oligarchs. As frequently noted by media

and human rights organizations during this period, vigilantes often
"reported" to city halls and local military detachments, where they
received various forms of support, including pseudo-official recognition, money, arms, and protection from legal prosecution.[39] While
members of military and police forces enjoyed virtual impunity from
human rights abuses due to the court-martial jurisdiction over
PC/AFP troops guaranteed under Presidential Decree 1850 (which
remained in effect until June 20, 1991), their close affinities with
vigilantes also seriously undermined the prospects for investigating
alleged violations by the latter. According to one of the government's own prosecutors, for example, there was "no cooperation
from local law enforcement in building a case when the accused
[were] connected to the police or military, like with vigilantes."[40]
The problem of impunity was further compounded by the widespread intimidation of witnesses.[41] In this regard, the Commission
on Human Rights, reconstituted by Executive Order 163 in May
1987 to investigate both government and nongovernment forces on
account of alleged human rights violations, introduced a series of
"quasi-judicial procedures" which "complainant and witnesses
alike must fulfill, often at considerable personal risk, without offering any prospect of the form of remedy available in civil or criminal
proceedings."[42] While allowing for considerable local variation, direct military contact and assistance in particular appeared so commonly associated with vigilantism as to suggest themselves as
"necessary, if not sufficient" conditions for the emergence of this
phenomenon. According to Calida, for example, without the prior
activation of local military detachments, there would be no vigilante
mobilization because the latter require the protection of the former.[43] In combination, informal support from civilian and military
officials contributed to a widespread pattern of de facto authorization and mobilization of vigilantism in the Philippines during this
period. With de facto impunity governing their extrajudicial
killings, vigilantes came to serve as "at once judge and executioner."

On October 3, 1988, in Bunaan, Davao City, the vigilante group
Alsa Masa reportedly apprehended a man named Blanco and two
others whom they suspected of being NPA members when the three
men failed to produce certificates of residency. Family members believe the three were tortured and then killed. According to the attorney representing the victims' relatives, the police in Bunaan refused

to investigate the killings or provide any assistance. A relative of one of the victims reportedly learned from friends on the local police force where the bodies were buried, and had them exhumed. Although witnesses who say they can identify the suspects subsequently came forward, the local police refused to undertake any investigation. The victims' lawyer did not make a complaint against the local police unit to its PC commander, explaining, "That would be unnecessarily risky and would just create more enemies."[44]

Vigilantism and Regime Transition

Beyond public declarations and informal practices by government officials, the process of regime transition itself lent additional impetus to vigilante mobilization in the Philippines after Marcos. This process involved not merely the resurrection of democratic institutions and procedures but also, as noted above, the intensification of counterinsurgency operations in the Philippines. Compared to its martial law predecessor (1972–86), the transitional regime under Aquino (1986–92) thus encouraged greater revitalization of *both civil and uncivil society* through the mobilization of, sometimes overlapping and mutually reinforcing, election and counterinsurgency campaigns. To that end, it is perhaps unsurprising that the rise of the peculiar "voluntarism" and spectacular violence associated with vigilantism coincided with what one author has referred to as the restoration of the pre-Marcos "ancien regime" (i.e., electoral democracy dominated by national oligarchy and local bosses).[45]

The most virulent manifestations of vigilantism appear to have emerged when and where the actual process of regime transition encountered especially powerful martial law legacies such as contracting civilian government and expanding armed struggle. While the martial law regime was never "properly" militarized, it had nonetheless served to weaken mechanisms and agencies of civilian governance in direct and indirect ways, ranging from the official abolition of Congress and the centralization of executive powers initiated in 1972 to the de facto neopatrimonialization of the Philippine presidency in subsequent years and, as a result, the virtual evacuation of many municipal government offices by the 1980s, especially in so-called NPA "strongholds." In this regard, the "patrimonial" concentration and eventual contraction of the Philippine economy further undermined the willingness—and, in places, the ability—of local officials to govern. As suggested by the increasing influence of the NPA, with an estimated 25,000 regulars in about 20 percent of the country's barrios by the mid-1980s, moreover, martial law served to deepen, rather than to resolve, political polarization in the Philippines. While the guerrilla army grew in size as well as experience during martial law, finally, the Armed Forces of the Philippines instead showed signs of increasing disrepair on all fronts, as suggested by the development of "live-and-let-live" arrangements with local guerrillas and the clogging of military promotions, as well as the concentration of government troops and resources near the presidential palace at considerable cost to those posted elsewhere.

In this context, the revival of elected civilian government in 1986–92 encountered distinct challenges in areas with a marked NPA presence even as, with presidential appointments of (anti- or non-Marcos) municipal and provincial officers-in-charge (OICs) and preparations for the first bi/multi-partisan local elections since 1971, the country's agro-industrial oligarchy and local political bosses once again moved into swift electoral action.[46] While far from clear-cut, a suggestive pattern of vigilantism and "democratization" in the Philippines emerges from this period. Most obviously, if the NPA and its supporting networks remained weak in a given community and its hinterlands, so did local manifestations of vigilantism, and the regime transition was achieved largely through elections without counterinsurgency. By contrast, the transitional regime and its designated OICs confronted a rather different situation within the broader sphere of NPA "strongholds" where the travails of mobilizing individual voters *and* demobilizing social revolution prefigured the rise of the vigilantes.[47] In this context, supportive military detachments typically provided an especially hospitable environment for the emergence of vigilantism. That is, the reassertion of military presence and the redeployment of government troops contributed to a marked expansion of possibilities for national resources trickling down and local groups linking up in many parts of the country. However, the patronage of local politicians and businessmen, plantation families, and/or mining companies often served to influence, separately or jointly, the nature and direction of individual groups mobilized as vigilantes during the regime transition.

In short, the phenomenon of vigilantism must be situated within the context of the regime transition itself. This is not to dispute the long history of election-related political violence, as well as predatory para- or perhaps pseudo-military formations in the Philippines. As suggested above, however, the rise of the vigilantes after the fall of Marcos was neither spurious coincidence nor spontaneous contagion. Significantly, unlike martial law, the transitional regime proclaimed itself a participatory one and contributed in other more tangible ways to the rejuvenation of mobilizational processes associated with electoral politics. While this renewed emphasis upon participatory politics echoed the much-celebrated "People Power" uprising in Manila, it also confronted the mounting mobilization of a decidedly more radical, mass-based, and widespread anti-Marcos opposition, anchored in the CPP and its New People's Army. In this context, the laudatory references to vigilantism as "people power" by Aquino and other high-ranking government officials took on added significance. That is, such public declarations invited comparisons which could not but underscore the very opposite of the celebrated affinity between people power and vigilantism. Sparked by an aborted coup and confined largely to Metro Manila, the February 1986 People Power revolt that ushered in the national transition from authoritarian rule emerged as a peculiarly nonviolent, urban upper/middle-class event without much in the way of either organized left or rural population present. Vigilantism, by contrast, accompanied more protracted and, in a sense, provincial processes of regime transition through the mobilization of spectacular violence and lumpen elements in communities where the CPP/NPA and its rural mass base loomed large in local power struggles. If these stark and salient differences were not lost on government officials at the time, the notion of vigilantism as people power beyond the defining moment and narrow experience of February 1986 nonetheless highlighted the extent to which participatory calls "from above" inspired mobilization "from below" in the name of civil *and* uncivil society.

Vigliantism and the Postcolonial State

While the activities of Aquino-supported government officials and the processes of post-Marcos regime transition thus encouraged the rise of vigilantism in the late 1980s, this phenomenon also reflected dynamics rooted deep in the colonial foundations of the Philippine state. That is, the peculiar coupling of expanded provisions for electoral participation with intensified campaigns aimed at pacification and (re)incorporation of mobilized populations mirrored critical moments in the history of modern state formation in the Philippines. Furthermore, the enduring structures of "Philippine colonial democracy"[48] contributed to the marked decentralization and privatization of coercive state apparatuses, which, in turn, prefigured a recurring pattern of subcontracted political violence.

From proclaimed "benevolent assimilation" to undeclared "savage war," American incursions into the Philippines at the turn of the century proceeded against the backdrop of the first nationalist revolution in Asia. Mobilized in 1896 and defeated in 1897, the anticolonial revolutionary forces regrouped with the onset of the Spanish-American War in April 1898, and in just a few weeks time, General Emilio Aguinaldo declared the first Philippine Republic. While the inauguration of a republican constitution and government followed in the next few months, the outbreak of the Philippine-American War interrupted this brief period of self-rule in Feburary 1899.

Once rid of Spain, one of the most backward of colonial powers at the time, the so-called "Philippine Insurrection" thus ran afoul of the arriviste imperialism of America at the turn of the century. If recycled conquistadores from the Spanish Americas had helped prepare the ground for more than 300 years of friar rule, men and methods associated with the American frontier instead carried the professed "mission" of the United States in the early stages of this second coming of colonial conquest to the Philippines. As a result of the decentralized nature of the American state and national army, which had yet to complete a highly contested process of "patchwork" civil and military institution building by the turn of the century,[49] it is perhaps unsurprising that the United States' first land war in Asia was fought much in the spirit and mode of so-called "Injun Warfare."[50]

While military administrative reform and domestic electoral politics might have discouraged American officers and the troops under their command from transgressing the boundaries of "civilized warfare" in the Philippines, this restraint increasingly gave way to a "savage war" doctrine developed during the Civil War and subsequently invoked from Sand Creek (1864) to Wounded Knee

(1890) in the so-called "Plains campaigns." Of course, this doctrine already reflected considerable "lived experience" among senior as well as junior American officers serving in the Philippines. That is, an overwhelming number of ranking U.S. officers posted to key positions in the Philippines, including Generals Elwell S. Otis, Wesley Merritt, Henry W. Lawton, Franklin J. Bell, Jacob Smith, and Adna Chaffee, had gained their (s)kills and stars in the American West. Recruited into service through so-called volunteer regiments of de facto state militias, moreover, the rank and file also earned a certain notoriety for its "lawless violence," encouraged perhaps as much by individual commanding officers as by the relative lack of military training, discipline, and experience that characterized these American troops in the Philippines.

Inasmuch as the American "state of courts and parties" remained entrenched despite the "patchwork" reform efforts to expand national administrative apparatuses in the late nineteenth century,[51] the new imperial regime in the Philippines also displayed notable colonial affinities as evidenced by the early introduction of local elections rather than a centralized bureacracy. In a process begun even as military campaigns continued in many parts of the islands, municipal mayors (1901), provincial governors (1902), and representatives to a national legislature (1907) were elected by restricted franchise and, once in office, granted extensive powers over local agents of coercive state apparatuses under the auspices of "Philippine colonial democracy." In the absence of a strong, colonial state bureaucracy, the Philippines thus developed a "highly decentralized, politicized, and privatized administration of law enforcement," where police and constabulary appointments, promotions, remunerations, and reassignments rested with municipal and provincial politicians.[52] This peculiar pattern of state formation was subsequently enshrined in the 1935 Commonwealth Constitution and reaffirmed with the Declaration of Independence in 1946.

While the electoral franchise was expanded to universal adult suffrage with independence, other local and increasingly national government measures aimed at the simultaneous demobilization and (re)incorporation of guerrilla organizations in the aftermath of the Japanese Occupation (1942–45) and its disruptive impact upon many "pre-war vertical ties" between landed oligarchy and peasantry.[53] Notably, the 1946 congressional election of six Democratic Alliance candidates closely identified with peasant organizations and guerrilla networks in the rice-bowl and high-tenancy region of Central Luzon—and enjoying the support of the Partido Komunista ng Pilipinas (PKP) and the Civil Liberties Union—prompted swift repression:

> Government authorities, for example, directed police, constabulary soldiers, and civilian guards—who were on the payrolls of landlords and the government—to raid offices of the Democratic Alliance and the PKP, break up political rallies, and beat up peasant leaders and spokesmen.[54]

In the aftermath of this election campaign, the unceremonious unseating of the Democratic Alliance Six and the eventual illegalization of the Huks and the National Peasant Union organized by them after the war, Pambansang Kaisahan ng mga Magbubukid (PKM), did little to undermine the guerrilla movement in Central Luzon during the late 1940s. Instead, abusive government troops and notoriously violent elections contributed to the strengthening of Huk/PKP organizational strength and revolutionary resolve.[55]

Against this backdrop, Cold War incursions into Asia could not but underscore in Washington the increasing geostrategic and enduring symbolic significance of the Philippines as host to U.S. military installations and as America's "showcase of democracy." By 1950, the newly appointed secretary of national defense, Ramon Magsaysay, was thus able to launch a concerted counterinsurgency campaign with critical American military assistance and cooperation, including the Manila-based Joint United States Military Aid Group (JUSMAG) and its "special mission" headed by then Lieutenant Colonel Edward G. Lansdale, an intelligence specialist borrowed from the U.S. Air Force. Leaving aside the intricate details and peculiar relations that helped shape this rejuvenated anti-Huk "psywar" campaign, it is nonetheless important to recall the mobilization of volunteers into "'hunter-killer' units called the Scout Rangers."[56] In addition to the contributions of such irregular outfits as the "Nenita Squad" with its rumored vampirelike bloodletting of victims, for example, the regular troops, reorganized into lighter, more mobile, and less conventional "battalion combat teams" by the early 1950s, also recruited among "all the law-enforcement capability in the area, including municipal police and especially the so-called civil guard, usually a rag-tag group of armed civilians."[57]

While the Huks were largely demobilized by the mid-1950s, their resurgence in Central Luzon in the late 1960s met with paramilitary repression at the hands of, for example, former Huks and criminals recruited by the PC into the infamous "Monkees"—"so-called to distinguish them from Huk liquidation squads commonly known, because of their long hair, as 'Beatles.'"[58] With their lumpen formation and spectacular violence, the vigilantes of the late 1980s thus reflected and reproduced a familiar pattern of paramilitary mobilization, albeit in the spirit and mode of the unprecedented contestation over "People Power" and "democratization" that characterized the Philippines during this period.[59]

"The Apocalypse Now" and History as State of Siege

In short, the decentralization and privatization of coercive state apparatuses encouraged under American auspices remained an enduring and powerful legacy of Philippine colonial democracy even after independence in 1946. Such legacies in turn served to blur the lines between state/society, civil/military, military/paramilitary, and legal/illegal, with a variety of peculiar coercive formations—notably so-called "lost commands," "private armies," and "fanatical sects"—operating at the behest of entrenched local "warlords" and landed oligarchs. Moreover, these familiar patterns for managing law enforcement and Philippine elections tended to prefigure a recurring cycle of intensified subcontracting and political violence during periods of declared "national emergency," as seen in the late 1940s and early 1950s and again in the mid to late 1980s. As if to confirm Walter Benjamin's notion of history as state of siege, postcolonial Philippine society and politics thus trace a tortuous trajectory on this slippery slope between officially sanctioned emergencies and the "normality of the abnormal."[60]

The vigilante phenomenon of the late 1980s emerged precisely as the Aquino government sought to promote reinvigorated counterinsurgency campaigns and revived electoral competition to counter a highly mobilized New People's Army and National Democratic Front under CPP auspices. In as much as the new government based its claims to popular legitimacy on Aquino's own status as martyred widow due to the political violence under Marcos and,

of course, the "People Power" origins of the regime itself, the staying power of an abusive military and the swift "return of the oligarchs" posed particular challenges for the successful military as
well as electoral countermobilization against the NPA/CPP.[61] This is
not to underestimate important continuities with Marcos-era paramilitary formations, such as the revived Barrio Self-Defense Units
(BSDU) and, eventually, the Civilian Home Defense Forces (CHDF).
In particular, the notorious CHDF had included "members of irregular quasi-military political, religious or criminal groups" since its
inception under PC command in 1976.[62] After the official lifting of
martial law on account of a papal visit to the Philippines in 1981,
such groups continued to proliferate and so-called "cults, fundamentalist sects and fanatic groups" were reportedly "armed and
trained by the military for counterinsurgency purposes [and] involved in massacres, murders, mutilations, cannibalism and torture."[63] However, it was only with the resurrection of formally
democratic institutions and procedures under Aquino a few years
later that vigilantism emerged as a distinct phenomenon with its
own peculiar discourse of "spontaneous voluntarism" and the spectacular circulation of its grotesque violence.

Beyond the noted historical affinity between the phenomenon of
vigilantism and the conditions of tenuous territorial as well as ideological government consolidation,[64] the nature and direction of mobilizational campaigns in the Philippines of the late 1980s also
revealed a peculiar and yet familiar dialectic of sorts. On the one
hand, mobilization "in the name of civil society" focused considerable energies on elections and political representation.[65] On the
other hand, mobilization in the name of uncivil society released
powerful forces for counterinsurgency and immanent violence. Thus
juxtaposed, the inviolate sacredness of electoral ballots and the sub-
mission to national citizenship celebrated in official political discourse appeared in sharp relief against the violent profanation of
human lives and the sovereignty of fanatic violence reverberating in
vigilante calls to *Kill for Democracy!* In this vein, the consolidation
of the regime transition ushered in with People Power revealed a curious but crucial slippage in the mobilization of volunteers under the
banner of Bantay Bayan ("Watchful/Vigilant Nation/People"). That
is, insofar as by 1987 such invocations extended to anticommunist
vigilantes, they served to transgress and thus to confirm the very
boundaries watched over by the much-celebrated national citizens'

movement for free elections with its calls for a Bantay (ng) Bayan campaign still resounding from the snap presidential election of February 1986. In combination, the mobilizational dynamic of civil *and* uncivil society helped to clinch the subsequent institutionalization of multiparty elections, the concomitant entrenchment of oligarchic dominance, and the effective marginalization of organized left politics in the post-Marcos Philippines.

With the advantage of hindsight, this essay has focused attention on the significance of protracted patterns of subcontracted state coercion and critical conjunctures of intensified political mobilization and demobilization for shaping the nature and direction of vigilantism in the late 1980s. Moreover, it has highlighted the simultaneous affirmation and disavowal of vigilantism implied by Philippine and U.S. government support for "low intensity conflict" with its characteristic "geographical, epistemological and military-strategic decenteredness."[66] In the shadow of the structured instrumentalities of vigilantism, however, there also lurked a grotesque violence and an "apocalypse-now mentality,"[67] stalking lived experience and haunting common sense with the circulation of severed heads and phantasmagoric rumors. On the one hand, the severed head served as a powerful reminder of a common vulnerability to the dangers associated with sovereign violence, including, of course, that of the NPA, while at the same time embodying a dismembered revolutionary movement. On the other hand, the phantasmagoric rumors (*tsismis* in Tagalog) arising from the very violence and fear that threatened everyday social relations and common sense also worked to order this terrifying insecurity and uncertainty into the familiar script and dominant discourse of binary contestation for power between, ultimately, government and antigovernment forces.

> *Tsismis* sorted out the mysteries, pieced together conspiracies, created "facts," and made sense of the madness. Tales of the murders traveled from witnesses to friends to enemies to the fish hawker in the marketplace, to the lady selling amulets, to Willy the meat vendor, and from them emerged multiple antinomies, contradictory explanations, epitaphs that gave voice to the ineffable. *Tsismis* . . . *Tsismis* of romance, sex, and petty rivalries, the *tsismis* of everyday life, gave way to the *tsismis* of the night, of horror and death, the kind of death most in need of *tsismis*: death by the untouchables, by the military, the NPA, the vigilantes, the death squads,

the fanatical cultists; death that precludes justice, that invites only forgiveness or revenge.[68]

Notes

1. Thanks to Arthur Brenner, Bruce Campbell, Sheila Coronel, and Geoff Robinson for some early inspirations for this chapter, and to Robert Cribb, Ron May, Rosanne Rutten, and John Sidel for helpful comments and criticism on a previous draft. As usual, the shortcomings are all mine.

2. On the doctrine of "low-intensity conflict," see *Low Intensity Conflict Field Manual No. 100–20* (Washington, D.C.: Headquarters, Department of the Army, 16 January 1981).

3. See, for example, Benedict Kerkvliet, *The Huk Rebellion: A Study of Peasant Revolt in the Philippines* (Berkeley: University of California Press, 1977); Alfred W. McCoy, ed., *An Anarchy of Families: State and Family in the Philippines* (Madison: University of Wisconsin Center for Southeast Asian Studies, 1993); and John T. Sidel, "The Underside of Progress: Land, Labor, and Violence in Two Philippine Growth Zones, 1985–1995," *Bulletin of Concerned Asian Scholars* 30, no. 1 (January-March 1998): 3–12.

4. Benedict J. Kerkvliet, "Patterns of Philippine Resistance and Rebellion, 1970–1986," *Pilipinas,* no. 6 (Spring 1986): 35–49.

5. Walden Bello, *Creating the Third Force: U.S.-Sponsored Low-Intensity Conflict in the Philippines* (San Francisco: Institute for Food and Policy Studies, 1987).

6. See, for example, Justus van der Kroef, "The Philippines: Day of the Vigilantes," *Asian Survey* 28 (June 1988): 630–49, and "The Philippine Vigilantes: Devotion and Disarray," *Contemporary Southeast Asia* 10, no. 2 (September 1988): 163–81; and Ronald J. May, *Vigilantes in the Philippines: From Fanatical Cults to Citizens' Organizations* (Honolulu: University of Hawaii Center for Philippine Studies, 1992).

7. David Kowaleski, "Vigilante Counterinsurgency and Human Rights in the Philippines: A Statistical Analysis," *Human Rights Quarterly* 12, no. 2 (1990): 257.

8. See esp. Amnesty International, *Philippines: Unlawful Killings by Military and Paramilitary Forces* (New York: Amnesty International, March 1988); Lawyers Committee for Human Rights, *Vigilantes in the Philippines: A Threat to Democratic Rule* (New York: Lawyers Committee for Human Rights, 1988); and Senate Committee on Jus-

tice and Human Rights, *Report on Vigilante Groups* (Manila: Republic of the Philippines, 1988).

9. Lawyers Committee, *Vigilantes in the Philippines,* 98.

10. Victor N. Corpus, *Silent War* (Quezon City: VNC Enterprises, 1989), 181. Of course, official military strategy as well as more localized initiatives by PC/AFP commanders in the field revealed considerable efforts to copy—or rather *counter*—the NPA's guerrilla methods. For an illuminating discussion of the NPA's strategic shift towards its own "Total War" in Negros Occidental, see Rosanne Rutten, "Popular Support for the Revolutionary Movement CPP-NPA: Experiences in a Hacienda in Negros Occidental, 1978–1995," in *The Revolution Falters: The Left in Philippine Politics After 1986,* ed. Patricio N. Abinales (Ithaca, N.Y.: Cornell University Southeast Asia Program, 1996), 110–53.

11. Cf. Alfred W. McCoy, "Demystifying LIC," *Kasarinlan* 4, no. 3 (First Quarter 1989): 31–40.

12. Eva-Lotta E. Hedman, "Beyond Beycott: The Philippine Left and Electoral Politics After 1986," in *Revolution Falters,* 87–89.

13. After the fall of Marcos, the Philippine Congress was reopened only in July 1987. While initial "seed money" had reportedly been made available in the amount of approximately 264 million pesos from the president's discretionary fund, a subsequent executive request for CAFGU budget allocations prompted critical senatorial scrutiny and public debate into the legality and funding of this paramilitary organization. As noted by the Lawyers Committee on Human Rights, "[w]hile Congress approved funding for the CAFGU, the program itself has never been legislated." Lawyers Committee for Human Rights, *Out of Control: Militia Abuses in the Philippines* (New York: Lawyers Committee for Human Rights, 1990), 71.

14. Lawyers Committee, *Vigilantes in the Philippines,* xi; Senate Committee, *Report on Vigilante Groups,* 10; and U.S. Department of State, "Citizens Self-Defense Groups in the Philippines," 28 April 1989, 12.

15. May, *Vigilantes in the Philippines,* 29.

16. Lawyers Committee, *Out of Control,* 31. See further Lawyers Committee, *Vigilantes in the Philippines,* and Amnesty International, *Unlawful Killings.*

17. Senate Committee, *Report on Vigilante Groups,* 16.

18. Kowaleski, "Vigilante Counterinsurgency and Human Rights in the Philippines," 257. See further Enrique Delacruz, Aida Jordan, and Jorge Emmanuel, *Death Squads in the Philippines* (San Francisco: Alliance for Philippine Concerns, 1987).

19. Kenneth M. George, *Showing Signs of Violence: The Cultural Politics of a Twentieth-Century Headhunting Ritual* (Berkeley: University of California Press, 1996), 96.

20. George, 93.

21. Lawyers Committee, *Out of Control*, 31.

22. Alfred W. McCoy, "The Restoration of Planter Power in La Carlota City," in *From Marcos to Aquino: Local Perspectives on Political Transition in the Philippines*, eds. Benedict J. Kerkvliet and Resil B. Mojares (Quezon City: Ateneo de Manila University Press, 1991), 130.

23. *Manila Chronicle*, 10 November 1988.

24. Lawyers Committee, *Vigilantes in the Philippines*, xiv.

25. See, especially, Rosanne Rutten, "'Mass Surrenders' in Negros Occidental: Ideology, Force and Accommodation in a Counterinsurgency Program" (paper presented at the 4th International Philippine Studies Conference, Australian National University, Canberra, 1–3 July 1992). The term "mass surrenders" refers to the well-publicized government initiatives offering amnesty and "rehabilitation" to surrendering NPA guerrillas. In actual practice, official figures on "mass surrenderees" were inflated as a matter of government propaganda as well as the willingness of nonguerrillas to be counted—and presumably rewarded in some fashion.

26. May, *Vigilantes in the Philippines*, 63.

27. Senate Committee, *Report on Vigilante Groups*, 15.

28. Lawyers Committee, *Vigilantes in the Philippines*, 50.

29. Cited in Sheila S. Coronel, *Coups, Cults, and Cannibals: Chronicles of a Troubled Decade (1982–1992)* (Manila: Anvil Publishing, 1992), 134. Other examples cited by Coronel included "Alsa Tasa" and "Alsa Baso" to refer to vigilantes with a noted weakness for drinking coffee or getting drunk, typically at the people's expense.

30. See further Bello, *Creating the Third Force*; Corpus, *Silent War*; and Gareth Porter, *The Politics of Counterinsurgency in the Philippines: Military and Political Options* (Honolulu: University of Hawaii Center for Philippine Studies, 1987).

31. As noted by Porter, for example, the counterinsurgency strategy underpinning this "Total War" had roots in the martial law period. With intensified U.S. backing, however, the PC/AFP enjoyed rejuvenation of military presence and resources, notably the reorganization of force structure into Regional Unified Commands (RUCs) and the reactivation of the National Capital Region District Command "to conduct security operations" in Metro Manila. Porter, *Politics of Counterinsurgency*.

32. See, for example, *New York Times*, 4 April 1987; *Manila Chronicle*, 16 March 1988; *Mindanao Daily Bulletin*, 17 July 1989.

33. Lawyers Committee, *Vigilantes in the Philippines*, 32.

34. *Asiaweek*, 12 April 1987.

35. *Manila Chronicle*, 6 September 1988.

36. Within a month, broadly similar "guidelines" were issued by an interagency subcommittee with representatives from the AFP, the Department of Local Government, the Department of National Defense, and the reconstituted Philippine Commission of Human Rights, but, according to a subsequent Philippine Senate Report, without proper authorization by executive order or an act of Congress. Nonetheless, these guidelines were formally adopted on October 30, 1987. See Senate Committee, *Report on Vigilante Groups*, 20.

37. Hong Kong AFP, March 16, 1987. In her State of the Nation Address on July 25, 1988, Aquino once again referred to an instruction to the chief of staff "to begin the process of disbanding all so-called vigilante groups in line with the Constitutional injunction against paramilitary groups." However, Ramos, who was appointed to succeed Ileto as secretary of defense, issued the following "clarification": "The Department of National Defense and the armed forces firmly believe that we must retain the Bantay Bayan." *Manila Chronicle*, 1 August 1988. An official designation in Tagalog for the government-sanctioned "Civilian Volunteer Self-Defense Organizations," Bantay Bayan (variously translated as "People's Guard" or "Nation Watch") echoed the Bantay ng Bayan campaign, which saw the Catholic Bishops Businessmen Conference of the Philippines in the vanguard of a mass mobilization for free and clean elections in 1986.

38. Lawyers Committee, *Vigilantes in the Philippines*, xv.

39. Lawyers Committee, *Vigilantes in the Philippines*, xv; Lawyers Committee, *Out of Control*.

40. Cited in Lawyers Committee for Human Rights, *Impunity: Prosecutions of Human Rights Violations in the Philippines* (New York: Lawyers Committee for Human Rights, September 1991), 32.

41. In this regard, former assistant director of the National Bureau of Investigation (NBI) Epimaco Velasco offers an illuminating comment: "I've never arrested anyone for intimidating witnesses. . . . If I did, it would take up all of my time." Cited in Lawyers Committee, *Impunity*, 146.

42. Amnesty International, "Philippines: 'Disappearances' in the Context of Counterinsurgency," Summary ASA 35/05/91 (February 1991), 17.

43. "*[K]ung walang* detachment, *hindi mag-aalsa ang mga yan. Kailangan ng proteksyon eh.*" ("If there is no [military] detachment, they will not rise up. After all, they need protection.") Lieutenant Colonel

Franco Calida, cited in Carolyn O. Arguillas, "The Davao Experiment," *Veritas*, 5–11 March 1987, Special Section, 18.

44. Cited in Lawyers Committee, *Impunity*, 32–3.

45. Benedict Anderson, "Cacique Democracy in the Philippines: Origins and Dreams," *New Left Review*, no. 169 (May-June 1988): 28.

46. See, especially, Temario Campos Rivera, "Class, the State and Foreign Capital: The Politics of Philippine Industrialization, 1950–1986" (Ph.D. diss., University of Wisconsin–Madison, 1991); and John T. Sidel, "Coercion, Capital and the Post-Colonial State: Bossism in the Postwar Philippines" (Ph.D. diss., Cornell University, 1995).

47. For example, the NPA reportedly issued—for a fee—"safe-conduct passes in guerrilla-controlled areas" during the 1988 elections. "Rebs admit bets gave them money," *Malaya*, 15 January 1988, 1. Moreover, NPA rebels allegedly campaigned for the new left party Partido ng Bayan in some areas. "Samar is no longer old politicos turf," *Manila Chronicle*, 17 January 1988, 5.

48. Ruby R. Paredes, ed., *Philippine Colonial Democracy* (Quezon City: Ateneo de Manila University Press, 1989).

49. Stephen Skowronek, *Building a New American State: The Expansion of National Administrative Capacities, 1877–1920* (Cambridge: Cambridge University Press, 1982).

50. Stuart Creighton Miller, *Benevolent Assimilation: The American Conquest of the Philippines, 1899–1903* (New Haven: Yale University Press, 1982), 196–218.

51. See further Skowronek, *Building a New American State*.

52. Sidel, "Coercion, Capital and the Post-Colonial State," 62.

53. Ronald King Edgerton, "The Politics of Reconstruction in the Philippines: 1945–48" (Ph.D. diss., University of Michigan, 1975), 19.

54. Kerkvliet, *The Huk Rebellion*, 262.

55. Kerkvliet, *The Huk Rebellion*.

56. Douglas S. Blaufarb, *The Counterinsurgency Era: U.S. Doctrine and Performance 1950 to the Present* (New York: Free Press, 1977), 28.

57. Blaufarb, *The Counterinsurgency Era*.

58. Otto D. van den Muijzenberg, "Political Mobilization and Violence in Central Luzon (Philippines)," *Modern Asian Studies* 7, no. 4 (1973): 702.

59. See further Rutten, "'Mass Surrenders' in Negros Occidental."

60. Walter Benjamin, "Critique of Violence," in *Walter Benjamin Reflections: Essays, Aphorisms, Autobiographical Writings*, ed. Peter Demetz (New York: Schocken Books, 1992), 277–300. See also Michael Taussig, *The Nervous System* (London: Routledge, 1992), 11–13.

61. Institute for Popular Democracy, *Political Clans and Electoral Politics: A Preliminary Research* (Quezon City: Institute for Popular Democracy, 1987), 95.

62. Amnesty International, *Report of an Amnesty International Mission to the Republic of the Philippines* (London: Amnesty International, 1982), 27.

63. Patricia Startup, M.M., and Eileen Laird, M.M., eds., *Truth Uncovered: Fact-Finding Mission Report—Cotabato—Zamboanga del Sur May 1985* (Quezon City: Claretian Publications, 1985), 15.

64. See, for example, H. Jon Rosenbaum and Peter C. Sederberg, eds., *Vigilante Politics* (Philadelphia: University of Pennsylvania Press, 1976).

65. Eva-Lotta E. Hedman, "In the Name of Civil Society: Contesting Free Elections in the Post-Colonial Philippines" (Ph.D. diss., Cornell University, 1998).

66. Taussig, *The Nervous System*, 21.

67. Coronel, *Coups, Cults, and Cannibals*, 120–31.

68. Alan Berlow, *Dead Season: A Story of Murder and Revenge on the Philippine Island of Negros* (New York: Pantheon Books, 1996), 56–57.

PART III

Social Control

CHAPTER 6

State Terrorism and Death Squads in Uganda (1971–79)

Edward Kannyo

BETWEEN 1971 AND 1979, DURING THE TYRANNICAL regime of Idi Amin, a large number of people were killed in Uganda at the hands of state agents.[1] Most estimates of the toll have ranged between 100,000 and 500,000 victims, though at least one scholar, Jan J. Jorgenson, has questioned the higher estimates and suggested the much lower range of 12,000–30,000.[2] All available evidence indicates that the overwhelming majority of these deaths were caused by three organizations that were central to the survival of the regime, namely the State Research Bureau (SRB), the Public Safety Unit (PSU), and the Military Police (MP). These institutions either operated as death squads or harbored units that acted as such within their ranks.

More than twenty years after the demise of the Amin regime, detailed knowledge of the internal operations of the State Research Bureau, the Public Safety Unit, and the Military Police remains scanty. Nobody who was a member of any of these organizations has made the kind of full confessions that have, for instance, come out of the Truth and Reconciliation Commission in South Africa or some of the perpetrators in Argentina's "dirty war."[3] The present study is based on a variety of sources, including accounts of people who lived within the country at the time and accounts and reports of the public media and international human rights organizations. The report of a commission set up in 1986 to investigate human rights violations since the country's independence also provides valuable material on the Amin regime.[4]

Death squads generally operate in the context of state terrorism, i.e., the regular use of violence, particularly homicide, by state agents against political opponents for the primary purpose of intimidation. Opponents are defined as anyone engaged in or suspected of engaging in activities and behavior that are deemed to threaten the government and its goals.[5] Fear is central to the politics of state terrorism.[6] It is evoked in a number of ways, including the criminalization of what would be regarded as legitimate political and social conduct under normal circumstances; the frequent imposition of harsh penalties, especially death, for infractions of draconian laws; collective punishments, such as destruction of villages and mass deportations; and torture and killings. The use of flawed judicial or pseudo-judicial procedures, such as special tribunals and broadly defined repressive legislation, serves to reinforce fear. Such conditions of state terrorism prevailed in Uganda during the period under study and explain the forms that official political violence took. State terrorism can be open or clandestine, but usually takes both forms. Under open state terrorism, military, police, and judicial institutions are used in arbitrary and draconian ways that blur the line between conformity and nonconformity, legality and illegality. Clandestine state terrorism involves the organization or condoning of violent and illegal activities such as abductions, torture, and murder carried out by the police, the military, intelligence agencies, and paramilitary "vigilantes."[7] This is also the context for the use of the death squads. It is political repression carried on outside the realm of law, "behind society's back."[8] Uganda under Amin sustained both open and clandestine forms of state terrorism.

State terrorism has often occurred in situations where regimes have come to power through violent means or survive through ferocious repression of opponents. Such regimes invariably perceive themselves to be constantly threatened by open or clandestine armed groups, "subversion," and "conspiracies."[9] States in which unbridled violence is the dominant method of dealing with opposition, dissent, and nonconformist behavior can be appropriately described as "terrorist states." Uganda under the rule of Amin was such a terrorist state.

This chapter begins with a brief historical and political background. This is followed by an analysis of the emergence of violence as the principal basis of the regime, the nature and activities of the death squads that sustained it in power, and the kinds of people who were targeted. The study concludes with a discussion of the major empirical and theoretical causes of state terrorism and death squad activities in Uganda in the period covered.

Political and Historical Background

The phenomenon of state terrorism and death squads emerged out of the failure of the incipient liberal democratic institutions that had been gradually introduced within the previous ten years of British colonial rule to take root. Shortly after the achievement of independence, the authoritarianism that had characterized the colonial and precolonial social and political structures was quickly reimposed. Under Amin, authoritarianism degenerated into state terrorism.

Uganda, a small East African state with an estimated population of 22 million people in 1998 (around 13 million during the time covered in this essay), was a creation of British imperialism. It was formed out of numerous precolonial polities at the beginning of the twentieth century.[10] When it achieved independence on October 9, 1962, Uganda, like the majority of the new states in Africa, lacked strong political institutions and had only the beginnings of a liberal democratic political culture. The colonial state was a bureaucratic authoritarian system. It sought to bring about only those economic, social, and political changes that were compatible with the exploitation of the imperial territories with the least expenditure of metropolitan resources. Modernization and the introduction of capitalist economic and social relations were curbed in order to avoid any massive disruption of traditional precapitalist structures that would have necessitated large-scale economic, social, and political restructuring.[11]

In the first nine years of independence, the country had two political regimes. From October 1962 to February 1966, it had an essentially liberal regime modeled on the Westminster system inherited from the former colonial power. A coalition government of the Uganda Peoples Congress (UPC) and the Buganda-based Kabaka Yekka ("The King's Party") governed the country until 1964. Milton Obote, the leader of the UPC, was the prime minister while the *kabaka* (king) of Buganda[12] occupied the ceremonial position of president from 1963 to 1966.

A split between the coalition partners and, more seriously, within the ruling UPC itself culminated in a series of moves by Obote resulting in the overthrow of the constitution. He began by arresting five of his ministers during a cabinet meeting on February 22, 1966, and ended up seizing supreme executive power as president in violation of the constitution on March 3, 1966. He expelled the *kabaka* from the presidency and, in May 1966, ordered the army to attack the royal palace when the *kabaka* declared his open opposition to the Obote coup. A large but undetermined number of people, many civilians, were killed in the ensuing battle that the *kabaka* lost. He eventually ended up in exile in Britain, where he died in 1969.

Between 1966 and 1969, the country became a de facto one-party state. Obote abolished the country's four monarchies, which had become essentially ceremonial, though still revered, institutions, and instead of holding elections in 1967, as mandated under the 1966 constitution, he introduced another constitution that provided for extreme centralization of power in the hands of the presidency. Thus his government remained in power without elections until January 1971. Moreover, he abolished internal democracy within his own party and subjected key party positions to appointment by the president rather than elections as before. Following an assassination attempt on Obote at the end of 1969, all opposition parties were banned and moves were made to create the typical institutions of a de jure one-party state. Political liberties were gradually extinguished as all forms of serious political dissent were suppressed through the threat of arbitrary arrest, curbing of opposition party activities, monopoly of the official electronic and print media, and intimidation of the private print media. Opponents were kept in check through a combination of coercion and cooptation. Although the Obote regime was negligent about disciplining the army and other security forces for occasional killings and abuses of civilians, there was no evidence of officially sanctioned homicide. It was an authoritarian rather than terrorist regime.

The Emergence and Survival of the Terrorist Regime

In January 1971, while Obote was out of the country, an army faction led by army commander General Idi Amin overthrew the government. Although he promised that his would be an interim administration, he soon concentrated all executive and legislative powers in his own hands and took steps to eliminate all public political forums. A proclamation of February 2, 1971, formally granted Amin the powers of the presidency, dissolved parliament (which, though docile, had continued to exist under the previous regime), and empowered him to legislate through decrees. Other key legal instruments included Decree No. 2, which dissolved district and municipal councils, and No. 14 (1971), which "suspended" (i.e., banned) all political activities. Throughout the life of the regime, there was a cabinet of ministers and a "Defense Council," composed of the most senior military officers under the chairmanship of Amin. It was the ostensible supreme decision-making body, but its deliberations were secretive. However, the general assumption was that whatever the nominal institutional framework, Amin arbitrarily made all the decisions, possibly with the advice of associates drawn from different sectors of society. In 1976, the Defense Council declared him "President for Life." Civilians drawn from all major parts of the country originally dominated the cabinet. However, by end of the regime, military men drawn from narrowly defined ethnic, religious, and geographical backgrounds dominated it.

During the first year, Amin drew substantial political support from various groups that had come to resent Obote's authoritarian regime. The Baganda, the single largest nationality that had seen its centuries-old monarchical institution violently destroyed in 1966, was one such group. Amin agreed to allow and support the return and state funeral of the remains of the late *kabaka*, who had been buried in Britain. He lifted the State of Emergency that Obote had imposed on the Buganda region in 1966 and extended to the rest of the country in 1969. It had provided for the means to legally circumvent the constitutional rights against arbitrary imprisonment. Scores of political prisoners who had been arrested under the terms of this provision were released at a big ceremony. His government also dissolved the feared General Service Department—the secret police—of the old regime and arrested its key operatives.

Amin rescinded a series of measures that the Obote regime had initiated in 1970 with the intention of bringing large sectors of the economy under state control. These moves had caused widespread unease among important segments of the country's elites and even ordinary people who were concerned about the future of private property and the market economy. The 1972 expulsion and distribution of the properties of the Ugandan-Asian community that had dominated the country's commercial sector provided the regime with an extra boost in popularity.[13] However, the fact that the lion's share of these properties was given to Amin's close associates, soldiers, and their clients, the continuing generalized physical insecurity and the failure to restore civilian government dissipated most of the initial support. The rapid decline of political support enhanced the role of violence in the maintenance of the regime.[14]

The coup had been a bloody affair, involving the elimination of hundreds, if not thousands, of soldiers who had resisted or were suspected of opposing the change of regime. The likelihood of vengeance from relatives and ethnic brethren of the soldiers was undoubtedly one factor that Amin and his supporters had to consider seriously. This fear was enhanced by the fact that Obote and his leading supporters settled in neighboring Tanzania, whose government refused to recognize the Amin regime and regularly denounced it. The exiles constantly threatened to invade and created underground networks that engaged in sabotage and endeavored to eliminate the regime.[15]

The most dramatic of these efforts was the abortive exile invasion of September 1972. Ugandan security forces easily defeated it, but it goaded Amin immediately to unleash a campaign of terror leading to the killing of numerous civilians associated with the Obote regime or the UPC. From the beginning, there were reports of plots and attempts on Amin's life. These were always hazy and difficult to verify. However, General Mustafa Adrisi, who was Amin's vice president, confirmed at least one of the reported attempts when he appeared before the 1986 Commission on Human Rights Violations.

In their public pronouncements and speeches, Amin and his officials made it clear that there was no distinction between active armed resistance, political opposition, and common crimes. They were all punishable by the most brutal measures. As early as 1973, a statement broadcast by an anonymous military "spokesman" (generally believed to be a covert description of Amin) declared:

"Those harboring guerrillas will be treated as guerrillas. . . . Villages in whose districts guerrillas are found will also be burned down. . . . Taxi drivers who give guerrillas lifts will be blown up in their cars, and house-owners hiding them will be blown up in their homes. People hiding guerrillas would lose their children and never see them again."[16] Similarly, Amin's tendency to publicly blame and threaten entire communities for the alleged sins of individuals undoubtedly contributed to the wide scope and high degree of political violence. In 1973, for instance, he accused the Langi ethnic group of engaging in "propaganda activities and creating confusion."[17] These kinds of accusations were often followed by the abduction and murder of prominent members of the communities who had been pinpointed as "troublemakers." Even artistic activities deemed politically suspect could result in the death of the authors. Thus, Byron Kawaddwa, a leading Luganda playwright, disappeared in 1977 after the presentation of a play he had written on the theme of the persecution and martyrdom of some of the first Ugandan Christians at the end of the nineteenth century. In the context of a terrorist regime identified with the Muslim minority (constituting 15 percent of the total population at the most), the regime most likely regarded the work as a political allegory.

Many aspects of Amin's rule increased the likelihood that it would resort to widespread violence. In its basic socioeconomic character, the regime was not very different from most authoritarian regimes that have emerged in many other parts of the developing world. It was characterized by patrimonial politics and the use of political power to gain access to wealth directly through financial emoluments and indirectly through the acquisition of privileged access to capital, monopolies, and protection money in semicapitalist state-dominated settings. State employment at all levels provided the main avenue for social mobility in the modern sector of the economic and social systems. Even a lowly private in the military led a relatively privileged life compared with others of similar social backgrounds and formal education. In a different and far less violent, though comparable, context, Richard Joseph has termed the resulting social and political dynamics "prebendalism," i.e., the treatment of power as "a congeries of offices which can be competed for, appropriated and then administered for the benefit of individual occupants and their support groups."[18] Under Amin, violence was widely used by state agents for personal enrichment.

The Amin regime was distinguished by the fact that it was personalist and lacked any clear or consistent ideological purpose. In addition, Amin's personality inclined him to the ready use of violence. It is generally agreed that his coup was motivated by personal factors, particularly the fear that Obote was about to arrest and charge him with alleged involvement in the murder of former deputy army commander Brigadier Pierino Okoya in 1970. Even before the coup, there was strong evidence of Amin's devious and brutal character. In the early 1950s, as a soldier in the British colonial King's African Rifles, he was believed to have used excessive force against civilians during military operations in Kenya. Similar charges were made but not pressed when he participated in military operations in the northeastern Ugandan region of Karamoja shortly before the country's independence in 1962.[19] In the mid-1960s when he was threatened with dismissal from his position as deputy army commander on suspicion of financial malfeasance, he is reported to have threatened his commander, Brigadier Shaban Opolot, with physical violence.

Amin lacked any clear political vision or goals that might have enabled him to gain political legitimacy. Within the first year of his regime, he had squandered numerous political opportunities to transform himself into a legitimate ruler. Threats and violent repression became his principal tools of governance. His pronouncements and policies, such as the expulsion of the Ugandan-Asian community and the later expropriation of British assets, reflected anticolonial and African nationalist impulses. However, Amin pursued these policies inconsistently, and the country became even more dependent on foreign economic interests. The only goals that he pursued with vigor and consistency were the constant search for personal physical security through the ferocious repression of opposition, and hedonist self-indulgence. His public conduct was marked by alternate demonstrations of insecurity, bombast, and megalomania.[20] Amin's regime fits the category of what has been termed, perhaps infelicitously, a "sultanistic" regime:

> It is based on personal rulership, but loyalty to the ruler is motivated not by his embodying or articulating an ideology, nor by a unique personal mission, nor by any charismatic qualities, but by a mixture of fear and rewards to his collaborators. The ruler exercises his power without restraint, at his own discretion and

above all unencumbered by rules or by any commitment to an ideology or value system.[21]

Economic, political, religious, ethnic, and, to some extent, class
interests drew Amin's supporters together. These links, underpinned
by fear and guilt, provide one key to the relatively long tenure of the
regime. Other factors included the extreme political and social fragmentation of civil society, the continuation of the political divisions
of the 1960s, and the monopoly of arms that the regime was able to
maintain until the end. Sporadic acts of armed resistance, such as attacks on soldiers, never reached the level of threatening the regime's
existence. State terror was undoubtedly a major obstacle to the consolidation of armed resistance.

The social marginality of Amin and the majority of his military
supporters appears to have increased their determination to ruthlessly cling to power. They had very limited formal education and
were both intimidated by and contemptuous of well-educated people. Although civilian technocrats dominated his first cabinet, Amin
gradually came to replace them with supporters of limited education
or experience. Within the military, in the wake of the coup, a number of junior and noncommissioned officers of very low formal education who had helped carry out the operation were promoted to
senior ranks. This catapulted them into positions in which they had
sudden access to power and wealth. Some were appointed to the
cabinet, ambassadorial posts, and governorships of provinces. The
fact that they knew that under normal circumstances they would not
have risen to such heights must have intensified their determination
to cling to power by all means, including criminal violence.

The political and military base of the Amin regime can be analyzed in terms of a model of concentric circles characterized by ethnic and religious identity. Amin was born a member of the small
Kakwa nationality. Through religious adherence to Islam, he became culturally associated with the Nubi community. Muslim Kak-
was, Nubis, and Muslim soldiers from other West Nile ethnic
groups formed the core of the group that helped Amin overthrow
the Obote government. They constituted the inner circle of Amin's
leadership cohort. Other soldiers from West Nile and Muslims from
the rest of the country formed the outer circles, respectively. The
regime also attracted aliens into the army, in effect mercenaries,
from members of ethnic groups that straddle the country's borders

with Sudan and Congo (then Zaire). In the late 1970s, Palestinians
and other foreigners also worked in the regime's security apparatus.

The regime operated within a complex setting marked by three
separate but interrelated spheres of arbitrary state violence. The first
sphere was the formal bureaucratic set of institutions, including the
regular judicial system. These institutions were allowed to operate
routinely as long as they did not adversely affect the members or
clients of the regime. When they did, the regime and its agents
would subject them to intimidation and, sometimes, violence. So,
for example, after the chief justice of the High Court, Benedicto Kiwanuka, made a major ruling in 1972 that Amin took to be a political challenge, the jurist was abducted and killed without a trace.[22]
A number of magistrates at lower levels of the system also disappeared or received death threats from soldiers and other agents of
the regime.[23]

The second sphere was constituted by the pseudo-judicial system of military tribunals and the brutal penalties that they were entitled to impose. Although they were designed to give an impression
of legality, they were in fact kangaroo courts in which the norms of
due process were never observed. They were at the heart of the
"open face" of state terrorism. The third sphere was the broadest
and most complex of the three. Its foundations lay in the institutionalization of unregulated coercion as a primary mechanism of
political and social control. This was facilitated by the extension of
the formal functions of the military and civilian intelligence agencies
to include repression of criminal activities. The results included official vigilantism; legalization of arbitrary arrest and extrajudicial
executions; and the generalization of military and police indiscipline
and criminality for the purposes of private gain behind the cover of
state authority. This was the sphere of the "masked face of state terrorism" and the domain of the death squads that operated behind
the screen of open state terrorism.

The Open Face of State Terrorism

A set of decrees promulgated in 1971 and 1972 provided the legal
framework for the unfolding of rule through violence. Decree No. 7
provided for maximum detention of six months for persons arrested
in the course of or after the coup and those who had belonged to the

General Service Department. Decree No. 13 (1971) authorized the military to arrest civilians suspected of criminal activities or intent, while Decree No. 8 (1972) permitted security forces to shoot to kill anyone "suspected" of being an armed robber. This provision in effect gave any member of the military, police, and paramilitary forces license to kill.

A major pillar in the structure of legalized state terrorism involved the activities of military tribunals that operated alongside the regular criminal justice system. The decision to bypass the regular judicial system in the repression of undesirable activities was formalized by the Trial by Military Tribunals Decree of 1973 (Decree No. 12). It provided for the trial of civilians and soldiers by military tribunals for offenses that would normally be tried by regular courts. The decision to set up such tribunals was left to the discretion of the Defense Council. An attempt was made to give the tribunals a facade of legality by a provision for the appointment of a senior magistrate to serve as a legal adviser to the jurists, who were military officers untrained in the law. In fact, there is no evidence that the legal advisers played any meaningful role in the proceedings. According to Peter Allen, who was a High Court judge at the time:

> It was a thankless task; most of the punishments handed out by the tribunals were extremely harsh, ranging from death by firing squad to terms of imprisonment ranging from fifteen to twenty years even for the most minor of offenses. The rules of evidence and procedure and the right to legal representation were all usually disregarded; indeed it was dangerous for an advocate even to apply for permission to appear on behalf of an accused person, for the military members of the tribunals seemed to take it as an affront or insult to them and some advocates were beaten up and some were locked up.[24]

Under the provisions of the Military Tribunals Decree, convicted persons could appeal to the Defense Council for clemency. However, there is no evidence that this ever happened in any case. All those charged and sentenced to death for political offenses were swiftly executed.

A few examples illustrate the way the military tribunals functioned. In February 1973, a military tribunal sitting behind closed doors tried 12 men on charges of engaging in guerrilla activities.

They were sentenced to death and publicly executed by firing squads in their hometowns in different parts of the country. Yoweri Museveni, now president of Uganda, has since revealed that the majority of them were part of an underground network he was organizing to initiate internal military resistance to the regime.[25] Between August and September 1977, a military tribunal tried 16 people on charges of conspiracy to overthrow the regime. Fourteen of them were sentenced to death by firing squad, and the other two were sentenced to 15 years in prison. The defendants were not represented by counsel and were convicted on the basis of their alleged confessions. The transcript of the proceedings presents a skeletal case with very few particulars and few clear dates for the alleged criminal activities. This appears to have been a show trial, probably intended to intimidate the public, which was beginning to stir and seek ways to get rid of the regime.[26] Finally, the 1975 trial of a British citizen resident in the country on charges of treason, based on a passage in an unpublished manuscript in which he described Amin as a "village tyrant" and made other disparaging comments, highlighted the role of the military tribunals as an instrument of intimidation. He was sentenced to death by firing squad but was spared and left the country following high-level diplomatic intervention by the British government.

By the mid-1970s, a combination of factors, including the expulsion of the Ugandan-Asian commercial class in 1972, uncontrolled government expenditures, the flight of skilled labor, and general insecurity, had led to a rapid decline in economic conditions. Inflation and a shortage of goods made the lives of most people harder and harder. Typically, the regime attempted to deal with the problem by applying the same pseudo-legal mechanisms of deterrence that it had set up and used against political dissent and opposition. In 1975, Amin declared that "overcharging, hoarding or cheating in any way" by traders would be treated as treason and those found guilty of these charges would face the firing squad.[27] In the same year, he promulgated the Economic Crimes Tribunal Decree, which established tribunals in each of the ten provinces of the country to try those involved in such "crimes" as embezzlement, smuggling, hoarding, overcharging, "corruption," and the "unauthorized" disposal of foreign currency.[28] A number of "economic crimes" that came before the military tribunals demonstrated the lack of due process even when the charges were not directly political. One involved two junior state employees who were charged with ordering and illegally selling textiles intended for a government store. One of the accused requested to have a lawyer represent him and was supported by the legal adviser. However, the chairman of the tribunal summarily rejected the request. One of the defendants was acquitted but the other was sentenced to 12 years in prison.[29] In another case, a prison warder and a policeman were charged with "corruption" for having attempted to extort money from a shopkeeper. They were both sentenced to death by firing squad. In a third case, three men were accused of smuggling goods abroad. One was acquitted but the other two were sentenced to death by firing squad. Later, all death sentences for economic crimes were commuted to prison terms. This rare show of relative generosity was probably motivated by the fact that the people concerned had not been accused of political offenses and by Amin's constant desire to present himself at home and abroad as a reasonable person.

The military and economic tribunals and the draconian sentences they could impose were an important part of the mechanisms of intimidation and fear. They conducted show trials intended to dramatize the hazards of antiregime activities or other forms of deviance. However, only a few cases were brought before these bodies. The more direct task of repression through physical elimination was entrusted to the death squads.

The Masked Face of State Terrorism

Shortly after the coup, information concerning mass killings in military barracks began to filter out. These were initially regarded by many as the unfortunate consequences of a violent coup. However, within a few months, civilians began to disappear under suspicious circumstances. In at least one case, a judge was found dead and incinerated in his car. In spite of official denials, many Ugandans and foreign observers began to suspect the regime. Public skepticism was reinforced by threats that Amin and his associates kept making about the opposition and "guerrilla activities."

The contradictions involved in the unbridled use of violence were reflected in Amin's occasional statements ostensibly designed to discourage the excesses of the death squads. Thus in 1974, he "warned" the Military Police not to harass the public or to use force on fellow soldiers. However, he stated that he was "pleased with their work" in getting rid of *kondos* (armed robbers) and arresting soldiers who were overcharging in the businesses they had obtained from the expelled Asians.[30] In the same year, domestic and international expressions of concern about the killings and, possibly, alarm at the apparent loss of control over the use of violence, led Amin to set up a commission of inquiry into the killings and disappearances. Its members were a High Court judge, who chaired it; two senior police officers; a junior military officer; and a lawyer in private practice. The commission received evidence concerning 308 people who had disappeared and were presumed dead. In its report, the commission absolved Amin and his government of any responsibility for the fate of the victims but recommended the prosecution or investigation of over 20 soldiers and policemen suspected of involvement in the disappearance of up to 66 specific individuals. Two of the police officers, Ali Towelli and Kassim Obura, both of whom became notorious during their respective tenures as heads of the Public Safety Unit, were tried by a military tribunal and "acquitted." The majority of the others were not subjected to any legal proceedings.

As the criminal violence of the death squads continued, the regime's leaders occasionally reflected the frustrations stemming from the difficulty of reconciling rule through terror and the quest for political normalcy. In October 1977, General Mustafa Adrisi, Amin's vice president, condemned the actions of security forces that looted property and used roadblock checks to extort bribes and generally broke the law. In January 1978, Amin admitted that members of the security forces were engaged in smuggling, a fact that could not have been a secret to the general public.[31]

In contrast to open state terrorism, clandestine state terrorism was virtually uncontrolled, with the selection of victims apparently left to the discretion of the agents of the death squads. In this sphere, political and private motives were intertwined. As has happened in similar circumstances elsewhere, absolute power over the lives of others inevitably attracted the most ruthless and cynical personalities and led to the perpetuation of a realm of state-protected criminality.[32]

The State Research Bureau

The State Research Bureau, also known as the State Research Center, was at the heart of clandestine state terrorism. It was created in

1971, ostensibly as a state intelligence organization within the presidential office, to replace the General Service Department, which had been eliminated with the demise of the Obote regime. It was led and initially primarily staffed by army officers from ethnic groups that Amin trusted, especially Nubians and nationalities from West Nile, his home region. The unit is believed to have had a full-time membership of 1,500 to 3,000.[33] Core personnel were soldiers, supplemented by many times more part-time informers. Members of the Presidential Escort Unit dominated the organization.

The SRB played a double role as an intelligence organization and a repressive organ. For purposes of the first function, it received training in and outside the country. It also acted as a training organization for intelligence operatives who were infiltrated into state institutions and the general population at home. They were sent under cover to the country's diplomatic missions in order to keep an eye on the country's diplomats and monitor the political activities of exiled nationals. Their tools of trade reportedly included typical intelligence and covert operations gear such as phone-tapping equipment, mobile radios, and antibomb blankets. It has been estimated that by 1977, some 12,000 people had passed through its training courses.[34]

The SRB and the PSU were considered the most dangerous repressive units. According to some sources, there was a core organization, known as the "Striker Unit," which was specifically responsible for the execution of targeted victims.[35] Thus the unit as a whole or its core, the Striker Unit, was definitely a death squad.

Knowledge of this as well as many other details of the operations of the organization remain scanty. Nevertheless, available evidence indicates that the principal modus operandi of the killers was abduction, sometimes in broad daylight but usually more discreetly. The victims would be bundled into cars, usually in the trunk, never to be seen again. They were usually imprisoned, tortured, and murdered by shooting, beating, battering with iron bars, and starvation. Among the torture instruments reportedly used at SRB headquarters were weights and pincers used on male genitals, saws used to cut off limbs, and blowtorches. There was also a cold room and a heated pool used for similar sinister activities.[36]

What is clear is that possession of an SRB card endowed its owner with absolute power of life and death over the rest of the population. The individual agent "used this power to settle private

scores and to silence, or eliminate, rivals in personal relations, business, or government."[37] Employees and associates of the organization enjoyed not only the direct benefits of salaries, houses, and
fancy cars that came with the job. They also in effect acquired a license to extort, imprison, and murder people outside the narrow
privileged circles of clients of the regime. A former minister in the
regime who later fled wrote: "The State Research staff are on the official payroll, but their salaries are negligible compared to the loot
they get from their jobs. They steal money from their victims; they
are paid lavish funds by Amin as a reward for gathering information; and they are given fantastic sums to spend when they go overseas. . . . They lead a life that no other Ugandan can now afford."[38]
In many cases the State Research Bureau seized individuals and incarcerated them for the purpose of extortion. Like the other death
squad units, the SRB had access to bank accounts. They could find
out the state of anyone's account, and that could be good enough
reason to take action against him.[39]

The Public Safety Unit

One of the principal justifications given by the Amin faction for taking power was the wave of armed robbery that had created a sense
of general insecurity in the country, particularly in Kampala, the
capital, toward the end of the Obote regime. The Public Safety Unit
was set up immediately after the coup as a special anticrime unit
within the regular police force to deal with this problem. Its headquarters were in Naguru, a suburb of Kampala. It consisted of
about 1,000 uniformed and plainclothes detective officers with
powers to arrest and detain criminal suspects. Through the PSU,
Amin adopted the kind of sledgehammer approach to fighting
armed robbery that he had used in dealing with the problems of
regime consolidation and survival immediately after the coup. The
PSU and other security agencies were permitted to use lethal force
without any obligation to follow the normal police and judicial procedures. A dramatic example of this was the public execution of
three alleged robbers before a crowd of thousands in a village outside the capital on July 3, 1972.[40] This impunity allowed the PSU to
function as a death squad.

Like other death squads described in this volume, the PSU,
though officially part of the regular police, became autonomous in

practice shortly after its establishment. It became especially notorious under the leadership of Ali Towelli. Peter Allen described the unit in the following terms:

> The PSU at first did some very useful work . . . but after Towelli had taken over, the personnel were soon replaced and he turned the unit into an organization for intimidation, terror and torture; it eventually became recognized as providing some of Amin's special murder squads. Those people lucky enough to be released or to escape from the hands of the PSU had many horrifying tales to tell of what went on there and of the many people who were murdered and whose unidentified bodies were openly taken to the city mortuary in PSU vehicles and just dumped there. No inquiries were made into those deaths because the rest of the police force feared the PSU as much as did the ordinary members of the public. PSU personnel openly boasted that they were above the law.[41]

At PSU headquarters, a former armory served as a prison. Two tiny cells held 50 captives. Former inmates estimated that on average only three of every ten people incarcerated there survived.[42] One of the PSU's most notorious acts involved Kassim Obura, its director, who shot and killed a businessman following a dramatic set of events that were played out in the streets of Kampala. The victim, who was the business partner of an army officer, had been framed by the latter with the charge of conspiracy to overthrow the regime while on a business trip abroad. Later, the charge was changed to theft from the business. He was arrested upon his return to Uganda and taken to PSU headquarters, where Obura and another senior commander demanded a large sum of money in return for his release. On payment of money by his family, the businessman was released, but he was rearrested after one week. He was hauled before a regular court, which dismissed the case for lack of merit. Fully aware of the threat he faced from the extortionists, he vainly sought protection from the court in the form of incarceration in a state prison. Subsequently, he fled from the court in a futile search for sanctuary. He was chased in the city streets and captured by policemen firing guns. He was transported to PSU headquarters, where he was shot dead by Obura in full view of a number of people, including the victim's lawyer. After the downfall of the Amin regime, Obura was captured, tried for the murder, and hanged.[43]

The Military Police

Like the Public Safety Unit, the Military Police was part of a preexisting state institution; and like its cousin, the PSU, it, too, operated as a death squad. The MP was set up in 1967 under the command of two of Amin's close associates, one of them Lieutenant Mustafa Adrisi, the future vice president.[44] Its official function was to deal with and eliminate indiscipline and lawlessness in the army, but, in keeping with the brutal atmosphere that characterized the Amin dictatorship, it went beyond this mandate both in its choice of victims and in the means it used to deal with them.

This death squad played a central role in the emergence and survival of the Amin regime. From the beginning, the majority of its members were soldiers with origins in the northwestern West Nile region of the country and Nubis. As a person whose ethnic origins were in this region, Amin enjoyed especially close relations with these officers and men. By 1971, they were regarded as his closest supporters in the conflict with Obote that was to culminate in the coup. In the immediate aftermath of the coup, the unit's principal occupation was the physical elimination of soldiers and other security officers from the defunct regime, but soon its role was expanded by the Military Police (Powers of Arrest) Decree No. 19 of 1971, which authorized it to arrest civilians. Throughout the life of the regime, the MP was a much-feared instrument of terror. Its headquarters in the Makindye suburb of Kampala was notorious for its underground torture rooms. Abduction and transfer to the MP usually meant certain death. Once again, hard figures or even reliable estimates for the number of people it killed are hard to come by.

The Victims

Ethnic, religious, and regional identities partially influenced the targets of political repression. The Obote regime had been primarily dependent on the support of the military, which was predominantly recruited from the northern region of the country. However, the region was not ethnically homogeneous. The biggest proportion of the army came from the north-central areas of Acholi and Lango. Obote was ethnically Langi, and the Acholi, who provided the single largest ethnic contingent, are culturally very close to the Langi. A smaller proportion came from the northwestern area of West Nile, which was the home of the Kakwa nationality with which Amin was culturally associated.[45]

The first victims of the regime were the hundreds, possibly thousands, of soldiers, policemen, and other members of the security forces who were killed resisting the coup or massacred in and outside military barracks subsequently on suspicion of opposition to the regime. They included 13 top military commanders and officers and a number of senior police officers under the previous regime. A disproportionate number, but not all, belonged to the Acholi and Langi ethnic groups, which had formed the core of Obote's support base in the army and police.[46] Two American citizens, a journalist and a university professor, who entered one of the military barracks seeking to confirm reports of these massacres were simply added to the list of victims. They disappeared, but their bodies were later found buried in the bush far from the barracks.

At the end of 1971, close to 600 military, police, and civilian intelligence operatives of the previous regime were massacred over a number of days in a makeshift barracks near the country's border with Tanzania. A year later, following an abortive invasion by armed exiles, the pogroms were extended to the civilian sector and became more indiscriminate in terms of the political and ethnic identities of the victims. Prominent civilian victims included the country's chief justice, who was abducted from the court chambers and disappeared; two successive presidents of the Industrial Court; Archbishop Janani Luwum, the head of the Uganda Anglican (Protestant) Church; two members of Amin's cabinet; a newspaper editor who was also a Catholic priest; former ministers and members of the National Assembly during the previous regime; and the head of the country's only university at the time. Amin's estranged former wife also met a violent death under mysterious circumstances. Contrary to the general pattern in other parts of the world, the repressive organs also struck down members of the regime who fell out of favor. Among erstwhile close associates of Amin who were liquidated were Brigadier Smarts Guweddeko, a former commander of the air force; Colonel Michael Ondoga, a former foreign minister; and two former army chiefs, Staff Brigadier Charles Arube (murdered after apparently leading an abortive coup) and Colonel Valentine Ochima.

The overwhelming majority of those killed were ordinary people and were drawn from all walks of life. Many were killed simply because members of the SRB, the PSU, or the MP sought to dispossess them. Others were victims of private vendettas and quarrels with people who could bribe or falsely denounce them to the agents of these institutions. The only common characteristic of the victims was political and social vulnerability. Generally, the most vulnerable persons were those who (a) had been members of the UPC, the ruling party under the previous regime, especially if they had held leadership positions; (b) members of the Acholi and Langi ethnic groups, presumed by Amin to be the strongest supporters of the UPC, especially if they had been connected to military and police forces; and (c) former members of the intelligence services of the old regime. Conversely, one was safe, if not entirely immune, if one was a member of the repressive organs, including the army, and not suspected of disloyalty; a Muslim Kakwa or Nubian; or a client of one of the "safe" groups.

State Terrorism and the Demise of the Regime

State terrorism is a blunt instrument that creates intractable problems for regimes that use it. One of the most important is the difficulty of controlling the scope of violence. The terrorist network can snare supporters and clients as readily as "enemies" of the regime. In addition, untrammeled violence tends to create conditions of anarchy, which threaten the political and economic bases of the regime. One of the common consequences is the flight of citizens, which deprives the country of skilled human resources. On the other hand, the coercive instruments must be given a substantial amount of freedom of action in order to keep actual and potential opponents off balance.

From beginning to end, the Amin regime was shaken by internal tensions that were reflected in the physical elimination or flight into exile of his former close associates. As the circle of supporters narrowed with time, fewer and fewer high-ranking members of the regime felt safe. By the late 1970s, Amin's political-military base had narrowed to such an extent that foreigners, particularly Libyans and Palestinians, were reportedly playing crucial roles as bodyguards and security operatives. It appears that by 1978, these tensions had reached a new height in the wake of the dramatic murder of Archbishop Luwum and the two former ministers the previous year. Mutinies in the army led to fighting in military barracks near the country's southern border with Tanzania. Amin then apparently sought to divert attention and possibly restore military discipline by claiming that Tanzanian forces had attacked across the border. Ugandan military units occupied an undefended portion of Tanzanian territory and wreaked havoc, killing, raping, and looting. This led to a massive Tanzanian counteroffensive that threw out the Ugandan units, crossed the border, and eventually drove Amin and his top associates into exile in early 1979.[47] In effect, Amin's lack of support and the internal contradictions of his regime led directly to his fall. While state terror served to prop up the regime initially, it ultimately prevented it from achieving the sort of legitimacy that would have allowed it to last. Amin's regime choked to death on its own violence.

Summary and Conclusions

Between 1971 and 1979, life for many Ugandans was "poor, nasty, brutish, and short." Contrary to the Hobbesian thesis, however, this was not because there was no Leviathan. The problem was that the Leviathan, in the form of Idi Amin and his associates, was dedicated to the satisfaction of its passions rather than the protection of civil society.

As in other postcolonial African societies that have struggled to create a stable economic, political, and social order, the roots of the problem lay primarily in the legacy of European imperialism. It undermined the preexisting political and social systems, amalgamated them into larger units, and left before new forms of social and political legitimacy had congealed. Under these circumstances, violence quickly became the primary, if not sole, basis of political power. In some of the most fragmented African states, the most ruthless individuals and groups managed to rise to the top and stay there as long as they could sustain regimes of terror.[48]

Amin often denied responsibility for the deaths that occurred during his regime. He was certainly not directly responsible for all of them. However, it is difficult to believe that he was not responsible for the slaying of most of the prominent victims. Some, like the Anglican archbishop and the two cabinet ministers, were killed shortly after they had been publicly accused of conspiracy to over-throw the regime at a mass rally of soldiers addressed by Amin him-self. Testimony presented to the 1986 Commission of Inquiry that investigated human rights violations pointed to Amin's direct in-volvement in the death of the archbishop as well as the chief jus-tice.[49] The State Research Bureau, the Public Safety Unit, and the Military Police all operated under Amin's ultimate authority. He ap-pointed and fired their heads. There is no evidence to suggest that he ever lost control over their leaders, who were themselves vulner-able to sudden physical elimination. More fundamentally, Amin used and condoned both legalized and clandestine forms of terror and was thus ultimately morally and legally responsible for all the killings by the death squads.

To date, the crimes of the Amin regime have not been effectively investigated and punished. The 1986 Commission of Inquiry into human rights violations heard from many victims and a few former leading officials of the regime, including the Mustafa Adrisi and Major Ozi, the founder of the State Research Bureau. All of them denied personal responsibility for the killings. Only two major fig-ures in the regime have been tried and convicted for murder: Kassim Obura, the notorious former head of the Public Safety Unit, and Colonel Abdalla Nasur, a reputedly sadistic former provincial gov-ernor. They were both convicted of murder and sentenced to death. Obura was subsequently hanged, and Nasur remains in prison. Amin continues to live in comfort in Saudi Arabia. Some of his close associates are either dead or in exile, but some have returned to the country. One of them, Moses Ali, has held various ministerial posi-tions under the current administration of President Museveni.

The political turbulence and complexity of the alliances formed during the regimes that succeeded Amin is one of the reasons why there has been no serious effort to investigate and punish those who were responsible for the carnage. There were four separate govern-ments between 1979, when Amin fled, and 1986, when the National Resistance Movement (NRM) took power following a long guerrilla insurgency. These administrations were primarily preoccupied with political infighting or struggling against the challenge of continued insurgency. The NRM, too, has been preoccupied with fighting per-sistent insurgency in various parts of the country as well as the ur-gent tasks of rehabilitation of the country's economic and social infrastructure and political reform.

Apart from economic and political preoccupations, other factors appear to have induced the current government to tolerate the continued impunity of those who are strongly suspected of having been involved in the atrocities of the Amin regime. Some of them cooperated with the NRM during the days of its guerrillas struggle. Others appear to enjoy a certain degree of influence in their home districts that have also been the scene of sporadic insurgency. As in some other parts of the world which have suffered human rights atrocities, the imperatives of national reconciliation and political stability might well have trumped the need to punish the guilty—at least for now. In the context of what is still a fragile political situation, the NRM government might have given priority to reconciliation and the preservation of peaceful conditions, but it has never issued a definitive statement on the problem of past human rights violations and the dilemma of balancing the imperatives of political stability with the need to punish those implicated in the brutal crimes of earlier regimes.

The phenomenon of death squads in Uganda was extraordinarily complex. They operated in a context of generalized state violence perpetrated by the army, the police, and the intelligence agencies. The leadership of the autocratic regime exercised loose control over the activities of these institutions. This allowed them to add private criminal activities, such as robbery and extortion, to their law-and-order functions. By using terror as an instrument of government, Amin reared a set of deadly monsters that he could not fully control. As a result, over a period of eight years, thousands of people lost their lives. Ultimately, the catastrophe of the Amin regime stemmed from the failure of the country's political elites to create viable, legitimate political institutions as well as the tyrant's vicious and amoral character. This case illustrates what has become clear in recent years: that failed states almost invariably create humanitarian and human rights disasters.

Notes

1. Henry Kyemba, *A State of Blood* (New York: Paddington Press, 1977); David Gwyn [pseud.], *Idi Amin: Death-Light of Africa* (Boston: Little, Brown, 1977); George Ivan Smith, *Ghosts of Kampala* (New York: St. Martin's Press, 1980); A.B.K. Kasozi, *The Origins of*

Social Violence in Uganda (Montreal: McGill–Queens University Press, 1994), 104–27.

2. Amnesty International, *Political Killings by Governments* (London: Amnesty International Publications, 1983), 44; Jan J. Jorgensen, *Uganda: A Modern History* (New York: St. Martin's Press, 1981), 315. A number of factors suggest the greater plausibility of the lower estimates. The Amin regime was in power for almost exactly eight years. An estimate of 500,000 victims would work out to an average toll of around 63,000 annually or 5,000 per month. In the first place, this was not case of genocide. Except for certain limited contexts and periods, no particular group was consistently targeted for physical elimination; victims came from all sectors of the population. Also, as Jorgensen has pointed out, the large number of killings occurred in four waves over the life of the regime. The first was during the first six months, when an estimated 1,500 soldiers were killed because of their ethnic and other presumed political associations with the previous regime. The other three waves occurred in 1972–73, 1974, and 1978. The rest of the killings were carried out intermittently by the various military and paramilitary organizations.

3. See, for example, Beth S. Lyons, "Between Nuremberg and Amnesia: The Truth and Reconciliation Commission in South Africa," *Monthly Review* 49, no. 4 (September 1997): 5–22; "The Science of Apartheid," *Harper's*, Sept. 1998, 19–21; Horacio Verbitsky, *The Flight: Confessions of an Argentine Dirty Warrior* (New York: New Press, 1996).

4. Republic of Uganda, *The Report of the Commission of Inquiry into Violations of Human Rights* (n.p., 1994).

5. Miles D. Wolpin, "State Terrorism and Death Squads in the New World Order," *Peace Research Reviews* 12, no. 3 (July 1992).

6. Raymond D. Duvall and Michael Stohl, "Governance by Terror," in Michael Stohl, ed., *The Politics of Terrorism*, 3rd ed. (New York: Marcel Dekker, 1988), 231–71.

7. Martha K. Huggins, ed., *Vigilantism and the State in Modern Latin America: Essays on Extralegal Violence* (New York: Praeger, 1991); Catholic Institute for International Relations, *State of Terror: Death Squads or Development?* (London: Catholic Institute for International Relations, 1989); Human Rights Watch, *Colombia's Killer Networks* (New York: Americas Human Rights Watch Arms Project, 1996); Martin Van Bruinessen, "Turkey's Death Squads," *Middle East Report* 26, no. 2 (April-June 1996): 20–23.

8. Carlos Figueroa Ibarra, "Guatemala: The Recourse of Fear," in Huggins, 74.

9. William Stanley, *The Protection Racket State: Elite Politics, Military Extortion, and Civil War in El Salvador* (Philadelphia: Temple University Press, 1996).

10. Kenneth Ingham, *The Making of Modern Uganda* (London: George Allen & Unwin, 1958); T.V. Sathyamurty, *The Political Development of Uganda: 1900–1986* (Aldershot, England: Gower, 1986).

11. See Anne Phillips, *The Enigma of Colonialism: British Policy in West Africa* (London: James Currey and Indiana University Press, 1989); Mahmood Mamdani, *Citizen and Subject* (Princeton, N.J.: Princeton University Press, 1996).

12. The largest of the precolonial polities.

13. John Cartwright, *Political Leadership in Africa* (London: Croom Helm, 1983), 244–45. The Ugandan-Asian community numbered close to 100,000 descendants of people who had migrated from the Indian subcontinent at the beginning of British colonial rule in East Africa at the end of the nineteenth century. They expanded and modernized the country's commercial networks and came to dominate them. At the time of their expulsion, some had become Ugandan citizens but many others held British or other foreign citizenships.

14. D. A. Low, "The Dislocated Polity," in H. B. Hansen and M. Twaddle, eds., *Uganda Now* (London: James Curry, 1988), 45–47.

15. Tony Avirgan and Martha Honey, *War in Uganda* (Dar es Salaam: Tanzania Publishing House, 1982), 28–52.

16. *Africa Contemporary Record, 1973–74*, Colin Legum, ed. (London: Rex Collings, 1974), B299.

17. *Africa Contemporary Record, 1973–74*, B299.

18. Richard A. Joseph, *Democracy and Prebendal Politics in Nigeria: The Rise and Fall of the Second Republic* (Cambridge: Cambridge University Press, 1987), 63.

19. Samuel Decalo, *Psychoses of Power: African Personal Dictatorships* (Boulder, Colo.: Westview Press, 1989), 96.

20. Aidan Southall, "Social Disorganization in Uganda: Before, During and After Amin," *Journal of Modern African Studies* 18, no. 4 (Dec. 1980): 627; Judith Listowel, *Amin* (Dublin: IUP Books, 1973), 175–88.

21. H.E. Chahabi and Juan J. Linz, eds., *Sultanistic Regimes* (Baltimore: Johns Hopkins University Press, 1998), 7. The term is drawn from what Edward Said has called "orientalist" discourse. See Edward W. Said, *Orientalism* (New York: Vintage Books, 1979).

22. Grace Ibingira, *African Upheavals Since Independence* (Boulder, Colo.: Westview Press, 1980), 271. Kiwanuka was also a major political figure. He had been the leader of the Democratic Party and the country's first prime minister just before the attainment of

independence. He was one of the political prisoners whom Amin released following the coup and later appointed the first African chief justice.

23. Republic of Uganda, 152–53.
24. Peter J. Allen, *Days of Judgment* (London: William Kimber, 1987), 129.
25. See Yoweri Museveni, *Sowing the Mustard Seed* (London: Macmillan, 1997), 84–85.
26. See the report of the transcripts and the commentary in Republic of Uganda, 157–201.
27. *Africa Research Bulletin,* Political, Social and Cultural Series 12, no. 1 (1975): 3496.
28. *Africa Research Bulletin,* Economic and Social Series 12, no. 3 (1975): 3460.
29. Republic of Uganda, 208.
30. *Africa Contemporary Record, 1974–75,* ed. Colin Legum (London: Rex Collings, 1975), B309.
31. *Africa Contemporary Record, 1977–78,* ed. Colin Legum et al. (New York: Africana Publishing Company, 1979), B441.
32. R. J. Rummel, *Death by Government* (New Brunswick, N.J.: Transaction Publishers, 1994).
33. Avirgan and Honey, 7–8; Republic of Uganda, 601.
34. Avirgan and Honey; Mahmood Mamdani, *Imperialism and Fascism in Uganda* (Trenton, N.J.: Africa World Press, 1984), 44; Republic of Uganda, 273; Kyemba, 112.
35. Gwyn, 103.
36. Republic of Uganda, 404–5.
37. Mamdani, *Imperialism and Fascism in Uganda,* 44.
38. Kyemba, 115.
39. Smith, 126.
40. *Africa Research Bulletin,* Political, Social and Cultural Series 9 (1972): 2543.
41. Allen, 181.
42. *Africa Contemporary Record, 1976–77* (London: Rex Collings, 1977), B374.
43. Republic of Uganda, 385–88.
44. Amii Omara-Otunnu, *Politics and the Military in Uganda* (New York: St. Martin's Press, 1987), 79.
45. Holger B. Hansen, *Ethnicity and Military Rule in Uganda* (Uppsala, Sweden: Scandinavian Institute of African Studies, 1977), 86–93.
46. David Martin, *General Amin* (London: Faber & Faber, 1974), 130–57.
47. Avirgan and Honey, 53–70.

48. See, for instance, Randall Fegley, *Equatorial Guinea: An African Tragedy* (New York: Peter Lang, 1989); Brian Titley, *Dark Age: The Political Odyssey of Emperor Bokassa* (Montreal: McGill–Queen's University Press, 1997).

49. Republic of Uganda, 553–55.

CHAPTER 7

From Petrus to Ninja: Death Squads in Indonesia

Robert Cribb

SINCE THE DECLARATION OF INDEPENDENCE IN 1945, Indonesia has had much experience of political violence. In addition to the war of independence, fought against the Dutch from 1945 to 1949, Indonesia has experienced civil wars, secessionist rebellions, pogroms, a bloody annexationist war, and state repression in various forms. A fundamentalist Muslim movement, Darul Islam, fought the Indonesian Republic in many regions from 1948 until the early 1960s; a conservative anticommunist rebellion in the late 1950s used several of the outer islands of the archipelago as a base for attempting to force a new government on Jakarta. Armed secessionist movements have been active in the provinces of Maluku, Aceh, and Irian Jaya (West New Guinea), while in 1965–66 anticommunist forces launched a massacre of leftists in which perhaps half a million people died. In 1975, moreover, Indonesia occupied the former Portuguese colony of East Timor and suppressed the local nationalist movement in a series of brutal campaigns. No reliable figures exist on the death toll from this occupation, but the figure for the fifteen years 1975–90 seems likely to exceed 60,000, or 10 percent of the Timorese population. In addition, Indonesian history has been marked by a long list of violent incidents and acts, some by the state, some by opponents of the state, and some in the service of local interests unconnected with the state, in which hundreds of people have died.

In this catalog of human woe, death squads resembling those in other parts of the world have intruded only occasionally. In the early 1980s, military death squads launched a campaign of extermination against "known" criminals in Indonesian cities. The military identity of the killers was not immediately clear, and Indonesians dubbed the events *petrus* (*penembakan misterius,* mysterious shootings).[1] These killings had subsided by the mid-1980s, and there were no further cases of death squad activity until the tangled events surrounding the fall of Suharto in 1998, when black-clothed killers, dubbed ninja from their resemblance in appearance to the clandestine warriors of Japan, launched campaigns of kidnapping and assassination against traditional Islamic leaders in the Japanese countryside. Both the curious absence of death squads from Indonesian history in general and these two specific cases require explanation.[2]

As the introduction to this book has made clear, death squads are primarily a surreptitious extension of the state. They exist when the legal framework (and perhaps international and public opinion) prevents a state from pursuing its enemies effectively, or when elements in society feel that the state is ineffective in defending itself or its people. For long periods of Indonesian history, however, the legal and practical constraints on state power have been so weak that authorities have been able to repress opposition groups openly and without resorting to clandestine means. Historically, moreover, the Indonesian military has been reluctant to countenance any kind of cultivation of serious armed force outside its own control. Although there is a long and only partly known history of cooperation between the authorities and criminal underworld groups, only in the special circumstances of 1965–66 has the military tolerated the emergence of semi-independent armed groups with the potential to pursue their own political agendas.

The historical weakness of legal constraints on Indonesian governments derives partly from the circumstances under which the Indonesian state emerged. Indonesia's first constitution was drafted during the closing weeks of Japan's occupation of the former Dutch colony during the World War II. Although Japanese supervision of the drafting process seems to have been weak, the constitution was initially intended for an Indonesian puppet state within Japan's Greater East Asia Co-Prosperity Sphere. Given the pressure of wartime and Imperial Japan's own statist traditions, it is not surprising that the resulting draft gave Indonesians few protections against state power. The constitutions of 1949 and 1950 gave better protection to democratic rights, but they were politically compromised by the fact that they were drafted under Dutch pressure, and in 1959 President Sukarno[3] unilaterally restored the 1945 constitution, which was not only retained under President Suharto's New Order from 1966 but was exalted as a national icon.

Indonesia's administrative-legal culture after independence, moreover, was remarkably unregulated. Indonesia's parliament passed relatively few laws, and those laws that were passed tended to be brief and general. Much was left to administrative regulation, and regulations in turn left much to the discretion of the authorities. The extent to which civil law constrained the military in its dealings with civilians was left vague. The court system was not separate from the civil bureaucracy, so that judges and prosecutors could not easily assert judicial independence of state power. There were thus few effective avenues for seeking recourse or redress against the actions of the state or its agents. Under Suharto's New Order, the authorities had available to them an extensive repertoire of legal means to control and harass any opposition groups that might emerge. Laws against subversion, the sowing of hatred, and insulting the head of state were couched in such general terms that almost any expression of political opinion was actionable. In the course of the New Order, dozens of intimidatory political trials were used to imprison dissidents for periods of five years or longer. In addition, the authorities could use such measures as prohibition on government employment, expulsion from educational institutions, and the cancellation of business licenses to add to the pressure on dissidents. Execution was rarely used within the legal system; rather, the capacity to ruin the lives and careers of political opponents meant that death squads were an unnecessary element in the political order.[4]

Historically, moreover, the Indonesian army was reluctant to tolerate any breach of its assumed monopoly of armed force and was therefore unwilling to allow the establishment of paramilitary forces of a kind that could develop into death squads. During the war of independence against the Dutch, the army was initially overshadowed by independent armed militia groups known as *lasykar*. In the early days of the revolution, the *lasykar* often fought more effectively and with a more dynamic spirit than the fledgling army, but their exuberance and indiscipline made them a hindrance to the plans of the army high command for a coordinated military struggle. To control the *lasykar*, the military adopted a strategy of both repression and co-optation, but even by the time the Dutch conceded Indonesian independence in late 1949 not all *lasykar* groups had been tamed.[5]

The civil wars and regionally based rebellions of the 1950s and early 1960s reinforced this military aversion to tolerating any independent source of armed force in the country. In 1965, therefore, when President Sukarno, backed by the Indonesian Communist Party, proposed the creation of an armed "Fifth Force" of workers and peasants to fight Sukarno's Confrontation with Malaysia, the military was deeply uneasy.[6] The proposal was never carried out, but its presence on the political agenda was an important element in the escalating crisis that culminated in the overthrow of Sukarno and the massacre of communists in 1965–66. Those massacres were a complex event, partly the result of intense political polarization, partly a deliberate initiative of conservative sections of the military led by General Suharto. It is a measure of the military's intense hatred of the left that on this occasion army units recruited and trained civilian vigilante groups, especially from the Muslim youth organization Ansor. These vigilantes, operating with military protection and encouragement, were responsible for a large part of the killings in some areas. This use of vigilantes seems especially to have been a device both to make use of local knowledge and to implicate broader sections of society in the killings. In this way the army tried to diminish the possibility that it might be held to account—at least politically if not judicially—for the massacres. In promoting the mass killings, the Indonesian military exploited fears and antagonisms that had developed deep roots during Indonesia's first 20 years of independence. Controversy over issues such as landownership and the place of Islam in the state had led to powerful divisions in Indonesian society, and there is no doubt that there would have been extensive violence in the countryside without military involvement. Nonetheless, the fact that the vigilante gangs were disarmed and dispersed by the military almost without demur once their work of violence had been completed is a powerful indication of the control that the military kept over the vigilantes.[7]

Even though the Indonesian military refused to tolerate the existence of serious paramilitary forces, General (later President) Suharto's New Order government made some political use of criminal gangs, especially at election times. Whereas the legal order was constructed so that there was no real constraint on state power, the political order of the Suharto era was devised so as to present an illusion of democratic procedure while being utterly undemocratic in reality. Thus, the New Order could point to its regular electoral cycle, a choice of contestants, secret balloting, and a high level of public participation, but the reality was that restrictions on recruitment, candidate selection, and campaigning by the two permitted nongovernment parties, together with a ban on participation by other groups, tight government control over parliamentary procedure, and the capacity of the parties to "recall" troublesome representatives, meant that election results were entirely without meaning for the government of the country.[8]

A part of the government's panoply of control and manipulation lay in the management of the five-to-six-week campaign period that preceded each general election. During this brief period, once every five years, some of the normal restrictions on political activity were lifted, and parties could rally and march to present themselves to the electoral public. Ostensibly a sign of democratic openness, the campaign periods were invariably marred by violence, including arson and looting. One of the government's recurrent slogans, "Together we make a success of the general election," reflects the way in which the authorities tried to portray each election as a time of potential crisis, a moment at which forces of social disorder threatened to well up and engulf society. There was a clear subtext: support the government party (Golkar), and all will be well.

The violence that emerged during election campaigns had many sources, but there have been many indications during successive campaigns that agents provocateurs working on behalf of the authorities were often responsible. These agents seem generally to have been drawn from the criminal underworld. Close connections between the authorities and criminal gangs in Indonesia are nothing new. Such liaisons were common during the colonial period,[9] and indeed many of the revolutionary-era *lasykar* had criminal roots despite their strong political orientation.[10] It is therefore not surprising that the authorities made use of criminals at election time, both to intimidate opponents and to sow alarm from which the government could hope to reap benefits.[11]

The criminals engaged in these activities were essentially small-to-medium-time hoods.[12] They were more practiced in menaces than in organization, and their influence seldom extended beyond a single town or region. Protection rackets, extortion, debt collection, burglary, pickpocketing, armed robbery, and occasional contract killings were the stuff of their normal existence. Many Indonesians, both in urban and rural areas, believed them to be powerful in magical arts that could give invulnerability, make them invisible, or confound the affairs of their enemies. Although they also engaged in supplying and controlling labor and in managing prostitution, the scale of their operations never reached that of Mafia-style organized crime. The more extensive rackets that Indonesian society had to offer were in the hands of establishment figures with a bent for criminal entrepreneurship—mainly military and Chinese—rather than under the control of small-time gangsters made good.

Of course, small-scale criminal gangs often worked for more powerful and respectable patrons as hit men and enforcers—as during the elections—but their ties with such patrons were inherently unstable. Most patrons, of course, kept links with more than one criminal band in order to avoid dependence on a single set of toughs, while the gangsters themselves were always on the lookout for lucrative opportunities with old or new patrons. Indonesia's criminal underworld, therefore, was in more or less constant flux, with gangs coalescing around effective leaders and moving from one patron to another, only to disperse and disappear as new leaders and opportunities emerged.

In the early 1980s, Indonesia experienced a serious crime wave. The term "serious crime wave," of course, is relative. In most modern societies people are willing to accept a certain level of criminal activity—in terms of frequency, kind, and scale—as part of the normal hazards of daily life. If these undefined and flexible limits are exceeded, a kind of social panic can arise. The Indonesian crime wave of the early 1980s was dominated by armed robbery, particularly on public transport. The crime that most clearly seemed to express the declining standards of public safety was the hijacking of overnight intercity buses, which were a key element in the movement of people about the country. In a typical instance, a group of robbers would board the bus as ordinary passengers but would leave their seats late at night and would force the driver at knifepoint to follow some deserted side road to a place where other gang members would be waiting to rob the passengers of their valuables. Local public transport in the larger cities was also vulnerable, and gangs of thieves could be seen in public buses brazenly making their way among the passengers, hands probing from pocket to pocket and bag to bag while the victims sat or stood in apparently helpless fear.[13]

Fear was paramount because of a perception that the robbers were desperate men who would meet any resistance with sadistic violence. Stories abounded of gratuitous cruelty, of women raped during a bus hijacking, of a young girl slashed because she refused to surrender a gold chain, of a child's finger cut off so that the robbers could take a gold ring.[14] There was a widespread perception at the time that such cruelty was unprecedented, but in fact fearsomeness is an ancient part of the stock-in-trade of criminals in the Indonesian archipelago. The pirates and bandit princes of precolonial times, the rural brigands of the colonial era, and the politicized gangsters of the revolutionary-era *lasykar* all sought to inspire a paralyzing terror among their enemies and victims. Terror, rather than cold, calculated murder, was the prime modus operandi of Indonesia's men of violence.[15]

The reasons for this crime wave are probably complex, but one element seems to have been that gangs that had grown in response to the employment opportunities offered especially by the government during the election campaign of 1982 were now short of work and income. As had happened after the elections of 1972 and 1977, many of them turned to regular crime to maintain their organizations and standing. The situation was made worse than in 1972 and 1977 by a downturn in the price of oil, which in turn reduced the availability of funds for construction projects, which both provide employment for men who might otherwise drift into criminal gangs and provide existing gangs with opportunities for extortion and labor management.[16]

Thoroughly undemocratic though it was, the New Order regime in Indonesia was never totally insulated from public opinion. The country's economic performance and the government's ability to deliver a steadily improving standard of living to most of its subjects was an important element in its legitimacy.[17] Throughout the thirty-two years of the New Order, Suharto enjoyed the enormous political advantage of being able to compare his performance with the economic misery Indonesia had suffered in the last years of the Sukarno era, when Indonesia was one of the poorest countries in the world. The crime wave of the 1980s undermined this legitimacy in two ways. First, it reinforced a feeling of insecurity that was inimical to confidence in the durability of the New Order's achievements.

There was a common feeling among the emerging middle class and those in general who benefited economically from the New Order without being in any way part of the central core that made enormous profits that the wheel of fortune that had carried them upward for a time would inevitably carry them down.[18] A part of the New Order's implicit promise to the Indonesian people was that repression and control were a reasonable price to pay for accelerated economic development and modernization. If development and prosperity, however, were fragile and temporary, then people were likely to find that price too high. And for those who already believed that the price was too high, complaints about criminality were an impeccably acceptable peg on which to hang veiled criticism of the regime. For the New Order, therefore, it was politically important not to permit the crime wave of the early 1980s to continue unchecked.

Widespread violence was also a symbolic rebuke to the New Order, because there was a general perception that crime was a result of poverty rather than, say, opportunity. The fearsomeness of criminals rested partly on the perception that they were social failures, outcasts from normal society who had nothing to lose. This perception ran counter to the awareness that some criminals at least made a rather good living from their activities, but it worked to undermine the Suharto government's claims to be delivering prosperity to all Indonesians. The New Order in fact was notoriously careless of the fate of victims of development: those who had lost land or homes to logging and mining activity or the construction of freeways, factories, and golf courses, who lost their livelihoods through changes in economic policy or regulation, or who lost life or health as a result of pollution or accident. At least some Indonesians, however, could tolerate such callousness as a price of achieving affluence and set the suffering of these victims against the putative other benefits that they might be receiving as a result of modernization. By contrast, the growing crime rate was not seen as a part of the price of affluence and modernity, but rather as a measure of the government's failure to deliver even a small share of the benefits of modernization to all its subjects.

The inability of the New Order to prevent the crime wave with the same ruthless efficiency that it used to suppress political dissent is puzzling at first glance, but it seems to have to do especially with developments in the police force under the New Order. Although the

Suharto regime came to power amid expectations that it would preside over a more regularized legal order than had Sukarno's Guided Democracy,[19] the new government paid remarkably little attention to enforcing rules of procedure and habits of honesty within the legal apparatus. On the one hand, the legal system was almost invariably ineffective in bringing to account people with good establishment connections; on the other hand, police and courtroom procedures became a means for policemen, prosecutors, and judges to extract bribes from members of the public on a dramatic scale.[20] The result was both that the professional expertise among the police in particular and the legal apparatus in general was poor, and that they could often be bought off, at least by more successful criminals. Even daring to report a crime to the police brought with it the risk of being caught up in a web of venal demands for payment, so that the level of public confidence in the police was very low. The perception of a crime wave in late 1982, therefore, was not so much a consequence of police reports as of the power of rumors and extensive reporting in the press, especially the down-market *Pos Kota*.[21]

Internal politics within the New Order elite also contributed to the feeling in government circles that firm action was needed. During the first decade and a half of the New Order, one of Suharto's most important political managers was General Ali Murtopo. Murtopo was the originator of many of the imaginatively restrictive political practices of the New Order, such as the "floating mass" principle, which kept the masses isolated from political activity except at election time. He was also an architect of the so-called "Act of Free Choice" in which carefully selected "representatives" of West New Guinea endorsed the region's formal inclusion in Indonesia in 1968. And he was particularly important in managing the national elections of 1977 and 1982 to ensure a comfortable victory for the government. This electoral management included the effective deployment of men of violence and agents provocateurs as mentioned above. Immediately after the 1982 elections, however, Suharto began to discard Ali Murtopo, cultivating in his place Murtopo's former protégé, General L. B. (Benny) Murdani. Aware of the potential a disgruntled Murtopo might have for making trouble, Murdani was interested in finding a pretext to dismantle Murtopo's network of supporters among the criminal underworld in Jakarta and other cities.[22]

A further reason for the action against criminals was the growing perception that high levels of crime were discouraging Western tourists from visiting Indonesia. The government was particularly concerned because a total eclipse of the sun, due on June 11, 1983, was expected to attract large numbers of tourists to the country.

On March 29, 1983, Murdani was installed as head of KOP-KAMTIB (Operational Command of the Restoration of Security and Order), the principal vehicle for military control of the political process. At approximately the same time, the first *petrus* killings took place in the Javanese city of Yogyakarta. They were soon followed by reports of similar killings in other centers in Java and later in cities on other islands.[23] Outside Java, the killers seem to have been especially active in Medan, the largest city on the island of Sumatra, which had a long-standing reputation for wild criminality, but reports also came from remote areas such as the provinces of East and West Kalimantan (Borneo), South Sumatra, and South Sulawesi.[24] Most of the killings followed a similar pattern. The victims were widely known local toughs. Many of them had been arrested on previous occasions, and both the police and the public regarded them as professional, or at least habitual, criminals. Some of them simply disappeared, but others were seen, often at dusk, being hustled away by muscular men with short haircuts who were dressed in civilian clothes. In most cases, the bodies of these alleged criminals were discovered the next morning, sometimes dumped into canals or ditches, sometimes deposited at prominent places on roadways, often shot neatly through the head at point-blank range. Many, but not all, showed signs of torture.[25]

The murders were dubbed "misterius" (*sic*), but the appellation was ironic. Suharto himself had hinted publicly that strong measures against criminals were in the offing, and some of the earliest killings, which took place in Yogyakarta in March 1983, were officially acknowledged as the work of local security forces.[26] Subsequently, government figures ingenuously suggested that the killings were a result of conflicts between gangs, but the fact that the presumed killers, when they were sighted, looked very much like soldiers in civilian dress and the fact that the authorities responded so calmly to the presence of armed assassins moving though society were enough to convince most people that the government's hand was behind the killings. By July 1983, senior figures in the regime openly described the killings in positive terms and came close to stating that they were the work of the military. A former senior general, moreover, placed the murdered criminals firmly in the New

Order's gallery of evil by suggesting that the "sadistic" activities of the criminals represented an attempt by the Communist Party to stage a comeback. Finally, some years later, President Suharto directly accepted responsibility for the killings in his ghostwritten memoirs, justifying them as necessary to put an end to the inhuman activities of the criminals.[27]

As with all other experiences of mass killing in Indonesian history, considerable uncertainty hovers over both the precise identity of the killers and the number of victims. Although local police and military officials seem to have been responsible in some cases, many observers attributed the killings to the army's special forces, Kopassanda (later called Kopassus), and to units hardened by battle and covert experience in East Timor. There was a perception that Kopassus assassins killed their victims quickly and cleanly, whereas local forces, especially police, were inclined to torture, and then stab or strangle, but such perceptions were inevitably difficult to disentangle from rumor.[28] Estimates of the number of people killed agree that at least hundreds perished, but the number is likely to be considerably greater. It was widely rumored that not all the bodies of victims were dumped in public places; some were hurled into rivers, creating consternation among fishermen, while others were reportedly dumped in caves. Pemberton reports a "local army man" as saying that five hundred were killed in the Surakarta area in Central Java alone. Indonesian Legal Aid Foundation figures estimated 3,000 to 4,000 deaths, while one outside estimate put the number as high as 8,500 in East Java alone. If the latter figure is true, then the national death toll may have been in the vicinity of 20,000, but it certainly seems safe to suggest that the figure lies between 5,000 and 10,000.[29]

No direct accounts of the killings have been published by those who undertook them, no arrests have ever been made in connection with the events, and no detailed journalistic investigations of the killings have been published.[30] Indications are, however, that the victims were generally selected and identified by local authorities, perhaps police, perhaps army (the Indonesian army maintains an extensive territorial establishment of soldiers whose task is to monitor and stay in touch with local communities in a way that is both supportive and intimidatory).[31] As in the mass killings of 1965–66, the *petrus* murderers seem to have been generally effective in targeting those whom they wanted to eliminate.[32] Only a small proportion of

those killed were "reformed" criminals whose past record was held
against them, while a few seem to have been sailors, targeted because of their tattoos, which were a distinctive adornment of many
gangsters. Clinics specializing in the removal of tattoos reportedly
did brisk business during those months and there were reports of individuals who feared they would appear on the death lists deliberately turning themselves in for petty crimes so that they would be
arrested and kept in jail, out of reach of the killers.[33]

Initially the public response to the killings was generally positive. Because the victims were known criminals and because the
killings were so clearly the work of government agents rather than
independent assassins, the public for the most part interpreted the
killings as an unorthodox attempt by the government to solve the
problem of street crime. It was, after all, hardly unusual for the police and security forces to depart from the letter of the law to achieve
what they thought would be politically desirable ends. With time,
however, some people, especially from human rights circles, began
to express misgivings over the lack of legal process.[34] Since the operations of more politically oriented death squads in Latin America
were widely known in elite circles, there was clearly not only a prin-
cipled objection to the killings but a fear that the New Order might
turn to assassination as a new and effective tool of political repression. It appears to have been this possibility that attracted increasingly hostile outside attention to the *petrus* murders. The somewhat
bemused tone that characterized early reports of the killings in
Western news media gave way to expressions of concern over
human rights that led the Indonesian government to ban further reports of the killings in the Indonesian press in August 1983.[35] A further reason for the ban may have been the emergence of suggestions
that *petrus* killers should now turn their attentions to corrupt officials, who, it was suggested, were just as much a blight on Indonesian society as small-time criminals.[36]

Despite fears that *petrus*-style killings would become a permanent feature of the New Order's political repertoire, the murders
gradually subsided. Although it was only obliquely reported in the
Indonesian press, the bodies of murdered criminals continued to
appear in the streets throughout 1984 and into early 1985, but by
mid-1985 the phenomenon appeared to be in decline. There was a
brief epilogue during 1984 and 1985 in which a considerable number of prisoners were "shot while escaping." There were many in-

dications that these "escapes" were set up to provide police or prison guards with a pretext to shoot prisoners. These unfortunates were said at the time to have been *disukabumikan.*[37] This campaign, however, also died out, and there was no systematic use of death squads for the remainder of the Suharto era. This is not to say that there were no illicit killings at the hands of the government. Killings in jail took place, and there were occasional kidnapping-murders of activists. Five people involved in a land dispute in East Java disappeared in September 1983, allegedly picked up by security forces, and in 1993 a labor activist, Marsinah, was kidnapped, tortured, raped, and killed, apparently by military authorities in East Java.[38] As a major tool of social and political control, however, death squads had disappeared.

In the aftermath of the fall of Suharto in May 1998, however, a new wave of mysterious killings suddenly struck East Java from the beginning of August 1998.[39] The earliest killings were in the easternmost region of Banyuwangi, but they soon spread to Jember, Pasuruan, Malang, and Madura, and there have been reports of isolated incidents in Central and West Java. Initially the victims of these killings were rural magicians, known as *bromocorah* or *tukang santet,* feared for their capacity to inflict suffering and disaster on their enemies and on those whom they are paid to plague. Soon, however, the victims came to include as well rural Islamic teachers called *kiai* with no particular reputation for black magic. Many of them suffered a horrible fate, stabbed, hanged, incinerated, or hacked to pieces. Their bodies were sometimes displayed in trees, sometimes thrown into mosques, sometimes left in the middle of the street. By the end of the year, at least 150 killings had taken place. The killings were attributed by all to shadowy gangs of black-clad masked men who quickly came to be called "ninja," because of a superficial resemblance to the celebrated Japanese shadow warriors. Terror descended on the regions affected. Nighttime activities such as markets and film-showings—highly important elements in social life in the tropics, where the days are hot and dusty—were abandoned. Instead, the young men of each community formed vigilante groups, which manned roadblocks and went on patrol around village perimeters to keep the ninja at a distance. Although the ninja initially targeted the practitioners of black magic, they themselves were widely believed to be proficient magicians, able for instance to change themselves into animals when confronted by village patrols.

When alleged ninja were captured by such patrols, they were often summarily executed. There were reports of the heads of alleged ninja being paraded through the streets while their naked headless bodies were dragged behind a convoy of motorcycles. In one reported incident, a petty market thief who was being chased by two undercover policemen turned the tables on them by pointing at them and shouting, "Ninja!" The policemen were reportedly beaten to death by the enraged crowd. In other cases, those killed as ninja seem to have been mental patients who wandered where they were not known and who were unable to give suspicious locals a convincing account of themselves. In November, the police in Central Java took the precaution of rounding up 200 mentally ill people who might have been suspected as ninja.

The ninja themselves made no public statement of their intentions, and so there was intense speculation over precisely what they intended and whom they might represent. In a style reminiscent of the early casual responses to the *petrus* killings, some government figures suggested that the ninja murders were simply a matter of local revenge-taking. Those who had suffered at the hands of *bromocorah*, it was suggested, were killing their tormentors, while the families of victims of the anticommunist killings of 1965–66 were taking revenge on the local Muslim leaders who had declared a holy war against the Communist Party in those days. Although the idea of revenge-taking is not itself implausible, Java's culture of revenge-taking tends to be public and collective, rather than secretive and delegated to assassins.[40] The apparent similarity of the assassinations, moreover, hinted at a centrally coordinated campaign, as did the evident professionalism of the assassins. They often, for instance, cut electricity to their victims' houses before attacking, and they seemed to be equipped with maps indicating escape routes. Some were seen carrying communications equipment and were heard to be talking with accents that were not local. As with the *petrus* killings, moreover, the insouciance of the government immediately aroused suspicion that other forces might be involved.

The meaning of the ninja affair remains highly uncertain, but if the reports of the ninja modus operandi are to be believed, then it seems highly likely that they were connected with the Indonesian armed forces. This does not itself mean that they were working under the direct or indirect authority of the army high command. One of the more complicated features of Indonesian politics during the last years of the New Order was the rise to prominence of General Prabowo Subianto, Suharto's son-in-law. Prabowo had long been identified as a rising star in the armed forces and as a potential military guarantor of the fortunes that other members of the Suharto clan had accumulated since the late 1960s. Prabowo's power base, however, lay not only within the special forces (Kopassus), which he had commanded, and among the veterans of Indonesia's long war in East Timor, where he had played a major role. He had also developed a shadowy constellation of gangsters, many of them displaced Timorese and Irianese (from West New Guinea), in Jakarta and other regions, which gave him a power base not unlike that which Ali Murtopo had commanded in the late 1970s. Moreover, he had also made a point of cultivating what in Indonesia were considered to be radical Muslim groups hostile both to Chinese business and to the traditionalist Islam that still has millions of followers in Java. In the weeks and days immediately before Suharto's resignation, Prabowo seems to have played a key role in fomenting violence and raising levels of tension in the capital, perhaps with the intention of bolstering the view that only his father-in-law could keep order in the country, perhaps with his own private ambitions in mind.[41] Whatever Prabowo's intentions may have been, however, he was evidently outmaneuvered by the armed forces commander, General Wiranto, who was able to have Prabowo first relieved of his commands, then honorably discharged from the military, and finally exiled to Jordan. Prabowo's fall from power caused consternation among his followers inside and outside the military, and there were reports that some 200 Kopassus troops deserted in mid-1998, possibly forming the backbone of the ninja operation in collaboration with sympathetic groups still inside the military.

Although it is possible that the ninja killings were intended simply to raise the level of public alarm in Indonesian society in order to pave the way for a return to authoritarian rule—the leading Muslim politician Amien Rais accused Suharto of attempting to achieve precisely this, and a small survey of public opinion conducted in October 1998 recorded that over 90 percent of respondents believed that the government had orchestrated the affair—it is possible that the killings had a narrower intention. The targets of the attacks were the rural Islamic teachers who were key supporters of one of the largest political parties to emerge in the aftermath of the fall of Suharto. This party, the Partai Kebangkitan Bangsa (National

Awakening Party), was effectively the political expression of the traditionalist Muslim organization Nahdatul Ulama (NU). Founded in
1926, NU had proved to be the most resilient and durable of all Indonesia's political organizations. It had played an important role in
cabinets in the democratic era of the 1950s and had consistently
commanded the backing of its rural heartland in East Java and parts
of Central Java under the successive regimes of Sukarno and
Suharto. Its leader, Abdurrachman Wahid, had been a focus for opposition to Suharto in the final months of the Suharto era and, except for the fact that he suffered serious health problems, was
expected to wield substantial influence in the contest for a president
to succeed Suharto's handpicked successor, B. J. Habibie. In the
months immediately after the fall of Suharto, indications were that
PKB support would go to Megawati Sukarnoputri, the daughter of
Indonesia's first president, who was seen as the main choice both of
those who wanted a more thoroughgoing dismantling of the
Suharto order and those who feared the influence of Islam. Without
PKB support, Megawati's ramshackle coalition of radicals, conservatives, and religious minorities was unlikely to prevail, and the most
plausible reason for the ninja killings seems to have been that they
were an attempt to convince the PKB's grassroots supporters that
backing Megawati was too dangerous to be worthwhile.

Of course, it is not necessary that the ninja killings have only a
single explanation. The killing of *bromocorah* in Banyuwangi was
reported as early as January 1998, and a similar episode took place
in neighboring Jember in late 1979 and early 1980.[42] On that occasion, too, the victims were apparently killed by outsiders operating
with the connivance of local authorities in an action that seems to
have been intended mainly to destroy the power of small-time rural
gangsters and influential local figures who had grown more ambitious than regional power-holders were willing to tolerate. It is thus
possible that the ninja killings of 1998 were in fact closer in spirit
and purpose to the *petrus* killings than initially appears.

Conclusion

The weakness of the rule of law in Indonesia and the extraordinary
legal powers that Indonesia's civil and military authorities have been
able to use for maintaining their control over society mean that

death squads have had little role to play in patterns of political repression. In most countries, death squads have been a tool used
against those who otherwise might claim and receive some protection from the legal system, or who have exploited weaknesses in the
legal system to evade apprehension. In Indonesia, by contrast, death
squads have been used primarily as a tool in intra-elite struggles and
the victims of the death squads have themselves been former practitioners of violence against other sections of society. The most important death squad episode, the *petrus* killings of 1983–85,
involved the elimination of underworld elements associated with a
losing side in internal elite politics. The *bromocorah* killings of
1998–99, which are still not fully explained, seem to have targeted
at least in part people who were formerly formidable practitioners
of black magic.

Indonesia after the fall of Suharto is still in a state of turmoil,
and it is by no means clear what eventual form of government will
emerge there, but there is widespread dissatisfaction with the lack of
rule of law during the New Order and a corresponding demand for
administrative regularity and for the application of proper procedures in the legal system. To the extent that these changes are implemented and to the extent that they are truly able to restrict arbitrary
use of the judicial system by the government, they may in fact
prompt a more frequent use of death squad techniques in the future.

Notes

1. The fullest and most carefully argued analysis of the *petrus* killings is
    David Bourchier, "Crime, Law and State Authority in Indonesia," in
    Arief Budiman, ed., *State and Civil Society in Indonesia* (Clayton,
    Vic.: Monash University Centre of Southeast Asian Studies, 1994),
    177–211. Also detailed, as well as valuable for the way it sets crimi-
    nality in a broader historical context, is W. J. O'Malley, "Criminals,
    Society and Politics in Java" (unpublished paper, 1984). Justus M.
    van der Kroef, "'Petrus': Patterns of Prophylactic Murder in Indone-
    sia," *Asian Survey* 25, no. 7 (July 1985): 745–59, is a useful but more
    general survey with particular attention to international responses.
    John Pemberton, *On the Subject of "Java"* (Ithaca, N.Y.: Cornell
    University Press, 1995), 311–14; and James T. Siegel, *A New Crimi-
    nal Type in Jakarta: Counter-Revolution Today* (Durham, N.C.:
    Duke University Press, 1998), esp. chap. 4, offer more idiosyncratic

analyses based on broad interpretations of New Order political culture. Zoher Abdoolcarim, "Behind the Secret Killings," *Asiaweek*, 20 January 1984, 21–22, 27–30; and Susumu Awanohara, "Rough Justice in Jakarta," *Far Eastern Economic Review*, 9 June 1983, 17–18, are the most important journalistic accounts of the killings.

2. For surveys of the human rights record of the New Order that reflect the relative absence of death squads from an otherwise depressing catalog of human rights infringements, see Hans Thoolen, ed., *Indonesia and the Rule of Law: Twenty Years of "New Order" Government* (London: Frances Pinter, 1987), and *Power and Impunity: Human Rights under the New Order* (London: Amnesty International, 1994).

3. Many Indonesian proper names are seen in more than one spelling. In particular, names with the letter "u" are often spelled using the older Dutch form "oe." In this chapter all names have been presented in their modern form.

4. For a general account of Indonesia's legal structure since independence, see Sudargo Gautama, *Indonesian Business Law* (Bandung: Citra Aditya Bakti, 1995), 1–30. On the flexible use of legal procedures to achieve political ends, see Thoolen, *Indonesia and the Rule of Law*, and Daniel S. Lev, "The Criminal Regime: Criminal Process in Java," in Vicente L. Rafael, ed., *Figures of Criminality in Indonesia, the Philippines, and Colonial Vietnam* (Ithaca, N.Y.: Cornell University Southeast Asia Program, 1999), 175–92.

5. Robert Cribb, *Gangsters and Revolutionaries: The Jakarta People's Militia and the Indonesian Revolution, 1945–1949* (Sydney: Allen & Unwin, 1991).

6. The state of Malaysia was formed in 1963 as a federation of several British colonial territories in Southeast Asia (the Malay Peninsula, Singapore, and Penang, together with the northern Borneo states of Sabah and Sarawak). Sukarno objected to these arrangements, partly because he feared that Malaysia would be a vehicle for continuing British influence in Southeast Asia, partly because he had good reason to believe that the peoples in northern Borneo were hostile to the federation, and partly simply because Britain had not consulted Indonesia over its plans. Indonesian forces engaged British and Commonwealth troops in a low-intensity war in Borneo until late 1965. The Indonesian armed forces at the time included the police force, along with the army, navy, and air force.

7. A further indication lies in the fact that few gangs were allowed to develop, and the killings consequently took place only on a very limited scale, in the province of West Java, where the military had only recently defeated the Darul Islam rebellion.

8. This said, it can be admitted that in the 1992 and 1997 elections the government made considerable use of pork-barrelling to win the vote in areas it considered to be important or sensitive.

9. Henk Schulte Nordholt, "De jago in de schaduw: misdaad en 'orde' in de koloniale staat op Java," *De Gids* 146, no. 8/9: 664–675; Ong-hokham, "The jago in colonial Java, ambivalent champion of the people," *Senri Ethnological Studies* 13 (1984): 327–44.

10. Cribb, *Gangsters and Revolutionaries*.

11. See Bourchier, "Crime, Law and State Authority," 180, 194–95.

12. The common Indonesian term for such criminals has changed over time. In the 1940s, the term *garong* was common, at least in the Jakarta area; by the early 1980s the most common term was *gali*; in the late 1990s the usual term was *preman*. Although the latter term is clearly derived from the Dutch *vrijman* (freeman), the commonly heard suggestion that *gali* is derived from *gabungan anak liar* (gang of wild children) seems to be fanciful. On *gali*, see Bourchier, "Crime, Law and State Authority," 179; on *preman*, see Loren Ryter, "Pemuda Pancasila: The Last Loyalist Free Men of Suharto's Order?" *Indonesia* 66 (October 1998): 45–73. For a brief discussion of the terminology for various categories of rural criminal in colonial Java, see O'Malley, "Criminals, Society and Politics in Java," 16 and 18–19.

13. Bourchier, "Crime, Law and State Authority," 181–82; *Prisma*, May 1982.

14. David Jenkins, "Angels of Death," *Far Eastern Economic Review*, 29 Sept. 1983, 29–30.

15. The cultural convention that the "safe" response to terror is paralysis may partly explain the passivity with which large numbers of communists (though not all) met their deaths in 1965–66. See Robert Cribb, "Introduction: Problems in the Historiography of the Killings in Indonesia," in Robert Cribb, ed., *The Indonesian Killings of 1965–1966: Studies from Java and Bali* (Clayton: Monash University, 1990), 20.

16. Pemberton, *On the Subject of "Java,"* 316. Bourchier, "Crime, Law and State Authority," 178–79, and van der Kroef, "'Petrus,'" 746–47, describe the general process of rapid social change and urbanization that tends to encourage crime in general.

17. R. William Liddle, *Leadership and Culture in Indonesian Politics* (St. Leonards, NSW: Allen & Unwin, 1996), 15–36.

18. Lea Jellinek, *Wheel of Fortune: The History of a Poor Community in Jakarta* (Honolulu: University of Hawaii Press, 1991).

19. Sukarno explicitly subordinated the legal system to broader political goals, and the colonial era laws that then still provided the vast bulk

of the country's legislation were considered valid only as long as they were subjectively judged to be consistent with the spirit of the constitution. See Gautama, *Indonesian Business Law.*

20.   See Daniel S. Lev, "The Criminal Regime: Criminal Process in Java," and John Pemberton, "Open Secrets: Excerpts from Conversations with a Javanese Lawyer, and a Comment," in Rafael, *Figures of Criminality in Indonesia,* 175–92 and 193–209.

21.   James Siegel, "I Was Not There, But . . . ," *Archipel* 46 (1993): 59–65.

22.   The term *petrus,* the Indonesian for (Saint) Peter, who admits the dead into Heaven, was itself an allusion to Murdani's Catholicism. See Bourchier, "Crime, Law and State Authority," 188. On the Murtopo-Murdani struggle, see 193–94.

23.   Pemberton, *On the Subject of "Java,"* 311, identifies two killings of gangsters in Jakarta in February 1983 as the start of the *petrus* killings, but these incidents did not mark the start of a campaign of killing in the capital.

24.   Bourchier, "Crime, Law and State Authority," 186; Van der Kroef, "'Petrus,'" 749–50.

25.   See O'Malley, "Criminals, Society and Politics in Java"; Bourchier, "Crime, Law and State Authority"; van der Kroef, "'Petrus'"; Pemberton, *On the Subject of "Java"*; Abdoolcarim, "Behind the Secret Killings"; and Awanohara, "Rough Justice in Jakarta."

26.   Bourchier, "Crime, Law and State Authority," 182–83; O'Malley, "Criminals, Society and Politics in Java," 1, 3.

27.   O'Malley, "Criminals, Society and Politics in Java," 4–5; Awanohara, 17; Pemberton, *On the Subject of "Java,"* 313; Bourchier, "Crime, Law and State Authority," 197. Another senior government official compared the gangsters to Italy's left-wing Red Brigades; see van der Kroef, "'Petrus,'" 750. Suharto's own account is in Soeharto, *Otobiografi: Pikiran, Ucapan dan Tindakan Saya* (Jakarta: Citra Lamtoro Gung Persada, 1988), 364.

28.   See Jenkins, "Angels of Death," 29; van der Kroef, "'Petrus,'" 748; Abdoolcarim, "Behind the Secret Killings," 21–22, 27–30.

29.   Bourchier, "Crime, Law and State Authority," 187; Pemberton, *On the Subject of "Java,"* 312. For various estimates of the number of victims, see Bourchier, "Crime, Law and State Authority," 186, and van der Kroef, "'Petrus,'" 754–55.

30.   Even when killers know that they act with impunity, many factors can make them reluctant to give open testimony about their actions. For the case of recent communal killings in West Kalimantan, see Richard Lloyd Parry, *What Young Men Do* (London: Granta, 1998); on the 1965–66 killings, see Cribb, "Problems in the Historiography."

31. See Jenkins, "Angels of Death."
32. Abdoolcarim, "Behind the Secret Killings," 30, suggests that officially sanctioned *petrus* killings became a cover for the unofficial settling of scores, but as with the 1965–66 killings there is neither anecdotal nor analytical evidence that this was the case.
33. O'Malley, "Criminals, Society and Politics in Java," 2; "Ada Dor, Ada Ya, Ada, Tidak," *Tempo,* 6 Aug. 1983, 14.
34. Bourchier, "Crime, Law and State Authority," 189–92; Awanohara, "Rough Justice in Jakarta," 17–18; O'Malley, "Criminals, Society and Politics in Java," 2; van der Kroef, "'Petrus,'" 749; Abdoolcarim, "Behind the Secret Killings," 27–28, 30; Pemberton, *On the Subject of "Java,"* 312–13. James T. Siegel's recent study of criminality in New Order Indonesia, *A New Criminal Type in Jakarta,* esp. chap. 4, presents a rather different explanation. He implies that the petrus killings were orchestrated, with the New Order first deliberately cultivating public fears of sadistic criminals in order to generate acquiescence in the authoritarian political order, and then applying similarly sadistic countermeasures in order to remind the public of the government's unfettered capacity for violence. In Siegel's explanation, the thin disguise of the killers was not cosmetic or designed to shield the regime from blame but rather a device to add mystery and thus terror to the killings.
35. Jenkins, "Angels of Death," 29–30; Susumu Awanohara, "Still Mysterious . . . ," *Far Eastern Economic Review,* 9 August 1984, 26–27. Van der Kroef, "'Petrus,'" 745, 748–49, and 752–54, discusses international reactions to the *petrus* killings in some detail.
36. Bourchier, "Crime, Law and State Authority," 192; Jenkins, "Angels of Death," 29–30.
37. This strange term, meaning "sent to Sukabumi" or "given the Sukabumi treatment," may refer to the fact that one of the earliest such incidents took place in the West Java town of Sukabumi, but it was also a play on the meaning of the town's name, "to like the earth," that is, to wish to be buried in it.
38. On the Marsinah case, see *Power and Impunity,* 62–64.
39. Major press reports on the ninja killings include Louise Williams, "Masked 'Ninja' Killer Gangs Terrorize Town," *Sydney Morning Herald,* 7 October 1998; Alex Spillius, "'Witch Doctors' Killed in Java," *Chicago Sun-Times,* 14 October 1998; Nicholas D. Kristof, "Fears of Sorcerers Spur Killings in Java," *New York Times,* 20 October 1998; Derwin Pereira, "Politics Behinds Killings in Java," *Straits Times,* 27 October 1998; Derwin Pereira, "Java's Ninja Terror: Politics at Play?" *Straits Times,* 30 October 1998; John Aglionby, "Mob 'Justice' Thrives in Wake of Ninja Killers,"

Guardian, 31 October 1998; "E. Java Killings Politically Orchestrated: Survey," *Jakarta Post,* 4 November 1998; "Soeharto Blamed for Terror Campaign in Java," *Sydney Morning Herald,* 6 November 1998; Louise Williams, "Indonesia's Black Death," *Sydney Morning Herald,* 7 November 1998. For an Indonesian analysis, see S. Darmadji et al., *Misteri Ninja dan Cara Antisipasinya* (Surabaya: Cipta Media Surabaya, [1998]).

40. See, for instance, the accounts of revenge against hated officials during the Indonesian revolution described in Anton Lucas, *One Soul One Struggle: Region and Revolution in Indonesia* (Sydney: Allen & Unwin, 1991), 103–32.

41. On Prabowo, see Ryter, "Pemuda Pancasila," 71, and Stefan Eklöf, *Indonesian Politics in Crisis: The Long Fall of Suharto, 1996–98* (Copenhagen: NIAS, 1999), 148–49, 214–17.

42. On this affair, see O'Malley, "Criminals, Society and Politics," 22–23.

CHAPTER 8

Modernity and Devolution: The Making of Police Death Squads in Modern Brazil

Martha K. Huggins[1]

DEATH SQUADS IN LATIN AMERICA HAVE A NOTORIOUS history. But they are much misunderstood. As Allan Nairn points out, they have been portrayed as totally informal and spontaneous—"as discrete bands of gangsters who roam the Latin American countryside randomly picking off victims."[2] The impression is that death squads have no connections with one another nor with the state. According to this outdated view, death squads are throwbacks, atavisms, tied to traditional premodern Latin American forms of social control, where power aspirants—the *poderosos*—and their geographically localized gangs, militias, and paramilitary forces battled it out with one another for regional power. Where the state is weak and ineffective, local politicos and their armed retainers, along with occasional rebels and bandits, take police and judicial power into their own hands.

But even if the absence of effective central government control explains vigilantism in Brazil's traditional past, how are we to explain it under Brazil's centralizing, industrializing military government (1964–85) and more recently in democratizing, postmilitary Brazil (1985-present)? In both sociopolitical situations, the state has penetrated civil society through sophisticated internal security bureaucracies, including well-developed police and intelligence systems modernized in part with U.S assistance during the military regime.[3] Thus, there is some question as to whether Brazil's death squads are really just a recrudescence of turn-of-the-century vigilantism.

To test this ordinary view of death squads, we first model the relationship among varieties of Brazilian vigilantism by placing them on a simple continuum. In the next section, we examine some recent historical roots of the symbiosis in Brazil between formal police systems and informal death squads, particularly death squads' origins in, and connections to, the state and the criminal justice system. In the third section, on devolution, we propose that death squads are a product of a consequent—if not fully intended—process of state centralization and subsequent deconstruction, where the former leads to the latter, as parts of the formal control system split off, debureaucratize, and increasingly carry out violence clandestinely and extralegally. The fourth section discusses the functions of such death squads for the national state, while the final section further analyzes one of these developments—police privatizing and subcontracting—as alternating, mutually symbiotic forms of modern social control.

Through several Brazilian examples in the body of this paper, we illustrate six sources of devolution into death squads, seeing it as (a) paradoxically rooted in formal organization—particularly in the bureaucratic centralization, specialization, and resulting competition among police agencies; (b) a product of domestic and/or international pressures against state violence; (c) generated by a real or perceived failure of the state and its social control system to control violence; and (d) furthered by national state reluctance to eliminate death squads, granting impunity to their murderous activities; (e) rooted in any case in state-related illegalities—where devolution spawns further devolution into decentralization and partial loss of state control; and finally (f) culminating in internal security as a free-market monetized commodity where "policing" is subcontracted out to interested bidders. While these may not include all possible sources of devolution, these patterns are most evident in the Brazilian data for this analysis.

Sources and Secrecy

Researching a subject held secret requires using a range of less-used and sometimes unusual sources because of people's unwillingness to talk about or even study illegal activities. However, Brazilian journalists have led the way in penetrating the shroud of secrecy around death squads; their investigations have been invaluable for this study. In fact, given the lack of academic research on this important subject, there would be almost no information about death squads in the various parts of Brazil without the work of Brazilian journalists. Their material links the death squad experience of Brazil's diverse regions with one another as few academic studies have been able to do.

Another source of data for this study is the few Brazilian government investigations into death squads, available via court testimony, police reports, and formal research.[4] Also used are previously unavailable government reports by the U.S. Agency for International Development (AID), released, apparently for the first time, under the Freedom of Information Act. Focusing on police activities in Brazil, these AID reports were submitted monthly from 1962 to 1972 by AID-Brazil to Washington, covering specifically the AID Office of Public Safety's police assistance program in Brazil. These reports frequently mention death squad activity in Brazil.[5] Another primary data source for this study is the author's interviews with Brazilian police torturers and killers, some of whom had been in or even commanded death squads. These interviews, collected for a study of torture,[6] provide personal accounts of police involvement in such violence. To protect the respondents' identities, each of these interviews is cited according to the interviewee's first initial and region of residence.

A Continuum of Vigilantism

To explore the questions raised about police death squads, these squads need to be related to the continuum of Brazilian extralegal vigilante violence. Such violence can range from relatively spontaneous, less formalized, less state-linked actions, such as mob lynchings, to systematic murders by individual "justice-seeking" assassins (*justiceiros*),[7] to the relatively organized state-linked violence by informal death squads, including off-duty police, to aggressive extralegal violence by units of on-duty police.[8] Such a continuum of extralegal violence is based on its degree of spontaneity, organization, and state involvement.

In Brazil, the most spontaneous of several forms of extralegal violence is the "anonymous" crowd lynching, involving previously unconnected civilians taking justice into their own hands under the sway of an immediate crowd reaction to a suspected lawbreaker. Such lynchings,[9] which erupt suddenly at the instigation of several unrelated informal leaders responding to crowd sentiment, are loosely organized and have no direct connections to government. The lynchers carry out their violence more as a "mob" than as a group. This distinguishes these "crowd" lynchings from "communal" lynchings,[10] which are more organized and less spontaneous and anonymous. The "communal" lynchings have roots in existing citizen bonds and community ties; such lynchers organize themselves to redress a perceived wrong affecting the community with which they identify.[11]

Less spontaneous than either type of relatively anonymous crowd lynchings, and thus more systematic and closer to the state— and so in the intermediate range of the vigilantism continuum—are murders by Brazil's *justiceiros*. These lone-wolf killers, usually common citizens, often live in the communities they purport to protect. Yet while community members may see *justiceiros* as Robin Hood–like figures who protect them against "criminals," many in fact kill for pay, so that their violence is not entirely altruistically communitarian. Moreover, some are off-duty police, which links their violence more closely to the state.[12]

At the continuum's most nonspontaneous and deliberately formal, organized, bureaucratic, state-controlled pole are state-appointed and -paid police who carry out extralegal killings while on duty. Brazilian police violence is usually deliberately planned and carried out during regular street sweeps and dragnets.[13] The police who perpetrate these killings are members of highly organized, usually elite, police units. The state, of course, has direct connections to such violence through its formal constitutional and operational control over the police, whose violence is officially justified by the state's declared war against drugs and crime, or, under the military, against "communists" and political "terrorists."

Very close to this formal pole on the vigilantism continuum is death squad violence. A Brazilian death squad is a team of murderers, entirely or mostly off-duty police, usually paid as a group by local businesses or politicos for their services. In effect, as privatized but official "security guards" they secretly serve commercial and/or political interests. Each death squad is usually linked to a network of similar extermination groups with connections to police through its members, who are also in the official state-hired, -paid, and -supervised police.[14] Many informal death squads are further linked to the state through personal connections with a variety of higher state officials who give them tasks, look the other way, and then reward them. The planned and state-linked nature of death squad operations makes their violence very far from spontaneous.

By placing lynchings, *justiceiro* murders, death squads, and on-duty police violence on a continuum—according to degree of spontaneity, organization, and state involvement—we can see how each of these types is related to the others and to state action and inaction; most of them are not as totally spontaneous and "disorganized" as popularly assumed. Indeed, the assumption that death squads are random and disorganized has hidden their true nature and seriously hampered an effective theoretical understanding of this phenomenon.

An Emerging Symbiosis:
Police and Death Squads

Most scholars date Brazil's modern death squads from 1958, when Brazilian army general Amury Kruel, chief of the state police forces in Rio de Janeiro, the then federal capital of Brazil, was being pressured by Rio's commercial association to do something about the rise in theft and robbery, which was affecting their businesses. Kruel directed his chief *delegado* (police district chief), Cecil Borer, to handpick a group of special police to be headed by state Civil Police inspector Milton Le Cocq de Oliveira. This policeman began his career in the Rio state's uniformed Militarized Police and later moved over to Rio state's Civil (i.e., investigative and nonuniformed) Police. Attached to the Civil Police's Serviço de Diligencia Especial, Le Cocq's new squad was made up of the force's reputed "bravest" men, who had declared their willingness to die in the pursuit of Rio's bandits. Hence the origin of their popular label: *homens corajosos* (courageous men).[15]

Kruel's bandit-hunters were a specialized motorized patrol unit—the Esquadrão Motorizada—within the Civil Police, not outside the formal police system. Popularly called the EM, Kruel's group had an explicit mandate to kill "dangerous criminals" on its own initiative.[16] *Time* magazine reported in 1969 that over the prior eleven-year period, Kruel's police unit had murdered an average of one person a week; this was verified by Brazil's national news weekly *Veja.*[17] Despite Kruel's later denial that his group had been a death squad—he said he had "merely ordered his police not to fail to kill"—this official police group quickly became just what it was later charged with being, a death squad.

Indeed, Kruel's Esquadrão Motorizada did not carry out its murders only while on duty. In 1958, its leader, Inspector Le Cocq, assembled a parallel eight-man Esquadrão de Morte, whose acronym was also EM. This group was informally dubbed the *turma da pesada* (hard duty group) to indicate its members' even greater willingness "to risk their lives pursuing *pistoleiros"* (armed criminals). For this, the group received additional outside remuneration from businesses and justice officials.[18] In Rio's slums, ditches, and fields, dead bodies began turning up showing signs of torture; they were carved with the death squad's imprint, a skull and crossbones. Notes were pinned to victims' bodies—"I was a thief," "I sold drugs," "I was a criminal"—and signed "EM."[19] A murder was commonly reported a day later in the Rio de Janeiro State Department of Public Security's internal newsletter, including the money paid for each assassination.[20] These murders were proudly reported on the radio, thanks to the death squad's "public relations" man, Ivo Americano Alves Brito, described by his colleagues as "*simpatico,* of good appearance, who used educated language." Before entering Rio's informal EM, Brito had been a Federal Police security agent at the Itamariti, Brazil's Foreign Ministry.[21]

The interpenetration in the late 1950s between Kruel's Esquadrão Motorizada and Le Cocq's Esquadrão de Morte marks the beginning of a new symbiosis between the "informal" murder teams, long a fact of Brazilian life, and the modern centralized police apparatus. It reflected the ease with which a formal police unit could spawn informal death squads; such devolution was an escalating by-product of official death squad "justice." Indeed, when, in August 1964, Inspector Le Cocq was murdered by "Cara de Cavalo" ("Horse Face") during a violent drive by the official EM police against Rio's "undesirables," Le Cocq's police friends established a "Scuderie Le Cocq," a "philanthropical" club of policemen sworn to avenge their colleague's murder by themselves carrying out off-duty death squad murders of "bandits"; the Scuderie also financially assisted the families of police killed by such "bandits."[22] Before long, this Scuderie had expanded into a statewide and then an interstate network of police-linked death squads, each vowing to kill ten "gangsters" for every policeman murdered. In some Rio police districts, statistics on death squad murders were logged and publicly posted, often published weekly in police newsletters, including the sums of money raised from private sources to pay for each killing.[23] By 1971, Rio's Scuderie had 2,000 associates, from inside and outside the police,[24] with up to 3,500 police associates in other parts of Brazil,[25] and even including some British and American police officers.[26] Once the State of Rio began to encourage informal death squads, they quickly proliferated. Each new death squad, whether directed at economic or political "criminals," had an increasingly distant relationship to the formal justice system.

Death squads started in Brazil's largest city, São Paulo, by a similar process: they usually evolved within formal police organizations and then partially devolved from them into a symbiosis between the formal and informal systems of social control. For example, some informal São Paulo death squads organized in the early 1960s. They developed out of a modernized São Paulo Civil Police motorized squad, the Rondas Noturnas Especials da Polícia Civil (RONE), according to a former head of the squad.[27] Established in 1957, at about the same time as the first automobile manufacturing plants arrived in the greater São Paulo City region, RONE served as night patrols whose emblem was an owl on a tree branch with a machine gun under its wing. The interviewee could "remember our concern was . . . that the elite has to be protected, so the RONE was created [to eliminate] . . . car thefts and house burglaries."[28] Popular discourse had it that the police in motorized patrols such as RONE were braver than most: they "never thought twice about drawing their guns or beating a suspect."[29]

The RONE police squad was defined by its operational autonomy, guaranteed in part by its deployment only at night and in part by its being headed by a *delegado,* a police district chief with a law degree. This helped ensure that almost any action of the elite RONE squad could be legalized as falling within its "legitimate mission." Pointing specifically to RONE and other such Civil Police motorized squads' shoot-to-kill policy and to the string of bodies left in their wake, one São Paulo newspaper described them simply and directly as "death squads,"[30] even though they were, in fact, formal police units.

In any case, before long São Paulo's RONE had devolved fully into an informal death squad. Its head, Civil Police DOPS (Political Police) *delegado* Sergio Paranhos Fleury, encouraged by the state's highest officials, invited some of his RONE colleagues to join him off-duty. Fleury reportedly got his victims' names from the state secretary of public security, who checked police "rap sheets" and selected victims, saying: "'This one. This one. This one here. Not this one, not yet.' They'd go out, arrest them, and then wait a few days to take them out of jail and kill [them]."[31] Commonly, death squad members received payment for their killings.

Under pressure to combat crime more effectively, São Paulo State's highest officials had apparently told Fleury that "society needed cleaning up because the courts were very slow about deciding things; the law was tying the hands" of the police.[32] Fleury's death squad was to eliminate hardened criminals who had allegedly escaped punishment under the official judicial system: "If you sent [the criminals] to jail, they [would] get . . . out, so [Fleury's men] killed a bunch [of them]."[33] In the process, an almost seamless symbiosis emerged between the formal state's RONE police and the seemingly not-state-connected informal death squads.

At the same time that Fleury's Political Police DOPS-linked Civil Police death squad was murdering alleged criminals and subversives in São Paulo, another São Paulo delegado in a different Civil Police division—the State Department of Criminal Investigations (Departamento Estadual de Investigações Criminais, or DEIC)—had assembled a "secret team within [his] directorate" (that is, an official death squad linked to his office) to take care of "very big, very important cases . . . [that other] specialized [police branches] were reluctant to deal with." For example, one day a police chief from another district telephoned the DEIC *delegado* and explained, "I can't do anything because my investigators . . . seem to be a little reluctant: They're not used to dealing with that kind of people."[34] The DEIC death squad, made up of "hard-nosed" men—"investigators who are . . . the best at violently hunting down bandits"[35]—set out to do what the overtly constituted police units would not do. The DEIC *delegado* had selected for his special death squad "guys who like taking risks, staying up all night, doing all those things you see in the [crime] movies." He explained that his men "really liked killing, killing outlaws. [They would be sent] to an ambush site [with the understanding that] even if [the criminal] didn't resist, they were going to kill him."[36] These DEIC-related death squad murders were carried out by police acting secretly under formal orders, while covertly attached to the DEIC special unit under command of this district police official.

Yet this DEIC team did not earn the negative label "death squad" until something happened to make public its possible autonomy from the larger official military internal control system. With this, its violence could no longer be ignored by Brazil's military government. In a particular incident that cast a dark shadow over DEIC, in late 1968, two DEIC investigators got into a brawl with three Federal Police agents in a São Paulo bar. After an exchange of insults at the bar, one of the DEIC investigators shot and wounded one of the Federal Police. When the military director of Brazil's Federal Police learned of this shooting, he demanded an investigation into DEIC's secret "death squad," charging that it was "a group of police operating on their own"—i.e., acting like a death squad.[37] Since the Civil Police group had already been operating for some time with its *delegado's* approval and with sufficient publicity for the Brazilian military to have known about it, we can only assume that the DEIC death squad's behavior had simply gone "too far"— e.g., unwittingly operated against members of a police organization that was hierarchically superior to it and closely connected to the military that was then running the country. At the very least, the public example of local police attacking members of Brazil's FBI-like Federal Police organization could not be tolerated. Clearly, fear of devolution was already spreading at higher levels.

The Brazilian examples point to the elements associated, at least there, with the emergence, growth, and privatization of death squads. First, their roots are in formal police organization, rather than being purely personal, traditional, or atypical "deviant" exceptions. Second, the political impetus for creating a death squad— whether market forces and demands (e.g., protection of business) and/or political ideologies (e.g., "Communist subversion")—is a real or perceived problem or situation not adequately dealt with by the formal social control structure. Third and fourth, death squads are encouraged on the one hand by the state's seeming failure to control violence and on the other by pressures, explicit or implicit, against the state using certain kinds of violence. Finally, devolution into death squads quickly engenders more devolution, with each new death squad spin-off less directly linked than the previous one to formal police organization. Finally, this privatization of internal security, driven ultimately by particularistic rather than communal and civic interests, institutionalizes an ever more privatized and sub-contractual social control response that at least appears to operate parallel to the formal system, yet in fact is syncretized with it. One result of this secret symbiosis is that death squads operate with an impunity that nurtures and sustains their terror—a dynamic granted legitimacy by the official social organizations that have generated informal death squad violence in the first place.

Organizational Roots of Devolution

We have seen that rather than being an outgrowth of "deviant" pre-modern social disorganization, Brazil's death squads have been firmly rooted in modern police organization, including the central-ization and specialization of social control. For example, in 1967, Brazil's military government—in an effort to further increase its control over internal order—promulgated a law for organizing po-lice on a national level (Organic Law Number 317), followed in 1969 by an even stronger version, Law 667. While Law 317 placed each state's municipal and state police forces under a state secretary of public security appointed by the military-installed state governor, Law 667 further subordinated all police to the military, making each state's highest police officials and the previously state-controlled po-lice forces simply auxiliaries of the Brazilian army. These laws rep-resented the military government's effort, in the name of "national security" and "internal war," to bring Brazil's previously federally decentralized police forces under tighter central government (i.e., military) control. In turn, the state police were renamed Polícia Mil-itar (i.e., Militarized Police) and stripped of their autonomous posi-tion as a state police force.

Such "rationalized" centralization, seen as a way of improving policing and making social control increasingly efficient, delineated more specifically the jurisdictions of each police force. The Milita-rized Police were to have full control over first-response street polic-ing, while the Civil Police—who had previously had responsibility for some street policing—were to relinquish this to the Militarized Police. In exchange, the Civil Police gained sole responsibility as "ju-dicial" police for post facto investigations of crime.

Yet, even as this more specialized division of labor was being created, it was being undermined. State Civil Police officials charged that the central military government was attempting to circumvent the Civil Police powers. The traditionally powerful Civil Police *delegados* (district chiefs) were especially vocal critics of Laws 317 and 667. As São Paulo Civil Police *delegados* saw it, "some officers of the [state Militarized Police] wanted to take over functions of the judicial [Civil] police," reducing the Civil Police to little more than investigators of crimes. In São Paulo, the *delegados* entered into "an open fight with the new Police Organic Law 317," actively resisting the Civil Police's being controlled by a military-appointed secretary of public security.[38] According to the São Paulo newspaper *Jornal da Tarde*, many São Paulo *delegados* described Law 317 as a " monster . . . a revocation of [the] rights of Civil Police."[39] The newspaper *O Estado de São Paulo* pointed out that the Police Organic Law 317, "made to resolve . . . police [organizational and turf] problems, . . . has served to increase [them] . . . and to unleash a crisis out of all proportion to its intrinsic importance."[40] In Minas Gerais, it was reported that Civil Police were "attack[ing] the Militar[ized] Police in the newspapers claiming that the [military-appointed] governor [has been] . . . silently giving all material and financial help to the Militar[ized] Police and neglecting the Civil Police."[41] Civil Police response to the loss of jurisdiction and the reduction in its autonomy was to create new death squads: these could operate outside state or military government regulation.

Besides fostering new death squads, centralization of internal security failed to control the devolution already well under way. For example, local police patrols like São Paulo's RONE had already gained considerable autonomy from even the state's police officials by the time Brazil's military had subordinated São Paulo city and state police to its own officers. RONE police were already "famous for violence: Their investigators never thought twice about drawing their gun or beating a suspect."[42] Perhaps in reaction to such autonomy on the part of both formal and informal police organizations and squads, in 1970 Brazil's military government moved toward even greater police centralization at the national level by establishing DOI/CODI, a formally constituted internal security organization of regionally interconnected elite police and military forces directly answerable only to regional military authorities. Besides collecting and analyzing intelligence information, DOI/CODI had separate specialized teams for "assault," "backup," and, explicitly, "murder." With the creation of DOI/CODI, Brazil's internal security system had become even more "Taylorized," with each social control function narrowly defined and sharply distinguished from other police functions. This had implications for internal conflict, devolution, and security force violence.

At the very least, the different security forces' proliferation of elite security units and squads, with their separate but overlapping jurisdictions, made it impossible not to violate one another's turf, as each entity sought to justify its existence over against other units and squads in seeking to control specific police operations and resources. For example, a structure like DOI/CODI that so narrowly defined and finely delineated the jurisdictions and functions of its own and the other security forces—through specialization and compartmentalization of work—could not avoid causing conflict within and between security forces and their specialized units. In part, this resulted from superimposing DOI/CODI on formally locally controlled municipal and states' police systems. The already existing competition between local and state police forces was now exacerbated by conflicts between these police and DOI/CODI.

Besides encouraging further internal competition and resistance, such competition also spawned illegal violence. Constant pressure to obtain information and make arrests in the shortest period of time, regardless of means, meant capturing as many criminals and subversives as possible and dealing with them quickly and forcefully. As one former intelligence operative explained, each part of the system "was in a race against time,"[43] as well as against other police units and divisions, since the rewards of extra income, power, and prestige went to those who most quickly gathered the most valuable information. This allowed particular police squads to disregard even the minimal legal, political, and social constraints in obtaining the necessary intelligence and of capturing, constraining, and eliminating the "enemy."

A particularly dramatic example of competition spawning devolution occurred on March 1, 1970, in São Paulo, when a DOI/CODI team raided Delegado Sergio Paranhos Fleury's São Paulo political police facility to "rescue" a prisoner there. DOI/CODI wanted to interrogate the prisoner in one of its own torture facilities; Fleury had no intention of letting his high-profile antiregime political militant—whom his group had captured—be transferred to a DOI/CODI facility. In the tumult, knowing that, if kept, the prisoner would be able to supply information that would help Fleury's political police capture other important militants, Fleury ordered the prisoner to lie on the floor and then jumped on the man's chest, breaking several of his ribs. Fleury wanted the prisoner to be too injured for DOI/CODI to torture him for information.[44]

Extreme specialization, compartmentalization, and competition among police organizations and units encouraged police operatives to instrumentalize their police tasks as ends in themselves, masking the wider moral implications of their violent actions.[45] In the process, for example, some DOI/CODI interrogators were transformed into specialized torturers—coldly calculating machines in a repressive system kept humming by the constant need for a rapid flow of information.[46] In fact, in carrying out its official mission to secure intelligence and neutralize "terrorists" and "subversives," DOI/CODI committed some of the military regime's most flagrant human rights violations.[47] DOI/CODI holding facilities were notorious for brutal torture—the acronym "DOI" is, in fact, homonymous with *doi* (to feel pain) in Portuguese. DOI/ CODI torture and murder squads, especially, behaved like informal death squads, secretly torturing and murdering unconvicted suspects, although, unlike their informal counterparts, DOI/CODI was formally linked to the legally rationalized military system of internal control.

Ironically, as we have seen, the military's more systematically violent internal security system—restructured to increase control from the top and to coordinate and eliminate competition and conflict below by centralizing and specializing—ended up exacerbating old conflicts and creating new ones. Much greater competition among police agencies and their units, unrestricted by legal and human rights considerations, spawned less formal groups whose violence could avoid official centralized control and thus national and international criticism, without severing completely their informal ties to the police and the state. Indeed, even as it was consolidating its control over internal security, Brazil's military was willing to overlook death squad activity—so long as informal "vigilantes" at least inadvertently promoted the national security state's "internal security" agenda.

Devolution Engenders Further Devolution

Pointing to official complicity nurturing still further devolution of social control, Brazilian journalist Helio Gaspari argues that the Brazilian military's security forces "working extralegally, inevitably start[ed] behaving illegally as well: The torturers bec[ame] smugglers and blackmailers and extortionists, and no one dare[d] to stop them." The Brazilian military's internal security apparatus "poison[ed] the [social] system. . . . A sort of gangrene set . . . in. [The] accumulation of peripheral debts contracted in clandestin[e] work could only be rewarded illegally," seen in the various illegalities carried out by death squads.[48]

Within such a dynamic of centralizing and specializing, illegality and violence, Brazil's internal control system turned against itself. A police interviewee explained that "everyone was spying on everybody else."[49] A former police intelligence agent reported that in the process of investigating "high-level smuggling, including guns and drugs, I got close to the aorta—even the governor and his secretary were suspects." Before long, "a friend began investigating [me]," and it followed that "you began not even trusting your friends." Threats against this policeman's life and family began—"They [even] threatened to kill [my] daughter."[50] Such devolution, in which different parts of the social control system begin to attack each other, fosters a downward spiral of distrust and violence. This in turn results in parts of the social control system moving still farther beyond centralized control. Naturally, under these fissiparous contradictions, there was no guarantee that, even in military Brazil, formal death squads would consistently act in the state's interests, as the following example illustrates.

In a politically disruptive death squad investigation of the early 1970s, while Brazil was under army rule, the military began looking into death squads in Espirito Santo State. There, two members of the state Civil Police publicly exposed state-connected death squads. They charged that gangs of off-duty Civil Police, under command of the state's military-appointed governor and his brother, the state secretary of public security, not only engaged in torture and summary executions—often burying their victims alive—but were also involved in fabrication of documents, robberies of cars and arms, and selling arms to nongovernment purchasers.[51] The Espirito Santo death squads were acting only in the interests of their own state and were answerable only to its governor and his secretary of public security, and not directly to the military. These informal police death squads gave local officials a power base independent of the military, diluting the recently passed Law 667 that subordinated all police to the military. Such decentralization of policing—where the authority over the "machinery of policing and its control . . . [shifted] to political sub-centers"[52]—became a possibility only when the death squads' profits from illegal activities freed them from the higher military regime authorities and strengthened a separatist, autonomous position for their own state.

The Brazilian military moved directly to investigate the Espirito Santo statewide death squad network, which it had previously allowed to flourish. When remuneration from illegal activities supported the central state, as Arendt has pointed out for any totalitarian regime,[53] there were few incentives for the military to suppress them. But at a time when Brazil's military government was struggling to consolidate its fragile technical and organizational hegemony over internal political and social control, the military seemed especially concerned that the Espirito Santo death squads might not report captured arms and might possibly even divert them to "subversives," defined as anyone who did not support the military government.[54] In other words, even though the military itself needed to support devolution to remain viable, once such devolution of social control got under way, it inevitably assumed a life of its own. Each locus of debureaucratized authority moved farther from the formal social control system that had spawned it, further privatizing social control.

Privatizing Social Control

As we have seen, some of Brazil's death squads emerged before the 1964 military coup at the behest of private businesses; these provided economic rewards to those focused primarily on economic criminals. The definition of "crime"—seen by businessmen as that which disturbed commerce—was shaped by market forces and demands and in turn shaped the content and focus of social control. For example, an eight-man São Paulo death squad, as late as the late 1960s and early 1970s headed by Civil Police member Ademar Agosto de Oliveira, "O Fininho" ("the Sly One"), was supported by local commercial interests.

O Fininho himself had been easily led into forming a death squad: His father, a policeman, had been killed in the line of duty by a common criminal. Fininho, who above all valued loyalty, selected the members of his death squad according to their "trustworth[iness]

to[ward Civil Police] *delegados,* [their not being] involved in any corruption," and their being able to keep the death squad a "secret, . . .
unknown even to [the rest of] the police." In the minds of participating death squad members, "The death squad had to be like a secret club."[55]

Loosely linked to the formal police system, O Fininho's death
squad was supported by a São Paulo business association that secretly gave each death squad member 400 cruzeiros a week (in those
days worth approximately U.S. $35) in a sealed envelope. The asso-
ciation also provided legal assistance to squad members, as well as
financial support to the families of those members killed "in the line
of duty."[56] In turn, death squad members provided their own arms,
ammunition, and other social control paraphernalia, using a portion
of their own earnings from murders-for-hire to cover the costs of
these killings—which were passed on to them as freelance workers
or subcontractors. For example, in early 1980, a member of a Rio
death squad had carefully figured out, in rational business style:

> Some bandits were killed in 10 shots, others in 2, 4, or 7. . . . With
> 6 shots for each execution, one box of bullets for a 39[-caliber re-
> volver] costs 3,500 cruzeiros, making each shot 70 cruzeiros [then
> worth $1.55]. If I kill 215 [people], each getting 6 shots, I spend
> for ammunition 90,300 cruzeiros [about $ 1,999.50, or $9.30 per
> victim].[57]

Since Fininho's freelance death squad was a sub-contracted service
rather than a subordinate unit of a larger organization, it was available to the highest bidder among a number of businesses, not under
contract to one alone.

Another death squad, headed in the mid to late 1970s by Silas
Pereira de Andrade, a former Militarized Police member known
popularly as "Sergeant Bob," was supported by the owner of a Rio
de Janeiro supermarket chain, Antonio Sartório Filho. Sartório
Filho is said to have paid 1,600 cruzeiros (by then worth U.S. $107)
a month to Sergeant Bob to coordinate security for his establish-
ments. Each man in Sergeant Bob's 15-man squad—which included
rank-and-file off-duty policemen from the Militarized Police 20th
Battalion—was paid 350 cruzeiros weekly (then about U.S. $24) to
protect Sartório Filho's supermarkets. Sartório Filho also guaranteed pensions to the widows of this private security force, which

again suggests the (albeit limited) social services sometimes attached to a death squad—a safety net ordinarily lacking for most Brazilian workers.[58]

Sergeant Bob's death squad, under weekly contract to one business as a group of private rent-a-cops, was nevertheless subordinated to a larger organization—the supermarket chain—and under relatively longer-term contract. In contrast, O Fininho's freelance death squad simply sold its services, to carry out a few murders, to the highest bidder among a series of private purchasers. The differences between the two Brazilian death squad examples suggest the varying types of privatization within Brazil's system of extralegal "justice."

Perhaps because Brazilian death squads usually seem fully privatized, rather than attached to the government or a business organization, both military and civilian governments over the last 25 years have been able to take an often contradictory approach to death squads—shifting between secretly working with and protecting them, to ignoring their existence, to sometimes trying them for crimes, to very infrequently punishing them with jail time. A recent example of the state's implicit support for death squads is the 1993 murder of eight sleeping street children by a police death squad outside Rio de Janeiro's Candelária Cathedral. Even though Brazil had already instituted a formally elected democratic government, these murderers might not have been caught and brought to trial had there not been a national and international outcry about the massacre.[59] In this case, eight of the death squad members were actually tried. Yet among the eight murderers indicted—the majority state Militarized Police members—only two, as of December 1998, had been found guilty and sentenced; three had won full acquittal and three trials were still going on.

The Functions and Risks of Death Squads for the State

As the historian Charles Tilly argues, "The managers of full-fledged [European] states [of the seventeenth and eighteenth centuries] often commissioned privateers, hired some-time bandits to raid their enemies . . . , and encouraged their regular troops to take booty."[60] Tilly, in fact, maintains that "European rulers could not successfully control the population of their lands without assistance even from their own competitors, so the builders of national power all played a mixed strategy: eliminating, subjugating, dividing, conquering, cajoling, buying, as the occasions presented themselves."[61] Predictably, therefore, even as Brazil was becoming more militarized and its social control more centralized and "modern," death squads proliferated. These gave the state great leeway in handling internal control. As Hannah Arendt remarks in *The Origins of Totalitarianism,* "One of the reasons for the duplication of secret services whose agents are unknown to each other is that total domination needs the most extreme flexibility."[62] A multiplicity of police services allows one branch of police to be used to support one course of action while another is used to undermine it, suggesting the value of extreme segmentation of police activities during Brazil's military period. As Arendt points out, the real "efficiency of . . . police [segmentation] consists in the fact that . . . contradictory assignments can be prepared simultaneously," allowing those who control the police to divide and rule. So devolution is useful at least in the short run for state hegemony over internal security. In fact, death squads, when dealt with effectively by the national state, can provide control options that neither national budgets nor political opinion could support.

Furthermore, through the creation of "subcenters of authority" within the formal social control system and through image management by "action at a distance,"[63] governments can lower the political costs of their repressive goals by refocusing national and international attention away from the state and toward supposedly random, unplanned, and at least officially "unofficial" violence. Thus repression could be maintained, while cloaked as "informal" and not state-related, shifting international attention away from the state's role in repression. As Maria Helena Moreira Alves has pointed out, death squads are "a less visible target for internal and international public opinion," and they "refocus . . . public attention and outrage" away from state violence when they do become visible.[64]

Yet if the state is to channel and shape extralegal violence into supporting its interests, it must maintain some connections with vigilante groups, even though such a state already runs the risk of losing control over the monster it has created.[65] Indeed, whenever state-fostered and -permitted "de-bureaucratizing" begins, the state needs to make efforts at, yet may have difficulty in, controlling the process, eventually finding itself "the sorcerer no longer able to control the powers of the nether world he has called up by his spells."[66] In the process, such a state—particularly where it lacks power to enforce its will in controlling death squads—risks losing whatever legitimacy it may have in national and international public opinion, as the death squads become increasingly brazen and visible.

Moreover, a state that covertly instigates and supports open vigilante violence could lose its claim to monopoly over force. Gilberto Dimmenstein compares such a state to the man who raises a lion cub to protect his house from robbers. At first he has a cute if fierce little pet; but when the lion is full-grown, although no one will try to rob his house, the lion is now as dangerous to its owner's welfare as any robber would be.[67] So the state, faced with its own death squads, is pressed to take action to counter the challenge of these alternative power entities. Nevertheless, as we have seen, even as Brazil's military state labored to centralize its control over internal security, it simultaneously fostered devolution toward a market of ever less controlled and ever more extralegal violent competitors carrying out ever more privatized and commercialized repressive and "protective" roles—thus further and further devolution.

Privatization and Invisibility

Segmentation and privatization of social control reduce the boundaries between the formal police teams that commit murder and the informal death squads, and between these two entities and the private rent-a-cops. The continuum of distinctions among these three social control entities—listed from apparently more to less controlled by public officials and less to more privatized—easily blur through their sharing of membership, allegiance to particularistic over civic interests, and an absence of state and popular oversight and control. In the process, there is an easy flow of policemen into and out of associated death squads and rent-a-cops, with few real differences between one social control entity and the other.

Where social control is privatized, commodified, and instrumentally defined as any activity that promotes the purchaser's interests (the latter seen as synonymous with "security"), social control becomes a customer-defined product: it is what "meet[s] . . . the demands of the 'sovereign' consumer."[68] This has resulted, in Brazil, in a working symbiosis between the formal police system, informal death squads, and rent-a-cops. Thus, Clifford Shearing could argue that in Brazil, the recent debureaucratizing of social control is a product of growth and expansion of the market economy and associated forms of privatization: "As the market comes to rule . . . it becomes increasingly important to anticipate and respond to whatever . . . threatens the range of interests that operate within" the marketplace. Consequently, from a market conception of social control, "partial, not impartial, policing is required."[69]

The market economy engenders death squads because, within the dynamic of a monetized exchange system among "free" participants who define their own interests irrespective of others' rights, "internal security" and policing are things that "not only can be, but should be, bought and sold within a market."[70] Within such logic, each increasingly market-type situation requires a different or slightly more privatized form of policing. This takes the form in Brazil of lone-wolf *justiceiros,* informal death squads for hire, formal specialized police squads, and a proliferation of private rent-a-cops. The many specialized formal police squads and the rent-a-cops, just like the more explicitly "informal" vigilante forms of social control—the *justiceiros* and death squads—operate to secure particular economic interests, whether or not this supports or runs counter to the "common good." Indeed, it is significant that in Brazil—where private economic interests often predominate over concerns for broader social well-being—the rent-a-cop business has grown to the point that many Brazilian cities' more prosperous areas have more rent-a-cops than official police,[71] while the poor squatter settlements are liberally "policed" by murderous *justiceiros* and death squads.[72]

Brazil's experience with death squads is not a completely deviant case in the privatizing of social control. Shearing declares that even in modern, highly rationalized European and U.S. social control systems, "policing has become . . . increasingly fractured, embedded, and decentered," resulting in both a decentralizing of the mechanisms of central rule and of the loci of rule itself. This gives rise to "'subpolitical' [clusters of localized authority] . . . that exist within a legal and political space that is neither purely public [i.e., state-ordered] nor [totally] private." As a result, there is no single center of control, but rather networks of localized authority that operate through alliances that involve "state and non-state authorities

[who] seek to manage each other . . . to produce effects that they regard as desirable."[73] This trend within modern, industrialized countries, pushed to the limit in modern Brazil, produces privatized death squads that provide largely short-term paid services to private contractors.

Conclusion: Alternating Control Systems

Two opposing processes have operated in tandem in Brazil, one recentering the state's control over internal security, as the state reins in the devolution that it had earlier fostered and even protected, and the other again decentering social control as the state "farms out" and partially loses control over some internal control to private groups. Such contradictory pressures in Brazil have contributed to a functional symbiosis between centralizing and debureaucratizing, with one by-product the death squads and *justiceiros*. Such initially state-engendered privatization helps Brazil's fragile democratizing state retain legitimacy by making it appear as if violent repression is occurring only from forces outside the state. Of course, in fact, this may increasingly be the case—to the state's ultimate disadvantage.

In any case, what helps promote the image of death squads as outside government control is that much discourse in Brazil configures all social life as falling simultaneously between and within opposed qualities—at once both rational and mystical, formal and informal.[74] According to this view, death squads—which are neither totally formal nor fully informal, whose members individually and collectively are both police and common citizens—could be cultural products of Brazilian liminality, that is, neither completely one thing nor another.

Yet, at the same time, as we have seen, Brazil's death squads are very compatible with structural rigidity, rationality, centralization, and specialization. Indeed, rather than being uniquely due to Brazilian cultural liminality, death squads are part of a decentering of authority that, in all market societies, grows out of a privatizing and commodifying of social control. As an institutionally attached yet secret arm of the formal police system, death squads carry out the state's dirty work from a socially and politically constructed liminal status that falls somewhere between being on and off duty—doing what the state cannot formally do if it still claims to be democratic.

The relative institutional invisibility of death squads makes them a perfect supplement and shield for failed regular policing by Brazil's democratizing yet still authoritarian state. Decades of police professionalization not only have not eliminated death squads but—especially because of the Brazilian state's continuing focus on a war against "crime"—may have indirectly spawned death squads. In the end, such an approach to Brazil's internal security problems inevitably leaves Brazil's fledgling democracy navigating a treacherous course between the Scylla of bureaucratically impersonal, directly state-supervised official police violence and the Charybdis of police death squads, unofficial and at most only indirectly state-controlled.

Notes

1. Thanks are due Malcolm Willison for editing various versions of this chapter and suggesting valuable theoretical insights. To Arthur D. Brenner and Bruce B. Campbell, organizers and co-presenters of the session on death squads at the American Historical Association meeting in Atlanta (January 1996), I am thankful for suggestions and encouragement. To my students Dena Mahar and Ericka Migliaccio, thanks for fact-checking, and to Carolyn Micklas for word-processing. This research was funded in part by my endowed Roger Thayer Stone Research Chair in Sociology at Union College. A version of this chapter was published as an article: "From Bureaucratic Consolidation to Structural Devolution" in *Policing and Society* 7, no. 4 (1997): 207–34.
2. Allan Nairn, "An Exclusive Report on the U.S. Role in El Salvador's Official Terror," *Progressive*, May 1984.
3. Martha K. Huggins, *Political Policing: The United States and Latin America* (Durham, N.C.: Duke University Press, 1998).
4. Helio Bicudo, *Meu Depoimento sôbre O Esquadrão da Morte* (São Paulo: Pontífica Comissão de Justiça e Paz, 1978); CPI-Menor, "Destinada a Investigar o Estermínio de Criancas e Adolescentes no Brasil," Relatório Final, Câmara dos Deputados, Brasília, March 1992; V.G. Boletim, "Boletim de Recortes sobre Vigário Geral," Ministério Público Procuradoria Geral da República, Assessoria de Comunicação Social, 1993.
5. Huggins, *Political Policing*.
6. Martha K. Huggins and Mika Haritos-Fatouros, "Tortured Consciousness: Secrets and Moralities in Brazilian Police Violence"

(unpublished paper, 1995); Martha K. Huggins and Mika Haritos-Fatouros, "Bureaucratizing Masculinities Among Brazilian Torturers and Murderers," in Lee H. Bowker, ed., *Masculinities and Violence* (Beverly Hills, Calif.: Sage, 1998); Huggins, *Political Policing*. I wish to thank my colleague Mika Haritos-Fatouros for encouraging me to use in this paper some of the data collected for our study of Brazilian police torturers.

7. Heloisa Fernandes, "Authoritarian Society: Breeding Ground for Justiceiros," in Martha K. Huggins, ed., *Vigilantism and the State in Modern Latin America: Essays on Extralegal Violence* (New York: Praeger, 1991).

8. Martha K. Huggins, "Vigilantism and the State: A Look South and North," in Huggins, *Vigilantism and the State;* Caco Barcellos, *ROTA 66: A Historia da Polícia que Mata* (São Paulo: Globo, 1992).

9. Maria-Victoria Benevides and Rosa Maria Fischer Ferreira, "Popular Responses and Urban Violence: Lynching in Brazil," and José de Souza Martins, "Lynchings—Life by a Thread: Street Justice in Brazil, 1979–1988," both in Huggins, *Vigilantism and the State.*

10. Benevides and Fischer Ferreira; de Souza Martins.

11. Benevides and Fischer Ferreira; de Souza Martins.

12. Heloisa Fernandes, "Authoritarian Society."

13. Paulo Sergio Pinheiro, "Police and Political Crisis: The Case of the Military Police," in Huggins, *Vigilantism and the State;* Paul Chevigny, *Edge of the Knife: Police Violence in the Americas* (New York: New Press, 1996).

14. GAJOP, *Grupos de Extermínio: A Banalização da Vida e da Morte em Pernambuco* (Olinda: GAJOP, 1991).

15. "O Esquadrão da Morte," *Jornal da Tarde,* 14 May 1968; "Esquadrão da Morte: Um Caso Nacional," *Globo,* 7 January 1973.

16. "De Cara de Cavalo a Ilha Grande," *Última Hora,* 31 March 1983. Many *Última Hora* sources came from the newspaper's own archive. In this and other Brazilian newspaper archives, article titles were often—and article page numbers almost always—omitted by archivists.

17. "The Death Squads of Rio," *Time,* 25 April 1969, 61; "Justiça e Feita," *Veja,* 29 July 1970, 31.

18. "O Esquadrão da Morte," *Veja,* 25 March 1970.

19. A.J. Langguth, *Hidden Terrors* (New York: Pantheon, 1978), 121; "De Cara de Cavalo."

20. "Ligue 234–2010 e Denuncie o Esquadrão da Morte," *Jornal do Brasil,* 28 September 1975.

21. "O Esquadrão da Morte," *Veja.*

22. "Ligue 234–2010."
23. "Ligue 234–2010"; Aderito Lopes, *O Esquadrão da Morte, São Paulo 1968–1971* (Lisbon: Prelo, 1978).
24. *Jornal da Tarde,* 11 October 1968.
25. R. S. Rose, "Vigilantism and the Police in Brazil: An Exploratory Investigation" (Paper presented at the International Sociological Association, Mexico City, 18 August 1982).
26. "Ligue 234–2010."
27. M, interview by the author, São Paulo, August 1993. M requested that his real name not be used.
28. M, interview.
29. "RUDI Não Moudou na Volta," *Estado de São Paulo,* 27 March 1969.
30. *Jornal da Tarde,* 20 and 22 June 1968; "ROSA e ROTA, Ordem e Medo," *Jornal do Brasil,* 10 October 1975.
31. M, interview.
32. M, interview.
33. M, interview.
34. S, interview by the author, São Paulo, 1993 (S requested that his real name not be used); see also *Jornal da Tarde,* 21 and 22 June 1968.
35. *Jornal da Tarde,* 20 June 1968.
36. S, interview.
37. *Jornal da Tarde,* "Os Federais Contra o Esquadrão," 9 December 1969.
38. *Monthly Report of the AID-OPS Police Training Program in Brazil,* 20 August 1968, TOAID, A-2079, 9.
39. "Policia Pode Parar a Qualquer Momento," *Jornal da Tarde,* 15 July 1968.
40. *Estado de São Paulo,* 26 July 1968.
41. *Monthly Report of the AID-OPS Police Training Program in Brazil,* 14 February 1968, TOAID, A-1215, 2.
42. *Estado de São Paulo,* 27 March 1969.
43. S, interview.
44. Antonio Carlos Fon, *A Tortura: A Historia da Repressão Política no Brasil* (São Paulo: Editora Global, 1986), 52; Huggins, *Political Policing,* 178.
45. Huggins, *Political Policing.*
46. Huggins and Haritos-Fatouros, "Tortured Consciousness"; Huggins and Haritos-Fatouros, "Bureaucratizing Masculinities"; Huggins, *Political Policing.*
47. Archdiocese of São Paulo, *Torture in Brazil* (New York: Vintage, 1985); Huggins, *Political Policing.*

48. Quoted in Lawrence Weschler, "A Miracle, a Universe II," *New Yorker,* 1 June 1987, 227; see also GAJOP.
49. LO, interview by the author, Brasília, October 1993. LO requested that his real name not be used.
50. S, interview.
51. "Documentos Denunciam Esquadrão," *Estado de São Paulo,* 14 January 1977; Ewerton Montenegro Guimarães, *A Chancela do Crime: A Verdadeiro História da Esquadrão da Morte* (Rio de Janeiro: Ambito Cultural Ediçoes, 1978).
53. Clifford Shearing, "Reinventing Policing: Policing as Governance," in Otwin Merenin, ed., *Policing Change, Changing Police: International Perspectives* (New York: Garland, 1996), 296.
52. Hannah Arendt, *The Origins of Totalitarianism* (New York: Harcourt Brace, 1951).
54. *Estado de São Paulo,* 14 January 1977; Guimarães.
55. "Fininho, O Foragido, Começa a Falar," *Estado de São Paulo,* 13 July 1972, 19.
56. "Fininho, O Foragido."
57. *Última Hora,* 28 April 1980.
58. *Globo,* 6–7 September 1977.
59. Martha K. Huggins and Myriam P. Mesquita, "Scapegoating Outsiders: The Murders of Street Youth in Modern Brazil," *Policing and Society 5* (1996); Martha K. Huggins and Myriam Mesquita, "Civic Invisibility, Marginality, Moral Exclusion: The Murders of Street Youth in Brazil," in Rozlyn Michelson, ed., *Children on the Streets of the Americas: Globalization, Homelessness, and Education in the United States, Brazil, and Cuba* (London: Routledge, 1999).
60. Charles Tilly, "War Making and State Making as Organized Crime," in Peter Evans et al., eds., *Bringing the State Back In* (New York: Cambridge University Press, 1985), 173.
61. Tilly, 175.
67. Arendt, 426.
62. Shearing, "Reinventing Policing."
63. Maria Helena Moreira Alves, *State and Opposition in Military Brazil* (Austin: University of Texas Press, 1985), 258.
64. Martha K. Huggins, "Violência Institucionalizada e Democracia: Ligações Perigosas" (lecture delivered at the University of São Paulo Núcleo de Estudos da Violência, 21 November 1992).
65. Karl Marx and Friedrich Engels, *The Communist Manifesto* (London: Penguin, 1985).
66. Gilberto Dimmenstein, *A Guerra dos Meninos: Assassinatos de Menores no Brasil* (São Paulo: Editora Brasiliense, 1991).

68. Shearing, "Reinventing Policing," 292. See also Clifford Shearing, "The Relation Between Public and Private Policing," in Michael Tonry and Norvil Morris, eds., *Modern Policing* (Chicago: University of Chicago Press, 1992).

69. Shearing, "Relation Between Public and Private Policing."

70. Steven Spitzer, quoted in Shearing, "Reinventing Policing," 291.

71. Teresa Pires do Caldeira, "City of Walls: Segregation and Citizenship in São Paulo" (Ph.D. diss., University of California at Berkeley, 1992).

72. Caldeira; Huggins and Mesquita, "Scapegoating Outsiders"; Huggins and Mesquita, "Civic Instability."

73. Shearing, "Reinventing Policing," 285–86.

74. Roberto Da Matta, *Carnivals, Rogues, and Heroes: An Interpretation of the Brazilian Dilemma* (Notre Dame, Ind.: University of Notre Dame Press, 1991); David Hess and Roberto Da Matta, *The Brazilian Puzzle: Culture on the Borderlands of the Western World* (New York: Columbia University Press, 1995).

PART IV

National, Ethnic, and Religious Identity Conflict

CHAPTER 9

The Rise and Fall of Apartheid's Death Squads, 1969–93

Keith Gottschalk

> *We were all drinking. We gave Kondile his spiked drink. After twenty minutes he sat down uneasily . . . then he fell over backwards. Then Major Nic van Rensburg said: "Well chaps, let's get on with the job." Two of the younger constables with the jeep dragged some dense bushveld wood and tyres and made a fire. . . . A man, tall and with blond hair, took his Makarov pistol with a silencer and shot him on top of his head. His body gave a short jerk. . . . The burning of a body on an open fire takes seven hours. Whilst that happened we were drinking and braaing [barbecuing] next to the fire. . . . The fleshier parts of the body take longer . . . that's why we frequently had to turn the buttocks and thighs of Kondile. . . . By the morning we raked through the ashes to see that no piece of bone or teeth was left.*

—Dirk Coetzee[1]

BEGINNING IN 1963,[2] THE SOUTH AFRICAN Government could detain anyone without trial for as many years as it pleased. This it did with tens of thousands of people, with and without the declaration of a formal state of emergency. But as the opening quotation shows, the South African government also resorted to a deliberate program of murder, including the use of death squads as well as other forms of state terror. Why then, with all the other power at its disposal, did the government decide to illegally kill thousands of its opponents and even completely innocent people? This chapter seeks an answer. It is largely confined to the period 1969–93, in which there were formal death squads. It will focus on the following questions: Who were the death squads? How far does evidence to date penetrate the camouflage of government denial and enable historians to allocate responsibility for authorizing or condoning such murder? How many people were killed?

This chapter starts by outlining as briefly as possible the matrix of political culture and precedents out of which death squads arose. It then shows how murder became a form of national security management. The South African government formed death squads both inside and outside the formal security forces. Of those formed within the security forces, this study will focus on the Z Squad, set up by the then Bureau of State Security (BOSS), 1969–79; the C1 Unit, set up by the South African Police (SAP) Security Branch (originally called the Special Branch of the CID; this was the political or secret police of the apartheid regime), c.1978–93; and the South African Defense Force (SADF) Special Forces. This will be followed by examination of private "vigilante" groups, which functioned as death squads from 1985 to 1993. A short look at the dismantling of the death squads at the end of the apartheid regime will then precede the conclusion.

The sources on state violence under the apartheid regime that are available to date have strengths and weaknesses. By far the most important source of information on the crimes of the apartheid government has been the work of the Truth and Reconciliation Commission (TRC), the most successful of a series of state commissions of inquiry.[3] This is true despite some shortcomings. The TRC's report was hastily compiled under impossible constraints of time, scale, and finance. It makes a few factual errors of early history,[4] and some of its findings on specific incidents have given rise to controversy and polemics.[5] Both radical and conservative commentators criticized it, yet it remains not only the best source of information on the death squads in South Africa but an example of how to deal with the aftermath of state terror. Another major source is autobiographies written by participants in the killing. These are, of course, partly shaped by commercial and legal realities, and much like testimony in amnesty hearings, they seek to put their authors in a mitigating perspective by shifting responsibility for their acts to others.[6] Those still awaiting the granting of amnesty, or under threat of prosecution, obviously do not wish to incriminate themselves. In some cases, testimony has been deliberately misleading for other reasons as well.[7] Moreover, the killings took place over such a long period and on such a wide scale that it is hard for many perpetrators to remember all the details of their crimes, even with the best of will. As with almost every case study of death squads, destruction of records by the *ancien regime* and contradictory accounts by veterans of secret units challenge scholars.[8]

A word is in order about what this chapter does not cover. It cannot do more than mention the brutal South African intervention in the affairs of its neighbors.[9] Similarly, this chapter mentions torture, and rape as torture, only in passing, as its focus is on killing. The TRC's revelation of security police and soldiers raping detainees and others, and other sexual molestation, requires a study in its own right.

The National Party government has entire, direct responsibility for over 1,090 killings at the lowest possible count. These were illegal even under its own laws.[10] In addition to these illegal killings, the apartheid regime legalized the use of maximum force by the police and other armed services to suppress rioting. Further, these riots probably would not have occurred had it not been for apartheid policies, disenfranchisement, and police brutality in the first place.[11] The apartheid regime also shares both direct and indirect responsibility for the fratricide between liberation movements. The weight of death is very heavy.

Origins

The death squads did not arise out of a vacuum. South Africa's colonial history of racial domination by white settlers included a deep-rooted pattern of unpunished brutality that extended from settler violence against workers, sharecroppers, and other tenants to virtually unchecked police and Prisons Department murders of black persons. In fact, during the South African epoch of farm jails, farm owners and prison commandants formed a continuum rather than separate categories. This chapter requires that readers invoke the sociological imagination to take cognizance of how apartheid South Africa's political economy, class and race structures, and dominant settler culture constituted the matrix within which the death squads arose and operated.

A further structural effect on the nature of apartheid violence lies in the fact that both the apartheid government and the liberation movements that opposed it believed they were fighting a revolutionary war. This state of mind led both parties (but particularly the apartheid government) to drop the distinction between combatants and noncombatants characteristic of conventional war and worked to increase greatly both the brutality and the scope of the killing.

The National Party government harshened various apartheid policies throughout the 1950s until they met with civil disobedience in the "native reserves," or remnants of precolonial commonage. The government responded with mass arrests, floggings, and fines that pauperized the migrant worker families. The "Bantu commissioners" and other bureaucrats pressured the tribal chiefs to reinforce police repression with coercion through setting up "bodyguards" or "home guards" vigilantes, or be deposed and replaced by compliant client chiefs.

This period already witnessed, in embryo, much of the later violence of the apartheid era. Note one of the consequences of the "subcontracting" of violence to the newly formed chief's bodyguards:

> I have come to warn the Father . . . the police were in our village . . . they meet the Bodyguard. They tell them how to stop your car. They tell them the best place to push it over the side. They say they must light it with petrol, they must burn you in the car. They must put rags on their hands to stop fingerprints. . . . The police have told them Father, it is okay, there is nothing to worry about, the police will be sent to investigate and they will make it okay.[12]

The above quotation from an Anglican parishioner in the Hurutse community dates from early 1958. In this case, the tip-off enabled the priest to escape assassination, but it illustrates several important points. First, earlier than is generally realized, many uniformed and detective police units felt comfortable with planning illegal killings, including political killings. Second, these units were comfortable with the strategy of organizing vigilantes into militias and death squads to kill illegally as surrogates for the government. Third, police units considered it legitimate to kill unarmed civilians who raised publicity about repression or merely organized legal assistance for the police's victims or their next of kin.

Even in this early period of apartheid rule, white (overwhelmingly Afrikaner) police, both uniformed and CID, routinely beat African suspects in nonpolitical crimes. The police carried out exceptionally widespread beatings of African detainees during the Pondoland Revolt of 1960 and the 1960 State of Emergency.[13]

The architect of the apartheid police state was Balthazar Johannes Vorster, minister of justice, police, and prisons in the early 1960s, who later became prime minister and then president. Within one year of his introduction of incommunicado solitary detention without trial,[14] the Security Police were able to torture detainees to death without fear of legal consequences. Even when the torture was noted in court, the media, or during postmortem proceedings, the most notorious perpetrators were often rewarded for their efforts with promotions.[15] Over 129 persons detained without trial are known to have been killed during torture, or tortured until they committed suicide to avoid further pain.[16] Many of the Bantustan security and other police routinely acted with such extraordinary brutality that their assaults could only be meant for deterrence and terror, rather than to help their interrogations.

Individual members of the SAP's Special Branch also sought to intimidate (white) liberals and radicals by firebombing and shooting at their homes and vandalizing their property. Among the hundreds of such incidents, a few amounted to attempted murder as early as 1964.[17] From this it is clear that a climate of terror and intimidation was building in South Africa by the early 1960s. Subsequent events, both nationally and internationally, caused this climate to intensify and led to even worse abuses.

Beginning in 1960, the National Party government perceived its rule to be radically threatened by domestic and foreign enemies who were seen to be growing in number and power. In the 1960s, urbanization grew a larger African working class inside South Africa, whose members joined the African National Congress (ANC) and the rival Pan-Africanist Congress (PAC) in unprecedented numbers. Both these liberation movements and their affiliated trade union federations launched campaigns of militant civil disobedience. When banned, they set up underground movements, which were aided by other African countries and which conducted sabotage and guerrilla operations. The government crushed the ANC's Mkhonto we Sizwe (MK, "Spear of the Nation") and the PAC's Poqo ("the Steadfast") between 1962 and 1964, yet these organizations continued to be active outside of South Africa and to threaten the South

African state. Pro-apartheid South Africans continued to feel embattled into the 1970s as they witnessed the growth of the black in-
telligentsia within South Africa and the popularization of the Black
Consciousness movement. By 1976, black protest led to what is
popularly termed the Soweto Revolt (in fact a national rebellion),
which took the government two years to crush and caused 700
deaths and a new wave of imprisonment.

Foreign developments, too, contributed to this sense of isolation
among white supremacists. Most African countries achieved independence from the British and French empires in the 1950s and
'60s, with South Africa's neighbors Angola and Mozambique becoming independent from the Portuguese empire in 1975. This enabled the South-West African People's Organization (SWAPO) to
start continuous guerrilla war in northern Namibia, a South African
colony. The end of white rule in Zimbabwe in 1980 stripped the
apartheid regime geographically of the last of its white-controlled
buffer states. This greatly facilitated MK logistics and made for
more frequent sabotage attacks and occasional large-scale guerrilla
hit-and-run raids throughout the 1980s. Also, continued industrialization produced ever larger black middle and working classes and
fostered a revival of militant African trade unions. The impact of
government monetary, pass laws, and public housing rental policies
triggered South Africa's largest-ever rebellion through 1984–89. The
international sanctions campaign, after a quarter century of marginal importance, grew to inflict significant military and economic
costs upon the apartheid regime. As a result of these developments,
the South African regime felt increasingly beleaguered and frustrated in its efforts to maintain apartheid. This led it to use murder
as a conscious element of internal security policy.

Murder as a Form of
National Security Management

Establishment of the National
Security Management System

The Afrikaner nationalist government responded to perceived
threats mainly by repression and the construction of a sizable mili-
tary-industry complex. Apartheid social engineering continued to

grow worse, moving from reactionary policy to a counterrevolution in an ethnicizing framework.

Increased repression and violence was rationalized ideologically. By the 1960s the Afrikaner nationalist governments sought to defend their acts of repression from criticism by liberal and leftist opponents by claiming that these were essential to combat the *swartgevaar* (black peril) and the *rooigevaar* (red peril). Afrikaner Nationalist politicians and clergy alike repeatedly denounced humanism, liberalism, and communism for undermining the white race. The head of the Security Police, General Hendrik van den Bergh, had such an authoritarian outlook that he denounced protest theater as "moral or spiritual sabotage." Army colonel J. K. Alheit denounced the permissive society as "ideological terrorism." The Security Police's Major General J. P. Venter denounced anyone who wore the peace sign used by the Campaign for Nuclear Disarmament as "the Anti-Christ."[18]

Since it increasingly saw itself fighting a war of survival against both internal and external enemies, the South African state was put on a war footing. Vorster, who was minister of justice, police, and prisons in the early 1960s, militarized both the South African Police and the Prisons Department. Policemen and prison warders were retitled with military ranks, as were the administrators of the Prisons Department, and placed under military-style discipline. The regime extended the censorship laws concealing military activity to cover police and prison warders' actions. During his years as prime minister (1966–79), Vorster also favored the Security Branch with large increases in its budget. In effect, a formal national security ideology came to pervade official thinking, which made the recourse to state terror easier.

This militarization of society was continued throughout the years that P.W. Botha served as minister of defense and General Magnus Malan as commandant general of the SADF. They popularized the propaganda doctrine of a Soviet-led international communist "total onslaught" to legitimate the SADF's "total strategy" propagated in the 1977 Defense White Paper.[19] This strategy sought a military-dominated coordination of the bureaucracy, and granted any authorization or funding increase that the SADF and Security Police might request. Later, as president, P. W. Botha set up a virtual shadow government after 1982. An older cabinet committee, the State Security Council (SSC), became the apex of an invisible nexus of Strategic Planning Committees ("Stratcoms"), Communication

Committees ("Comcoms"), and Joint Intelligence Committees ("GIKcoms," in this blitz of Afrikaans acronyms). This invisible government comprised at all levels mixed military-civil institutions, always chaired by military officers, which became the bureaucratic organs responsible for the death squads.

This military domination within government was accompanied by greater readiness than before to kill enemies, and kill them on a larger scale. As appropriate for covert war, the language of State Security Council documents bears witness to the increased emphasis on killing, using words such as *elimineer* (to eliminate), *neutraliseer* (to neutralize), *uitwis* (to wipe out), and *vernietig* (to destroy).[20] Lower down the hierarchy, officers and other ranks used both these terms and euphemisms such as *raak ontslae van hom* (get rid of him), *vat hom uit* (take him out), *los die probleem op* (to solve the problem), *maak 'n plan met* (make a plan with), "steal him," and "we are reducing the files."[21] As government policies provoked rebellion on the largest scale known in South Africa's history, these dynamics led to a vicious spiral of events.

As far back as the 1976 Soweto Revolt, in the Vorster era, Jimmy Kruger, minister of police, proposed that the high school student movement "must be broken, and the police should perhaps act a bit more drastically and harshly, bringing about more deaths." The cabinet adopted his proposal.[22] When the military in turn dominated policy-making, they had the same predilection for killing, this time on a larger scale. Their key policy directives included the May 2, 1985, decision of the GIS (Afrikaans acronym of the Joint Intelligence Structure) of the Joint Security Staff: "Ringleaders must be selectively eliminated. The idea around elimination is twofold: the physical gunning-down of leaders in riot[s . . . and] the removal of intimidators. In the latter case specific thought is given to schools and labor situations."[23] On paper, the recommendation qualified this. Rioters should be shot only when committing serious offenses against the common law. "Elimination" can, after all, have two meanings, gunning down, or (for schoolchildren) to be "restricted physically to such an extent that they are removed from circulation and kept away." On the face of it, this appeared to refer not to shooting, but to house arrest and preventive detention. However, the conduct of the police during 1976–77 and between 1984 and 1989, towards both school students and trade union leaders, indicates that both types of "elimination" were practiced.

Namibia: The Testing Ground
for Apartheid State Terror

A striking number of the Security Police and SADF death squad leaders fought, all told, in three wars in three countries over two decades.[24] They later applied their foreign experience to South Africa. The Namibian War of Independence in particular became the crucible in which the apartheid regime forged aspects of the counterrevolutionary strategy it later imposed on South Africa itself.[25] This included the use of death squads.

For example, the "contra-mobilization" strategy, which set rival liberation movements against one another and which was later used with much success in South Africa, was pioneered in Namibia. In South Africa's contra-mobilization in Namibia, the Security Police and the National Intelligence Service (NIS) competed to claim credit for setting up the Democratic Turnhalle Association party (DTA),[26] while the SADF tried to set up explicitly ethnic political parties,[27] which failed to gain support. All these were intended as rivals to the South-West African People's Organization (SWAPO). This presaged the SSC strategy inside South Africa during the 1980s of aiding rivals of the ANC and local vigilante groups with protection from the law, funds, and weapons.

Even the internal death squads established for use within South Africa had strong links to the Namibian campaign. For coercion in Namibia, the Security Police founded Unit K in 1976, which expanded into a counterinsurgency motorized infantry unit called Koevoet (Crowbar).[28] Koevoet was later disbanded after the Namibian war ended, but the Security Police formed similar units for use within South Africa in the late 1970s at Vlakplaas (the "C1 Unit"), the Eastern Cape, and KwaZulu-Natal.[29]

Many of the other murderous tactics later used in the domestic struggle within South Africa were pioneered in the war in Namibia. One example is the routine killing of POWs after interrogation.[30] Another was the Koevoet practice of driving armored combat vehicles through huts and shanties, which was later adopted by riot police units inside South Africa and made arrest improbable and death intentional. The SADF also set the precedent in Namibia in 1988 of using infantrymen in mufti to attack SWAPO political meetings and assassinate political leaders. Then president P.W. Botha personally forbade the prosecution of six such assassins.[31] In a similar fashion

within South Africa, between 1990 and June 1993, private "vigilantes" were permitted to make *pangas* (machetes) and other
weapons in state railway workshops. Joined by SADF Special Forces
soldiers in mufti, they killed 572 train commuters on the Johannesburg-Soweto line over a period of several years, a tactic intended to
cause random terror.[32]

The SADF claimed that by 1990, when it left Namibia, it had
killed 8,000 SWAPO and Angolan "terrorists."[33] The murderous
tactics to which the South African security forces had become accustomed when fighting a guerrilla campaign on foreign soil quickly
found application at home. With increasing domestic and international pressure coming to bear on the apartheid government, and
with the intervention in Namibia to show the way, violence within
South Africa increased.

Elimineer: The Policy of Murder

> "I shot [Tiso] three times in the chest," Gevers said. . . ."They
> took the dead man's clothes off. . . . They put the dead man in a
> sitting position—which Vlakplaas operatives called the 'Buddha
> position'—and tied the explosives to him.
>
> "We drove a kilometre away and detonated the explo-
> sives. . . . There was just a big hole in the ground where he had
> sat. . . . Late that night we burnt his clothes in a big drum. Tiso
> had brown leather shoes which Brits took because he said they
> were too nice to destroy," said Gevers. The men drank until they
> fell over.
>
> Early the next morning . . ."for three hours we walked
> around looking for pieces of human flesh to make certain that we
> had destroyed all evidence. The biggest piece we got was the size
> of a finger nail, [in all] only about half a kilogram of flesh and
> bone. We held this in our hands. We put the pieces of flesh in the
> hole and blew them up. We searched again for pieces of flesh and
> blew them up again."[34]

The gruesomeness and depravity of this quotation is typical of many
hit squad assassinations, as revealed in confessions to the TRC.
These practices raise certain questions: Why was murder used and
not other methods? Why was murder used in some cases but not others? Many of the answers are illustrated by the following: In one
joint SADF Special Forces–Security Police killing of ten youths

"probably involved in school boycotts, consumer boycotts and even arson," Security Police brigadier Jan Cronje testified that he made no attempt to prosecute them because "[a]t that time I had no testimony I could use in a case against them." The killing was staged to make the youths look like incompetent "terrorists" who had blown themselves up. This gave the public the impression that the SADF and SAP were effective, "created confidence in the apartheid government and persuaded white people" to vote for it.[35] The writer Jacques Pauw, himself from a conservative Afrikaans family, reflects:

> They were apartheid's ultimate and most secret weapons. When all else had failed—detention without trial, harassment and dirty tricks, state of emergency regulations and criminal prosecution—the death squads were sent out to finally "solve the problem." They acquired the power to decide over life and death. In the process, they not only abandoned their police or SADF oaths to serve and uphold law and order, but were also forced to abandon their own morality. . . . These were men who had their own rules, their own language, their own culture. Informal rules required that only two people should ever be present when orders were given, turning the only witnesses into co-conspirators. . . . The death squad's culture, its techniques and methods had much in common with those of a gang of ordinary thugs. What distinguished the squad's members from common criminals was that they believed themselves to be fighting a secret twilight war against an evil enemy. Any method that could lead to the destruction and disruption of the enemy was permitted and tacitly condoned. In committing these atrocities, there was one golden rule: never get caught. They referred to it as the "eleventh commandment."[36]

The "eleventh commandment" meant that the apartheid regime could retain the moral high ground among the white minority. Its officials could portray themselves as anticommunist crusaders of the Free World defending South Africa against a Soviet-led "total onslaught" of terrorists who committed murder and other atrocities on civilians, including women and children.

Death Squads Within the State Security Forces

Soon after Vorster became prime minister, his protégé General H. J. van den Bergh set up a secret service, the Republican Intelligence

Service (RID), which he then separated from the Security Branch. He renamed and greatly expanded it into the Bureau of State Security (BOSS) in 1968. Sometime around 1969, BOSS founded its Z Squad, a death squad seemingly named metaphorically for the letter that terminates the alphabet. According to a former BOSS agent, Gordon Winter, General van den Bergh told a Government Commission of Inquiry in 1979:

> I can tell you here today, not for your records, but I can tell you I have enough men to commit murder if I tell them to kill. . . . I do not care who the prey is, or how important they are. Those are the kind of men I have. And if I wanted to do something like that to protect the security of the State nobody would stop me. I would stop at nothing. But that is such a damaging admission that, my dear honorable gentlemen, for the sake of the South African government, you will be compelled to omit it from your findings.

The general's arrogant confidence in the old-boy loyalty of the judicial commission was not misplaced. Winter comments that the commission just paraphrased his words in a watered-down version.[37]

The earliest known illegal killings for which Security Police members (both brigadiers) later applied for amnesty occurred in 1969–70 and 1972.[38] Similarly, Winter claims to have received "broad hints" from top BOSS officials that in January 1970 they had assassinated a sacked agent who they feared might expose them.[39] This killing was one of the earliest assassinations by BOSS's Z Squad, and it set a precedent as well. BOSS committed the assassination in a foreign country, the United Kingdom, and (as the Special Branch sometimes did to detainees who died under torture) disguised the fatal assault as a fall from a building. Winter also recorded that Z Squad assassination attempts included the February 1974 parcel-bomb killings of a student leader, Ongopotse Tiro, who had fled to Botswana, and John Dube, an MK saboteur who had fled to Zambia, along with the murders of Namibians.[40] The sensational 1974 assassination of Tiro may well mark the initiation of top-level government endorsement of death squads targeting unarmed civilian political and student leaders, as opposed to captured guerrillas and secret service defectors. After 1979, BOSS, now renamed the National Intelligence Service (NIS), was forced to disband its Z Squad and was confined to intelligence analysis as a result of interagency rivalry.[41] The Security Police and SADF hit squads now stepped into the breach.

In the future, historians might coax revelations about the extent of illegal killings from members of the SADF's Buffalo Battalion and the Civil Cooperation Bureau (CCB). But as this book goes to press, the "Vlakplaas unit," as South Africa's media dubbed the C1/C10 unit, got more high-profile publicity than any other hit squad. C1 came to epitomize the lawlessness of the National Party regime. It was perhaps the most notorious South African death squad throughout the 1980s. Government attempts to distance itself from the unit or to deny knowledge of its acts are made futile by the simple question posed by C1's last commander, police colonel Eugene de Kock: If the government knew nothing, then why was C1 the most decorated police unit? Why did the minister of police and numerous police generals come to the unit's barbecues and to its bar to congratulate the men on their successful operations and award them medals?

The Afrikaans poet and writer Antjie Krog puts her finger on one pertinent point about the C1 unit (nicknamed the Vlakplaas unit after the state-owned farm that was its base):

> Even though the official task description for Vlakplaas was simply to track down and arrest guerrillas, in the eighteen months of [CO Dirk] Coetzee's stay, there was only one arrest. Nevertheless, and despite spending millions of rands at the taxpayer's expense, the unit was never criticized or accused of wasting money.
>
> The reason is obvious: the unofficial task, namely to train a hit squad that could be called out to take care of activists, was carried out perfectly. The orders were given orally, one-to-one. No diaries, no written reports. Amongst ourselves, says Coetzee, "we developed our own body language. The wink of an eye, the nod of a head, could spell someone's end."[42]

Other units established within the South African security apparatus included the Civil Cooperation Bureau (alias *die organasie* [the organization], alias Triplane), created by the SADF Special Forces in 1986 and officially disbanded in 1990; and TREWITS (Afrikaans acronym for Counter-Revolutionary Information Task Team), established by the SADF and the Security Police around 1987.[43] TREWITS eventually became responsible for drawing up hit lists for the death squads, and because of its status as "judge," the Security Police jokingly called it the Sanhedrin. TREWITS considered all ANC diplomats and the entire executive committee of the ANC, the South African Communist Party (SACP), and the United Democratic Front (UDF, an organization of ANC sympathizers) as potential targets for assassination, although the ANC did not target corresponding members of the South African government such as cabinet ministers, the National Party executive committee, and government diplomats. TREWITS is known to have authorized 82 extrajudicial killings and seven attempted killings.

First in Namibia, and then in South Africa, the SADF and SAP policy was to pay *kopgeld* (bounty) of 2,000 rands for each corpse,[44] which encouraged security forces to take no prisoners. The Security Branch routinely legalized its extrajudicial killings by planting weapons beside the corpses, prior to the arrival of the media or CID police in charge of any postmortem inquiries.[45]

Killing techniques varied. Most killings were low-tech, involving beatings with fists or iron implements.[46] Poison figured in many Special Forces assassination attempts,[47] as did explosives. The brutal inventiveness of this activity indicates the cold planning of most death squad murders. The SADF even had an entire section called the Electronic Magnetic Logistical Component, whose job it was to construct explosive devices, which it built into letters, washing powder boxes, briefcases, cars, radios, TVs, and umbrellas.[48] This premeditation is also borne out by the frequency with which both the security forces and their covert death squads entrapped their victims. For example, youth organization activists were recruited into false MK cells in Chesterville, KwaNdebele, Nietverdiend, and elsewhere. In most cases, their recruitment culminated in ambush killings. C1 and its *askaris* (POWs "turned" under torture and used as double agents) took the initiative in 52 known killings of this kind, including some where the provocateurs gave out booby-trapped grenades and mines so that the victims would blow themselves up.[49]

Those responsible for these murders were not a handful of rogue officers or isolated psychopaths, but were instead part of a cold-blooded murder machine with the full resources of a modern state behind them. Nevertheless, even they were not enough for the apartheid government, which also subcontracted killing to private groups and individuals.

Subcontracting Death:
Murder by State-Sponsored Vigilantes

Other contributions to this volume have uncovered a process of sub-contracting whereby governments encourage and collaborate with nonstate actors in the formation or work of death squads. In South Africa, aside from the use of Namibian and Angolan soldiers, a peculiar and characteristic form of subcontracting took place. This involved the exploitation of existing divisions within the black and "colored" communities through the covert organization of and support for "vigilantes." Not only could these vigilante groups work as unofficial state adjuncts, their violence could also cover up the killings of the government death squads. The Security Police sought to popularize the notion that one of the main roots of the increasing level of violence in South Africa was "black-on-black" conflict. The propaganda that ANC and communist factions killed each other was simply one part of this larger campaign. The police smear that the parcel bomb that killed Ruth First was sent by her husband, Joe Slovo, became the most successful of these propaganda plants in the conservative media.

The military-bureaucratic establishment during the Botha era was keen on what it called "contra-mobilization," otherwise known as a "third force" strategy. In the context of counterrevolutionary doctrines, this referred to the government use of popular or indigenous rivals of a revolutionary movement against it. Such rivals may be armed and aided by the government where they already exist, or the government may create them. These popular rivals to an insurgent movement are then used as a third armed force, which attacks the insurgents on their home front, while the government's special forces, sometimes in mufti, also stage raids. The government of South Africa instituted such a policy, which had several major benefits. Politically, the government maintained plausible deniability for war crimes and other atrocities whenever its security forces acted outside the law, for such acts could easily be blamed on popular anti-insurgent vigilantes. Government propagandists presented such war crimes as tribal, factional fighting and as "black on black" violence. The government then pointed to this violence to justify ethnic segregation and strong government repression. Also, it was cheap: instead of hiring extra police and soldiers with salaries and fringe benefits, the government obtained the services of tens of thousands of militia members merely for the cost of firearms, or even for free. The government simply used the medieval strategy of letting vigilantes loot the bodies and homes of those they killed.

As far back as 1982, the SADF urged the SSC to "exploit and encourage the division between" the African National Congress, Inkatha, and the Black Consciousness movement.[50] The second prong of this strategy was elaborated in a November 1985 National Intelligence Service document. In addition to an allusion to detention, it recommended:

> The activities of the comrades should be rendered inoperative by the neutralization of the leadership . . . in a clandestine manner, to make them the target of the vigilantes or *mbangalala*. . . . The action against intimidation from anarchists and revolutionaries by the so-called vigilantes or *mbangalala* should, taking into consideration an organization such as Inkatha, in a clandestine manner be reinforced, extended and portrayed as a natural resistance by moderates against anarchy.[51]

The SSC adopted the National Strategy Against the Revolutionary War Against the Republic of South Africa in December 1986. Strategy 44 of the National Strategy, which was minuted in January 1987, reaffirmed that the government should "mobilize groups and individuals to . . . offer resistance against revolutionary actions [and ensure that counterrevolutionary organizations should be] developed on an ethnic basis to prevent radicals from utilizing the political vacuum."[52]

These cabinet directives were a series of ascending steps in the mid-1980s repression of insurrection. They are snapshots of a smoking gun that led to the SADF's and Security Police's various hit squads, and also to the government's aid to the Inkatha Freedom Party (IFP), code-named Operation Marion. Operations Palmiet, Xenon, and a variety of other code names were used for aid to the Witdoeks (White Bandannas), Amasolomzi (Eyes of the Home), and other local vigilante groups similarly encouraged by the government.[53]

During the years 1984–94 there were up to possibly 19,000 political killings in South Africa, most of which were the result of government efforts to turn rival liberation movements against one another.[54] Until 1987, two-thirds of the killings were the result of direct conflict between the government forces and the popular upris-

ing, and only one-third were due to conflicts between rival liberation movements. After that year, these proportions were reversed.
From 1990, killings were overwhelmingly due to fratricide between
the supporters of rival liberation organizations, such as the ANC
and Inkatha. The IFP claims that over 400 of its officeholders (as
opposed to rank-and-file members) were assassinated. For a sample
that the TRC was able to investigate, over three-quarters were killed
by ANC supporters, the others being victims of the police, of fratricide within the IFP, and of nonpolitical violence.[55]

The old regime has varying levels of responsibility for this fratricide. By banning the political parties that had the largest support
in the country and harshly suppressing opposition, it bears historical responsibility for the conclusion by most South Africans that this
was a tyranny only rebellion could overthrow. Such a dynamic had
side effects, including the militarization of opposition organizations
and the militarization of political struggle. The conflict between the
police state and the liberation movements created its own dynamics,
which in turn led to secondary conflicts such as the militarization of
rivalry between competing liberation movements. Ultimately it led
to tertiary conflicts as well, in which combat spread from interparty
to intraparty rivalry. That point made, the actual situation was quite
complex, and simplistic formulations must be avoided. For example, unlike RENAMO in Mozambique, the IFP had not been set up
by the South African Security Police. To the contrary, the apartheid
security apparatus was suspicious of the IFP in its first five years and
initially made two attempts to set up rival organizations against it.
It was only later that the special partnership between the IFP and the
security forces developed.

While scholarship on South Africa must be both wary and
weary of populist conspiracy theories,[56] it is clear that the apartheid
government was responsible for many of these fratricidal killings. Its
strategy directives to exploit and maximize fratricide have already
been documented above. Provincial HQs of the Security Branch implemented this strategy on a wide scale. In May 1985, for example,
Major General Dirk Genis told Port Elizabeth Security Police, "The
conflict between the UDF and AZAPO should be exploited as soon
as possible. ComCom [Communications Committee] is busy planning in this regard."[57]

The SADF provided variegated support for a wide range of
African counterrevolutionaries from the *witdoeks* (Operation Xenon)

in Crossroads and Cape Town to the AmaAfrika in Uitenhage and Port Elizabeth. The scale of these actions was, however, dwarfed by Operation Marion to support Inkatha. Police constable William Harrington testified about the police role in the ANC-IFP clashes around Pietermaritzburg. At night, disguised in ski masks, his police unit went from home to home, searched for weapons, and demanded to see IFP membership cards. If the house was without one, they burned it down: "'I fired on any ANC house or group from my vehicle. I distributed weapons to IFP chiefs, I transported Inkatha members and ammunition. It was days of death and blood.'"[58]

During 1992, the C10 unit (the C1 unit renamed) supplied Inkatha vigilantes on the Witwatersrand and in KwaZulu-Natal with shotguns, AK-47 rifles, hand grenades, land mines, RPG launchers and ammunition, and mortars in a quantity that filled six ten-ton trucks.[59] These actions coincided with the 1990–92 alliance of the National Party (NP) and the IFP against the ANC at the Conference for a Democratic South Africa (CODESA) and other negotiations. In 1999, a former Security Police member, now an IFP member of the Provincial Legislature, led police to one buried cache which alone contained seven tons of weapons in a bunker four meters underground.[60] At least one IFP executive member, Themba Khoza, was reportedly simultaneously a paid double agent for two rival secret services—the National Intelligence Service and the Security Police's C1 unit.[61]

Murder to Enforce Loyalty Among the Murderers

There are over nine known cases where white Security Police killed, or gave the order to kill, African informers and African colleagues in the Security Police because they were suspicious of the victim's loyalty.[62] A tenth illegal killing is perhaps the most revealing example of the level of white racism in the police, even at the Police College at Hammanskraal. Sergeant Mothasi, an African, accused a Colonel van Zyl of beating him severely enough to burst his eardrum. When Mothasi refused to withdraw the charge, three Security Police shot both him and his wife.[63] As the professional increasingly merged with the criminal, one Security Police captain, Michael Bellingan, tried to justify murdering his wife in 1991 on the grounds that she was allegedly going to leak information about the Security Branch.[64] In another case, the Security Police killed a Military Intelligence (MI) double agent inside Botswana, plus his wife and two deaf young children. This was merely because in their mopping-up operations in Botswana, some of the insurgents he had double-crossed caused the C1 unit some trouble.[65]

Nor were the police the only government agency affected by the climate of violence. In the SADF, 31 Angolans press-ganged into military service were killed in 1979, simply because they were *kakmakers* (troublemakers). In 27 of these cases, their wives and children were also killed.[66] During the 1980s, the KwaZulu Police (KZP) killed "a handful" of other KZP members because they refused to cover up Inkatha or KZP crimes.[67] As late as 1994 the SADF killed one white conscript with snake serum because he was suspected of being an ANC sympathizer. They also attempted to kill another dissenter by impregnating his shirt with nerve poison. The SADF chemical warfare researchers who developed these poisons were themselves repeatedly threatened by their commanding officer, Brigadier Wouter Basson, who warned that he would kill them if they revealed these secrets.[68] In 1991, the C1 unit tried to assassinate its former commanding officer, Dirk Coetzee, with a booby-trapped cassette player after Coetzee had revealed the nefarious doings of the unit to the press. The Security Branch was particularly anxious to kill Coetzee before he could testify about General Lothar Neethling's issuing poison to Special Branch policemen.[69]

In a climate in which the value of human life was increasingly cheapened, assassination and planned assassinations spread even to the ruling establishment itself. There is strong circumstantial evidence, such as a contemporary cover-up and current threats to the surviving daughter, that in 1977 the Z Squad assassinated a National Party parliamentary candidate, Robert Smit, and his wife.[70] Within five years, the political confidence of the secret services grew with P.W. Botha's accession to the premiership. Military Intelligence eclipsed BOSS, but showed a potentially more lethal paranoia toward even its political bosses. When the Zimbabwean army overran a base of the SADF-supplied RENAMO counterrevolutionary party in Mozambique, it captured papers of one of the South African military liaison officers, Colonel van Niekerk. These included an MI political assessment of every member of the contemporary South African cabinet. The MI assessment included words to the effect that in any future major crisis, Mr. R. F. "Pik" Botha, then minister of foreign affairs, was the cabinet minister most likely to betray the

Afrikaner volk—and in such circumstances should be eliminated. When he was shown this particular captured document on his next visit to Mozambique, the Mozambican minister noted that Pik Botha "turned as white as a sheet."[71] Pik Botha had no doubts as to its authenticity, and that it meant what it said. The Security Police did in fact carry out grenade attacks on the homes of its allies, including cabinet ministers Allan Hendrickse and Chris April, because they had voted against a bill that President P. W. Botha wanted parliament to pass.[72] In 1986, the Security Branch and SADF Special Forces also assassinated a cabinet minister of a satellite regime—the minister of internal affairs in KwaNdebele, Piet Ntuli, with a car bomb—after his reign of terror through mass floggings had become embarrassing to the South African government.[73] In a climate in which the government decided to suspend the rule of law and to employ murder against its opponents, no one was safe, not even the executioners themselves.

Unravelling:
Demoralization, Defections, Dismantling

Ultimately, the actions of the apartheid government and particularly its employment of death squads could not be kept secret. In 1989, Butana Nofemela, a Security Police assassin, was sentenced to death for the nonpolitical murder of an Afrikaner farmer. The night before his hanging, after he had realized that senior policemen who had promised to save him had double-crossed him, he revealed all that he knew to the *Weekly Mail,* which published his exposé on October 20, 1989: "Death Row Policeman Tells of Special Branch Hit Squad." This was swiftly followed by an article in the *Vrye Weekblad* on November 17, 1989, entitled, "Bloody Trail of the SAP. Meet Captain Dirk Johannes Coetzee, commander of a police death squad."[74] The initial reaction of the police establishment was to smear the reputations of the whistle-blowers and to try to cover its tracks by shooting potential whistle-blowers such as *askari* Brian Ngqulunga.[75] It also tried to hide its death squads by changing their names or organization. For example, Security Police Unit C1 was renamed Unit C10.[76] When the SADF's Civil Cooperation Bureau was officially disbanded in 1991, its personnel were transferred to Military Intelligence's Directorate of Covert [Information] Collection

(DCC). It continued as a unit of the DCC until exposed in November 1992 by investigators from the Goldstone Commission. Since the DCC's task was to try to compromise ANC leaders via hired prostitutes, homosexuals, and drug dealers,[77] this implied the government was negotiating with the ANC in bad faith.

During 1989, the cabinet forced P. W. Botha to resign as president, and the National Party parliamentary caucus voted for F. W. de Klerk as the new president. De Klerk immediately started to demilitarize state structures. His first reforms were to dismantle the invisible government of the National Security Management System, starting with the State Security Council. The new president responded to the two media exposes of police hit squads by appointing the Harms Judicial Commission to "cut to the bone. . . . No stone will be left unturned to establish the full truth." Despite de Klerk's pledge, the Security Police successfully deceived Judge Harms, whose expertise lay in patent laws. Security Police assassin Joe Mamasela admitted, "Oh, I lied. We all lied" to the commission. Security Police assassin Craig Williamson recalled, "They believed totally the nonsense that was fed to them. The whole Harms Commission was a farce. It was fed manure and it was kept in the dark and it grew the type of mushrooms it was supposed to grow."[78]

Nevertheless, de Kock asked police general "Krappies" Engelbrecht to disband C10. He told de Kock that it was too early, because the ANC could withdraw from negotiations and resume the armed struggle, in which case the government might still need the "sharp edge" of the police.[79]

But, de Kock claims, the C10 unit found out about three months in advance of the impending unbanning of the liberation movements. The men of C10 became demoralized, especially when even other Security Police officers suddenly started avoiding them.[80] He also claims that in this paranoid atmosphere, Engelbrecht asked him to kill Joe Verster, the "managing director" of the SADF's Civil Cooperation Bureau. In addition to this bizarre interservice hostility, C10 members now so mistrusted one another as to tape-record each other at meetings and to ask one colleague to kill another.[81]

The political transition from minority to majority rule and democracy culminated in the dismantling of the death squads such as C10, the CCB, and the Buffalo Battalion during 1992–93. When the Goldstone and Steyn commissions reported to de Klerk the DCC's continuing covert actions against the ANC, de Klerk in

December 1992 purged 19 Military Intelligence officers and operatives, including four brigadiers and two generals.[82]

When the death squad members realized all too late how the official euphemisms used on paper gave the National Party president, cabinet ministers, and generals a measure of credible deniability, they felt betrayed. When any of them applied to the TRC for amnesty, the others named as murderers in the amnesty application would in turn apply for amnesty. This facilitated unraveling the broad outlines of a representative sample of, but not all, death squad crimes.

De Klerk first became aware of opposition to his reforms by hard-liners in the police and military in January 1990. The ex-president later wrote in his autobiography that when he discovered the secret atom bomb program that was never discussed in any cabinet meeting or even in the State Security Council, he suspected that other matters might also have been kept secret.[83] Yet de Klerk denied to the end that he had been aware of the death squads. He recalled that his early opposition to the military's proposals and their growing power meant that the security establishment did not trust him with their secrets, and he frankly preferred it that way.[84] As if truly discovering the state of affairs in his country for the first time, De Klerk noted that the establishment and funding of the undercover units must have required high-level authorization. Putting his finger on some of the central issues discussed in this chapter, he wrote that such units

> soon acquired a high degree of autonomy and often carried out operations on their own initiative. They became a law unto themselves. They recruited some agents who were criminals.... At some further stage, probably about the time that I became president, these murky elements in the undercover structures of the security forces began to formulate their own policy.[85]

The TRC agreed. In its report, it noted

> the extent to which covert action, the existence of large amounts of secret funds and a climate of unaccountability led to an increasingly criminalized set of networks between members and ex-members of the security forces. In such cases, considerable financial interests were clearly furthered by a destabilized political

situation. There is considerable evidence of ex- and serving security force members engaged in, for example, gun-running, as well as a range of other criminal activities.[86]

When democracy came, some soldiers resigned from the Special Forces to become mercenaries in other countries.[87] Of known death squad members, Joe Mamasela became a born-again Christian and Paul van Vuuren a farmer. Only a handful are in jail: Security Police colonel Gideon Nieuwoudt was sentenced to 20 years jail for killing four people with a car bomb, and Colonel Eugene de Kock was sentenced to life imprisonment plus 212 years jail.[88] Ferdi Barnard was jailed for his drive-by killing of David Webster. Captain Jeff Benzien still serves in the police and was neither disciplined nor demoted. Dirk Coetzee, Brood van Heerden, and Willie Nortje serve in the National Intelligence Agency. None of the Security Police generals who gave the orders to kill have been charged, nor even sued to return the money they looted from secret service funds.[89] Like their surviving victims, many of the retired death squad operatives and soldiers suffer from post-traumatic stress disorder. In interviews, many of them say they experience feelings of waste; have insomnia or nightmares of swimming pools filled with blood; and engage in heavy drinking to combat their troubles.[90]

Precisely because they had been official parts of the government apparatus (as opposed to being privately organized and supported), members of the SADF Civil Cooperation Bureau and the C10 squad had no interest in continuing as an ultraright political movement after the end of apartheid. Their focus was instead on golden handshakes, retirement packages, and hoping to preserve their benefits by staying as far away from the limelight as possible. Those without pensions got involved in criminal activities such as setting up brothels, stealing, and drug-dealing.[91] The few independent death squads on the ultraright were broken up, their members arrested and jailed after murdering 54 Africans by 1994.

Conclusions

Two years after liberation, the government coalition partners (the ANC and IFP) ensured that their national executives implemented what amounted to joint cease-fire committees at the provincial, district, and branch levels. These finally succeeded in disentangling their political parties' moral and material resources from local warlords who continued feuding in some countryside communities, shantytowns, and working-class wards. Retired president De Klerk later wrote, "There is no evidence that the assassination of opponents had the slightest effect on the final outcome of the struggle—other than causing further personal suffering and bitterness. The activities of these elements during my presidency to undermine the transformation process bordered on treason."[92] The killings, and the general climate of lawlessness and arbitrary rule of which they were a part, were unable to preserve the apartheid regime. All the death, the suffering, and the oppression, which were used to combat the regime's real and imagined enemies, were useless.

The epoch of apartheid, the police state, and the death squads made it necessary for the post-apartheid democracy to devote much effort to transforming political culture, and particularly to demilitarizing party structures, rhetoric, ideology, and political practice. The liberation movement had to choose an inclusive strategy toward its rivals, almost co-optation, and offer the former ruling race and ruling classes both the symbols and substance of a negotiated compromise. The first democratic constitution explicitly outlaws torture and execution and promotes both a justiciable Bill of Human Rights and a human rights culture. It provides for a public protector, a Human Rights Commission,[93] and, specifically for the police, an Independent Complaints Directorate. So far, South Africa has been remarkably successful as a multiparty democracy.

In South Africa's first five years as a democracy, virtually no hit squads have arisen from the ultraright and none from the ultraleft. Social movements have sprung up in response to a crime wave temporarily overwhelming police and prosecutors. These movements, from Mapogo a Mathamaga (idiomatically, "Defend Ourselves Like a Tiger") in the north to People Against Gangsterism and Drugs (PAGAD) in the south, have spawned some vigilantes and hit squads. This poses a challenge to democracy both to suppress the crime wave and the vigilantism and to suppress them only by the rule of law.[94] Still, these limited and apparently spontaneous vigilante groups are a far cry from the death squads and government-sponsored vigilantes of the apartheid era.

The absolute power that successive National Party governments granted the police state and the military included legal protection from prosecution for murder and rape. This was another case study of how absolute power corrupts absolutely.[95] Analysis of the extrajudicial killing makes striking how many of them were gratuitous. Time and again, when the Security Police already had the extreme power to lawfully detain their opponents for as long as they chose and to hold them incommunicado, and when censorship of the media was legal, they murdered presumed enemies of the state and sometimes killed the spouses and children of their victims as well.

Extrajudicial killing was also skewed by the racial hierarchy of a racist state. With very few exceptions, only Africans, Asians, and Coloured Persons were illegally killed inside South Africa; very few whites were targeted and murdered. It is also conspicuous that before 1990, the sole prosecutions and convictions of Security and other police for extrajudicial murder over three decades were of one Coloured and one English-speaking officer, January van As in the Protea police station and Brian Mitchell of the New Hanover police station. They did not enjoy the same degree of protection afforded to those in the Afrikaner old boy network. Ironically, from the late 1980s, the reduction of the unequal status of black and white as apartheid was phased out had its perverse mirror image in the world of the death squads. It became acceptable to illegally kill whites ranging from academics such as David Webster to suspect conscripts or even a former commanding officer. "Red" lives became as cheap as black lives.

Clearly, the racism and violence that South African society inherited from colonial times made the apartheid government more prone to choosing violent solutions to perceived problems. The fact that these problems were seen as growing and nearly insurmountable as the apartheid regime faced both external pressure and internal resistance to apartheid also greatly increased the potential for a resort to state terror. Events as they unfolded in the 1980s and '90s sent the country into a downward spiral of violence and state terror culminating in the use of death squads both abroad and at home.

Special mention must be made here of two peculiarities of the South African situation. The first is the importance of foreign intervention—particularly in Namibia—in increasing the state's willingness to use violence. Time and again, tactics first used in imperialist intervention in a foreign war eventually came to be applied against domestic insurgents and "enemies," often by the same members of the security forces who first developed them.

The second peculiarity of the South African case is the importance of fomenting and exploiting divisions within society and particularly within the opposition movements. In the context of attempting to preserve a white, minority government against an overwhelming black majority, a "divide and conquer" strategy had particularly strong appeal. Supporting bands of "vigilantes" became a central strategy of the apartheid government in its illegal war against the opposition ANC. In effect, the commission of illegal acts, up to and including the formation of death squads and the use of murder on a wide scale, was "subcontracted" to nonstate forces among the black population. The most notorious case was the clandestine support for murderous elements of the IFP, but in fact such subcontracting had a long history in apartheid South Africa, as evidenced by police attempts to use members of a "chief's bodyguard" to kill an Anglican priest (as presented at the beginning of this chapter). Not only were death squads created within the security forces, but time and time again, black collaborators were used as agents of illegal government terror.

Notes

1. Antjie Krog, *Country of My Skull* (Johannesburg: Random House, 1998), 60–61.
2. The General Law Amendment Act 37 of 1963 legalized detention without trial for up to 90 days. The courts in fact permitted the Special Branch (political police) to repeatedly redetain the person for as long as it wished. The de jure legalization of indefinite imprisonment without trial came with the Terrorism Act 83 of 1967.
3. The TRC was set up by the Promotion of National Unity and Reconciliation Act, 34 of 1995. In its second year of power the ANC-led government set up the machinery to enable all combatants in organizations on all sides of liberation war to apply for amnesty for virtually any war crime. Almost the sole condition for amnesty was truthfully reporting all that they knew, who gave the orders, and where the bodies were buried. With this incentive, the TRC could uncover more war crimes than all previous commissions combined.
4. For example, it refers to *British* settlers killing San and Khoi-khoi "in the seventeenth and eighteenth centuries." Truth and Reconciliation Commission, *Truth and Reconciliation Commission of South Africa Report* (Cape Town: Juta, 1998), 2: 25.

5. Rian Malan, "Boipatong. A Question of Spin," *Frontiers of Freedom,* Second Quarter 1999, 26–35, is the longest single critique to date of the TRC's finding on a specific pogrom. This critique generated in turn a debate in the media. See also Robert Kirby, "Gaudy Rumour and Tabloid Hearsay," *Frontiers of Freedom,* no. 22 (1999): 23–25; and Anthea Jeffery, *The Truth About the Truth Commission* (Johannesburg: South African Institute of Race Relations, 1999).

6. The accounts by Captain Jacques Hechter, Paul van Vuuren, and Joe Mamasela of how they killed Richard and Irene Mutasa are one classic example of this. Krog, *Skull,* 82, 85, 87.

7. For example, many members of the security services in KwaZulu-Natal falsely confessed to involvement in political killings to protect their superordinates. *Cape Times,* 2 March 1999.

8. When the start of democracy loomed closer, one secret service department alone burned 44 tons of paper and microfilm records in a blast furnace. *TRC Report,* 1: 219.

9. It must not be forgotten that the apartheid regime, in its attempts to defeat the liberation movement and its real and perceived foreign allies, not only launched military raids into Angola, Botswana, Lesotho, Mozambique, the Seychelles, Swaziland, Zambia, and Zimbabwe but also ruled Namibia as a de facto colony. Its destabilization strategy also immensely aggravated and prolonged a 30-year civil war in Angola and organized in Mozambique a civil war that would not otherwise have occurred. For this study it has to suffice to draw scholars' attention to the ultimate responsibility of South Africa for at least hundreds of thousands of Angolans and Mozambicans who were killed, or who as war refugees and displaced persons died from hunger and other depredations, ostensibly because of other Angolans' and Mozambicans' actions. It is startling that in this broad sense, the majority of persons killed by South African–armed forces were Angolans and Mozambicans.

10. These comprise:

—129 detainees known to have been tortured to death, or in a few cases to have committed suicide to avoid further torture. See *TRC Report,* 2: 205–21.

—250 known secret, illegal burials of killed POWs. All skeletons so far disinterred show evidence of torture, as opposed to combat injuries, inflicted prior to killing. See *TRC Report,* 2: 543.

—100 persons killed by three members of the death squads who admitted their crimes. One of the perpetrators also petrol-bombed over 350 houses in and around Pretoria, Mamelodi, and Atteridgeville, in which additional persons must have been killed. Another assassin in a different death squad, a veteran of between 200 and 500 operations, remembers killing 40 persons, often by electric torture, but notes that he bombed, tortured, and killed too many persons to ever compile a full list. See Jacques Pauw, *Into the Heart of Darkness: Confessions of Apartheid's Assassins* (Johannesburg: Jonathan Ball, 1997), 15, 170, 185, 197. To prevent any possibility of double-counting, the 87 illegal killings known to have been ordered by TREWITS (Counter-Revolutionary Information Task Team) are excluded. Many acts have clearly been successfully concealed, so that the true number will never be known.

—572 train passengers killed by death squads on the Johannesburg-Soweto lines between 1990 and June 1993. The killers were Buffalo Battalion soldiers in mufti and sometimes vigilantes permitted to organize and make *pangas* (machetes) and other weapons in railway workshops. See *TRC Report*, 2: 477, 585; and *New Nation*, 14 March 1997.

11. *TRC Report*, 2: 176.
12. Charles Hooper, *Brief Authority* (Cape Town: David Philip, 1989), 371–72.
13. *TRC Report*, 2: 195, 197.
14. General Law Amendment Act, 37 of 1963; Criminal Procedure Amendment Act, 96 of 1965; Terrorism Act, 83 of 1967.
15. For a typical case, see *Cape Times*, 19 December 1980 and 1 July 1983.
16. *TRC Report*, 2: 205–21.
17. For example, several liberal and radical lecturers and students at the University of Cape Town left their cars parked daily at the top of the steepest road in the suburb, which ended at the bottom in a T-junction. They discovered, in addition to repeated vandalism, that nuts had been loosened on a car wheel, and that the steering had been tampered with. *Varsity*, 7 April 1971.
18. *Cape Times*, 30 September 1966 (van den Bergh), 16 July 1971 (Alheit), and 6 July 1972 (Venter).
19. *TRC Report*, 2: 25–27.
20. *TRC Report*, 2: 38.
21. Pauw, *Assassins*, 16, 196, 197.
22. *TRC Report*, 2: 175.
23. *TRC Report*, 2: 176.
24. Brigadier Jan Cronje and Colonel Eugene de Kock served with the Security Police expeditionary force in Rhodesia (now Zimbabwe) during the early 1970s, in South-West Africa (now Namibia) during the late 1970s, and in South Africa, primarily the Transvaal,

throughout the 1980s. (Pauw, *Assassins*, 36–40, 186.) The same was true of Vossie de Kock, Riaan Stander, and many others.

25. Keith Gottschalk, "Restructuring the Colonial State: Pretoria's Strategy in Namibia," in *Namibia in Perspective*, eds. Gerhard Totemeyer, Vezera Kandetu and Wolfgang Werner (Windhoek: Council of Churches in Namibia, 1987), 27.

26. Gottschalk, "Restructuring the Colonial State," 31.

27. *Namibian,* 13 December 1985.

28. Koevoet killed between 300 and 500 persons per year during the 1980s. Those killed were unknown proportions of SWAPO guerrillas, POWs routinely killed after interrogation, and civilians. *TRC Report,* 2: 61, 69, 70, 71, 74.

29. *TRC Report,* 2: 317.

30. *TRC Report,* 2: 61, 70, 253; Eugene de Kock, *A Long Night's Damage: Working for the Apartheid State* (Saxonwold: Contra, 1998), 79, 160.

31. *TRC Report,* 2: 69, 257.

32. *New Nation,* 14 March 1997; *TRC Report,* 2: 477, 585; *Cape Times,* 5 June 1998.

33. *TRC Report,* 2: 59. It is not easy to quantify what proportion of these were in fact armed insurgents, what proportion were civilian supporters of SWAPO, and what proportion were nonpolitical Namibians.

34. Pauw, *Assassins,* 119.

35. Pauw, *Assassins,* 186–87.

36. Pauw, *Assassins,* 16, 17, 19–20.

37. Gordon Winter, *Inside BOSS: South Africa's Secret Police* (Harmondsworth, U.K.: Penguin, 1981), 559.

38. *TRC Report,* 2: 19.

39. Winter, *BOSS,* 312.

40. Winter, *BOSS,* 559–67.

41. The demotion of BOSS and the phase-out of its Z Squad occurred because of interagency rivalry. When P. W. Botha replaced van den Bergh's ally Balthazar J. Vorster as president in 1978, van den Bergh immediately resigned. Botha completed the downscaling of BOSS, even renaming it, by 1981. His government stripped it of its operational functions, and there is no evidence of its Z Squad existing in the 1980s. Botha's ascension from minister of defense to prime minister, then president, ensured that the military displaced the police as dominant among the state security agencies. See *TRC Report,* 2: 318.

42. Krog, *Skull,* 60.

43. Pauw, *Assassins,* 224–26; *TRC Report,* 2: 286.

44. *Cape Argus*, 6 November 1996.
45. For examples, see *TRC Report*, 2: 288, 592.
46. Pauw, *Assassins*, 179.
47. *TRC Report*, 2: 116; *Cape Argus*, 23 September 1997 and 10 June 1998.
48. *Cape Argus*, 9 June 1998; *TRC Report*, 2: 138.
49. *TRC Report*, 2: 257–67.
50. *TRC Report*, 2: 299.
51. *TRC Report*, 2: 299.
52. *TRC Report*, 2: 298.
53. *TRC Report*, 2: 175, 460–61, 464–74, 527.
54. The TRC statistics confirm closer to half of such a total. Up to 5,000 persons were killed between 1984 and 1989, while the ANC, SACP, and PAC were banned. From 1990 until the April 1994 election, up to 14,000 may have been killed. *TRC Report*, 2: 389, 584.
55. *TRC Report*, 2: 343–44.
56. For example, one political analyst itemized every single calamity that politicians and others had blamed on a "third force," now grown to the proportions of an urban legend. See John Kane-Berman, letter to the editor, *Mail & Guardian*, 27 February–5 March 1998.
57. *TRC Report*, 2: 305.
58. Krog, *Skull*, 70.
59. de Kock, *Damage*, 235–42.
60. *Cape Times*, 12 May 1999.
61. Pauw, *Assassins*, 127.
62. *TRC Report*, 2: 269–72.
63. Pauw, *Assassins*, 271.
64. *Cape Argus*, 28 January 1999.
65. *TRC Report*, 2: 592.
66. *TRC Report*, 2: 23; *Cape Times*, 15 July 1999.
67. *TRC Report*, 2: 475.
68. *Cape Argus*, 10 June 1998.
69. de Kock, *Damage*, 203–10.
70. *TRC Report*, 2: 267.
71. Source B, oral communication with the author, 1984.
72. *TRC Report*, 2: 294. In 1983 the apartheid government set up a latter-day equivalent to the prerevolutionary French Estates General. The South African House of Representatives was a segregated colored (i.e., mixed-race) Third Estate that could always be outvoted by the white First Estate, the House of Assembly.
73. *TRC Report*, 2: 492. Kwandebele was one of the "Bantustans" set up by the *ancien régime*. These were autonomous polities run by satellite regimes.

74. Both cited in Pauw, *Assassins,* 80, 162.
75. Pauw, *Assassins,* 89–91.
76. de Kock, *Damage,* 320.
77. Pauw, *Assassins,* 279–80.
78. Pauw, *Assassins,* 82, 86.
79. de Kock, *Damage,* 84–85.
80. de Kock, *Damage,* 189; Pauw, *Assassins,* 79, 87.
81. de Kock, *Damage,* 200; Pauw, *Assassins,* 105–6.
82. Pauw, *Assassins,* 280.
83. Frederik de Klerk, *The Last Trek—A New Beginning* (London: Macmillan, 1998), 153, 273.
84. de Klerk, *Trek,* 116–17.
85. de Klerk, *Trek,* 123.
86. *TRC Report,* 2: 695.
87. *Cape Times,* 28 January 1999.
88. *TRC Report,* 2: 318–19; Pauw, *Assassins,* 181.
89. Pauw, *Assassins,* 180–81, 317–19.
90. Pauw, *Assassins,* 20, 21, 55, 95, 101, 120–21, 130, 205, 290.
91. de Klerk, *Trek,* 123.
92. de Klerk, *Trek,* 124.
93. Act 108 of 1996. Chapter 2 is the Bill of Rights.
94. *Sunday Independent,* 25 July 1999.
95. One conscript, a psychologist, recalled in his memoirs, just published as this chapter went to press, that when he was posted to an SADF base in northern Namibia, the military bar "was decorated with the jawbones of two slain enemies." One cannot imagine the South African army during the World War II ever decorating its bases in North Africa or Italy with the jawbones of killed German or Italian soldiers. See Anthony Feinstein, *In Conflict* (Claremont: David Philip, 1999), here cited from review in *Mail & Guardian,* 9–15 July 1999.

CHAPTER 10

India's Secret Armies[1]

Patricia Gossman

THE INDIAN GOVERNMENT'S RESORT TO DEATH SQUADS as an instrument of counterinsurgency is symptomatic of a much larger crisis in governance, in particular the state's failure to counter threats to its internal security through legal means and to accommodate the demands of subnationalist movements and other opposition groups within the political system. The emergence of a violent secessionist movement in Punjab and the eruption of full-scale conflict in the long-troubled state of Jammu and Kashmir can both be traced to the government's efforts to centralize power at the expense of democratic processes and institutions. Central government manipulation of state elections and party politics and repeated failures to deliver on promised reforms in both states nurtured extremist groups whose access to arms soon made them more powerful than any local authority. The state's response included illegal measures from the start; the decision to go even further and organize death squads was apparently motivated by the perceived need for greater deniability as state forces began targeting known individuals and political figures. The Punjab crisis preceded the outbreak of the insurgency in Kashmir, and the "Punjab solution," as it was known, came to be seen by many in India's internal security bureaucracy as a model for counterinsurgency operations elsewhere.

This is not to say that human rights violations by the Indian police began with these conflicts. In the early 1970s, Indian security forces committed atrocities on a large scale during a brutal crackdown against Maoist insurgents in Bengal[2] and against ethnic Nagas in the country's northeast.[3] But in general, the army and police

forces involved in these conflicts did not organize separate, secret
units to carry out these abuses. Deaths in custody were denied or
covered up, massacres were explained away as crossfire killings, and
the protests of India's small human rights movement were ignored.
It was not until the Emergency of 1975–77, when Prime Minister Indira Gandhi suspended civil liberties and jailed thousands of her opponents, that concern about fundamental rights and the behavior of
the police found a mainstream audience in India. By the mid-1980s,
human rights abuses in Punjab had become a source of some embarrassment for the Indian government. Under greater scrutiny by
both the Indian public and the international community, and under
pressure from extremist Sikh militant groups that by 1990 were
wreaking havoc in the state, the Punjab police pursued a two-track
approach. Police continued to execute suspected militants in custody and claim that they had been killed in armed "encounters"; for
most of these routine killings, no elaborate cover-up was considered
necessary. At the same time, senior police officials in the state began
to organize clandestine units to infiltrate extremist militant organizations and target known militant leaders and prominent activists
whose murders would be harder to disguise. Ironically, the public
demand for greater accountability from the government may have
been a factor in the decision by the Punjab police to set up death
squad operations.

    In Punjab, death squads were almost exclusively made up of
out-of-uniform police officers, although they frequently included informers who were often former members of extremist groups. In
Kashmir, all of the security forces involved in the conflict—the army
and federal paramilitary forces, as well as police—have made use of
former members of guerrilla forces to infiltrate militant organizations and assassinate or threaten militant leaders and other opposition figures. This same practice has been employed in Assam, a state
in India's northeast, where pro-independence guerrilla forces have
been locked in conflict with the Indian army for more than 50 years.
There, former members of the most prominent militant group, the
United Liberation Front of Assam (ULFA), have been recruited into
a pro-government militia—the Surrendered United Liberation Front
of Assam (SULFA)—that has been used by the army to assassinate
journalists and activists as well as ULFA members. In Andhra
Pradesh, a southern Indian state plagued by conflict over land reform, a police death squad called the Green Tigers has assassinated

human rights activists and others suspected of sympathizing with Maoist radicals.

Police Death Squads in Punjab

For most of the 1980s the state of Punjab in northern India was in the grip of one of the bloodiest conflicts in India's post-independence history. The origins of the conflict lay in a power struggle between political leaders who represented the state's majority Sikh[4] population and central government politicians eager to maintain control over the resources of one of the country's most prosperous states.

In the early 1980s, a movement by Sikh leaders for greater autonomy turned violent when some militant Sikhs embarked on a campaign of terror, murdering elected officials, civil servants, and Hindu and Sikh civilians. 1984 marked a turning point in the conflict. In June of that year, the Indian army stormed the Golden Temple in Amritsar, the Sikhs' holiest shrine, which had been turned into an armed fortress by the militants. More than 1,000 were killed, many of them unarmed pilgrims who were staying in the temple compound at the time.[5] Outraged by the assault, some separatist Sikhs demanded an independent state called Khalistan ("Land of the Pure"). On October 31, 1984, Indian prime minister Indira Gandhi was assassinated by her own Sikh bodyguards, and in the aftermath of her death, mobs led by ruling Congress Party politicians slaughtered thousands of Sikhs in New Delhi and other cities across northern India. The connivance of local officials in the massacres and the failure of the authorities to prosecute the killers alienated many ordinary Sikhs who had not previously supported the separatist cause.

In the years that followed, the Punjab police adopted increasingly brutal methods to stem the insurgency, including arbitrary arrests, torture, and prolonged detention without trial. Increasingly, large numbers of young Sikh men "disappeared" in police custody, the victims of secret executions and cremations by police death squads. At the same time, violence by militant organizations escalated as they engaged in indiscriminate attacks on civilians in buses and trains and in other public places. While some militant groups were organized into guerrilla forces with an identifiable command structure, others operated as criminal gangs that found in the political crisis a lucrative business in extortion and arms smuggling.

Efforts by Sikh political leaders and central government officials to negotiate a political settlement met with repeated failure largely because of the central government's failure to follow through with promised reforms and measures to meet Sikh demands. For its part, the Sikh political leadership, torn by internal rivalries, was never able to distance itself publicly from the militants. By taking up genuine grievances that Sikh politicians had failed to address and enforcing their will through terror, the militants effectively eliminated any moderate political rivals for power. Violence in the state by all parties reached unprecedented levels in late 1990.

The upsurge in violence gave senior police officers the rationale they needed to convince skeptics in the central government of the need for a no-holds-barred offensive on the militants. The counterinsurgency operation that ultimately crushed most of the militant groups by mid-1993 represented the most extreme example of a policy in which the end appeared to justify any and all means, including torture and murder. It was a policy that had long been advocated by senior police officials, in particular Director General of Police (DGP) K.P.S. Gill, who has had overall authority for counterinsurgency operations in the state. The goal was to eliminate, not merely arrest, militant Sikh leaders and members. Gill also expanded a bounty system of rewards for police who killed known militants—a practice that encouraged the police to resort to extrajudicial executions and disappearances.[6]

In their efforts to find and kill the militants, the police conducted massive search operations, frequently arresting persons who may merely have lived in an area known to be frequented by militant groups or who belonged to an organization suspected of supporting the militants. In some cases, the police recruited informers, some of whom were former militants themselves, to identify the victims and carry out the killings. Although there was little effort to disguise the nature of these executions, police reports generally claimed the victim was killed in an "encounter" or, occasionally, that he committed suicide to avoid capture.

The systematic execution of detained civilians and suspected militants by the Punjab police has been one of the most heinous features of counterinsurgency operations in the state. No precise figure of the number of those killed in custody is available, but in more than ten years of conflict, the number is certainly well into the thousands. One police officer admitted that he estimated that over a five-year period, 500 people were killed by police from his police station alone.[7] So-called "encounter" killings became so much a part of Punjab's political landscape that few police officials denied the practice existed and many tacitly admitted that it was condoned.[8]

In one case, a senior officer's use of police to carry out acts of reprisal caused controversy within the police force itself. After Senior Superintendent of Police (SSP) Sumedh Singh Saini narrowly escaped an assassination attempt in Punjab on August 29, 1991,[9] that same day police from Saini's station came to the home village of the leader of the Babbar Khalsa militant group and took down the names of five of his relatives who lived in one house. Later that night, gunmen surrounded the house and opened fire, killing three women and a five-year-old child, and then set fire to the house. The next morning, a plainclothes policeman advised the relatives to search for five bodies. The cremation was ordered to be carried out in the presence of the police. Although police officials claimed that the incident was the result of intergang rivalry, no group claimed responsibility. On October 17, 1991, Dinesh Kumar reported in the *Times of India* that the SSP of Ropar, Mohammad Mustafa, had "accused the SSP of Chandigrah, Mr. Sumedh Saini, of ordering the execution of family members of top Babbar Khalsa [group] militant Balwinder Singh of Jatana, in retaliation for an unsuccessful attempt by militants to assassinate him. The accusation has been leveled in a confidential letter sent to the Punjab police chief. . . ."[10] Three days after it was published, Mustafa reportedly denied the story.

The pattern of "encounter" killings was well established early in the conflict. In most cases, the victim would be detained during police raids on villages or city neighborhoods and tortured for several days before being killed. One police officer described these raids:

During my career with the Punjab police, I participated in approximately five raids per day. The orders to conduct the raids were issued by the senior superintendent of police or the station house officer (SHO). On a typical day, approximately three of the raids were conducted for the purpose of apprehending suspected criminals. These raids were usually conducted during daylight hours. The other two raids typically took place during hours of darkness and were targeted against Sikh families who were suspected of collaborating with armed Sikh militants. The information for these raids was usually provided by paid informants.[11]

Young Sikh men were the most likely to be detained, particularly those who resided in areas known to be militant strongholds or those who belonged to political groups suspected of sympathizing with or supporting the militants. In many cases, the victims had relatives or acquaintances who were suspected to have joined militant groups, and the family members were detained as hostages in order to compel the wanted relative to turn himself in. Detaining relatives was also a way of punishing the family for "harboring" a militant. In most cases these hostages were tortured; in some cases, even after the wanted relative surrendered to the police, the hostages were killed or "disappeared." A police officer described the kinds of persons most likely to be arrested:

> Forty percent of those arrested were militants, 50 percent were people suspected of collaborating with militants, and 10 percent were informants whose identity we wanted to protect by making it look like they were wanted by the police. The 50 percent who were arrested on suspicion of collaborating with militants consisted of two basic types of people—*amritdhari* (baptized) Sikhs and suspected militant collaborators. *Amritdhari* Sikhs are considered suspect by the police because of their orthodox observance and practice of the Sikh religion. Police authorities maintain intelligence on all *amritdhari* Sikhs in a given geographic area. They are routinely characterized as supporters of the movement for an independent state known as Khalistan. When the police have no suspect for a case or need to arrest someone in order to fulfill an arrest quota, *amritdhari* Sikhs are often the victims. Once an *amritdhari* Sikh is arrested, it is probable that he will continue to be rearrested after release.[12]

Journalists have also reported that the police singled out *amritdhari* Sikhs. A report in *India Today* noted, "The police do appear to attach sinister importance to the partaking of *amrit* [the act of being baptized]. The State Intelligence Department updates its dossier on amritdharis every month."[13]

The second group of people targeted were young Sikh men suspected of collaborating with the militants or of being sympathizers with the Khalistan movement. A police officer admitted that

> [a]t the time of Operation Bluestar in 1984 when an armed confrontation occurred between Sikhs and government forces sur-

rounding the Golden Temple in Amritsar, a profile was developed of who was considered to be antigovernment and pro-Khalistan. Based on that profile, young Sikh men between the ages of 18 and 40, who have long beards and wear turbans, are considered to be pro-Khalistan. Whenever the police receive a report from an informant or any other individual that Sikh militants have visited the home of a Sikh family, the police are dispatched to raid the home of that family. Pursuant to that raid, any Sikh male who fits the profile described above is arrested.[14]

Police persecution in Punjab drove large numbers of Punjabi Sikhs to seek asylum abroad. According to police familiar with the arrests, those who are denied asylum and returned home face grave risks. Upon arrival they would be taken into custody and a message would be sent to the police in Punjab asking if the person was on the police blacklist for political activities. Some would be executed.[15]

Where legal remedies existed in Punjab, they proved ineffective in ending the abuses because the police routinely disregarded court orders to produce detainees. A police officer confirmed this practice:

> Once a person suspected of harboring militants or of being pro-Khalistan is arrested, he is subjected to detention procedures which circumvent normal police routine. The arrest is not recorded in the daily log which includes the names of all criminals arrested on a given day. There is no official record of the arrest or detention. Instead, the name is placed on a secret "blacklist" which is maintained by the SHO. . . . Even an unsolicited visit by Sikh militants condemns a person to the blacklist. . . . It is also common knowledge that the list is circulated to the SHOs who administer the Punjab police department. Once a person's name is on the police blacklist he is subject to repeated arrests . . . and . . . torture.[16]

Detainees were also frequently moved from police station to police station to obstruct the efforts of families and lawyers to locate them. Although the Indian penal code requires that every detainee be produced before a magistrate within 24 hours of arrest, the Punjab police consistently ignored the law. Similarly, Indian law requires that every unnatural death be investigated by a magistrate and that a postmortem be performed. The Punjab police routinely flouted these regulations by performing postmortems not in civil hospitals but on the premises of police stations, and by cremating the bodies of victims before any investigation could take place. In the cases in which bodies were returned to the families, the police usually oversaw the cremation. In most cases of "encounter" killings, the police never acknowledged that a detainee had been in custody. Efforts by local community leaders, including *panchayat* (village council) members and *sarpanches* (heads of the councils), to serve as witnesses to arrests in an attempt to hold police accountable also proved unsuccessful in stopping the killings. While the police routinely evaded responsibility for these killings by claiming either that those killed had never been in their custody or that they were killed in armed encounters, the police did not go out of their way to disguise their own identities.

The government practice of providing cash rewards for police who eliminated wanted militants encouraged the police to engage in extrajudicial executions. The existence of police hit lists was widely reported by Indian and international human rights groups. But because the lists themselves were kept secret, police could easily claim after a killing that the victim was one of the "wanted terrorists" who was on the list. A police officer explained the use of the blacklist:

> Once a person's name is on the police blacklist, he faces very severe consequences if he absconds or leaves his home [changes residences]. If a person suspected of pro-militant, pro-Khalistan activities absconds, the police authorities conclusively believe that individual has joined the ranks of armed Sikh militants. If a police patrol discovers that an individual on the police blacklist has left his home, the name is passed on to the SHO for identification as a Sikh militant. Based on the patrol report that the "suspect" individual has absconded, a police order is broadcast by wireless to all police stations in Punjab identifying the "suspect" and requesting that the local station be informed if he is detained.... It is commonly understood by police authorities in Punjab that once the name of a suspect individual who has absconded is broadcast over the wireless, he is considered to be a Sikh militant and is subject to a "shoot on sight" order. Pursuant to police policy, it is acceptable police practice for any officer in Punjab to assassinate in an "encounter" an individual on the list of those who have absconded from their homes.[17]

In addition to the routine elimination of suspected militants, by
the late 1980s the police were also operating clandestine units to infiltrate militant organizations and employing undercover agents to
act as death squads to identify, kidnap, and kill suspected militants.
This was the most secret of the police operations against the militants and the one that required the greatest deniability. While almost
any police officer could expect a reward for killing an identified militant, only these agents, known as "black cats," operated completely
under cover. A police officer whose husband worked undercover as
a "black cat" for the police described how the system worked:

> We lived in a civilian locality under undisclosed names. He had a
> van, and in addition to his official Mauser pistol, he was given
> four AK-47 guns that were captured from the militants and a
> bolt-action rifle. He and the others he traveled with dressed in
> civilian clothes and often had untrimmed beards to make them
> appear like Sikh militants. They kept their police identification
> with them, just in case they were accidentally picked up by the
> regular police. Once they got any information on militants, they
> would get verbal orders from the SSP to abduct those persons if
> possible and bring them to the police station for interrogation
> and torture. If they were unable to abduct someone, then they
> had orders to shoot and kill.[18]

India's central government created a special fund to finance
Punjab's death squads, to pay the network of informants who provided information about militants and those suspected of supporting militants, and to reward police who captured and killed them.
The reward for each person abducted or killed was about 50,000
rupees ($1,670).[19] The money was generally divided among the SSP
and other ranking officers. In many cases, the SSP was the one who
recruited informants and decided who was to be arrested and killed.
The corruption that accompanied this bounty system has been reported in the Indian press. According to a report in *India Today,*

> The rush for claiming cash rewards is turning police into merce-
> naries. Besides the rewards for killing listed militants (annual out-
> lay for the purpose: Rs. 1.13 crore [$338,000]), the department
> gives "unannounced rewards" for killing unlisted militants. . . .
> The amount can vary from Rs. 40,000 [$1,333] to Rs. 5 lakh
> [$16,666]. . . . [T]he operation of the secret fund is only known to

a handful of senior police officers. . . . Whatever records are maintained are erased after a few weeks.[20]

The Indian government has repeatedly claimed that it has taken
action against police responsible for human rights abuses in Punjab,
but in fact, many police officials responsible for numerous "encounter" killings have been promoted to more senior positions.

The Punjab police also detained the relatives of suspected militants and others accused of having links to the militants who resided
outside Punjab. In some cases, they bypassed the local police in carrying out arrests; in others, the local police were involved. Under
DGP Gill, police hit squads tracked down and killed suspected militants in neighboring states and in cities as far away as Bombay and
Calcutta. One 1993 case in Calcutta led the state government of
West Bengal to file a protest with the state government of Punjab.[21]

Although mass executions of suspected militants and their supporters dropped after 1993, targeted assassinations continued. The
militant organizations were decimated by the campaign, and violence by the groups declined precipitously. In the changed political
climate, human rights lawyers in Punjab began to make some head-
way bringing cases against police who had been involved in the
killings. In January 1995, Jaswant Singh Khalra, general secretary of
the human rights wing of the Akali Dal political party, filed a peti-
tion in the High Court claiming that hundreds of individuals had
been killed and secretly cremated by the Punjab police. On September 6, 1995, Khalra was arrested outside his home in Amritsar. His
body was never recovered. In a report to the Supreme Court on July
30, 1996, the Central Bureau of Investigation (CBI) named nine police officials responsible for the abduction, and India's Supreme
Court directed that the officers face trial, that further investigations
be carried out to ascertain the fate of Jaswant Singh Khalra, and
that key witnesses be offered protection during the investigations.
On July 22, 1996, the CBI stated in a report to the court that it had
found *prima facie* evidence that the Punjab police had secretly dis-
posed of 984 bodies between 1990 and 1995, a period in which
hundreds of Sikh men "disappeared" in police custody. Most
human rights activists believe this to be a fraction of the number
killed during this period. The investigation remained stalled following appeals by the state government, but in September 1998, the
Supreme Court ruled that the official National Human Rights Com-

mission could proceed in its investigation of mass cremations carried out by the Punjab police. Still, for many in the government, the lesson from the Punjab crisis was that the illegal means had served them best—the death squad operations, together with the mass arrests, disappearances, and "encounter" killings, had succeeded in crushing the militant organizations.

India's Secret Army in Kashmir

Kashmir has been at the heart of a territorial dispute between India and Pakistan since the two nations gained their independence in 1947.[22] Both nations claim Kashmir. Following an invasion by Pakistani raiders and an uprising of villagers in the western part of the state, the then ruler of the princely state of Jammu and Kashmir, Maharaja Hari Singh, acceded to India on condition that the state retain autonomy in all matters except defense, currency, and foreign affairs. Fighting between India and Pakistan ended with UN intervention; since 1948 the cease-fire line, now known as the Line of Actual Control, has been monitored by a UN observation force. The far northern and western areas of the state are under Pakistan's control; the Kashmir Valley, Jammu, and Ladakh are under India's control.

But India never delivered on its promise of autonomy for Kashmir. Instead, New Delhi made every effort to control the state government by propping up chosen political leaders and ensuring that dissent within the state was suppressed. It was not until 1986, however, that discontent within the state found wider popular support. In that year the ruling National Conference (NC) party, widely accused of corruption, struck a deal with India's Congress Party administration that many in Kashmir saw as the final betrayal of Kashmir's autonomy. As a result, a new party, the Muslim United Front (MUF), began to attract the support of a broad range of Kashmiris, including pro-independence activists, disenchanted Kashmiri youth, and the pro-Pakistan Jama'at-i Islami, a religious organization, and appeared poised to do well in state elections in 1987. Blatant rigging assured an NC victory, which was followed by the arrests of hundreds of MUF leaders and supporters. In the aftermath, young MUF supporters swelled the ranks of a growing number of militant groups who increasingly crossed over to Pakistan for arms and training. The major militant organizations were divided between those who advocated an independent Kashmir and those who supported accession to Pakistan. These organizations began assassinating NC leaders and engaging in other acts of violence. Some groups also targeted Hindu families, and a slow exodus of Hindus from the valley began.

In December 1989, the most popular of the pro-independence groups, the Jammu and Kashmir Liberation Front (JKLF), abducted the daughter of Home Minister Mufti Mohammad Sayeed, then freed her when the government gave in to demands for the release of five detained militants. That event, together with a surge in popular protest against the state and central governments, led New Delhi to launch a massive crackdown on Kashmir. On January 19, 1990, the central government imposed direct rule on the state. From the outset, that Indian government's campaign against the militants was marked by widespread human rights violations, including the shooting of unarmed demonstrators, civilian massacres, and summary executions of detainees. Militant groups—which continued to obtain arms and training from Pakistan—stepped up their attacks, murdering and threatening Hindu residents, carrying out kidnappings and assassinations of government officials, civil servants, and suspected informers, and engaging in sabotage and bombings. By May 1990, rising tension between Pakistan and India following the escalation of the conflict in Kashmir raised fears of another war between the two countries.

The Indian government was well versed in the use of death squads as a counterinsurgency tactic by the time tensions over the status of Kashmir erupted into a full-blown insurgency. But it was not until 1992 that hawks in the government's home ministry and intelligence agencies began to push hard for a "Punjab solution" for Kashmir—a reference to the extensive use of police informants, collaborators, and death squads that resulted in the secret murders of thousands of suspected militants in Punjab in the early 1990s. By 1995 the use of turncoat "countermilitants" as informers and assassins became a central component of the government's strategy, and ultimately it decimated the ranks of the militants.

Throughout the years of insurgency, the Indian government (through various changes of party and administration) vacillated between trying to manage its Kashmir policy from Delhi or handing over control to its appointed representative, the state governor, and the security agencies. The latter usually prevailed, because while New Delhi wanted control over the policy, the security forces wanted direct control over the day-to-day management of operations. This was the case in late 1992 when Kashmir policy was directed not so much from Delhi as from the governor's house in Srinagar, the state capital, and the headquarters of the security agencies operating in the state, particularly the Border Security Force (BSF). At the time, the governor was Girish Saxena, the former head of India's state intelligence agency RAW (Research and Analysis Wing). The security forces launched a campaign dubbed "Catch-and-Kill," the goal of which was the elimination, through murder, of suspected militants. By all accounts, it was a successful campaign. But this was not yet a death squad operation. Although the victims were frequently found shot execution-style, with bullet holes in the backs of their heads, the government did little to disguise the nature of the killings beyond issuing press statements claiming that suspects were killed in encounters with security forces or while trying to escape. In April 1993, a senior security official in Srinagar told the *New York Times,* "We don't have custodial deaths here, we have alley deaths. . . . If we have word of a hard-core militant, we will pick him up, take him to another lane and kill him."[23]

But the murder of human rights activist H. N. Wanchoo marked a turning point and the beginning of genuine death squad tactics in the state.[24] Wanchoo, a retired trade unionist and a communist, had assumed a prominent role as a human rights activist by 1992, documenting cases of torture, extrajudicial executions, and disappearances and, together with a local lawyer, bringing these cases to the attention of the High Court and international human rights organizations. According to colleagues, he planned to submit information to the United Nations Human Rights Commission in early 1993. Because Wanchoo was a Hindu, the government found his work particularly embarrassing; it could not dismiss him as a militant.

On the morning of December 5, 1992, Wanchoo left his house accompanied by two Kashmiri men who had asked for his assistance. They told him that a boy had been picked up by the security forces and asked Wanchoo to see the boy's mother and reassure her that he would be able to go to court and get the boy released. According to family members, Wanchoo had never seen the two men before, but he often received visits from unknown people who came to him for help.

Wanchoo's body was found on a street in a nearby neighborhood at about 10:15 A.M. He had been shot three times, once in the back of the head, once in the upper back, and once in the abdomen. In the weeks following the murder, Indian officials claimed that they had arrested the persons responsible and that they were members of "a fundamentalist organization." They later claimed that one of the killers remained at large and the other had been killed while trying to escape BSF custody.[25] In fact, human rights activists who investigated the case have argued that two militants of the Jamiat-ul Mujahidin were released from jail on condition that they kill Wanchoo.[26] At least one of the militants was subsequently killed by Indian security forces.

Five months later, another prominent human rights critic was assassinated, again in what was apparently a death squad operation. Dr. Abdul Ahad Guru, a renowned Kashmiri cardiothoracic surgeon, was abducted and later shot dead on March 31, 1993. Dr. Guru was a member of the governing council of the JKLF and an outspoken critic of human rights abuses by Indian security forces in Kashmir. He met frequently with the international press and international human rights groups.

Dr. Guru left the grounds of his hospital at about 2:00 P.M. on March 31, accompanied by two other doctors. About 100 meters from the hospital, a man stopped the car and asked for a lift. He got into the front seat of the car, and a second man who abruptly joined him got into the back. The men then forced Dr. Guru to get out of the car and into another vehicle. They then left. At about 9:00 P.M. Dr. Guru was brought to another neighborhood of Srinagar, taken out of the car, and shot. A government source later alleged that a member of the pro-Pakistan militant organization Hizb-ul Mujahidin, a man named Zulkar Nan, was released from custody specifically to carry out the murder.[27] Shortly after the murder, the security forces shot and killed Zulkar Nan, thus eliminating the only witness to their involvement in Guru's murder.

The killings served their purpose: two of the most visible critics of the government's human rights record had been silenced, and the few remaining human rights activists scaled back their activities and kept a lower profile. At the same time, the government escaped censure from the international community. By using former militants to carry out the assassinations, it was able to distance itself from the incidents and instead blame "internecine rivalries" among the militant groups for the killings.

The Recruitment of "Renegade" Countermilitants

In the Wanchoo and Guru killings, former militants were recruited specifically to carry out those killings. Afterward, the recruitment of militants who had been "turned' while in custody, persuaded by promises of release and money to join with the government, became a central part of the government's counterinsurgency strategy. Why and how former militants were persuaded to switch sides is not clear, but the promise of money, arms, and protection was clearly sufficient to convince a number of those who were either not ideologically committed to independence or had themselves become embittered by corruption and abuses within the ranks of the militant groups.

In 1994–95, the government made several attempts to hold elections in Kashmir, and to that end, Indian security forces intensified their efforts against militant groups, stepping up cordon-and-search operations and summarily executing captured militant leaders. Alongside them, operating as a secret, illegal army, were a number of these state-sponsored countermilitant groups, composed of captured or surrendered former militants described as "renegades" by locals and "friendlies" by the Indian government. Most operated as death squads. The security forces made systematic use of these irregular militias, in effect subcontracting some of their abusive tactics to groups with no official accountability. Wearing no uniforms, their members could not be easily identified. There was no one to whom civilians could register complaints about their behavior. As one Kashmiri doctor told a Human Rights Watch investigator, in the past, "when someone misbehaved, he was wearing a uniform, so he was accountable. We could call his commander. Now, when these renegades misbehave, there is no one to call. No one accepts responsibility for them, though we know the government is sponsoring them."[28]

Human rights activists continued to be a target for the countermilitants. One of the most prominent victims was Mian Abdul Qayoom, who was until April 1995 the president of the Jammu and Kashmir Bar Association and one of Kashmir's most prominent human rights monitors. Under his direction, the bar association produced voluminous records of human rights violations by Indian security forces in Kashmir. On April 22, 1995, he was shot by two men who had come to his house claiming to seek his services in a human rights case. The incident left Qayoom permanently disabled.[29] Journalists were also singled out. In the first such incident of its kind in Kashmir, on September 7, 1995, a parcel bomb exploded in the offices of the British Broadcasting Corporation (BBC) in Srinagar. The parcel was addressed to BBC correspondent Yusuf Jameel, who had been a target of both the security forces and various militant groups over the years. Mushtaq Ali, a photographer with Agence France Press, who was with Jameel in the office that day, died in the explosion. Jameel and Habibullah Naqash, photographer with *Asia Age* and UNI, were injured. According to sources in Srinagar, the bomb had been sent by a countermilitant group.[30] On December 8, 1995, Zafar Mehraj, a veteran Kashmiri journalist, was shot and critically injured as he returned from an interview with Koko Parray, the head of the state-sponsored countermilitant group Ikhwan-ul Muslimoon (Muslim Brotherhood), at Parray's headquarters in Hajan, a small town 50 kilometers from Srinagar. Mehraj was working for Zee television, an independent television corporation.[31] He had previously been threatened by both the security forces, who suspected him because of his ties to militant group and his travel in Pakistan, and some militant groups who resented his contacts with Indian officials. The gunmen were later identified as members of Ikhwan-ul Muslimoon.[32]

The Murder of Jalil Andrabi

The murder of Jalil Andrabi attracted international scrutiny and criticism largely because Andrabi, a human rights lawyer and a leading member of the JKLF, was well known, a frequent caller at diplomatic missions in New Delhi, the United Nations Human Rights Commission, and the United States State Department. Even so, the interest in his case was short-lived.

Most of the facts in the case are not disputed. In January 1996, Andrabi told a lawyer conducting a fact-finding mission for Human Rights Watch that he had received threats from members of a local "renegade" countermilitant group working with the army.[33] Two men had come to his house on the pretext of soliciting his help in a human rights case—a ruse that had been used in other attacks on human rights activists. Suspicious of the motives of his visitors, Andrabi asked them to return at a later time and then surreptitiously photographed them as they were leaving his house. After leaving Srinagar, Andrabi contacted the press, international human rights groups, and officials at the United States embassy in New Delhi about the incident, drawing considerable attention to the case, particularly to the fact that he could identify the men through the photographs as members of a countermilitant group.

His efforts backfired. Officials at the U.S. Embassy refused to take the affair seriously; one went so far as to suggest that Andrabi was using the threat to bolster his own standing within the JKLF.[34] Andrabi's abduction caught those who had not taken his earlier allegations of renegade threats seriously by surprise, and by that time, diplomatic efforts to intervene on his behalf were too late.

According to Andrabi's wife, Rifat, she and her husband were returning home at about 5:45 P.M. on March 8 when their car was pulled over by Major Aftar Singh, known as "Bulbul" (Nightingale), of the 35th Rashtriya Rifles unit of the Indian army, who arrested Andrabi.[35] When she and her brother attempted to file a report with the police accusing the major of illegal detention, the police cautioned her to say "unidentified men" instead, claiming they could not register a case against the army. "You are telling me the law," one of them said. "But that's not the practice in Kashmir." She stated that Director General of Police K.P.S. Gill himself told the family the morning after that Andrabi was "with us" and would be "released very soon." Three weeks later, Andrabi's body was floating in the Jhelum River; an autopsy showed that he had been killed days after his arrest. According to local sources, after his arrest, he was handed over to a countermilitant group to be killed.[36] True to the pattern established in the Wanchoo and Guru cases, the five men responsible for Andrabi's murder were shot dead by Indian security forces a month later. Widespread international condemnation of Andrabi's killing prompted Indian authorities to initiate an investigation that ultimately indicted Major Bulbul. However, the army claimed the major had been on a temporary assignment and was no longer on duty and was untraceable.

The Chain of Command

Officials in Kashmir routinely describe extrajudicial killings, abductions, and assaults by the countermilitant groups as resulting from "intergroup rivalries," giving the regular security forces deniability about the role these groups play in the counterinsurgency effort.[37]

As a result, Indian authorities have been able to point to an "improvement" in the number of human rights complaints against uniformed soldiers while at the same time counting fewer casualties among its own forces. But there is no question that the countermilitants constitute an integral part of India's security apparatus in Kashmir.

In some cases, attacks by these paramilitary groups are carried out on orders from police or army officers. In other cases, the groups operate on their own, within broadly defined limits to their discretionary powers and the full expectation on the part of the security forces that they will use their discretion to take initiatives within the overall counterinsurgency strategy of fighting terror with terror. Their actions are taken with the knowledge and complicity of official security forces. When arrested by local police, members of these groups are released on orders of the security forces.[38] In its report of human rights practices, the U.S. State Department noted that in 1996, "[k]illings and abductions of suspected militants and other persons by pro-government countermilitants emerged as a significant pattern in Kashmir. . . . There are credible reports that government agencies fund, exchange intelligence with, and direct operations of countermilitants as part of the counterinsurgency effort."[39] In March 1996, the Indian biweekly newsmagazine *India Today* highlighted the role of paramilitary groups:

> [They have become the] centerpiece of the counterinsurgency operations in the [Kashmir] Valley. . . . Used initially as intelligence sources—to help in flushing-out operations—they are now also being used as "prowlers": they take part in the security forces' armed encounters with militants. . . . In fact, the security forces are raising "small armies" of surrendered militants in the Valley and, in the militancy-affected areas of Doda, are relying on them to even neutralize hard-core outfits like the Harkat-ul-Ansar (HUA), the Hizbul Mujahedin and the Lashkar-e-Toiba, all dominated by battle-hardened Afghan mercenaries. The police too are helping, though in a limited way. . . ."Special Operation Groups" comprising the police and the surrendered militants, holding high-powered wireless sets, masquerade as ultras [militants] and catch the genuine ones by surprise.[40]

The government uses the groups in a number of ways: as informers who watch and report on the activities of the militants; as spies to infiltrate existing militant organizations; and as members of paramilitary "renegade" organizations to attack members of militant groups. In a report published in the *Times of India* on March 9, 1996, Colonel K. P. Ramesh of the Rashtriya Rifles stated that surrendered militants were provided arms for their protection and given reward money for providing information.[41]

The number of former militants in the state-sponsored militias is impossible to determine. One of the most prominent groups, Ikhwan-ul Muslimoon, is reportedly composed of former members of many of the militant organizations, most of whom had been detained by the security forces before joining the group. In 1999 it was headed by Javed Ahmad Shah, who is now a member of the state legislative council and works with the army's Rashtriya Rifles unit and with the State Task Force, a division of the Jammu and Kashmir Police created in 1995 of recruits from mostly outside the state.

The name of another paramilitary group, Taliban, was reportedly deliberately chosen to create confusion with the militant Islamic Afghan group of the same name.[42] Since the conflict in Kashmir began in 1990, the Indian government has attempted to discredit militant organizations by claiming that the insurgency in Kashmir was entirely provoked by Pakistan and was not indigenous in origin. It has also accused the militants of espousing a militant Islamic ideology when that characterization is true of only some of the groups. The BSF and the Rashtriya Rifles reportedly finance their own countermilitants.

Members of these militias are also used to support Indian government policies. In public statements, Ikhwan-ul Muslimoon leader Koko Parray has indicated his group's support for the elections and intention to field candidates and ensure that people in areas under its control vote despite the opposition's boycott. One former Ikhwan-ul Muslimoon leader, a man called Papa Kishtwari, has founded his own "party" called Tehrik Wattan. His militia group is believed responsible for dozens of death squad crimes in the Pampore region. In March 1996, Ghulam Rasool, a young journalist who had attempted to expose crimes committed by Papa Kistwari in Pampore, was "arrested" by Kistwari's forces and murdered. Rasool had been the head of the *waqf* committee, which oversees local schools and mosques. Villagers have attempted to file charges against Kistwari, but nothing has come of it because he has had the protection of the army.

Victims of abuse by these groups have testified that the government has deliberately avoided arresting members of these groups even when there was clear evidence of their committing crimes.[43] Residents angry at extortion by the groups have demanded that the administration either disarm the groups or give them uniforms.[44] After four journalists were abducted by Ikhwan-ul Muslimoon forces in July 1995, the security forces made no effort to apprehend leaders of the group, even after Koko Parray acknowledged publicly that he had ordered the kidnapping. Parray admitted involvement in the abduction at a press conference he held, but was never arrested or even questioned about the incident by the security forces. During the kidnapping, Ikhwan forces were waved through security checkpoints after they had given a pre-arranged password.[45] The countermilitants operate in close proximity to army and BSF camps, and some members of these groups have been housed in the camps.[46]

The election of a state government in October 1996, the first since 1990, did little to rein in the countermilitants, although there have been fewer incidents of assassination. Although Chief Minister Farooq Abdullah criticized the use of the countermilitant groups and called for their disbandment or integration into the regular security forces, the army and the Special Task Force have continued to recruit new members and to use the groups to act as informers, carry out "arrests," and intimidate family members of suspected militants. For their part, the countermilitants blame Farooq Abdullah for failing to provide jobs and for "stealing" the election from them. In an interview in October 1998, Papa Kistwari dismissed charges that he and his men had killed social workers and other activists in his district and proudly displayed a photograph of himself posing with Indian army officers. "My boys get 1,500 rupees a month from the government" for killing militants, he boasted. "My boys are disciplined."[47]

By providing intelligence to the security forces about militant hideouts and identifying and assassinating militant leaders, the countermilitants have played a critical role in eliminating or severely weakening many of the militant groups. By early 1999, the militants had been largely driven from Kashmir's urban areas. At the same time, militant groups with strong links to Pakistan have assumed a new prominence, carrying out killings of Hindu civilians in the state's Doda district and other border areas. Such killings are new; the more popularly based groups like the JKLF targeted government officials but did not carry out whole-scale attacks on civilians. As a result of the violence, the center of the conflict has shifted away from Srinagar and the Kashmir Valley to Doda's rugged terrain. There the army has engaged in a familiar pattern of brutality: extrajudicial execution, rape, and torture. It has also armed local Hindus, organized as Village Defense Committees (VDCs), to work with the army. In June 1998, a joint VDC-army operation shot dead four family members of a suspected militant. The role of the VDCs has raised concerns that tensions in Doda might erupt along communal lines, with more violence between the Muslim and Hindu communities. Convinced of its "success" with the countermilitants, there is every indication that the army could grant the VDCs a similar "death squad" role. If that is the case, it will herald a new period of lawlessness in Kashmir.

Conclusion

Why the Indian government has permitted its police and other security forces to engage in death squad operations says a lot about India's own self-image and its sense of place in the international community. The world's largest democracy may find a way to defend some repressive tactics in the name of fighting terrorism, but at a certain point, the need for greater deniability about illegal police practices led almost inevitably to the creation of death squads. Despite the exposure of some of these operations, for many in the government, the lesson from both Punjab and Kashmir has been that the illegal means—the death squad operations, together with the mass arrests, disappearances, and "encounter" killings—have served them best and have succeeded in crushing the militant organizations, and that this victory has been worth the other costs. And those costs have been high. The legacy of the conflicts in Punjab and Kashmir can be counted not only in the numbers of dead and disappeared but in the damage to many of India's democratic institutions: the undermining of judicial powers, the expansion of systematic police corruption, the lack of accountability, and the routinization of extreme measures to combat threats to the state.

Notes

1. Much of this article is excerpted from Human Rights Watch/Asia and Physicians for Human Rights, *Dead Silence: The Legacy of Abuses in Punjab* (New York: Human Rights Watch, 1994), and Human Rights Watch/Asia (now the Asia division of Human Rights Watch), *India's Secret Army in Kashmir* (New York: Human Rights Watch, 1996). Research on Kashmir was funded in part by the John D. and Catherine T. MacArthur Foundation.

2. In March 1967, a breakaway Maoist group in the Indian state of West Bengal split from the Communist Party (Marxist) because of differences between the two groups over whether to support the parliamentary path to change or the path of armed struggle. The group initiated a series of peasant uprisings, beginning in the district of Naxalbari in West Bengal, from which the party was given the name Naxalite. Over the next few months, peasant committees in Naxalbari seized land, burned property records, and assassinated oppressive landlords and others identified as "class enemies." The uprising was crushed in July, but over the next two years, similar revolts broke out in other villages in West Bengal and across India. For more on the origins and impact of the Naxalbari uprising see Sumanta Bannerjee, *In the Wake of Naxalbari* (Calcutta: Subarnarekha, 1980). See also Marcus F. Franda, *Political Development and Political Decay in Bengal* (Calcutta: Firma K. L. Mukhopadhyay, 1971), chap. 5.

3. The inclusion of Nagaland, a state in India's far northeast, as part of the Indian state is disputed by many Naga leaders who claim that India has violated the Nagas' right of self-determination. Pro-independence forces in the state have been in conflict with the Indian army since the 1950s.

4. Sikhs represent a small but significant religious minority in India, constituting about 2 percent of the country's 900 million people. In Punjab, they make up approximately 60 percent of the population. They are not a homogeneous community, however, and divisions among them have contributed to the conflict. The Sikh religion was founded in India by Guru Nanak (1469–1539), a mystic poet who rejected both Islam and Hinduism, yet drew on elements of both to construct a monotheistic religion that teaches escape from rebirth through devotion and discipline. Sikhism arose at the time of the height of power of the Mughal Empire in India (1526–1757). Wary of the growing power of the Sikhs, the Mughals took brutal steps to suppress them, executing their leaders and creating a tradition of mil-

itancy and martyrdom that resonates in contemporary Sikh politics. For more on the history of the Sikhs in Punjab, see generally Robin Jeffrey, *What's Happening to India?* (New York: Holmes & Meier, 1986); Kuldip Nayar and Khushwant Singh, *Tragedy of Punjab* (Delhi: Vision Books, 1984); and Mark Tully and Satish Jacob, *Amritsar: Mrs. Gandhi's Last Battle* (London: Jonathan Cape, 1985).

5. Many of the bodies of those killed were cremated en masse by the army and police, making it impossible to know for certain how many were killed. The government's *White Paper on the Punjab Agitation* gave official figures as 493 "civilians/terrorists" killed and 86 wounded, and 83 troops killed and 249 wounded. Citizens for Democracy, *Report to the Nation: Oppression in Punjab* (New Delhi: Citizens for Democracy, 1985), 65. According to Tully and Jacob, more than 3,000 people were inside the temple when Operation Blue Star began, among them roughly 950 pilgrims, 380 priests and other temple employees and their families, 1,700 Akali Dal supporters, 500 followers of Bhindranwale, and 150 members of other armed groups. "According to eye-witnesses about 250 people surrendered in the temple complex and 500 in the hostel complex after the two battles were over. The White Paper says that 493 people were killed and eighty-six injured. These figures leave at least 1,600 people unaccounted for. It would obviously be wrong to assume that they were killed in the battle, but there must be a big question mark over the official figures of civilian casualties in the operation, a figure which is appallingly high anyhow for an operation conducted by an army against its own people." Tully and Jacob, 184–85.

6. Sources in Punjab and New Delhi, interviews by the author, December 1990 and October 1992. These sources asked that their names not be used. [Editors' note: According to the author, most of the sources whose interviews by the author or Human Rights Watch are cited here asked that their names not be used and must remain anonymous for reasons of security.]

7. Police officer, interview by the author, Punjab, October 1992.

8. In fact, the killings were so widespread and so routine that they became the subject of black humor by journalists covering the conflict. In a conversation with HRW in March 1993, a senior journalist who had covered Punjab for years recounted a meeting he had had with Director General of Police K. P. S. Gill, during which Gill threatened a waiter who was too slow in refilling the DGP's beer that he would "have him killed in an 'encounter.'"

9. Saini had been identified in many cases of extrajudicial killings, disappearances, and torture. See Human Rights Watch, *Punjab in Crisis: Human Rights in India* (New York: Human Rights Watch,

1991). Although the Babbar Khalsa was originally believed responsible, according to a *Times of India* report, later on, the Khalistan Liberation Force was accused of the assassination attempt. Dinesh Kumar, "Police Accused of Killing Militant's Kin," *Times of India* (Bombay), 17 October 1991.

10. Kumar, "Police Accused of Killing Militant's Kin."
11. Police officer, interview by the author, Punjab, October 1992.
12. Police officer, interview by the author, Punjab, October 1992.
13. Kanwar Sandhu and Ramesh Vinayak, "Punjab: Area of Darkness," *India Today* (New Delhi), 15 July 1992, 24.
14. Police officer, interview by the author, Punjab, October 1992.
15. Police officer, interview by the author, Punjab, October 1992.
16. Police officer, interview by the author, Punjab, October 1992.
17. Police officer, interview by the author, Punjab, October 1992.
18. Police officer whose husband was a member of a police death squad, interview by the author, Punjab, October 1992.
19. Police officer and other sources, interviews by the author, Punjab, October 1992.
20. Kanwar Sandhu, "Official Excesses," *India Today*, 15 October 1992, 31–32.
21. See United States Department of State, *Country Reports on Human Rights Practices for 1993* (Washington, D.C.: U.S. Government Printing Office, 1994).
22. The conflict is situated in the valley of Kashmir in the north Indian state of Jammu and Kashmir. The valley of Kashmir lies between the Pir Panjal and Karakoram mountain ranges of the Himalayas. When we use the term "Kashmir" we are referring to the valley, which includes the towns and villages along the Jhelum River, from Handwara and surrounding towns in the northwest to Anantnag in the southeast.
23. See Edward Gargan, "Indian Troops Are Blamed as Kashmir Violence Rises," *New York Times*, 18 April 1993.
24. The author and other colleagues at Human Rights Watch investigated these cases and conducted interviews with a number of witnesses and other sources in Kashmir and New Delhi from March 1993 until the present. For reasons of security, most of the sources must remain anonymous.
25. In an interview in New Delhi in March 1993, Madhukar Gupta, joint secretary in the Home Ministry, told the author that the Indian government had arrested the persons responsible for Wanchoo's murder and that they were members of "a fundamentalist organization" which opposed Wanchoo because he was a politically prominent Hindu. When asked about the government's intentions to

prosecute the accused persons and make it known publicly that the murder suspects had been apprehended, Joint Secretary Gupta stated, "It was a very difficult time," and he "could not say any more."

26. Madhukar Gupta, interview by the author, March 1993.

27. Indian government official, interview by the author, December 1998.

28. Doctor, interview by Human Rights Watch consultant, Srinagar, January 1996; Human Rights Watch/Asia, *India's Secret Army in Kashmir.*

29. Witnesses, interviews by Human Rights Watch, Srinagar, January 1996.

30. Witnesses, interviews by Human Rights Watch, Srinagar, January 1996.

31. Interview by Human Rights Watch, January 1996.

32. Interview by the author, Srinagar, October 1996.

33. Interview by Human Rights Watch, January 1996.

34. The reaction from U.S. officials was colored by their frustration with the JKLF's unwillingness—or inability—to help negotiate the release of five Westerners kidnapped by a shadowy militant group called Al-Faran in July 1995.

35. Rifat Andrabi, interview by the author, Srinagar, October 1996.

36. Interviews by the author, Srinagar, October and November 1996.

37. During interviews with the author, senior officials in Srinagar routinely responded to questions about the countermilitants by claiming that the violence was due to feuds between rival militant forces.

38. Author's interviews with sources in Srinagar, October and November 1996; Human Rights Watch interviews, January 1996 and October 1998.

39. United States Department of State, *Country Report on Human Rights Practices for 1996* (Washington, D.C.: U.S. Government Printing Office, 1996), 1436–37.

40. Harinder Baweja and Ramesh Vinayak, "A Dangerous Liaison," *India Today,* 15 March 1996, 52–53. The English rendering of some of the names of the groups varies.

41. Cited in A. G. Noorani, "State Terror-I, Repeating Punjab in J & K," *Statesman,* 17 April 1996.

42. The name Taliban comes from the Arabic word for student. In Afghanistan, the Taliban militia controlled most of the country by late 1998.

43. Human Rights Watch interviews, January 1996, and author's interviews in Kashmir, October and November 1996.

44. Baweja and Vinayak, "A Dangerous Liaison," 55.

45. Author's interview with one of the journalists who had been abducted, Kashmir, October 1996.

46. Human Rights Watch interviews in Kashmir, January 1996 and October 1998; author's interviews in Kashmir, October and November 1996.

47. Papa Kistwari, interview by Human Rights Watch, October 1998.

CHAPTER 11

Territoriality and Plausible Deniability: Serbian Paramilitaries in the Bosnian War

James Ron

DURING THE FIRST MONTHS OF THE 1992 BOSNIAN civil war, ethnic Serb paramilitaries played a key role in forcibly displacing Bosnian Muslims and Croats from their homes, using classic death squad methods such as killing, torture, theft, and rape. Although socialist Yugoslavia's increasingly Serb-led Yugoslav People's Army (JNA) aided the Bosnian Serb military effort during the initial round of fighting, some of the most intense violence was done by ethnic Serb irregulars hailing both from Bosnia and from Serbia proper.[1] This chapter will offer one explanation for this excessive reliance on irregular paramilitary forces during the first months of the Bosnian war. Conventional wisdom in the Western press suggests that brutal paramilitaries are inherent to "Balkan" or "Serbian" culture. Instead, I will argue that the paramilitaries' centrality stemmed from local and international norms prohibiting Serbian military action beyond Serbia's official borders. These limitations prompted Serbian officials to enter into a subcontracting relationship with semiprivate groups in both Bosnia and Serbia proper, which were able to use violence without directly incriminating the Belgrade regime.[2]

In a concluding section, I address issues of definition: were the Serbian paramilitaries indeed "death squads" in any sense of the word? If so, in what way? I will argue that the Serbian groups assumed some, but not all, of the characteristics we typically associate with the death squad label. The paramilitaries resembled the classic Latin American–style death squads in that they were clandestine, semiautonomous state agents using extreme, illegal violence to achieve political goals against a clearly defined target population. They differ from the conventional model, however, in that they also engaged in military or guerrilla operations and targeted victims who were not citizens of the Serbian state. In the popular Western imagination, death squads use murder to eliminate internal enemies, typically leftists. The Serbian paramilitaries, on the other hand, killed Bosnian Muslims and Croats to eliminate their presence within contested regions claimed by nationalist activists for the Serbian ethnos. The Serbian paramilitary victims were thus neither purely "external" nor "internal" enemies, and they were targeted for their ethnic identity rather than their political affiliation.

The differences between the Serbian paramilitary units and the Latin American death squads highlights the need for a more robust definition than the one commonly used. Although most death squads originate in the state's quest for plausible deniability, they come in many shapes and forms, as is evident from the cases surveyed in this volume. Until now, most observers have associated the "death squad" label with Latin America's anticommunist gunmen of the 1970s and 1980s. The global death squad phenomenon encompasses a much broader spectrum of cases, however, suggesting that we adopt a more inclusive analytical framework.

Background

Serbian paramilitary action first emerged during the summer 1991 battles between ethnic Serbs and Croat forces in the Krajina region of Croatia, which at the time was still a republic of the now-defunct Socialist Federal Republic of Yugoslavia (SFRY). A typical report described the former Yugoslavia in 1991 as a "land where former football hooligans and neofascist ganglords run riot with assault rifles and mortar bombs instead of boots and bottles."[3] Another talked about a "bizarre assortment of soldiers of fortune, self-styled dukes, guerrillas and local warlords,"[4] while a third spoke of "The Duke, the King of Slavonia, Captain Dragan . . . and many other colorful characters. . . . They govern, plunder and defend their patches of land in exchange for fairly nominal pledges of loyalty to distant governments. . . ." The paramilitaries, this last account argued, had become "cult heroes in their local towns, mopping up unemployment among the jobless youth and, as a result, winning far more popularity than their leaders in Belgrade and Zagreb."[5] By the end of the Croatian war, paramilitaries on all sides of the conflict had made a deep impression on journalists and citizens alike, promoting an image of thuggish violence, rape, and plunder. From 1991 onward, the terms "paramilitary" and "Serb" would be linked together in the Western press.

When the Bosnian war began in April 1992, reports of paramilitary atrocities accelerated. As one reporter argued, the Bosnian war "is being waged by a kaleidoscope of militias, armies and freelance groups. Accurate numbers are impossible to ascertain, loyalties overlap, and who really controls whom, if anyone, is a moot point."[6] In spring 1992, journalists were increasingly eager to uncover Serbia's clandestine links to the paramilitaries because Western powers and the United Nations had sought to block direct Serbian state intervention in the Bosnian fighting. One British daily, hinting at the Belgrade-Bosnia link, wrote: "[A]s Bosnia is ripped apart at its ethnic seams, a notorious band of Serbian veterans of the dirtiest fighting in neighboring Croatia is leading the assault. The warlords, usually products of Belgrade's underworld, are television celebrities, icons of national heroism for many Serbs, and powerful players on the republic's political stage. . . . [F]ighters annexing territory for the self-styled Serbian Republic of Bosnia-Herzegovina declare their allegiance to 'Arkan,' 'the Duke,' or Jović—two underworld figures and a political thug. But the militia also provides a front for crack [Serbian] professional soldiers masquerading as local volunteers. . . ."[7] Concrete evidence of a Belgrade link to the Bosnian paramilitaries was hard to come by, as both the paramilitaries and Serbian officials denied their relationship. Serbia had sworn publicly to keep its military forces within its own territory, and the paramilitaries, if they agreed to be interviewed, stressed their autonomy from Serbian leaders.

Systematic investigations of the fighting confirm that the paramilitaries played a central role in the 1992 ethnic cleansing campaign in Bosnia. A 1994 United Nations report by the "Commission of Experts," the prelude to the Yugoslav war crimes tribunal, found that reports of serious human rights violations co-varied positively with reported paramilitary activity in given municipalities. The UN investigators identified 55 different ethnic Serb paramilitary groups and 67 different municipalities in the former Yugoslavia that experienced Serb paramilitary action, the overwhelming majority of which were in Bosnia.[8] The irregulars were often the first troops to engage Bosnian Muslim and Croat civilians firsthand, and it was during this time that much of the worst violence took place. The old Yugoslav People's Army, which was officially stationed in Bosnia only until May 14, 1992, reportedly lent support to the irregulars but did not, for the most part, partake directly in acts of ethnic cleansing. The Yugoslav federal troops often deployed near Muslim- or Croat-held areas, but left much of the close-in action to the paramilitary irregulars.[9]

Serbian paramilitaries from Bosnia and Serbia proper thus played a key role in driving Muslims and Croats from areas claimed by nationalist activists for a future Bosnian Serb state. Thousands of non-Serbs were killed in the process, with the murders serving both as a way of inducing flight and as an end in themselves. Official agents of the Serbian republic were involved in the killings, but the extent and precise nature of that involvement remains unclear.

Territorial Limitations on Official Serbian Military Action: The Bosnian Border, 1992

During the Yugoslav socialist period, the hundreds of thousands of Serbs living in Bosnia and Croatia were separated from the Serbian republic by the Yugoslav federation's internal administrative boundaries. Bosnia-Herzegovina, Croatia, and Serbia were all separate republics of socialist Yugoslavia, and each had its own internal security apparatus within the republican-level Ministry of Interior. Powerful federal norms prevented one Yugoslav republic from intervening militarily in the internal affairs of another.[10] These inter-republican norms were particularly significant in 1991, when socialist Yugoslavia still existed. The sole military body authorized to cut across republican boundaries was the federal Yugoslav People's Army, which was inculcated with a strict nonpartisan and ethnically blind ethos. Although Serbia increasingly influenced the army's senior command, it could not rely on the federal army in the early stages of the conflict to fully back the Serbian cause.

In 1992, constraints on cross-border Serbian military intervention were reinforced by international recognition of Bosnia's independence, a move that deepened the divide between Serbian ethnos and state. The U.S. and European Union governments recognized Bosnia's independence on April 6 and 7 respectively, threatening Serbia with punitive action if it intervened militarily in the deepening Bosnian conflict. The Western powers hoped thereby to prevent outside stimulation of the Bosnian fighting and to secure a lasting cease-fire. Throughout spring 1992, Western intelligence services, reporters, and human rights groups continued to charge Serbia with continued involvement in the Bosnian fighting, both through the remnants of the Yugoslav People's Army and through cross-border paramilitaries. On May 30, the Security Council imposed comprehensive mandatory sanctions on rump Yugoslavia—now composed of a dominant Serbia and a much smaller Montenegro—for its suspected cross-border activity, ordering all UN member states to cut commercial ties with the country.[11]

Serbia outwardly seemed to comply with these restrictions on extraterritorial military action, promising international observers it would respect Bosnia's territorial integrity. A key part of this effort was Serbia's order to withdraw from Bosnia the remnants of the Yugoslav People's Army, which by this time was almost entirely staffed by ethnic Serbs. On May 4, 1992, rump Yugoslavia officials, directed for the most by Serbian leader Slobodan Milošević's Socialist Party, announced that they were ordering all soldiers who were citizens of Serbia and Montenegro to withdraw from Bosnia within fifteen days, explaining that there were "no longer any grounds" for rump Yugoslavia to "decide on military questions" in Bosnia.[12] In reality, some 80 percent of the Yugoslav People's Army remained in Bosnia, since these men were local Bosnian Serbs.[13] The withdrawal of soldiers with Serbian and Montenegrin citizenship, however, was aimed at reassuring Western powers that the new rump Yugoslavia intended to respect Bosnian sovereignty.

Belgrade officials also declared a ban on paramilitary infiltration from Serbia into Bosnia. "Irregular formations are prohibited in Serbia by law," the Serbian prime minister stated, adding that the government was launching efforts to thwart "armed individuals" from Serbia from getting involved in the Bosnian fighting. The "occasional appearance of armed individuals and groups," the government said on another occasion, is a "marginal phenomenon subject to strict control." In late April 1992, as reports of Serbia-based paramilitary activity in Bosnia escalated, Serbian leader Slobodan Milošević stated emphatically that the "organs of . . . the Republic of Serbia fully control" its territory and were blocking cross-border infiltrations.[14] This public relations effort was supported even by Serbian ultranationalist Vojislav Šešelj, who vowed he had "no paramilitary formations and no need to intervene militarily" in Bosnia, and Arkan, who promised that he too had "no forces in Sarajevo."[15] Throughout the spring and summer of 1992 officials repeatedly stressed their public commitment to blocking the irregular forces.

Protestations of innocence to the contrary, Serbian state representatives continued to contribute clandestinely to the Bosnian Serb military effort throughout the spring and summer of 1992. Although some members of Serbia's ruling Socialist Party might have been willing to let the Bosnian Serbs fend for themselves, Serbia's far-right opposition and sympathetic allies inside the regime lobbied hard for the Bosnian Serb cause. Serbia's political leaders faced a difficult dilemma. If they abandoned the Bosnian Serbs entirely, they would face censure at home for leaving brother Serbs in the lurch. If they openly sent Serbian state forces to fight for Bosnian Serbs, however, they would face stiff international pressure.

In an effort to resolve this dilemma, Milošević and his fellow leaders turned to the Serbian paramilitaries, many of whom had already cut their teeth on the Croatian fighting. The Serbian republican regime devised a series of clandestine connections to Serbian irregulars recruited by their own agents as well as by far-right political leaders, links they could and did deny when pressed. Serbian officials would help equip and transport the irregulars into Bosnia, and in return they would portray themselves as private patriots concerned only with defending endangered diaspora Serbs. Serbia's leaders thus hoped to fulfill their nationalist duties while simultaneously evading Western censure for extraterritorial military adventurism.

The Serbian Paramilitaries as State Subcontractors

As the cases in this volume suggest, many death squads are initiated by state officials as part of a subcontracting arrangement by state officials seeking to bypass existing constraints on internal state violence. In these cases, the need for secrecy and clandestine organizing is generated by the surrounding legal and normative environment, which bars torture, extrajudicial executions, and other forms of state thuggery.

Like most death squads, the Serbian paramilitaries' services were clandestinely used by state agents seeking to avoid responsibility for illegal actions. The normative restrictions the Serbian state sought to avoid differed somewhat from those facing other states, however, in that they were chiefly territorial in nature. Although millions of ethnic Serbs lived in the Serbian diaspora, the Serbian republic was blocked from openly intervening on their behalf by a host of local and international territorial restrictions. In one sense, this was a conflict between different definitions of the areas held as "sovereign" by the Serbian nation. For Serbian nationalists and many Serbian state officials, sovereign Serbian territory was the area inhabited by the Serbian ethnos, encompassing Serbia as well as portions of Bosnia and Croat territory. For the international community and local non-Serbs, however, sovereign Serbian territory was defined more narrowly, referring only to the areas within the Serbian republic.

Normative restrictions prevented the Serbian state from acting openly throughout the Serbian ethnos, prompting Serbian officials to support the extraterritorial paramilitaries. These groups could fight in Bosnia without directly implicating the Serbian leadership, providing Belgrade's leaders with plausible deniability. The paramilitaries could operate with relative freedom abroad, whereas Serbia's formal security forces remained bottled up within Serbia proper. The paramilitaries were a rational solution to an immediate problem faced by the Serbian state, not a cultural phenomenon hardwired into Serbian or Balkan society.

The Serbian Nationalist Movement

Many of the paramilitary leaders began their careers as dissidents in the anticommunist Serbian national movement of the 1980s. Debates over Serbia's constitutional status within socialist Yugoslavia had promoted the arguments of dissidents critical of the communists for subordinating Serbia, suppressing democracy, and rewriting World War II history to legitimize communist rule.[16] Toward the mid-1980s, some of the leading dissidents launched an increasingly cogent critique of the Serbian communists' political and economic performance, drawing on widespread public dissatisfaction with the economy and interrepublican wrangling. Serbian nationalist intellectuals wrote about formerly taboo subjects such as Serbia's suffering during the 1941–45 civil war, communist discrimination against Serbia, and the need for Serbian political and territorial unity. The Serbian state had failed in its mission to unify the Serbian ethnos under one political roof, the nationalists said, and this failure lay at the root of many contemporary Serbian problems. Nationalist writers even began to depict Serbia's World War II royalist guerrillas in a more positive light, criticizing the Communist Party's official version of the civil war, which had tagged the pro-monarchist fighters as cowards and fascist collaborators. The irregular royalist units would later provide inspiration and a rough blueprint for contemporary Serbian paramilitaries.

In 1987, Slobodan Milošević's faction assumed a leading role in the Serbian Communist Party branch. Rather than confront the dissident nationalists head on, Milošević resolved to co-opt them by adopting many of their arguments as his own. The result was a unique "left-right" agenda that merged socialism and nationalism. Milošević promised to reinvigorate Serbia by shaking up the bureaucracy, reasserting centralized control over Serbia's provinces, and demanding respect for Serbia in Yugoslav federal forums.[17] When multiparty elections came to Serbia in 1990, the ex-communists—now campaigning as the renamed Socialist Party of Serbia—performed well, largely as a result of Milošević's nationalist credentials.

As Serbia entered the new, multiparty era, a group of radical parties emerged to Milošević's right, seeking to push the Serbian political agenda in an increasingly nationalist direction. These groups, veterans of the anticommunist crusade of the 1980s, were frustrated with Milošević's skillful co-optation of their agenda and his electoral success. Although postcommunist elections had allowed dissidents to replace the *ancien régime* in many Eastern European countries, Serbia's dissidents had remained in the opposition, outmaneuvered by Milošević's political agility and quick incorporation of the nationalist agenda.[18]

Once war broke out in Croatia and then in Bosnia, however, these radical parties assumed a vital role as paramilitary subcontractors. In effect, the Belgrade-based political leaders acted as middlemen positioned halfway between state agencies and semiprivate Serbian gunmen. Faced with territorial constraints blocking Serbia from intervening directly in the fighting, the state turned to the right-wing politicians, using them to open their own recruitment operation for individuals willing to fight and kill for those portions of the Serbian ethnos lying beyond Serbia's legal boundaries.

Serbia- and Bosnia-Based Paramilitaries

Broadly speaking, ethnic Serb paramilitaries active in Bosnia can be divided into those originating from Serbia proper and those from Bosnia. Many of the Serbia-based paramilitaries clustered around nationalist politicians based in Belgrade, while the Bosnia-based groups were typically recruited by locally prominent businessmen, municipal officials, or Bosnian Serb political activists.

When tensions mounted between ethnic Serbs and Croatian republican forces in 1991, activists in Serbia's right-wing parties began to double as paramilitary organizers. Nationalist Belgrade activists such as Mirko Jović and Dragoslav Bokan of the Serbian National Defense Party, Vojislav Šešelj of the Serbian Radical Party, and Vuk Drašković of the Serbian Renewal Movement took on their new military role with relish, viewing it as their patriotic duty for the endangered Serbian ethnos. Jović and Bokan hastened to form the White Eagles, Šešelj created the Serbian Četnik Movement, and Drašković founded the Serbian Guard (he later disassociated himself from the movement). A fourth paramilitary chieftain, Željko Raznjatović, better known by his alias Arkan, was in a category of his own. Although he later displayed some political ambition, Arkan had no independent political base and was not a card-carrying member of the nationalist dissident movement, although he occasionally adopted its symbols and language. Instead, he was reportedly close to the intelligence services of the old socialist Yugoslavia, the Serbian Ministry of Interior's State Security service, and perhaps even to Slobodan Milošević himself. This set Arkan off from the political paramilitary leaders such as Šešelj and Drašković, who saw themselves as Milošević's rivals for leadership of the Serbian nation.

According to two Belgrade journalists who closely followed the paramilitaries during the 1991 Croatian fighting, the Serbia-based irregulars had their own separate organizational structure that was "different than the organization of regular army units. They had their own special platoons, units, battalions and divisions. They appointed their own commanders in the field. . . . They had different insignia from the military . . . they had their own flags and emblems, and they always went to church before battle."[19] Belonging largely to the most radical strands of the Serbian national movement, the paramilitaries were often virulently anticommunist.

The paramilitary commanders claimed publicly that they were protecting ethnic Serbs from deadly assaults by Croatian fascists and Muslim fundamentalists, and they charged Milošević's Socialists with treason for betraying diaspora Serbs in Croatia and Bosnia. Milošević had bowed to Western pressure, refusing to send Serbian Ministry of Interior forces or rump Yugoslav army troops to support ethnic Serb fighters abroad. Given this failure, the nationalists said, it was up to the irregular "volunteers" to step in. In 1991, some paramilitary leaders even discussed the option of creating a new, all-nationalist army that would replace the communist-tainted Yugoslav federal army and aggressively defend the Serbian ethnos. Although the irregulars shelved those plans and agreed to work clandestinely with Milošević for a time, they continued to regard the Socialists with the utmost suspicion. In the early years of the fighting, the paramilitaries preferred to play down their relationship with the state, keeping quiet about the vital support they received from Yugoslav army officers and officials of the Serbian Ministry of Interior. Later, when the tacit state-paramilitary alliance broke down in 1993, the paramilitary leaders would begin to hint at their 1991–92 linkages to the Serbian regime.

Although most had their headquarters in Belgrade, the Serbia-based irregulars recruited widely throughout rump Yugoslavia, composed of Serbia and Montenegro, sending busloads of volunteers to the front lines. The most prolific organizer was Vojislav Šešelj, who was rumored to receive greater quantities of official support than the others. According to war correspondents based in Belgrade, Šešelj sent 5,000 men to Croatia during 1991 and perhaps as many as 30,000 to Bosnia during 1992. Other paramilitaries mustered a few thousand volunteers, with their numbers fluctuating dramatically over time and space.

In addition, a few small-time Serbian paramilitaries were recruited by local entrepreneurs who put together their own fighting bands and traveled independently to Bosnia from Serbia. Given the lack of formal, direct state control over the paramilitary recruitment process, it was easy for these independent gunmen to insinuate themselves into the fighting, following their own agenda amid the broader nationalist effort. One such group was the "Yellow Wasps," a band of 66 men who gathered during the spring of 1992 in Zvornik, a Bosnian border town. One Yellow Wasp commander was a former judo instructor from the town of Šabac near Belgrade, while the other was his brother and a Šabac auto mechanic. Both men had fought in 1991 with Vojislav Šešelj's forces in Croatia, but had then decided to strike out on their own during the Bosnian fighting, organizing their own militia to "defend the Serbian people" in Zvornik. The Yellow Wasps, however, seemed more intent on looting and extortion than anything else. In addition to assaulting members of Zvornik's Muslim community, the Wasps also reportedly extorted well-to-do Serbs, angering local Bosnian Serb authorities so much that they eventually threw the Wasps back over the border into Serbia.[20]

Although the paramilitary leaders consistently articulated high-sounding patriotic ideals in the press, promising to defend the embattled Bosnian Serb ethnos through selfless sacrifice, the reality was much nastier. Many of the "volunteers" were unemployed Serbian males in search of booty and cheap wartime thrills. In some cases, the men had been recruited directly from Serbian prisons, agreeing to fight in return for rehabilitation or a reduction in sentence. The results must have been anticipated by their recruiters: many of the irregular fighters behaved atrociously in the field, using methods far more brutal than anything required for strictly military purposes. Theft was an integral part of the Bosnian paramilitary mission, with Muslims, Croats, and even some Serb civilians assaulted for cash and possessions. Sexual assaults were also common, as were other forms of gratuitous torture and violence.

In addition to the paramilitaries hailing from Serbia proper, a plethora of local irregular fighting groups emerged from among the Bosnian Serb population. Many were recruited by locally prominent Bosnian Serbs, including businessmen and political entrepreneurs who hoped to contribute to the national cause while also looting ethnic "enemies." In the Banja Luka region of Bosnia, for example, Veljko Milanković, a prominent local businessman, recruited and armed the "Wolves from Vučjak."[21] By his own account, Milanković was a significant financial backer of the Serb Democratic

Party, the Bosnian Serbs' main political movement. When fighting began in Croatia in 1991, Milanković sent his Wolves to support the ethnic Serb military effort there, but redeployed them back to Bosnia several months later when tensions rose at home.[22] Their first Bosnian operation, Milanković said, was the seizure of a local television transmitter, which allowed the Bosnian Serb Democratic Party to replace broadcasts from Zagreb and Sarajevo with news from Belgrade. Although Milanković portrayed himself as a selfless contributor to the Bosnian Serb national cause, a nearby major in the Bosnian Serb army saw it differently. "Only riffraff and thieves" joined the Wolves in 1992, he charged, attracted chiefly by the prospect of war booty. "Those men had joined up early to steal during the Croatian fighting," he said, "and wanted to continue the same here by stealing from Muslims."[23] The major's opinion was seconded by another local Bosnian Serb soldier, who said that although the Wolves might have fought well in Croatia, they had become some of the most ardent ethnic cleansers and looters in the Bosnian fighting.[24] Slavica, a former key Bosnian Serb intelligence officer based in Banja Luka, came to the Wolves' defense, explaining that their main function was not to ethnically cleanse Muslims, but rather to guard Milanković 's property and business interests. "It was a chaotic time," she explained, "and rich men like Milanković wanted to protect their money."[25]

A detailed study of 1992–95 events in two Bosnian Serb towns, Doboj and Teslić, revealed an extensive set of ties between local Bosnian Serb paramilitary activists, Bosnian Serb municipal officials, and activists from the Serb Democratic Party. The study by Human Rights Watch claimed that a "group of local Bosnian Serb political leaders, police chiefs, party leaders, officials and civilians" had established an "underground mafia-type network" in the early stages of the war.[26] By way of example, the study mentioned the central role of Milan Ninković, president of the Doboj town branch of the Serb Democratic Party as well as president of the local municipal council. Ninković "was one of the principal organizers of the overall plan and strategy to 'ethnically cleanse' the Doboj area," maintaining contacts with locally recruited paramilitaries through his brother, who managed two large local businesses and procured weapons for the fighters. In the Bosnian town of Teslić, the Human Rights Watch report alleged, Milovan Mirkonjić, chief of the local "territorial defense" unit, was one of "the five principal organizers of 'ethnic cleansing'" in the area. Mirkonjić allegedly worked closely with local paramilitary chiefs from the "Red Berets" and "Predo's Wolves."

The Ethnic Cleansing of Zvornik

The April 1992 ethnic cleansing of Zvornik, the Bosnian border town, is one of the better-documented examples of paramilitary action, having been researched extensively by a Vienna-based human rights group.[27] Zvornik, a town of some 80,000 located just over the Drina River from Serbia, was approximately 60 percent Muslim in early 1992. Its strategic importance to the Serbian military effort stemmed from its location on a major highway leading from Serbia proper into Serb-controlled areas in eastern Bosnia. On April 8, the day after European recognition of Bosnian sovereignty, Serbian paramilitary forces attacked Zvornik, crossing the Drina River from Serbian republican territory. The initial assault was led by Arkan's Serbian Voluntary Guards. According to refugee testimony, Arkan himself led the operations and seemed autonomous of both the local Bosnian Serb authorities and the nearby Yugoslav federal troops, who had not yet withdrawn from Bosnia. The second assault wave included less exclusive paramilitaries such as Vojislav Šešelj's Serbian Movement and Dragoslav Bokan's White Eagles.

Jovan Dulović, a longtime Serbian crime reporter from the Belgrade daily *Politika,* was on the Serbian side of the river when the fighting began. He followed the second wave into Zvornik, recalling that the paramilitaries "looked like a bunch of gangs. All the scum of Serbia were there, and it was total chaos."[28] Dulović made his way to the office of the chief of Zvornik's Bosnian Serb Territorial Defense, Marko Pavlović, the man theoretically in charge of the local Serbian military effort. Dulović found Pavlović virtually powerless, however, because none of the paramilitaries felt obliged to follow his instructions. "I felt almost sorry for him," Dulović said. "He didn't have any of his own men and the paramilitaries weren't listening to him. They were a bunch of bandits."

The paramilitaries quickly subdued Muslim resistance in Zvornik. During and immediately after the fighting, they looted the stores and homes of Muslims, killing civilians in the process. The first wave of Arkan-led troops, more disciplined and professional than the others, soon left the town and moved on to other fighting. New paramilitaries came in and began stripping the homes more thoroughly. Differences arose between the local Bosnian Serb authorities and the paramilitaries. The authorities were issuing "safe passage" exit permits to Zvornik's Muslims, encouraging them to flee the region in a relatively secure and orderly process. The paramilitaries did not respect the police-issued permits, however, grabbing civilians as they exited the police station, ripping up their passes, physically abusing them, and even taking some off to impromptu detention camps.

The picture painted by refugee testimony is one of paramilitary-induced chaos. According to one group of researchers who interviewed dozens of refugees, "the various paramilitary units marauding [sic] around Zvornik all had unlimited freedom of action (terrorizing the civilian population, randomly performing executions and arrestations [sic])." Refugee testimony indicated that the "paramilitary units only accepted the authority of their own respective 'leaders,' . . . [while] many of the less strictly organized paramilitary groups regarded their complete freedom of action as a kind of 'remuneration' for their work."[29] In his diary, Belgrade reporter Dulović noted details of interviews with several paramilitary commanders whom he recognized from other battlefields. There was "Miroslav, from the Serbian Četnik Movement, who was commander of a big unit," as well as "Pedja, from Arkan's unit." Dulović spoke with men who identified themselves as belonging to the White Eagles and Yellow Wasps, as well as some who boasted they belonged to some unheard-of group known as "the silent liquidation units," who tried to "make their jobs sound more important by giving themselves scary names."

Dulović's diary estimates that some 5,000 Serb paramilitary fighters were deployed through Zvornik and its surrounding villages. In areas where the fighting had ended, the irregulars were loading trucks with looted refrigerators and other appliances. Dulović noted a hierarchy of looters, with the elite Arkan-led troops enjoying preferential access to the most lucrative Muslim-owned assets, such as gold and cash. Next came men from the Serbian Četnik Movement and the White Eagles, who seized the larger appliances. Bringing up the rear were local militias and the smaller Serbia-based paramilitaries, who were forced to settle for whatever remained. "These guys stripped the wires out of the walls and dismantled windows and doorframes," Dulović said. The more prestigious the unit, the better access one received to looted goods.

The Zvornik model of paramilitary violence was repeated throughout the spring and summer of 1992, as paramilitaries from Serbia proper swept through eastern Bosnia, attacking large border cities such as Foča, Gorazde, and Višegrad, as well as smaller towns and villages. From their bases along the Bosnia-Serbia border, men from the larger paramilitary formations sallied forth to join smaller local militias, jointly consolidating ethnic Serb military and political control in eastern Bosnia and forcing out the bulk of the non-Serbian population.

The Clandestine Belgrade-Bosnia Paramilitary Connection: How Did It Work?

The dearth of reliable information about Serbia's links to the Bosnian fighting has generated multiple interpretations of the "Belgrade connection." At one extreme, critics view Milošević as the key architect of Bosnian ethnic cleansing, micromanaging the entire brutal process. The image these analysts prefer is of a smoothly functioning death machine spreading its tentacles from Belgrade down to the most remote Bosnian detention camps and massacre sites. Military analyst Milan Vego, for example, argued that while "the regime in Belgrade consistently tries to . . . muddle the issue," the reality was that "the operational chain of command runs . . . from the Supreme Defense Council [in Belgrade] . . . through the General Staff in Belgrade, to . . . the Army of the Serbian Republic of Bosnia Herzegovina. . . ."[30] At the other end of the spectrum are denials by Serbia's leaders, seen above, who insisted that Serbia was uninvolved in the Bosnian events.

A third interpretation rejects both extremes, arguing that while Milošević facilitated, encouraged, and supported the Bosnian Serb war effort, he only set the general tone by providing guidance and weapons. Sonja Biserko, the head of Belgrade's Helsinki Commission, for example, believes that "Bosnia got away from Milošević; he started something he didn't know how to stop."[31] Bosnia was a confusing place in the spring of 1992, with a multitude of paramilitaries, army units, and local leaders wielding political and military power. According to Nataša Kandić, director of the Belgrade-based

Humanitarian Law Center and a vigorous war crimes investigator, there "may in fact be no one chain of command" for individual atrocities.[32]

The "Military Line" Hypothesis

Although we cannot know with certainty the details of Serbia's relationship to the paramilitaries, several Western journalists, drawing heavily on insights from independent Belgrade reporters (who prefer to remain anonymous), have developed a plausible scenario involving something they call the "Military Line." The Military Line, these reporters claim, was the name assumed by a group of key Socialist Party politicians, Serbian Interior Ministry officials, and Yugoslav army officers, all of whom broadly supported the goal of consolidating Bosnian Serb control in key areas by pushing out Muslims and Croats. The term "Military Line" was first used publicly by Tim Judah, a Belgrade-based British war correspondent, whose book briefly states that the group sought to help Serbs in Bosnia and Croatia carve out their own enclaves.[33] Julian Borger, another British reporter, wrote a more detailed account that same year, arguing that the Military Line was a "parallel chain of command" that allowed Milošević to privately control Serbia-based paramilitaries and Bosnian Serb forces.[34] Borger said that in 1991–92, the Military Line's main coordinator was Jovića Stanišić, then head of the Interior Ministry's secret service, known as State Security. Stanišić 's chief aides, according to Borger, were Radovan Stojičić ("Badža"), an officer in the Interior Ministry's uniformed division—known as Public Security—and Franko Simatović ("Frenki"), another State Security officer. Badža and Frenki, Borger said, trained and armed the Serbia-based paramilitaries and even traveled with them to battlefields in Croatia and Bosnia. Borger wrote that Badža, Frenki, and other key leaders stood at the top of a pyramid working to coordinate Belgrade's plans throughout Bosnia and Croatia. This "network of state security agents," he concluded, "coordinated the process of ethnic cleansing." Borger also highlighted the key logistical role of Mihalj Kerteš, a leading member of the ruling Socialist Party. Kerteš, Borger said, distributed guidance, intelligence, and weapons to the Serb Democratic Party in Bosnia and Croatia just prior to the wars in both republics. Journalist Misha Glenny added more details about Kerteš's work as an arms supplier: In 1990 and 1991, Glenny wrote, Kerteš was the architect of a major Serbian weapons distribution program aimed at carving a Greater Serbia from parts of Bosnia and Croatia. "Throughout 1990, Kerteš ordered the dispatch of hundreds of thousands of pieces of weaponry mainly to the two militant Serb regions of Bosnia-Herzegovina. . . . Throughout 1991, Kerteš' secret convoys of lorries bulging with guns and munitions ploughed their furrow with . . . diligence. . . ."[35]

Borger's ground-breaking article drew on interviews with unnamed Serbian officials as well as some key named individuals, including Branislav Vakić, a Serbian Radical Party legislator and former paramilitary commander, who told Borger that Serbian Interior Ministry officials "Badža" and "Frenki" were both heavily involved in supplying, training, and coordinating his paramilitaries. In an earlier, 1994 interview with *Dnevni Telegraf*, an independent Belgrade daily, Vakić had made a similar claim, saying that thousands of his fighters had received fuel and uniforms from the federal army's military police, naming a string of helpful military officers and Interior Ministry officials.[36] Vojislav Šešelj, the Serbian Radical Party's leader and Vakić's political boss, made similar statements during a public dispute with Slobodan Milošević in 1993. Šešelj, who was seeking to counter Milošević's charges that he was a war criminal and an adventurer, told Serbian reporters that his men had in fact worked closely with Serbian government officials throughout the 1991–92 fighting in Bosnia and Croatia. "Our volunteers took part in combat as part of special units of the police from [Serbia], under the command of Mihalj Kerteš," Šešelj said, adding that "we fought on many battlefields alongside Frenki."[37] Thus Šešelj and Vakić, both former clandestine paramilitary subcontractors for the Serbian regime, independently offered information supporting the Military Line scenario.

I found fragments of additional evidence during my own interviews. For example, a former U.S. State Department official dealing with Bosnia in 1992 told me that he and his colleagues believed in 1992 that the Bosnian ethnic cleansing was choreographed by agents of Serbian State Security. In the first months of the war, he said, "State Security operatives fanned out across Bosnia initiating, leading, and controlling the fighting in different districts."[38] The United States had satellite imagery and radio intercepts in support of his claim, he said, but refused to specify details. Dejan Pavlović, an independent Serbian journalist, painted a similar picture. "State Security sent men to each Bosnian municipality looking for trusted persons who would act as allies," he told me in Belgrade. "These 'trusted persons' would be told that the area needed to be secured for reasons of convoy security or military strategy, and that as a result, the Muslims needed to be cleared out."[39] At times these operations were run by local chiefs of police, or at other times by the director of a hospital or the mayor. "You'll never find one method or one chain of command for ethnic cleansing," Pavlović explained, "because in each area, the person or group responsible for carrying out the ethnic cleansing was different. Each commander used a different method based on the different tools he had." Filip Švarm, another war correspondent at the independent Belgrade weekly *Vreme,* said State Security typically would recruit men in Croatia and Bosnia with valuable assets such as a warehouses, transportation companies, or municipal offices. "Those people were most useful because they could store weapons and provide vehicles when necessary," he explained.[40] Saša, a young man who fought with ethnic Serb forces in the Krajina area of Croatia, recounted an experience that seems to support Švarm's thesis.[41] In early 1991, Saša said, a local merchant in his village was recruited by Serbian State Security as their main local contact. "I don't know why he was chosen," Saša said. "Perhaps because they trusted him, or because he was generally respected in the village." The merchant organized a local group who trained together in 1991 in preparation for fighting with Croat republican forces. Every week, Saša said, the group would meet a representative of Yugoslav military intelligence in a nearby forest, who would occasionally arrive with a truckload of weapons.

The most persuasive piece of evidence attesting to the cross-border role of Serbia's State Security was supplied to me by Daniel Snidden, an ethnic Serb from Australia who reportedly once served in that country's armed forces. Snidden, known popularly in Belgrade as "Kapetan Dragan," came to Belgrade in 1991 and soon assumed command of a Serbian paramilitary unit in Croatia.[42] Snidden said that when he first came to Belgrade he was approached by Serbian State Security agents who asked if he would travel to Croatia briefly to assess the military potential of local Serbs. He reported back that "the situation was bloody awful. These guys had been trained by Communist officers who had no concept of a modern, professional fighting force." State Security asked Snidden to organize a training course, and his trainees, schooled in warfare at the "Alpha center" in the Serb-held Krajina region of Croatia, became the elite of the ethnic Serb army in the Krajina, many of whom went to Bosnia in 1992 to support the Bosnian Serb military effort. One of Snidden's top lieutenants claimed that the Alpha center forces were on the direct payroll of Serbian State Security, explaining that Snidden's men were given Serbian State Security dog tags and that Snidden himself took orders directly from State Security officers in Belgrade.[43] "Other units may have been under the local Serb authorities," the lieutenant said, "but we were the direct responsibility of State Security in Belgrade."

Most of the men recruited by State Security were not as glamorous as Daniel Snidden, however, who now runs a high-profile veterans' assistance organization in Belgrade and enjoys considerable positive media exposure. Perica, a former truck driver and paramilitary fighter in both Bosnia and Croatia, exemplifies the fate of the "little men" active at the lower rungs of the Military Line's cross-border network.[44] When I met him in early 1997, Perica worked for a small, marginal veterans' association in Belgrade, unsuccessfully lobbying the Serbian government for benefits on behalf of former paramilitary "volunteers." Prior to that, Perica said, he fought with the Serbian irregulars in Croatia and Bosnia, although he would not specify his unit. Perica said the main obstacle his association faced in seeking compensation after the war was Serbia's official denial of having ever recruited the paramilitaries in the first place. "When they needed men to fight their wars they called us volunteers and patriots," Perica said bitterly, "but now they pretend we never existed. They keep saying, 'Serbia was never involved in the war, Serbia never sent any soldiers to fight.'" Perica revealed a few details of his recruitment by Serbian State Security, explaining that he was initially contacted during 1990 or 1991 in his home town of Smedrevo "because my father had once been a police chief." At the time, Serbian State Security was then searching for "guys like me, whom they could trust, to see if we would fight abroad for the Serbian people." Perica explained that State Security was recruiting heavily among all his friends at the time. "Everybody was either an agent, working part-time for State Security, or pretending to be an agent," he recalled. Some of the men were true patriots, he said, seeking to defend Serbs in Croatia and Bosnia from genocide, while others were simply seeking war booty. "People said you could make money in the field," he explained.

Perica's recruitment tale underlines the importance of the Serbian police linkages to the Military Line. His father had been a police chief, making him a visible and potentially trustworthy worker in the eyes of the State Security recruiters, themselves secret policemen in the Interior Ministry. Recruitment was not just limited to the offspring of police officers, however. Julian Borger, the above-quoted British correspondent and Military Line theorist, cited in his article a former Belgrade police chief as saying that criminals serving time in Serbian prisons were recruited to fight in both Croatia and Bosnia. "The convicts were told, 'if you go to the front line, we will cut your sentence,'" the former chief told Borger.[45] Miroslav Mikuljanac, then a reporter for the Belgrade-based *Borba* newspaper, told me he had witnessed similar events in 1991, when he met convicts riding on Serbian Radical Party buses to fight in Croatia.[46] "They had been told their sentences would be reduced if they fought for their country," Mikuljanac recalled. "They hadn't even been given a chance to call home and tell their mothers; they were pulled out of prison and sent directly to the front lines." Mikuljanac accompanied the paramilitaries from Belgrade into Croatia, where they received weapons from the Yugoslav People's Army and joined other ethnic Serb fighters on the front lines.

Jovan Dulović, the Serbian reporter who covered the paramilitary attack on Zvornik, explained that when the fighting began beyond Serbia's borders, the police "turned to the people they knew best for help: informers and criminals."[47] It was a natural move, since "when the police needed a secret job done; who else would they turn to?" Nikola Barović, a criminal defense lawyer who worked with former paramilitaries after the war, said the police had "slowly crossed the line from working with informers to gain information about criminals, to recruiting informers to act as paramilitary leaders outside of Serbia."[48] Barović's argument was supported by the former Belgrade police chief, who explained to Borger that "in using criminals, for example as informants, there is always a narrow line you walk along. The police here crossed that line by a mile."[49]

Using the Interior Ministry's uniformed and plainclothes police, officials close to the top ranks of the Serbian state had generated a series of covert relationships with individuals and groups in an effort to quietly transfer influence, weapons, and guidance from Serbia to ethnic Serb fighters in the diaspora. Secrecy was important because of restrictions on official Serbian cross-border military action. The state-paramilitary connection thus provided the Serbian leadership with plausible deniability, facilitating an ethnic cleansing policy for which the Serbian government hoped to avoid responsibility.

Were the Serbian Paramilitaries "Death Squads"?

In many respects, the Serbian paramilitaries described here fit this volume's definition of death squads. They were clandestine, irregular forces enjoying significant backing from elements of the Serbian state, namely the clandestine Military Line group. To a certain extent, the paramilitaries originated among private sectors, including the Serbian nationalist movement and the Belgrade underworld. This private/public overlap is a typical quality of contemporary death squads. Like most death squads, moreover, the Serbian paramilitaries carried out extrajudicial executions and other violent acts against a clearly defined group of persons, most of whom were noncombatants, in order to further a political agenda articulated by private and state interests alike.

The unequivocal classification of the paramilitaries as death squads encounters some problems, however, when we note their range of activities, which include some bona fide military missions, and their use of violence beyond Serbia's internationally recognized borders. On the first count, it is important to note that the paramilitaries did not limit themselves to attacks on Muslim and Croat civilians. In many cases, paramilitary units were reported to have fought against Muslim and Croat militias, in both Bosnia and Croatia, in an effort to secure ethnic Serb military control in the region. The attacks on civilians and combatants were fused into a larger, unified mission because of the inherently political nature of the non-Serb civilian population living in areas claimed by Serb national activists. As long as non-Serbs lived in regions slated for Serb control, the Serb claims of ownership would be prone to dispute by Western powers and Bosnian and Croat officials. The Serbian paramilitaries were thus not designed exclusively for acts of terror against civilians, although that was certainly a significant part of their program.

Instead, they were devised by the Serbian state as a way of circumventing territorial restrictions on Serbian state action, and their mission was broadly defined as "defense of the Serbian nation" living in the diaspora. According to the reigning Serbian strategy, that "defense" mission included the mass, forced displacement of non-Serbs from areas slated to be part of a future Greater Serbia. Displacement, in turn, was facilitated by murder, terror, rape, and other paramilitary violence. The paramilitaries thus did not start out solely as agents of terrorization, but rather as extraterritorial agents capable of clandestinely projecting Serbian state power abroad. In so doing, they also occasionally engaged in bona fide combat with Croat and Muslim military forces. Murder of civilians was not their only task.

The second definitional problem relates to the paramilitaries' area of operation. Were they irregular combatants operating abroad in a war between two sovereign states (Serbia and Bosnia), or were they internal forces of repression and violence? If the former is the case, then the paramilitaries would not fit the definition of death squads used in this book, which stresses the role of internal repression. There is no clear resolution of this dilemma, but according to the Serbian nationalist position, the paramilitaries were operating within the Serbian ethnos, and were thus eliminating "internal" enemies and thus fit comfortably within the death squad definition. Although Bosnian government officials and Western diplomats might define eastern and northern Bosnia as sovereign Bosnian territory and thus "external" to Serbia, Serbian nationalists saw those areas as part of Greater Serbia.

This chapter has highlighted the role of rules and regulations in producing paramilitary and death squad activism. International and domestic activists have generated dense webs of rules, regulations, and norms surrounding state action, hoping to create more just, transparent, and predictable social order.[50] Although some of these rules produce their desired outcomes, others create perverse incentives for states to engage in clandestine action, including death squad recruitment. Thus today's enhanced sensitivity to human rights norms, as well as more traditional norms such as sovereignty and territorial integrity, may in fact be part of the problem. Although human rights monitors seek to limit state violence to create a better world, they may sometimes simply drive the violence underground. Faced with restrictions on who and how they can kill, state actors may hand the violence over to semiprivate gunmen, hoping these fighters can accomplish what the state was prevented from doing by courts and human rights activists. Death squads are thus not always simply violations of human rights norms, but may in some cases be those norms' unanticipated offspring.

Notes

1. Norman Cigar, *Genocide in Bosnia: The Policy of "Ethnic Cleansing"* (College Station: Texas A & M University Press, 1995), 54–55.
2. The material for this chapter draws on Part I of James Ron, "Frontier and Ghetto: The Institutional Underpinnings of State Violence in Bosnia and Palestine" (Ph.D. diss., University of California at Berkeley, 1999).
3. Branko Milinković, "Yugoslavia: Who Is in Charge of This War," *Inter Press Service,* 18 November 1991.
4. Andrej Gustinčić, "Yugoslav Conflict Creates Bizarre Assortment of Folk Heroes," Reuters North American Wire, 20 August 1991.
5. Marcus Tanner, "Assassination Divides Serbs," *Independent* (London), 7 August 1991.
6. Tim Judah, "Kaleidoscope of Militias Fights over Bosnia," *Times* (London), 30 May 1992.
7. Philip Sherwell, "Serbia's Warlords Walk Tall in Benighted Bosnia," *Sunday Telegraph* (London), 26 April 1992.
8. United Nations, *Final Report of the UN Commission of Experts Established Pursuant to Security Council Resolution 780 (1992)* (New York, 1994), Annex IIIA, para. 24.
9. Former United States State Department official, interview by author, Washington, D.C., February 1998. The official asked that his name not be used.
10. Sabrina Petra Ramet, *Nationalism and Federalism in Yugoslavia, 1962–91* (Bloomington, Ill.: Indiana University Press, 1993).
11. United Nations Security Council Resolution 757 (30 May 1992).
12. "FRY Citizens to Leave Bosnia," Tanjug, 4 May 1992, available through FBIS [cited 5 May 1992], EEU-92-087; and "Presidency Asks Bosnian Leaders to Absorb JNA," Tanjug, 5 May 1992, available through FBIS [cited 6 May 1992], EEU-92-088.
13. "Blames Muslim, Croat Leaders for Bosnia," Tanjug, 10 May 1992, available through FBIS [cited 11 May 1992], EEU-92-091.
14. "Božović Denies Territorial Claim," Tanjug, 22 April 1992, available through FBIS [cited 22 April 1992], EEU-92-078; "Government Issues Statement on CSCE Document," Radio Beograd Network, 24

April 1992, available through FBIS [cited 24 April 1992], EEU-92-080; "Milošević Comments on Peace Talks, U.S. Policy," RTB Television Network, 23 April 1992, available through FBIS [cited 24 April 1992], EEU-92-080.

15. "Šešelj Denies Existence of Paramilitary Forces," Tanjug, 23 April 1992, available through FBIS [cited 24 April 1992], EEU-92-08; "Arkan: Only Bosnian SDG Members in Sarajevo," Borba, 30 May and 31 May 1992, available through FBIS [cited 10 June 1992], EEU-92-112.

16. Audrey Helfant Budding, "Serb Intellectuals and the National Question, 1961–1991" (Ph.D. diss., Harvard University, 1998); and Veljko Vujačić, "Communism and Nationalism in Russia and Serbia" (Ph.D. diss., University of California at Berkeley, 1995).

17. For an excellent, concise account see Julie A. Mertus, Kosovo: How Myths and Truths Started a War (Berkeley: University of California Press, 1999), 175–87. For an overview of contemporary Serbian politics, see Robert Thomas, The Politics of Serbia in the 1990s (New York: Columbia University Press, 1999).

18. Ognjen Pribičević, "The Serbian Exception: Why Communists Never Lost Power," Uncaptive Minds, Fall/Winter 1995–96, 119–25.

19. Miroslav Mikuljanac and Gradiša Kapić, "Exiting with Trumpets and Cameras," Borba, 21 November 1993.

20. Louise Branson, "Scapegoat Goes into the Dock," Times (London), 20 November 1994. The Vučković brothers, who commanded the Yellow Wasps, were indicted in 1994 for war crimes by Serbian authorities. Details about their activities can be found in a Šabac District Court indictment dated 28 April 1994 (doc. #398/93). Additional information was supplied by Dragoljub Džordžević, lawyer for the defense, in an interview by the author in Belgrade on 31 May 1997.

21. Vučjak Mountain was the unit's headquarters. Unit members reportedly wore a White Wolf patch on their left shoulder.

22. "Wolves from Vučjak, Col. Veljko Milanković," Duga (Belgrade), 24 October 1992.

23. Bosnian Serb army major, interview by author, Banja Luka, May 1997. The officer requested that his name not be used.

24. Bosnian Serb soldier, interview by author, Banja Luka, May 1997. The soldier requested that his name not be used.

25. Slavica, interview by author, Banja Luka, April 1997. Slavica, a former officer in the 1st Krajina Corps intelligence division, requested that her last name not be used.

26. Human Rights Watch/Helsinki, *Deadly Legacies: The Continuing Influence of Bosnia's Warlords*, Vol. 8, No. 17 (New York: Human Rights Watch, 1996), 2.

27. Ludwig Bolzmann Institute of Human Rights, *Report on Ethnic Cleansing Operations in the Northeast-Bosnia City of Zvornik from April through June 1992* (Vienna: Ludwig Bolzmann Insitute, 1994).

28. Jovan Dulović, interview by author, Belgrade, 26 May 1997.

29. Ludwig Bolzmann Institute, *Report on Ethnic Cleansing*, 23.

30. Milan Vego, "Federal Army Deployments in Bosnia and Herzegovina," *Jane's Intelligence Review* 4, no. 10 (October 1992): 445–46.

31. Sonja Biserko, interview by author, Belgrade, April 1997.

32. Nataša Kandić, interview by author, Belgrade, February 1997.

33. Tim Judah, *The Serbs: History, Myth and the Destruction of Yugoslavia* (New Haven and London: Yale University Press, 1997), 145–67.

34. Julian Borger, "Milošević Case Hardens," *Guardian* (London), 3 February 1997.

35. Misha Glenny, *The Fall of Yugoslavia* (Harmondsworth, England: Penguin Books, 1992), 150.

36. "Četnik Duke," *Telegraf* (Belgrade), 28 September 1994.

37. Cvijetin Milivojević, "I Am Ready, Awaiting Arrest," *Spona* (Belgrade), 18 December 1993, as translated in Paul Williams and Norman Cigar, *War Crimes and Individual Responsibility: A Prima Facie Case for the Indictment of Slobodan Milošević* (Washington: Balkan Institute, 1996), 7.

38. United States State Department official, interview by author, Washington D.C., February 1998. The official asked not to be identified by name.

39. Dejan Pavlović, interview by author, Belgrade, February 1997.

40. Filip Švarm, interview by author, Belgrade, February 1997.

41. Saša, interviews by author, Belgrade, March and April 1997. Saša requested that his last name not be used.

42. Daniel Snidden, interview by author, Belgrade, March 1997.

43. Lieutenant under Snidden, interviews by author, Belgrade, February and March 1997. The lieutenant asked that his name not be used.

44. Perica, interviews by author, Belgrade, February, March, and April 1997. Perica requested that his last name not be used.

45. Borger, "Milošević Case Hardens."

46. Miroslav Mikuljanac, interview by author, Belgrade, April 1997.

47. Dulović, interview.

48. Nikola Barović, interview by author, Belgrade, March 1997.

49. Borger, "Milošević Case Hardens."

50. James Ron, "Varying Methods of State Violence," *International Organization* 51, no. 2 (1997): 275–300. See also Margaret E. Keck and Katheryn Sikkink, *Activists Beyond Borders: Advocacy Networks in International Politics* (Ithaca, N.Y.: Cornell University Press, 1998).

APPENDIX

DEATH SQUAD CASES: A SHORT SUMMARY

THE PURPOSE OF THIS APPENDIX IS TO PROVIDE AS comprehensive a list as possible of death squad cases in light of available information. It is meant to be a starting point for further research on death squads. The following makes no claim to be definitive or thorough, as the editors, who have compiled the list and written the descriptions, are not experts on the countries and developments described here. The list is divided into two sections: the first identifies cases where death squads have definitely been active and identified as such; the second lists and describes episodes in which death squads may have been active, but which require further research in order to validate the application of the term and to elaborate on the circumstances surrounding their formation and activity. In some of the latter cases, there is no information beyond the name of the country. Inclusion here is based both on reliable published sources and on references from scholars who are mentioned in the Preface to this volume.

The editors welcome suggestions, corrections, and emendations from interested readers. Contact them at: www.siena.edu/brenner/deathsquads.html

Part A: Known Cases of Death Squads

I. South America

Argentina: In the 1840s–early 1850s, the dictator Brigadier General Juan Manuel de Rosas (1829–52) created and controlled a secret parapolice organization called *mazorcas*. This small unit was composed of former or existing members of the police and militia and carried out extrajudicial executions and other violent acts against designated enemies of the Rosas regime. The violence was intended to eliminate some opponents and to intimidate others. Rosas publicly kept a distance from this shadowy outfit, but justified its existence as a necessary response to a crisis caused by a combination of internal rebellion and external intervention. *Sources:* John Lynch and Tony Robben, communications with Arthur D. Brenner; and John Lynch, *Argentine Dictator: Juan Manuel de Rosas 1829–1852* (1981), ch. 6.

In the modern Argentine era, the first right-wing death squad (known as AAA or Triple A) operated from January 1974 to July 1975. In October 1975, the paramilitary task forces organized by the army began to operate clandestinely. These included the Justicalist Restorationist National Command, Argentine Anti-Communist Alliance, Christina Viola Commando, José Ignacio Rucci Commando, Liberators of America Commando, and the Lieutenant Colonel Duarte Ardoy Commando for Marxist Repression. They operated with full force after the March 1976 coup d'état and throughout the military dictatorship that lasted until 1983. *Sources:* Tina Rosenberg, *Children of the Chain: Violence and the Violent in Latin America* (New York: William Morrow, 1991); Emilio F. Mignone, *Derechos Humanas y Sociedad: el caso Argentino* (Buenos Aires: Centro de Estudios Legales y Sociales, 1991); Graciela Fernández Meijide, *Las Cifras de la Guerra Sucia* (Buenos Aires: Asamblea Permanente por los Derechos Humanos, 1988); Horacio Verbitsky, *The Flight* (New York: New Press, 1996); and María José Moyano, *Argentina's Lost Patrol: Armed Struggle 1969–1979* (New Haven, Conn.: Yale University Press, 1995).

Brazil: Police death squads in São Paulo and other cities have operated since the 1960s to eliminate known or suspected criminals and street children. See above, Chapter 8.

Chile: With support from Argentina, Bolivia, Brazil, Paraguay, and Uruguay, the dictatorship of Augusto Pinochet created "Operation Condor," which operated from the early 1970s to the 1990s. This was a joint effort to collect, exchange, and store information about leftists, communists, and Marxists so that Marxist political and terrorist activity could be eliminated in South America. Among its tasks was the murder of alleged terrorists or supporters of terrorist organizations, whether or not these were found within the countries named above. Special hit squads were formed and dispatched to carry out these assassinations. Information about Operation Condor became public in 1998 when a Spanish court sought the extradition of former Chilean president Augusto Pinochet to Spain to stand trial for his responsibility, as Chilean head of state, for the disappearance or death of several hundred Spanish nationals during the course of his dictatorship, from 1973 to 1990. The Chilean secret police, DINA, may also have utilized death squads among its many nefarious activities under Pinochet. *Sources:* News reports on Pinochet's detention in England, 1998; Mary Helen Spooner, *Soldiers in a Narrow Land: The Pinochet Regime in Chile* (Berkeley: University of California Press, 1994); B. Paz Rojas, *Tarda pero llega: Pinochet ante la justicia española* (Santiago: LOM Ediciones; CODEPU, 1998).

Colombia: Following a long history of civil violence involving private and state-supported paramilitary forces, Colombia has been immersed since the 1960s in a multifaceted war among leftist guerrillas, the armed forces, and paramilitary groups affiliated either with the armed forces or drug cartels. Death squads have been a regular feature of this conflict. Some are the product of a partnership between the armed forces and paramilitary units that are equipped and financed by the armed forces; some work at the behest of the drug cartels; still others are composed of off-duty police hired by multinational corporations to "clean up" urban areas. Throughout this period, government forces have claimed that extralegal measures were necessary to suppress communist rebellion, but the state has often denied its involvement, claiming that the paramilitaries and death squads were working at the behest of private right-wing interests. The Colombian government tolerated or encouraged the formation of some death squads so that it could continue to seek foreign aid and investment, especially from the United States. *Sources:* Human Rights Watch/Americas, Human Rights Watch Children's Rights Project, *Generation Under Fire: Children and Violence in Colombia* (New York: Human Rights Watch, 1994); Germán Alfonso Palacío Castañeda, "Institutional Crisis, Parainstitutionality and Regime Flexibility in Colombia: The Place of Narcotraffic and Counterinsurgency," in *Vigilantism and the State in Latin America: Essays on Extralegal Violence,* ed. Martha K. Huggins (New York: Praeger, 1991); Jenny Pearce, *Colombia: Inside the Labyrinth* (London: Latin American Bureau, 1990); Charles Berquist, Ricardo Peñaranda and Gonzalo Sánchez, eds., *Violence in Colombia* (Wilmington, Del.: Scholarly Resources, 1992); Paul Oquist, *Violence, Conflict and Politics in Colombia* (New York: Academic Press, 1980).

Peru: Since the 1980s, the government has been challenged by a Maoist insurgency called Sendero Luminoso (Shining Path). In addition to regular military operations, the government encouraged the formation of paramilitary organizations that at times acted as death squads. Among these was CRF (Roderigo Franco Democratic Command), which may, in fact, have been a cover for regular security forces. *Source:* Elena S. Manitzas, "All the Minister's Men: Paramilitary Activity in Peru," in Huggins, *Vigilantism,* 85–103.

II. Central America

El Salvador: Death squads formed at the behest of right-wing interests, sometimes acting privately and sometimes while in control of the government, killed thousands of leftist guerrillas and their presumed supporters in the 1970s and 1980s. See above, Chapter 4.

Guatemala: In one of the most notorious cases of death squads in the world, security forces and private right-wing interests supported or operated death squads on a vast scale between 1954 and the early 1990s for the purpose of eliminating guerrilla movements and their alleged supporters among the mixed-race and Indian peasants. The government tried to justify this widespread violence by claiming that it was intended to preserve democracy, and was rewarded with U.S. government aid and support for the death squads by the CIA. Estimates for the number of victims range from 150,000 to 200,000. *Sources:* Carlos Figueroa Ibarra, "Guatemala: The Recourse of Fear," in Huggins, *Vigilantism,* 73–83; Susanne Jonas, *The Battle for Guatemala: Rebels, Death Squads, and U.S. Power* (Boulder, Colo.: Westview Press, 1991); Guatemala Commission for Historical Clarification, *Report* (Guatemala City, 1999).

Honduras: The "Department of Special Investigations" founded in the late 1970s by Gustavo Alvarez Martínez evolved into a death squad known as Battalion 3–16. It was directed by several figures of the regular Honduran security and intelligence agencies and regularly carried out kidnappings and "disappearances," with separate squads and personnel assigned for interrogation, torture, and executions. Most of the members of the latter teams were ex-soldiers recruited from the country's jails, where they were serving time for violent crimes, and Alvarez ordered many of them executed in order to maintain secrecy. A second death squad headed by the Nicaraguan Contra intelligence chief, Ricardo Lau, and reportedly funded by the CIA, also began to operate in Honduras by the end of 1981, helping the Honduran military eliminate labor and student leaders, alleged Salvadoran gunrunners, and Sandinista spies. Lau's assassins worked closely with the Honduran Army's 101st Brigade and managed between 1982 and 1984 to kill scores and possibly hundreds of such victims in and around the Contra bases in Honduras.

Honduran human rights organizations also accused the country's military in early 1996 with reactivating the death squads, including Battalion 3–16, which, they assert, murdered at least six people in 1995. *Sources:* Donald E. Schulz and Deborah Sundloff Schulz, *The United States, Honduras, and the Crisis in Central America* (Boulder, Colo.: Westview Press, 1994); Leticia Salomon, *La Violencia en Honduras, 1980–1993* (Tegucigalpa: Centro de Documentación de Honduras [CEDOH], Comisionado Nacional para la Protección de los Derechos Humanos, 1993); Freddy Cuevas, "Rights Chief Claims Honduras has Reactivated Death Squads," *Houston Chronicle,* 22 February 1996.

Nicaragua: In the aftermath of civil war, political gangs working as clients of wealthy landowner patrons acted as death squads in the mountainous Segovias region between 1926 and 1934. Death squads reappeared in Nicaragua during and after Sandinista rule, i.e., from 1981 to 1995. See above, Chapter 2.

III. North America/Caribbean

United States: In the period from roughly 1850 to 1940, several private detective and security guard firms fought the nascent labor movement in the United States. In some cases, they carried out deliberate murders of labor organizers, union members, and ordinary workers.

Immediately after the end of the civil war, a group of former Confederate veterans founded a secret terror society, the Ku Klux Klan. It fought northern political control and the political, social, and economic influence of non-Protestants, Northern "carpetbaggers," and, above all, the newly emancipated black population. In its early years, it functioned as a death squad. *Source:* Scott Nelson, *Iron Confederacies: Southern Railways, Klan Violence, and Reconstruction* (Chapel Hill: University of North Carolina Press, 1999).

IV. Europe

Germany: In the early years of the Weimar Republic, paramilitary organizations such as the Free Corps and illegal auxiliaries of the regular army spawned death squads that murdered members or civilians who were presumed (likely) to have betrayed illegal arms caches or military formations to Entente arms inspectors. See above, Chapter 3.

German SS and police units, in the so-called Operation Silbertanne, carried out covert murder in German-occupied Holland, ca. 1942–43. In contrast to near all other Nazi murders, these were covert and the identities of the perpetrators were concealed.

Serbia: At the outset of its war for control of Bosnia in 1992, the Serbian government secretly supported the activities of ethnic Serb paramilitary forces operating in Bosnia. See above, Chapter 11.

Spain: As part of its strategy to oppose the Basque separatist movement ETA, the Spanish government in 1983 established a secret unit, the Group for Anti-Terrorist Liberation (known by its Spanish acronym, GAL). From then until its dissolution in 1987, it allegedly murdered 27 people and wounded 30 more, most (but not all) linked to ETA. GAL and its ties to the government were kept secret until the mid-1990s, when the wall of secrecy surrounding it began to crumble after several of this death squad's members testified in their murder trials that they had been working in the service of the government of Prime Minister Felipe Gonzales. Several high government officials of the Ministry of State Security were implicated and later convicted for having financed this illicit operation and ordering GAL assassinations. *Sources:* Newspaper reports on the investigation and trials of police and government officials tried for the deaths, March 1995-April 1996; Antonio Rubio and Manuel Cerdan, *El Origen de GAL: Guerra Sucio y crimen de estado* (Madrid: Temas de Hoy, 1997); Javier Garcia, *Los GAL al Descubierto: La Trauma de la Guerra Sucio contra ETA* (Madrid: El Pais; Aguilar, 1988).

Turkey: Since the early 1990s, security forces have committed extrajudicial executions of Kurdish nationalists in southeastern Turkey. By 1994, the number of death squad victims in this area had surpassed 300, and the use of death squads by the Turkish military has continued to the present. *Source:* "Turkey: Responses to an Emerging Pattern of Extrajudicial Executions," in *"Disappearances" and Political Killings: Human Rights Crises of the 1990s. A Manual for Action* (Amsterdam: Amnesty International, 1994), 55–67. See also numerous reports in major newspapers during this period.

V. Africa

Burundi: May-June 1972 and 1994-present.

    Congo-Brazzaville

    Kenya

    Liberia

    Rwanda: Death squads were among those responsible for the genocide of 1994 and continuing reprisals between Tutsi and Hutu militants and vigilantes.

    Somalia

    Sierra Leone

    South Africa: The apartheid regime formed death squads both among its security forces and among vigilante groups from the 1960s to the early 1990s, and there have been a few smaller episodes of privately directed death squads since the transition to multiethnic democracy in 1994. Additionally, South Africa security forces operated a death squad called Koevoet in Namibia in the 1970s and 1980s, and South African death squads assisted the white Rhodesian government in its fight in the 1970s against the Black African parties ZANKU and ZAPU. See above, Chapter 9.

    Uganda: During the violent reign of Idi Amin (1971–79), three segments of the official security apparatus acted as or harbored within them death squads that were responsible for hundreds and possibly thousands of murders. See above, Chapter 6.

    Zaire (now Republic of Congo): In the 1980s, the armed forces (FAZ) harbored death squad units that were infamous for the arbitrary arrest, torture, and extrajudicial execution of individuals suspected of being sympathetic to the opposition Parti Révolutionnaire du Peuple (PRP). *Source:*

Michael Z. Schatzberg, *Dialectics of Oppression in Zaire* (Bloomington: Indiana University Press, 1988).

VI. Middle East

Algeria: The secret French underground Organisation de l'Armée Secrète (OAS) fought against the insurgent Algerian Front de Libération National (FLN), "traitors," and French leftists from 1960 to 1962. It formed death squad units called Delta Commandos, led by Roger Degueldre. *Source:* Martha Crenshaw, "The Effectiveness of Terrorism in the Algerian War," in *Terrorism in Context,* ed. Martha Crenshaw (Philadelphia: University of Pennsylvania Press, 1995).

VII. South Asia

Bangladesh: "Razikars" in the 1970s.

India: India's police and armed forces, acting at the request of the central government, created death squads to deal with intractable insurgencies by Sihk separatists in Punjab and by separatists in the northern state of Jammu and Kashmir. These episodes took place in the 1980s and 1990s. See above, Chapter 10.

Sri Lanka: Government-backed death squads have annually murdered hundreds and perhaps thousands of presumed opponents since the 1970s. These death squads are popularly known as "vigilantes" in Sri Lanka and are made up primarily of members of the security forces. They operate outside the law to murder students and other civilians suspected of sympathizing with radical Sinhalese organizations. To date, the victims number in the tens of thousands. *Source:* Asia Watch, *Journalist Murdered in Sri Lanka as Death Squad Killings Continue* (New York: Asia Watch, 1990).

VII. East Asia and Pacifica

Indonesia: In the early 1980s, military death squads launched a campaign of extermination *(petrus)* against "known" criminals in Indonesian cities. These killings subsided by the mid-1980s and there were no further cases of death squad activity until the tangled events surrounding the fall of Suharto in 1998, when unidentified killers ("ninja") launched campaigns of kidnapping and assassination against traditional Islamic leaders in the Javanese countryside. See above, Chapter 7. Through much of 1999, anti-independence militias in East Timor, which were equipped and supported by the regular Indonesian armed forces, conducted a violent campaign of terror against pro-independence activists leading up to and in the aftermath of a vote to determine the future of this province. While the Indonesian army watched without intervening, the militias, which often acted as death squads, killed hundreds and possibly thousands of East Timorese, particularly in the weeks after the vote of September 1999, in which an overwhelming majority voted for independence.

Philippines: At the time of the transition from the rule of Ferdinand Marcos to the democratic regime of Corazon Aquino in the late 1980s, army-backed "vigilantes" conducted campaigns of terror against alleged leftist insurgents in various parts of the Philippines. See above, Chapter 5.

Section B: Possible Death Squad Cases

I. Central America

Mexico: There are strong but unsubstantiated charges that Mexican security forces have used death squads as a tool in their effort to quell a peasant rebellion in Chiapas state since 1994.

II. North America and Caribbean

Haiti: It is difficult to discern where vigilantism and state-sponsored terror have included death squads in the long history of violence in Haiti. Shortly after his inauguration as president in 1957, François Duvalier encouraged the formation of Cagoulards, "masked men" whose function was to suppress political opposition by murder, rape, arson, and the terrorization of entire neighborhoods. These evolved into the Tonton Macoutes when they were permitted to take off their masks. Incipient death squads known as the Seventh Fleet and the Red Berets were also formed in the late 1960s under Duvalier's dictatorship in order to protect nascent industries against the working class.

Following the coup that deposed President Jean-Bertrand Aristide in 1991, vigilantes called *attachés* working under order of police chief Lieutenant Colonel Michel François terrorized the country and may have had death squads operating with them. By late 1993, after Aristide returned to the country, military terrorism against his supporters and their families was carried out both by the *attachés* and by FRAPH (Front for the Advancement and Progress of Haiti; *fraph* in French roughly means "to strike"), a paramilitary formation under the direction of Emmanuel Constant. FRAPH was responsible for rape, kidnapping the small children of pro-Aristide activists, and mutilation of bodies and dumping them in public places. Between 1991 and 1994, these forces, and the military, were responsible for some 2,000 to 3,000 murders, and they may continue to function in Haiti. *Sources:* Jean Jacques Honorat, "Terror and Poverty in Haiti: A Legacy of the Duvalier

Era," in *States of Terror? Death Squads or Development* (London: Catholic Institute for International Relations, 1989), 115–22; Roland I. Perusse, *Haitian Democracy Restored, 1991–1995* (Lanham, Md.: University Press of America, 1995).

United States: Histories of the early Mormon Church describe the formation in Missouri, in 1838, of extralegal "vigilantes" or a "paramilitary" unit organized under the name Danites. Though it was created to protect Mormons against persecution by an unwelcoming Missouri populace, it quickly became a feared force within the Mormon community as its work spread to enforcing orthodoxy among the faithful. Numerous studies of the Mormon faith speak of the Danites, and while none says that they committed murder, the dread that they raised among the Mormons and their neighbors suggests that this might have been the case. See, for example, Donna Hill, *Joseph Smith. The First Mormon* (Garden City, N.Y.: Doubleday, 1977).

IV. Europe

Belgium: 1918–23

Bosnia: There have been unsubstantiated allegations that during and after the Bosnian war of 1991–96 the Bosnian government engaged the services of death squads to clandestinely murder both non-Bosniak foes and putative Bosniak collaborators with Croatian or Serbian forces.

France: Among the reprisals carried out by members of the French Resistance against putative collaborators with the Nazis between 1944 and 1947, which numbered in the thousands, some vigilante groups may have become or acted as death squads. In the 1950s, there may also have been right-wing death squads actively attacking leftists and intellectuals.

Germany: At the end of World War II, so-called *Werwolf* units were formed by the Nazi regime to conduct guerrilla warfare against the invading Allied armies. Among their assigned tasks was to eliminate "traitors" and potential collaborators whose acts threatened to undermine partisan activity against the Allies. Several units undertook such in the spring of 1945, particularly in the Wilhelmshaven in Hannover. *Source:* Perry Biddiscombe, *Werwolf! The History of the National Socialist Guerrilla Movement, 1944–1946* (Toronto: University of Toronto Press, 1998).

Greece: Death squads may have been active in two episodes: In the years 1944–49, during a civil war, the Greek antifascist resistance may have used death squads to kill putative collaborators; and in the period from 1979 to the 1990s, the Greek army is sometimes alleged to have formed death squads to help it fight a communist movement.

Hungary: During the revolution of 1956, detachments of Hungarian officers under Soviet control murdered and tortured real or presumed "counterrevolutionaries," i.e., revolutionaries. *Sources:* Tom Sakmyster,

Hungary's Admiral on Horseback: Miklos Horthy, 1918–1944 (1994); Nicholas Nagy-Talavera, *The Green Shirts and the Others* (1970); Margit Szollosi-Janze, *Die Pfeilkreuzlerbewegung in Ungarn* (1989); and Gyorgy Litvan, ed., *The Hungarian Revolution of 1956* (Longman, 1996); also, István Deák, communication with Arthur D. Brenner.

Northern Ireland: Three groups are alleged to have used or to use death squads at various times from the 1970s to the present: (a) Protestant paramilitary associations, fighting Catholics and supporters of Irish independence, specifically the IRA/Sinn Fein Party; (b) the IRA, fighting Protestant paramilitary organizations, Protestants and supporters of remaining part of Great Britain (in the late 1990s, these forces are also believed to be used for social control against drug dealers, other criminals, and recalcitrant Catholics); and (c) British security forces. Specific allegations have been made against the police, Royal Irish Constabulary, SAS, and other special forces and intelligence units. British death squads have also been implicated in murdering to support Protestant paramilitaries. *Sources:* Various reports in the contemporary press; see, for example, John Ware, "Time to Come Clean over the Army's Role in the "Dirty War," *New Statesman* 127, no. 4382 (24 April 1998): 15–17.

Rumania: Death squads are alleged to have been formed in the dying days of the Ceausescu dictatorship in 1989–90.

Russia: In the late 1990s, Russian and Western journals began to report the existence of the Felix group (named after the founder of the Soviet secret police, Felix Dzerzhinsky). It was allegedly established just prior to the end of the Soviet Union in 1991 and the disbanding of the KGB. Its 60 members were mostly former operatives of the KGB and other state security agencies. Its function was supposedly to liquidate corrupt Russian government officials, but reports suggest that it may also be a task force engaged by Russian businessmen to protect their illicit activities from government interference. *Source:* Victor Yasmann, "Does Russia Need Death Squads?" *Jamestown,* 14 July 1995.

V. Africa

Algeria: The ferocious civil war between the secularist military and Islamic fundamentalists, which raged from 1992 to 1998, resulted in the deaths of over 50,000 people. Death squads appear to have been used on both sides, by radical Islamists to enforce religious orthodoxy and by the security forces to eliminate Islamist leaders via extrajudicial executions. The exceptionally perilous situation has made accurate reporting about the existence of death squads in this conflict difficult, if not impossible, and scholars, human rights activists, and journalists must await a calming of the situation in order to facilitate further study. See, for example, John-Thor Dahlburg,

"Women Lose in Algeria's Civil War," *Guardian* (Manchester), 26 June 1996.

Ethiopia: Following the overthrow of Haile Selassie, the Provisional Military Council (Dirgue) in 1977–78 carried out violent repression against revolutionary students, but because the students were allies of a sort, the repression had to be carried out by covert units operating amid an atmosphere of urban guerrilla warfare. It is possible that in these circumstances, the Dirgue used death squads against its erstwhile student allies.

> *Ghana*
> *Kenya*
> *Liberia*

Nigeria: Under the so-called Structural Adjustment Programme of 1986–96, Nigerian businessmen and industrialists struggled with each other for the control of immense wealth and resources. This provided an atmosphere in which these elites transferred mutual agreements to mutual hostilities and ultimately began to engage hired killers, successful businessmen to eliminate their partners and aggrieved ones to avenge those who had double-crossed them. The government, the police, and the society watched helplessly as the hit squads perpetrated numerous killings without fear and without respect for class, creed, religion, sex, or status. *Source:* Olutayo Adesina, communication with Arthur D. Brenner, 15 July 1997.

VI. Middle East

Egypt: Unsubstantiated reports by journalists and human rights agencies in the 1980s and 1990s suggest that death squads spun off or trained by regular security forces have been responsible for the deaths of Islamic militants who seek to replace the secular with an Islamic republic. *Source: The Political Role of the Military,* eds. Constantine P. Danopoulos and Cynthia Watson (Westport, Conn: Greenwood Press, 1996): 107–21.

Israel: There have long been suspicions and allegations that during the Palestinian uprising (Intifada) of 1987–93, Israeli security forces began to form death squads to murder specified leaders and instigators of anti-Israel violence. According to James Ron (communication with the editors), these incipient units were absorbed and "regularized" after their existence was reported in the press and before they actually turned into death squads.

Palestinians: There have been suspicions and allegations since the 1970s about the existence of Palestinian murder outfits whose targets are presumed or known Palestinian "collaborators" with Israel. Dozens of such murders have taken place, but it remains unclear whether and how many of them may be ascribed to death squads rather than to unorganized vigilante activity.

VII. Central Asia

Tadzhikistan: After factional violence erupted in this former Soviet Republic in 1992, Tadzhikistan government security forces extrajudicially executed approximately 300 people. *Source:* Amnesty International, *Tadzhikistan. Hidden Terror: Political Killings, 'Disappearances' and Torture since December 1992* (New York: Amnesty International, U.S.A., 1993).

VIII. South Asia

Afghanistan: 1970s-present
    Pakistan: Following her dismissal from a second period as prime minister in 1996, Benazir Bhutto was accused not only of corruption but also of sanctioning death squads. Whether this took place during her first term as prime minister (1988–90) as well as the second (1993–96) is unclear, and to date Western sources have not provided details about the death squads she is alleged to have approved. *Source:* "Benazir Bhutto Faces Uphill Fight After Being Ousted—Again," *St. Louis Post-Dispatch,* 6 November 1996.

IX. East Asia and Pacifica

Cambodia
    China
    Indochina: Some of the details about Operation Phoenix, conducted by the U.S. military in the war in this region between 1944 and 1973, suggest that some of its murders of both civilians and military figures were the work of death squads.
    Laos
    Malaysia

BIBLIOGRAPHY

Abdoolcarim, Zoher. "Behind the Secret Killings," *Asiaweek,* 20 January 1984, 21–22, 27–30.

Abinales, P. N. *Militarization in the Philippines.* Diliman; Quezon City: Third World Studies Center, University of the Philippines, 1982.

Abrahams, Ray. *Vigilant Citizens: Vigilantism and the State.* Cambridge: Polity Press, 1998.

Acevedo C., Dario. *La mentalidad de las elites sobre la violencia en Colombia, 1936–1949.* Bogotá, Colombia: Instituto de Estudios Politicos y Relaciones Internacionales/El Ancora Editores, 1995.

Adams, Richard Newbold. *The Reproduction of State Terrorism in Central America.* Texas papers on Latin America, 89–01 0892–3507. Austin: Institute of Latin American Studies, University of Texas at Austin, 1989.

Agee, Philip. *Inside the Company: CIA Diary.* New York: Bantam Books, 1975.

Agger, Inger. *Trauma and Healing Under State Terrorism.* London; Atlantic Highlands, N.J.: Zed Books, 1996.

Ali, S. Mahmud. *The Fearful State: Power, People, and Internal War in South Asia.* London; Atlantic Highlands, N.J.: Zed Books, 1993.

Allen, Peter J. *Days of Judgment.* London: William Kimber, 1987.

Americas Watch. "El Salvador Extradition Sought for Alleged Death Squad Participant." *News from Americas Watch,* 14 August 1991.

———. *El Salvador's Decade of Terror: Human Rights Since the Assassination of Archbishop Romero.* New Haven, Conn.: Yale University Press, 1991.

———. *Human Rights in Nicaragua: Rhetoric and Reality.* New York: Americas Watch Committee, 1985.

———. *Violations of the Laws of War by Both Sides in Nicaragua, 1981–1985.* New York: Americas Watch Committee, 1985.

Americas Watch and American Civil Liberties Union. *Report on Human Rights in El Salvador.* New York: Vintage Books, 1982.

Americas Watch Committee and American Civil Liberties Union. *Report on Human Rights in El Salvador.* New York: Random House, 1982.

Amnesty International. *El Salvador "Death Squads"—A Government Strategy*. London: Amnesty International Publications, October 1988.

———. *Philippines: The Killing Goes On*. London: Amnesty International Publications, February 1992.

———. *Philippines: Unlawful Killings by Military and Paramilitary Forces*. New York: Amnesty International USA, March 1988.

———. *Political Killings by Governments*. London: Amnesty International Publications, 1983.

———. *Power and Impunity: Human Rights Under the New Order*. London: Amnesty International, 1994.

———. *Report of an Amnesty International Mission to the Republic of the Philippines 11–28 November 1981*. London: Amnesty International Publications, November 1981.

Anderson, Benedict. "Cacique Democracy in the Philippines: Origins and Dreams." *New Left Review* 169 (May-June 1988): 3–31.

———. *Imagined Communities*. London: Verso, 1985.

Anderson, Scott, and John Lee Anderson. *Inside the League: The Shocking Exposé of how Terrorists, Nazis and Latin American Death Squads Have Infiltrated the World Anti-Communist League*. New York: Dodd, Mead, 1986.

Anderson, Thomas. *Matanza; El Salvador's Communist Revolt of 1932*. Lincoln: University of Nebraska Press, 1971.

———. *Politics in Central America: Guatemala, El Salvador, Honduras, and Nicaragua*. New York: Praeger, 1988.

———. *The War of the Dispossessed*. Lincoln: University of Nebraska Press, 1981.

Andreopoulos, George J., and Harold E. Selesky. *The Aftermath of Defeat: Societies, Armed Forces and the Challege of Recovery*. New Haven, Conn.: Yale University Press, 1994.

Apter, David E. *The Political Kingdom in Uganda: A Study in Bureaucratic Nationalism*, 2nd ed. London: Frank Cass, 1997.

Archdiocese of São Paulo. *Torture in Brazil*. New York: Vintage, 1985.

Arendt, Hannah. *The Origins of Totalitarianism*. New York: Harcourt Brace Jovanovich, 1973.

Armony, Ariel C. "The Former Contras." In *Nicaragua Without Illusions*, ed. Thomas W. Walker. Wilmington, Del.: Scholarly Resources, 1997.

Armstrong, Robert and Janet Shenk. *El Salvador: The Face of Revolution*. Boston: South End Press, 1982.

Arnson, Cynthia. *Crossroads: Congress, the President, and Central America, 1976–1993*, 2nd ed. University Park, Pa.: Pennsylvania State University Press, 1993.

———. *El Salvador: A Revolution Confronts the United States*. Washington: Institute for Policy Studies, 1982.

Arnson, Cynthia, Aryeh Neier, and Susan Benda. *As Bad as Ever: A Report on Human Rights in El Salvador.* 4th Supplement. New York: Americas Watch Committee; Washington: American Civil Liberties Union, 1984.

Asia Watch Committee. *Bad Blood: Militia Abuses in Mindanao, the Philippines.* New York: Human Rights Watch, 1992.

Asmal, Kader, Louise Asmal, and Ronald Roberts. *Reconciliation Through Truth: A Reckoning of Apartheid's Criminal Governance.* Cape Town: David Philip Publishers, 1996.

Attir, Mustafa O., Burkart Holzner, and Zdenek Suda, eds. *Directions of Change: Modernization Theory, Research, and Realities.* Boulder, Colo.: Westview Press, 1981.

Austin, Dennis, and Anirudha Gupta. *The Politics of Violence in India and South Asia: Is Democracy an Endangered Species?* London: Research Institute for the Study of Conflict and Terrorism, 1990.

Avirgan, Tony and Martha Honey. *War in Uganda.* Dar es Salaam: Tanzania Publishing House, 1982.

Awanohara, Susumu. "Rough Justice in Jakarta." *Far Eastern Economic Review,* 9 June 1983, 17–18.

———. "Still Mysterious . . ." *Far Eastern Economic Review,* 9 August 1984, 26–27.

Awwad, Amani Michael. "State Terrorism in the Arab-Israeli-Palestinian Conflict: Social Constructionism and the Question of Power." Ph.D. diss., Western Michigan University, 1995.

Baloyra, Enrique. *El Salvador in Transition.* Chapel Hill: University of North Carolina Press, 1982.

Barata, Ronaldo. *Inventario da violencia: crime e impunidade no campo paraense, 1980–1989.* Belem, Paraguay: Editora Cejup, 1995.

Barcellos, Caco. *ROTA 66: A Historia da Polícia que Mata.* São Paulo: Globo, 1992.

Barnes, Bob. *NicaNotes.* Nevada City, Calif.: Friendsview Press, 1987.

Bello, Walden. *Creating the Third Force: U.S.-Sponsored Low-Intensity Conflict in the Philippines.* San Francisco: Institute for Food and Policy Studies, 1987.

Bendaña, Alejandro. *La tragedia campesina.* Managua: Ediart-CEI, 1991.

Benevides, Maria-Victoria, and Rosa Maria Fischer Ferreira. "Popular Responses and Urban Violence: Lynching in Brazil." In *Vigilantism and the State in Latin America: Essays on Extralegal Violence,* ed. Martha K. Huggins, 33–46. New York: Praeger, 1991.

Benítez Manaut, Raúl. *La Teoría Militar y la Guerra Civil en El Salvador.* San Salvador: UCA Editores, 1989.

Benjamin, Walter. "Critique of Violence." In *Reflections: Walter Benjamin Essays, Aphorisms, Autographical Writings,* ed. Peter Demetz and trans. Edmund Jephcott, 277–300. New York: Schocken Books, 1992.

Best, Geoffrey. *War and Law Since 1945*. Oxford: Clarendon Press, 1994.

Betz, Hans-Georg. *Postmodern Politics in Germany: The Politics of Resentment*. New York: St. Martin's Press, 1991.

Bicudo, Helio Pereira. *Do esquadrão da morte aos justiceiros*. São Paulo: Ediçoes Paulinas, 1988.

———. *Meu Depoimento sôbre o Esquadrão da Morte*. São Paulo: Pontífica Comissão de Justiça e Paz, 1978.

Blandón, Miguel Jesús. *Entre Sandino y Fonseca Amador*. Managua: Departamento de Propaganda y Educación Política del FSLN, 1981.

Blaufarb, Douglas. B. *The Counterinsurgency Era: U.S. Doctrine and Performance 1950 to the Present*. New York: Free Press, 1977.

Blutstein, Howard, ed. *Area Handbook on El Salvador*. Washington: U.S. Government Printing Office, 1971.

Bonner, Raymond. *Weakness and Deceit: U.S. Policy and El Salvador*. New York: Times Books, 1984.

Bourchier, David. "Crime, Law and State Authority in Indonesia." In *State and Civil Society in Indonesia*, ed. Arief Budiman, 177–211, Clayton, Australia: Monash University Centre of Southeast Asian Studies, 1994.

Bridgeman, Edward R. *The Outlaws—The Terrorist Threat in America: A History and State of Homegrown Violence in America*. San Diego, Calif.: Monday Communications, 1982.

Brody, Reed. *Contra Terror in Nicaragua: Report of a Fact-Finding Mission: September 1984-January 1985*. Boston: South End Press, 1985.

Brown, Cynthia G. *The "MAS Case" in Colombia: Taking on the Death Squads*. New York: Americas Watch, 1983.

Browning, David. *El Salvador: La Tierra y El Hombre*. San Salvador: Dirección de Publicaciones, Ministerio de Educación, 1975.

Brysk, Alison. *The Politics of Human Rights in Argentina*. Palo Alto: Stanford University Press, 1994.

Buchrucker, Bruno. *Im Schatten Seeckts. Die Geschichte der Schwarzen Reichswehr*. Berlin: Kampfverlag, 1928.

Burgess, J. Peter, ed. *Cultural Politics and Political Culture in Postmodern Europe*. Amsterdam; Atlanta, Ga.: Rodopi, 1997.

Burns, E. Bradford. *At War in Nicaragua: The Reagan Doctrine and the Politics of Nostalgia*. New York: Harper & Row, 1987.

———. *Patriarch and Folk: The Emergence of Nicaragua, 1798–1858*. Cambridge: Cambridge University Press, 1991.

Burns, Peter. "Crime wave in Indonesia: negara hukum tidak jadi." *Kabar Seberang. Sulating Maphilindo* (North Queensland, Australia), no. 15 (July 1985): 51–59.

Byrne, Hugh. *El Salvador's Civil War: A Study of Revolution*. Boulder, Colo.: Lynne Rienner, 1996.

Cabestrero, Teofilo. *Blood of the Innocent: Victims of the Contras' War in Nicaragua.* New York: Orbis Books, 1985.

Caldeira, Teresa Pires do Rio. "City of Walls: Segregation and Citizenship in São Paulo." Ph.D. diss., University of California at Berkeley, 1992.

Calder, Bruce J. *The Impact of Intervention: The Dominican Republic During the U.S. Occupation of 1916–1924.* Austin: University of Texas Press, 1984.

Carazo, Jaime Morales. *La Contra.* Mexico City: Grupo Editorial Planeta, 1989.

Carey, Peter, and G. Carter Bentley, eds. *East Timor at the Crossroads: The Forging of a Nation.* New York: Social Science Research Council, 1995.

Cartwright, John. *Political Leadership in Africa.* London: Croom Helm, 1983.

"Catch and Kill": A Pattern of Genocide in Kashmir: A Bestial Method of Breaking the Will of a People. Institute of Kashmir Studies, Human Rights Division, Report No. 6. Srinagar: Human Rights Division, Institute of Kashmir Studies, 1993.

Catholic Institute for International Relations. *Right to Survive: Human Rights in Nicaragua.* London: CIIR, 1987.

Chahabi, H. E., and Juan J. Linz, eds. *Sultanistic Regimes.* Baltimore: Johns Hopkins University Press, 1998.

Chambers, David M. *Hooded Americanism: The History of the Ku Klux Klan.* Durham, N.C.: Duke University Press, 1989.

Chandler, David P. *The Tragedy of Cambodian History: Politics, War, and Revolution Since 1945.* New Haven: Yale University Press, 1991.

Chevigny, Paul. *Edge of the Knife: Police Violence in the Americas.* New York: New Press, 1996.

Chingono, Mark F. *The State, Violence and Development: The Political Economy of War in Mozambique, 1975–1992.* Aldershot, England; Brookfield, Vt.: Avebury, 1996.

Christoph, Jürgen. *Die politischen Reichsamnestien 1918–1933.* Frankfurt a.M.: Peter Lang, 1988.

Cigar, Norman. *Genocide in Bosnia: The Policy of "Ethnic Cleansing."* College Station: Texas A & M University Press, 1995.

Comissão Pastoral de Direitos Humanos da Arquidiocese de Belo Horizonte. *Esquadrão do Torniquete: cultura de morte.* Belo Horizonte, Brazil: Editora FUMARC, 1991.

Coronel, Sheila S. *Coups, Cults, and Cannibals: Chronicles of a Troubled Decade (1982–1992).* Manila: Anvil Publishing, 1993.

Coronel Urtecho, José. *Reflexiones sobre la historia de Nicaragua, de Gainza a Somoza.* 3 vols. Leon, Nicaragua: Tall. Tip. de la "Editorial Hospício," 1962.

Corpus, Victor N. *Silent War.* Quezon City: VNC Enterprises, 1989.

Corradi, Juan E., Patricia Weiss Fagen, and Manuel A. Garreton Merino, eds. *Fear at the Edge: State Terror and Resistance in Latin America.* Berkeley: University of California Press, 1992.

Craig, Gordon. *The Politics of the Prussian Army, 1640–1945.* Paperback ed. New York: Oxford University Press, 1964.

Crelinsten, Ronald D., and Alex Peter Schmid, eds. *The Politics of Pain: Torturers and Their Masters.* Boulder, Colo.: Westview Press, 1994.

Cribb, Robert. *Gangsters and Revolutionaries: The Jakarta People's Militia and the Indonesian Revolution, 1945–1949.* Sydney: Allen & Unwin, 1991.

———, ed. *The Indonesian Killings of 1965–1966: Studies from Java and Bali.* Monash papers on Southeast Asia, 21. Clayton, Australia: Monash University Centre of Southeast Asian Studies, 1990.

Dallin, Alexander, and George W. Breslauer. *Political Terror in Communist Systems.* Stanford, Calif.: Stanford University Press, 1970.

Da Matta, Roberto. *Carnivals, Rogues, and Heroes: An Interpretation of the Brazilian Dilemma.* Notre Dame, Ind.: University of Notre Dame Press, 1991.

Danner, Mark. *The Massacre at El Mozote.* New York: Vintage Books, 1994.

Darmadji, S., et al. *Misteri Ninja dan Cara Antisipasinya.* Surabaya, Indonesia: Cipta Media Surabaya, [1998].

de Klerk, Frederik. *The Last Trek—A New Beginning. The Autobiography.* London: Macmillan, 1998.

de Kock, Eugene. *A Long Night's Damage: Working for the Apartheid State.* As told to Jeremy Gordin. Saxonwold; Johannesburg: Contra Press, 1998.

de Souza Martins, José. "Lynchings—Life by a Thread: Street Justice in Brazil, 1979–1988." In *Vigilantism and the State in Latin America: Essays on Extralegal Violence,* ed. Martha K. Huggins, 21–32. New York: Praeger, 1991.

De Swaan, Abram. "Terror as a Government Service." In *Repression and Repressive Violence,* ed. Mario Hoefnagels, 40–50. Amsterdam: Swets & Zeitlinger, 1977.

Decalo, Samuel. *Psychoses of Power: African Personal Dictatorships.* Boulder, Colo.: Westview Press, 1989.

Delacruz, Enrique, Aida Jordan, and Jorge Emmanuel. *Death Squads in the Philippines.* San Francisco: Alliance for Philippine Concerns Press, 1987.

Denny, Harold N. *Dollars for Bullets.* New York: Dial Press, 1929.

Deutsche Liga für Menschenrechte, ed. *Weißbuch über die Schwarze Reichswehr: "Deutschlands Geheime Rüstungen?"* Berlin: Verlag der Neuen Gesellschaft, 1925.

Dickey, Christopher. "Behind the Death Squads." *New Republic*, 26 December 1983, 16–21.

Diehl, James M. *Paramilitary Politics in the Weimar Republic*. Bloomington: Indiana University Press, 1977.

Dimmenstein, Gilberto. *A Guerra dos Meninos: Assassinatos de Menores no Brasil*. São Paulo: Editora Brasiliense, 1991.

Dixon, Marlene, ed. *On Trial: Reagan's War Against Nicaragua*. San Francisco: Synthesis Publications, 1985.

Dixon, Marlene, and Susanne Jonas, eds. *Revolution and Intervention in Central America*. New rev. ed. San Francisco: Synthesis Publications, 1983.

Duvall, Raymond D., and Michael Stohl. "Governance by Terror." In *The Politics of Terrorism*, 3rd ed., ed. Michael Stohl, 231–71. New York: Marcel Dekker, 1988.

Eckstein, Harry, "On the Etiology of Internal Wars." *History and Theory* 4, no. 2 (1965): 133–63.

Edgerton, Ronald King. "The Politics of Reconstruction in the Philippines: 1945–58." Ph.D. diss., University of Michigan, 1975.

Eisenstadt, S. N. *Patrons, Clients, and Friends: Interpersonal Relations and the Structure of Trust in Society*. New York: Cambridge University Press, 1984.

Eklöf, Stefan. *Indonesian Politics in Crisis: The Long Fall of Suharto, 1996–98*. Copenhagen: NIAS, 1999.

Engineer, Asghar Ali, ed. *Ethnic Conflict in South Asia*. Delhi: Ajanta Publications, 1987.

Enloe, Cynthia H. *Ethnic Soldiers: State Security in Divided Societies*. Athens: University of Georgia Press, 1980.

———. *Police, Military and Ethnicity: The Foundations of State Power*. New Brunswick, N.J.: Transaction Books, 1980.

Enríquez, Laura. *Harvesting Change: Labor and Agrarian Reform in Nicaragua, 1979–1990*. Chapel Hill: University of North Carolina Press, 1991.

Fegley, Randall. *Equatorial Guinea: An African Tragedy*. New York: Peter Lang, 1989.

Feinstein, Anthony. *In Conflict*. Claremont; Cape Town: David Philip, 1999.

Feitlowitz, Marguerite. *A Lexicon of Terror: Argentina and the Legacies of Torture*. Oxford: Oxford University Press, 1998.

Feldman, Allen. *Formations of Violence: The Narrative of the Body and Political Terror in Northern Ireland*. Chicago: University of Chicago Press, 1991.

Fellman, Michael. *Inside War: The Guerrilla Conflict in Missouri during the American Civil War*. New York: Oxford University Press, 1989.

Fernandes, Heloisa. "Authoritarian Society: Breeding Ground for Justiceiros." In *Vigilantism and the State in Latin America: Essays on Extralegal Violence,* ed. Martha K. Huggins. New York: Praeger, 1991.

FitzGerald, Francis. *Fire in the Lake: The Vietnamese and the Americans in Vietnam.* Boston: Little, Brown, 1972.

Fon, Antonio Carlos. *A Tortura: A Historia da Repressão Política no Brasil.* São Paulo: Ed. Global, 1986.

Ford, Franklin L. *Political Murder: From Tyrannicide to Terrorism.* Cambridge: Harvard University Press, 1985.

From Madness to Hope: The 12 Year War in El Salvador. Report of the United Nations Commission on the Truth for El Salvador. New York: United Nations, 1993.

From Max Weber: Essays in Sociology, eds. H. H. Gerth and C. Wright Mills. New York: Oxford University Press, 1946.

Gagnon, V. P. "Ethnic Nationalism and International Conflict: The Case of Serbia." *International Security* 19, no. 3 (1994–95): 130–66.

GAJOP. *Grupos de Extermínio: A Banalização da Vida e da Morte em Pernambuco.* Olinda: GAJOP, 1991.

Galtung, Johan. "Cultural Violence." *Journal of Peace Research* 27, no. 3 (1990): 291–305.

———. "Self-Reliance: An Overdue Strategy for Transition." In *Toward a Just World Order,* ed. Richard Falk, Samuel S. Kin, and Saul H. Mendlovitz, 602–22. Boulder, Colo.: Westview Press, 1982.

Garfield, Richard, and David Siegel. *Health and the War Against Nicaragua, 1981–1984.* New York: Central America Health Rights Network/LINKS, 1985.

Gautama, Sudargo. *Indonesian Business Law.* Bandung: Citra Aditya Bakti, 1995.

George, Alexander, ed. *Western State Terrorism.* New York: Routledge, 1991.

Glenny, Misha. *The Fall of Yugoslavia.* Harmondsworth, U.K.: Penguin Books, 1992.

Gordon, Harold J. "Politischer Terror und Versailler Abrüstungsklausel in der Weimarer Republik." *Wehrwissenschaftliche Rundschau* 16, no. 1 (January 1966): 36–54.

———. *The Reichswehr and the German Republic, 1919–1926.* Princeton: Princeton University Press, 1957.

Gottschalk, Keith. "Restructuring the Colonial State: Pretoria's Strategy in Namibia." In *Namibia in Perspective,* eds. Gerhard Totemeyer, Vezera Kandetu, and Wolfgang Werner, 27–35. Windhoek: Council of Churches in Namibia, 1987.

Gottschalk, Keith, and Vincent Maphai. "The Changing Nature of Policy-Making in Government." In *State of the Nation 1997/8,* ed. B. de Villiers, 107–37. Pretoria: Human Sciences Research Council, 1998.

Gould, Jeffrey. *To Die in This Way: Nicaraguan Indians and the Myth of Mestizaje, 1880–1965.* Durham, N.C.: Duke University Press, 1998.

Gow, James. *Triumph of the Lack of Will.* New York: Columbia University Press, 1997.

Graziano, Frank. *Divine Violence: Spectacle, Psychosexuality and Radical Christianity in the Argentine "Dirty War."* Boulder, Colo.: Westview Press, 1992.

Grimm, Dieter, ed. *Staatsaufgaben.* Frankfurt a.M.: Suhrkamp, 1996.

Grossman, Dave, Lieutenant Colonel. *On Killing: The Psychological Cost of Learning to Kill in War and Society.* Boston: Little, Brown, 1995.

Grossman, Richard. "'Hermanos en la patria': Nationalism, Honor, and Rebellion: Augusto Sandino and the Army in Defense of the National Sovereignty of Nicaragua, 1927–1934." Ph.D. diss., University of Chicago, 1996.

Guelke, Adrian. *The Age of Terrorism and the International Political System.* London: Tauris Academic Studies, 1995.

Guimarães, Ewerton Montenegro. *A Chancela do Crime: A Verdadeiro História da Esquadrão da Morte.* Rio de Janeiro: Ambito Cultural Ediçoes, 1978.

Gumbel, E.J. "Femeliteratur." *Die Justiz* 4 (August 1929): 532–53.

———. *"Verräter verfallen der Feme." Opfer/Mörder/Richter 1919–1929.* Berlin: Malik-Verlag, 1929.

———. *Verschwörer. Zur Geschichte und Soziologie der deutschen nationalistischen Geheimbünde seit 1918.* Vienna: Malik-Verlag, 1924.

———. *Vier Jahre politischer Morde.* Berlin: Verlag der neuen Gesellschaft, 1922.

Gurr, Ted Robert. "The Political Origins of State Violence and Terror: A Theoretical Analysis." In *Government Violence and Repression,* ed. Michael Stohl and George A. Lopez, 46–48. Westport, Conn.: Greenwood Press, 1986.

Gwyn, David [pseud.]. *Idi Amin: Death-Light of Africa.* Boston: Little, Brown, 1977.

Hannover, Heinrich, and Elisabeth Hannover-Drück. *Politische Justiz 1918–1933.* 2nd ed. Bornheim-Merten: Lamuv, 1987.

Hannson, Desirée, and Dirk van Zyl Smit, eds. *Towards Justice? Crime and State Control in South Africa,* Cape Town: Oxford University Press, 1990.

Hansen, Holger B. *Ethnicity and Military Rule in Uganda.* Uppsala, Sweden: Scandinavian Institute of African Studies, 1977.

Hansen, Holger B., and Michael Twaddle, eds. *Uganda Now: Between Decay and Development.* London: J. Currey; Athens: Ohio University Press, 1988.

Harris, Peter. "The Role of Right-Wing Vigilantes in South Africa." In *States of Terror: Death Squads or Development?* ed. Mike Kirkwood, 1–13. London: Catholic Institute for International Relations, 1989.

Haysom, Nicholas. *Mbangalala: The Rise of Right-Wing Vigilantes in South Africa.* Johannesburg: University of the Witwatersrand, Centre for Applied Legal Studies, 1986.

Hedman, Eva-Lotta E. "Beyond Boycott: The Philippine Left and Electoral Politics After 1986." In *The Revolution Falters: The Left in Philippine Politics After 1986,* ed. Patricio N. Abinales, 83–109. Ithaca, N.Y.: Cornell University Southeast Asia Program, 1996.

———. "In the Name of Civil Society: Contesting Free Elections in the Post-Colonial Philippines." Ph.D. diss., Cornell University, 1998.

Helfant Budding, Audrey. "Serb Intellectuals and the National Question, 1961–1991." Ph.D. diss., Harvard University, 1998.

Helsinki Watch. *War Crimes in Bosnia-Herzegovina.* 2 vols. New York: Human Rights Watch, 1992–93.

Henderson, Conway W. "Conditions Affecting the Use of Political Repression." *Journal of Conflict Resolution* 35, no. 1 (1991): 120–42.

Herman, Edward. *The Real Terror Network.* Boston: South End Press, 1982.

Hess, David, and Roberto Da Matta. *The Brazilian Puzzle: Culture on the Borderlands of the Western World.* New York: Columbia University Press, 1995.

Heydeloff, Rudolf. "Staranwalt der Rechtsextremisten. Walter Luetgebrune in der Weimarer Republik." *Vierteljahreshefte für Zeitgeschichte* 32, no. 4 (1984): 373–421.

Historia y violencia en Nicaragua. Managua: Instituto de Investigaciones y Acción Social "Martin Luther King," Universidad Politecnica de Nicaragua, 1987.

Hoefnagels, Mario, ed. *Repression and Repressive Violence: Proceedings of the 3rd International Working Conference on Violence and Non-violent Action in Industrialized Societies.* Amsterdam: Swets & Zeitlinger, 1977.

Homer-Dixon, Thomas Fraser. "On the Threshold: Environmental Changes as Causes of Acute Conflict." *International Security* 16 (Fall 1991): 76–116.

Hooper, Charles. *Brief Authority.* Cape Town: David Philip, 1989.

Horowitz, Irving Louis. *Taking Lives: Genocide and State Power.* 4th expanded and rev. ed. New Brunswick, N.J.: Transaction Publishers, 1997.

Horváth, Ödön von. *Sladek.* Gesammelte Werke, 2. Frankfurt: Suhrkamp, 1983.

"How to Control Quangos." *Economist,* 6 August 1994, 45–47.

Howard, Michael, George J. Andreopoulos, and Mark R. Shulman, eds. *The Laws of War: Constraints on Warfare in the Western World.* New Haven: Yale University Press, 1994.

Huggins, Martha K. "From Bureaucratic Consolidation to Structural De-
volution." *Policing and Society* 7, no. 4 (1997): 207–34.
———. *Political Policing: The United States and Latin America.* Durham,
N.C.: Duke University Press, 1998.
———. "Vigilantism and the State: A Look South and North." In *Vigilan-
tism and the State in Latin America: Essays on Extralegal Violence,* ed.
Martha K. Huggins, 1–18. New York: Praeger, 1991.
Huggins, Martha K., and Mika Haritos-Fatouros. "Bureaucratizing Mas-
culinities Among Brazilian Torturers and Murderers." In *Masculini-
ties and Violence,* ed. Lee H. Bowker. Beverly Hills, Calif.: Sage,
1998.
———. "Tortured Consciousness: Secrets and Moralities in Brazilian Police
Violence." Unpublished study, 1995.
Huggins, Martha K., and Myriam Mesquita. "Civic Invisibility, Marginal-
ity, Moral Exclusion: The Murders of Street Youth in Brazil." In *Chil-
dren on the Streets of the Americas: Globalization, Homelessness, and
Education in the United States, Brazil, and Cuba,* ed. Rozlyn Michel-
son. London: Routledge, 1999.
———. "Scapegoating Outsiders: The Murders of Street Youth in Modern
Brazil." *Policing and Society* 5 (1996).
Human Rights Watch. *Colombia's Killer Networks.* New York: Americas
Human Rights Watch Arms Project, 1996.
Human Rights Watch/Helsinki. *Bosnia and Hercegovina: The Unindicted,
Reaping the Rewards of "Ethnic Cleansing."* Human Rights
Watch/Helsinki (Newsletter) 9, no. 1. New York: Human Rights
Watch/Helsinki, 1997.
———. *Bosnia-Hercegovina: The Continuing Influence of Bosnia's War-
lords.* Human Rights Watch/Helsinki (Newsletter) 8, no. 17. New
York: Human Rights Watch, 1996.
Ibingira, G.S.K. *African Upheavals Since Independence.* Boulder, Colo.:
Westview Press, 1980.
———. *The Forging of an African Nation: The Political and Constitutional
Evolution of Uganda from Colonial Rule to Independence,
1894–1962.* New York: Viking Press, 1973.
Ignatieff, Michael. "Human Rights: The Midlife Crisis." *New York Review
of Books,* 20 May 1999, 58–62.
Ingham, Kenneth. *The Making of Modern Uganda.* London: George Allen
& Unwin, 1958.
Inglehart, Ronald. *Modernization and Postmodernization: Cultural, Eco-
nomic, and Political Change in 43 Societies.* Princeton, N.J.: Princeton
University Press, 1997.
International Commission of Jurists. *Review,* "El Salvador," June 1978.
"Israel's Death Squads." *Middle East International,* no. 441 (8 January
1993): 19.

Izz al-Din, Ahmad Jalal. *Terrorism and Political Violence: An Egyptian Perspective*. Trans. Sanaa Ragheb. Chicago: Office of International Criminal Justice, the University of Illinois at Chicago, 1987.

Jackson, Steven, et al. "Conflict and Coercion." *Conflict Resolution* 22, no. 4 (Dec. 1978): 627–57.

Jalal, Ayesha. *Democracy and Authoritarianism in South Asia: A Comparative and Historical Perspective*. Cambridge: Cambridge University Press, 1995.

Jeffery, Anthea. *The Natal Story: Sixteen Years of Conflict*. Johannesburg: South African Institute of Race Relations, 1997.

Jellinek, Lea. *Wheel of Fortune: The History of a Poor Community in Jakarta*. Honolulu: University of Hawaii Press, 1991.

Jenkins, David. "Angels of Death." *Far Eastern Economic Review*, 29 September 1983, 29–30.

Jonas, Susanne. *The Battle for Guatemala: Rebels, Death Squads, and U.S. Power*. Boulder, Colo.: Westview Press, 1991.

Jonas, Susanne, and Edward J. McCaughan, eds. *Latin America Faces the Twenty-first Century: Reconstructing a Social Justice Agenda*. Boulder, Colo.: Westview Press, 1994.

Jonas, Susanne, and Nancy Stein. *The Construction of Democracy in Nicaragua*. San Francisco: Global Options, 1989.

Jorgensen, Jan J. *Uganda: A Modern History*. New York: St. Martin's Press, 1981.

Joseph, Richard A. *Democracy and Prebendal Politics in Nigeria: The Rise and Fall of the Second Republic*. Cambridge: Cambridge University Press, 1987.

Judah, Tim. *The Serbs: History, Myth, and the Destruction of Yugoslavia*. New Haven, Conn.: Yale University Press, 1997.

The Kabaka of Buganda. *Desecration of My Kingdom*. London: Constable, 1967.

Karugire, Samwiri R. *A Political History of Uganda*. Nairobi: Heinemann Educational Books, 1980.

Kasfir, Nelson. *The Shrinking Political Arena: Participation and Ethnicity in African Politics with a Case Study of Uganda*. Berkeley: University of California Press, 1976.

Kasozi, Abdu Basajabaka Kawalya, with the assistance and collaboration of Nakanyike Musisi and James Mukooza Sejjengo. *The Social Origins of Violence in Uganda, 1964–1985*. Montreal; Buffalo: McGill–Queen's University Press, 1994.

Kay, Bruce H. "Violent Democratization and the Feeble State Political Violence, Breakdown, and Recomposition in Peru, 1980–1995." Ph.D. diss., University of North Carolina at Chapel Hill, 1996.

Kerkvliet, Benedict J. "Patterns of Philippine Resistance and Rebellion, 1970–1986." *Pilipinas*, no. 6 (Spring 1986): 35–49.

Kessler, Richard J. *Rebellion and Repression in the Philippines.* New Haven: Yale University Press, 1989.

Kinzer, Steven. *Blood of Brothers: Life and War in Nicaragua.* New York: Anchor Books, 1991.

Kirkwood, Mike, ed. *States of Terror: Death Squads or Development?* London: Catholic Institute for International Relations, 1989.

Kohler, Gernot. "Global Apartheid." In *Toward a Just World Order,* vol. 1, ed. Richard Falk, Samuel S. Kin, and Saul H. Mendlovitz, 315–25. Boulder, Colo.: Westview Press, 1982.

Kowalewski, David. "Countermovement Vigilantism and Human Rights. A Propositional Inventory." *Crime, Law and Social Change* 25 (1996): 63–81.

———. "Vigilante Counterinsurgency and Human Rights in the Philippines: A Statistical Analysis." *Human Rights Quarterly* 12, no. 2 (1990): 246–64.

Krennerich, Michael. *Wahlen und Antiregimekriege in Zentralamerika. Typologien und Erklärungen.* Opladen: Leske und Budrich, 1996.

Krieger, Joel. *The Oxford Companion to Politics of the World.* New York: Oxford, 1993.

Krog, Antjie. *Country of My Skull.* Johannesburg: Random House, 1998.

Kuhn, Robert. *Die Vertrauenskrise der Justiz (1926–1928). Der Kampf um die "Republikanisierung" der Rechtspflege in der Weimarer Republik.* Cologne: Bundesanzeiger, 1983.

Kyemba, Henry. *A State of Blood.* New York: Paddington Press, 1977.

Lampel, Peter Martin. *Verratene Jungen. Roman.* Frankfurt a.M.: Frankfurter Societäts-Druckerei, 1929.

Langguth, A.J. *Hidden Terrors.* New York: Pantheon, 1978.

Laqueur, Walter. *Guerrilla: A Historical and Critical Study.* Boston: Little, Brown, 1977.

La Resistencia no violenta ante los regimenes salvadoreños que han utilizado el terror institucionalizado en el periodo 1972–1987. San Salvador: Universidad Centroamericana "Jose Simeon Canas," Departamento de Sociologia y Ciencias Politicas, Instituto de Derechos Humanos: Harvard University, Center for International Affaires, 1988.

Laurence, Patrick. *Death Squads: Apartheid's Secret Weapon.* London: Penguin, 1990.

Lauria Santiago, Aldo. *The Social-Historical Construction of Repression in El Salvador.* New York: Columbia University–New York University Consortium, 1991.

Lavelle, William Anthony. "State Terrorism and the Death Squad: A Study of the Phenomenon." M.A. thesis, California State University Sacramento, 1992. Reprinted as unclassified Technical Information Report by the Defense Information Agency, Alexandria, Va., 1993.

Lawyers Committee for Human Rights. *Impunity: Prosecutions of Human Rights Violations in the Philippines.* New York: Lawyers Committee for Human Rights, September 1991.

――――. *Out of Control: Militia Abuses in the Philippines.* New York: Lawyers Committee for Human Rights, 1990.

Leogrande, William. *Our Own Backyard: The United States in Central America 1977–1992.* Chapel Hill: University of North Carolina Press, 1998.

Lernoux, Penny. *Cry of the People.* New York: Doubleday, 1980.

Lev, Daniel S. "The Criminal Regime: Criminal Process in Java. In *Figures of Criminality in Indonesia, the Philippines, and Colonial Vietnam,* ed. Vincente L. Rafael, 175–92 Ithaca, N.Y.: Cornell University Southeast Asia Program, 1999.

Liddle, R. William. *Leadership and Culture in Indonesian Politics.* St. Leonards, NSW: Allen & Unwin, 1996.

Listowel, Judith. *Amin.* Dublin: IUP Books, 1973.

Lopes, Aderito. *O Esquadrão da morte. São Paulo: 1968–1971.* Lisbon: Prelo, 1973.

Lopez, George A. "National Security Ideology as an Impetus to State Violence and State Terror." In *Government Violence and Repression,* eds. Michael Stohl and George A. Lopez, 73–95. Westport, Conn.: Greenwood Press, 1986.

――――. *Terrorism and World Order.* The Whole Earth Papers, 18. New York: Global Education Associates, 1983.

Lopez, George A., and Michael Stohl, eds. *Dependence, Development, and State Repression.* New York: Greenwood Press, 1989.

Los Escuadrones de la Muerte en El Salvador. El Salvador: Editorial Jaraguá, 1994.

Low, D. A. "The Dislocated Polity." In *Uganda Now,* eds. Holger B. Hansen and Michael Twaddle. London: James Curry, 1988.

Lowenthal, Abraham F., and J. Samuel Fitch, eds. *Armies and Politics in Latin America.* Rev. ed. New York: Holmes & Meier, 1986.

Lucas, Anton. *One Soul One Struggle: Region and Revolution in Indonesia.* Sydney: Allen & Unwin, 1991.

Ludwig Boltzmann Institute for Human Rights. *Report on Ethnic Cleansing Operations in the Northeast-Bosnia City of Zvornik from April through June 1992.* Vienna: Ludwig Boltzmann Institute of Human Rights, 1992.

Lule, Yusef. *Human Rights Violations in Uganda under Obote.* Pasadena: California Institute of Technology, 1982.

Lungo Uclés, Mario. *El Salvador en los 80: Contrainsurgencia y Revolución,* 2nd ed. San Salvador: Editorial Universitaria, 1991.

Lütgemeier-Davin, Reinhold. *Pazifismus zwischen Kooperation und Konfrontation. Das Deutsche Friedenskartell in der Weimarer Republik.* Cologne: Pahl-Rugenstein, 1982.

Lyons, Beth S. "Between Nuremberg and Amnesia: The Truth and Reconciliation Commission in South Africa." *Monthly Review* 49, no. 4 (September 1997): 5–22.

Malamud Goti, Jaime E. *Game Without End: State Terror and the Politics of Justice.* Norman: University of Oklahoma Press, 1996.

Malan, Rian. "Boipatong. A Question of Spin." *Frontiers of Freedom,* Second Quarter 1999, 26–35.

Mamdani, Mahmood. *Citizen and Subject.* Princeton, N.J.: Princeton University Press, 1996.

———. *Imperialism and Fascism in Uganda.* Trenton, N.J.: Africa World Press, 1984.

———. *Politics and Class Formation in Uganda.* New York: Monthly Review Press, 1976.

Manuel, Anne, with Jemera Rone. *Nightmare Revisited 1987–88: 10th Supplement to the Report on Human Rights in El Salvador.* New York: Americas Watch Committee, September 1988.

Mao Tse Tung. *On Revolution and War.* Garden City, N.Y.: Doubleday, 1969.

Martin, David. *General Amin.* London: Faber & Faber, 1974.

Marx, Karl, and Friedrich Engels. *The Communist Manifesto.* London: Penguin, 1985.

Mason, T. David, and Dale A. Krane. "The Political Economy of Death Squads: Toward a Theory of the Impact of State-Sanctioned Terror." *International Studies Quarterly* 33 (1989): 175–198.

Mauceri, Philip. *The Impact of Violence on a Weak State: Peru, 1980–1990.* Washington, D.C.: Latin American Studies Association, 1991.

Mauch, Hans Joachim. *Nationalistische Wehrorganisationen in der Weimarer Republik. Zur Entwicklung und Ideologie des 'Paramilitarismus'.* Frankfurt a.M.: Peter Lang, 1982.

May, Ronald J. *Vigilantes in the Philippines: From Fanatical Cults to Citizens' Organizations.* Honolulu: University of Hawaii Center for Philippine Studies, 1992.

McClintock, Michael. *The American Connection.* Vol. 1, *State Terror and Popular Resistance in El Salvador.* Bath: Pitman Press, 1985.

———. *Instruments of Statecraft: U.S. Guerrilla Warfare, Counterinsurgency and Counter Terrorism 1940–1990.* New York: Pantheon, 1992.

McCoy, Alfred W. "Demystifying LIC." *Kasarinlan* 4, no. 3 (First Quarter 1989): 31–40.

———. "The Restoration of Planter Power in la Carlota City." In *From Marcos to Aquino: Local Perspective on Political Transition in the*

Philippines, ed. Benedict J. Kerkvliet and Resil B. Mojares, 105–42. Quezon City: Ateneo de Manila University Press, 1991.

Mendieta, Salvador. *Alrededor del problema unionista de Centro-América.* 2 vols. Barcelona: Tip. Maucci, 1934.

———. *La enfermedad de Centro-América.* 3 vols. Barcelona: Tip. Maucci, 1932.

Menzel, Sewall H. *Bullets Versus Ballots: Political Violence and Revolutionary War in El Salvador, 1979–1991.* New Brunswick, N.J.: Transaction Publishers, 1994.

———. *Fire in the Andes: U.S. Foreign Policy and Cocaine Politics in Bolivia and Peru.* Lanham, Md.: University Press of America, 1996.

Merkl, Peter, ed. *Political Violence and Terror: Motifs and Motivations.* Berkeley: University of California Press, 1986.

Merrett, Christopher. *A Culture of Censorship: Secrecy and Intellectual Repression in South Africa.* Claremont; Cape Town: David Philip, 1994.

Mertens, Carl. *Verschwörer und Fememörder.* Berlin: Verlag der Weltbühne, 1928.

Mignone, Emilio Fermin. *Derechos Humanos y Sociedad: el Caso Argentino.* Buenos Aires: Centro de Estudios Legales y Sociales: Ediciones del Pensamiento Nacional, 1991.

Miles, John. *Kroniek uit die doofpot. 'n polisie roman* (Chronicle of the cover-up. A police novel). Cape Town: Taurus, 1991.

Miller, Stuart Creighton. *"Benevolent Assimilation": The American Conquest of the Philippines, 1899–1903.* New Haven, Conn.: Yale University Press, 1982.

Miranda, Felipe B. *The Politicization of the Military.* State of the Nation Reports, 2. Quezon City, Philippines: UP Center for Integrative and Development Studies in cooperation with University of the Philippines Press, 1992.

Mittelman, James H. *Ideology and Politics in Uganda: From Obote to Amin.* Ithaca, N.Y.: Cornell University Press, 1975.

———. *The Uganda Coup and the Internationalization of Political Violence.* Munger Africana Library Notes, 14. Pasadena: Munger Africana Library, 1972.

Mohindra, Satish. *Terrorist Games Nations Play.* New Delhi: Lancer Publishers; Hartford, Wis.: Spantech & Lancer, 1993.

Montgomery, Tommie Sue. *Revolution in El Salvador: From Civil Strife to Civil Peace.* 2nd ed. Boulder, Colo.: Westview Press, 1995.

Moreira Alves, Maria Helena. *State and Opposition in Military Brazil.* Austin: University of Texas Press, 1985.

Morgan, J. H. "The Disarmament of Germany and After." *Quarterly Review* 242, no. 481 (October 1924): 415–57.

Moyano, María José. *Argentina's Lost Patrol: Armed Struggle 1969–1979.* New Haven: Yale University Press, 1995.

Museveni, Yoweri. *Sowing the Mustard Seed.* London: Macmillan, 1997.

Nagel, Irmela. *Fememorde und Fememordprozesse in der Weimarer Republik.* Cologne: Böhlau, 1991.

Nairn, Allan. "Behind the Death Squads." *Progressive,* May 1984, 9, 20–29.

———. "Confessions of a Death Squad Officer." *Progressive,* March 1986, 26–30.

Neier, Aryeh, and Juan Mendez. *July 19, 1983: Report on Human Rights in El Salvador.* 3rd Supplement. New York: Americas Watch Committee, 1983.

Nelson, Scott. *Iron Confederacies: Southern Railways, Klan Violence, and Reconstruction.* Chapel Hill: University of North Carolina Press, 1999.

Nobre, Carlos. *Maes de Acari: una historia de luta contra a impunidade.* Rio de Janeiro: Relume Dumara, 1994.

Nordstrom, Carolyn, and JoAnn Martin, eds. *The Paths to Domination, Resistance, and Terror.* Berkeley: University of California Press, 1992.

Nunn, Frederick M. *The Time of the Generals: Latin American Professional Militarism in World Perspective.* Lincoln: University of Nebraska Press, 1992.

Núñez, Orlando, et al. *La guerra y el campesinado en Nicaragua.* 3rd ed. Managua: CIPRES, 1998.

Nwankwo, Arthur Agwunka. *African Dictators: The Logic of Tyranny and Lessons from History.* Enugu: Fourth Dimension, 1990.

O'Malley, W. J. "Criminals, Society and Politics in Java." Unpublished paper, 1984.

Omara-Otunnu, Amii. *Politics and the Military in Uganda, 1890–1985.* New York: St. Martin's Press, 1987.

Onghokham, "The Jago in Colonial Java, Ambivalent Champion of the People." *Senri Ethnological Studies* 13 (1984): 327–44.

Organization of American States: Inter-American Commission on Human Rights. *Report on Human Rights in El Salvador.* Washington, 1978.

Osanka, Franklin M. *Modern Guerrilla Warfare.* New York: Free Press of Glencoe, 1962.

Papaioannou, Kostas, *Politike dolophonia: Thessalonike '63: hypothese Lambrake.* Athens: Ekdoseis To "Pontiki," 1993.

Paredes, Ruby R., ed. *Philippine Colonial Democracy.* Quezon City: Ateneo de Manila University Press, 1989.

Paret, Peter, and John Shy. *Guerrillas in the 1960s.* New York: Praeger, 1962.

Parry, Richard Lloyd. *What Young Men Do.* London: Granta, 1998.

Pauw, Jacques. *Into the Heart of Darkness: Confessions of Apartheid's Assassins.* Johannesburg: Jonathan Ball, 1997.

———. *In the Heart of the Whore: The Story of Apartheid's Death Squads.* Halfway House, South Africa: Southern Book Publishers, 1991.

Pemberton, John. *On the Subject of "Java."* Ithaca, N.Y.: Cornell University Press, 1995.

Penglase, Ben. *Final Justice: Police and Death Squad Homicides of Adolescents in Brazil.* New York: Human Rights Watch, 1994.

Perdue, William D. *Terrorism and the State: A Critique of Domination Through Fear.* New York: Praeger, 1989.

Petersen, Klaus. *Literatur und Justiz in der Weimarer Republik.* Stuttgart: Metzler, 1988.

Philippine Commission for Human Rights et al. *Truth Uncovered: Fact-Finding Report—Cotabato—Zamboanga del Sur May 1985.* Quezon City: Claretian Publications, 1985.

Philippine Senate Committee on Justice and Human Rights. *Report on Vigilante Groups.* Manila: Bureau of Printing, January 1988.

Phillips, Anne. *The Enigma of Colonialism: British Policy in West Africa.* London: James Currey; Indiana University Press, 1989.

Phillips, Mark. "Divide and Repress: Vigilantes and State Objectives in Crossroads." In *States of Terror: Death Squads or Development?* ed. Mike Kirkwood, 15–36. London: Catholic Institute for International Relations, 1989.

Pinheiro, Paulo Sergio. "Police and Political Crisis: The Case of the Military Police." In *Vigilantism and the State in Latin America: Essays on Extralegal Violence,* ed. Martha K. Huggins, 167–88. New York: Praeger, 1991.

Pion-Berlin, David. "The Ideological Governance of Perception in the Use of State Terror in Latin America: The Case of Argentina." In *State Organized Terror: The Case of Violent Internal Repression,* ed. P. Timothey Bushnell et al., 135–52. Boulder, Colo.: Westview Press, 1991.

———. *Of Victims and Executioners: Argentine State Terror, 1976–1983.* Notre Dame, Ind.: Helen Kellogg Institute for International Studies, University of Notre Dame, 1989.

Porter, Gareth. *The Politics of Counterinsurgency in the Philippines: Military and Political Options.* Honolulu: University of Hawaii Center for Philippine Studies, 1987.

Rafael, Vicente L., ed. *Figures of Criminality in Indonesia, the Philippines, and Colonial Vietnam.* Ithaca, N.Y.: Cornell University Southeast Asia Program, 1999.

Riley, Kevin Jack. "The implications of Colombian drug industry and death squad political violence for U.S. counternarcotics policy." Rand note, N-3605-USDP. Santa Monica, Calif.: Rand, 1993.

Rivera, Temario Campos. "Class, the State and Foreign Capital: The Politics of Philippine Industrialization, 1950–1986." Ph.D. diss., University of Wisconsin–Madison, 1991.

Robinson, Geoffrey. *The Dark Side of Paradise: Political Violence in Bali.* Ithaca, N.Y.: Cornell University Press, 1995.

Röhm, Ernst. *Geschichte eines Hochverräters.* 7th ed. Munich: F. Eher Nachf., 1934.

Ron, James. "Frontier and Ghetto: The Institutional Underpinnings of State Violence in Bosnia and Palestine." Ph.D. diss., University of California at Berkeley, 1999.

Rose, R. S. "Vigilantism and the Police in Brazil: An Exploratory Investigation." Paper presented at the International Sociological Association, Mexico City, 18 August 1982.

Rosenbaum, H. Jon, and Peter C. Sederberg. "Vigilantism, an Analysis of Establishment Violence." In *Vigilante Politics,* ed. H. Jon Rosenbaum and Peter C. Sederberg, 9–19. Philadelphia: University of Pennsylvania Press, 1976.

———, eds. *Vigilante Politics.* Philadelphia: University of Pennsylvania Press, 1976.

Rubenstein, Richard E. *Alchemists of Revolution: Terrorism in the Modern World.* New York: Basic Books, 1987.

Rubín, Paul, and Jan P. de Groot, eds. *El debate sobre la reforma agraria en Nicaragua.* Managua: INIES, 1989.

Rummel, R.J. *Death by Government.* New Brunswick, N.J.: Transaction Publishers, 1994.

Rushdie, Salman. *The Jaguar Smile.* New York: Viking, 1987.

Rutten, Rosanne. "'Mass Surrenders' in Negros Occidental: Ideology, Force and Accommodation in a Counterinsurgency Program." Unpublished paper, 4th International Philippine Studies Conference, Australian National University, 1–3 July 1992.

Ryter, Loren. "Pemuda Pancasila: The Last Loyalist Free Men of Suharto's Order?" *Indonesia* 66 (October 1998): 45–73.

Sabrow, Martin. *Der Rathenaumord: Rekonstruktion einer Verschwörung gegen die Republik von Weimar.* Munich: Oldenbourg, 1994.

Said, Edward W. *Orientalism.* New York: Vintage Books, 1979.

Salewsky, Michael. *Entwaffnung und Militärkontrolle in Deutschland 1919–1927.* Munich: Oldenbourg, 1966.

Sathyamurty T.V. *The Political Development of Uganda: 1900–1986.* Aldershot, England: Gower, 1986.

Schmid, Alex P., and Albert J. Jongman. *Political Terrorism: A New Guide to Actors, Authors, Concepts, Data Bases, Theories and Literature.* 2nd ed. Amsterdam: North-Holland Publishing Company, 1988.

Schroeder, Michael J. "Horse Thieves to Rebels to Dogs: Political Gang Violence and the State in the Western Segovias, Nicaragua, in the Time of Sandino, 1926–1934." *Journal of Latin American Studies* 28 (May 1996): 383–434.

———. "The Sandino Rebellion Revisited: Civil War, Imperialism, Popular Nationalism, and State Formation Muddied Up Together in the Segovias of Nicaragua, 1926–1934." In *Close Encounters of Empire: Writing the Cultural History of U.S.–Latin American Relations,* ed. Gilbert Joseph, Catherine LeGrand, and Ricardo Salvatore. Durham, N.C.: Duke University Press, 1998.

———. "To Defend Our Nation's Honor: Toward a Social and Cultural History of the Sandino Rebellion in Nicaragua, 1927–1934." Ph.D. diss., University of Michigan, 1993.

Schulte Nordholt, Henk. "The Jago in the Shadow: Crime and 'Order' in the Colonial State in Java." *Review of Indonesian and Malayan Affairs* 25, no. 1 (Winter 1991): 74–91.

Schulze, Hagen. *Freikorps und Republik, 1918–1920.* Boppard: H. Boldt, 1969

———. *Staat und Nation in der Europäischen Geschichte.* 2nd ed. Munich: C. H. Beck, 1995.

———. *Weimar. Deutschland 1917–1933.* 2nd ed. Berlin: Siedler Verlag, 1982.

Sederberg, Peter C. "The Phenomenology of Vigilantism in Contemporary America: An Interpretation." *Terrorism* 1, no. 3–4 (1977): 287–305.

Seegers, Anette. *The Military in the Making of Modern South Africa.* London: Tauris, 1996.

Selochan, Viberto. *The Armed Forces of the Philippines: Its Perceptions on Governing and the Prospects for the Future.* Monash University Centre of Southeast Asian Studies Working papers, 53. Clayton, Australia: Monash University Centre of Southeast Asian Studies, 1989.

———. *Could the Military Govern the Philippines?* Australian National University Strategic and Defence Studies Centre Working Paper, 160. Canberra: Strategic and Defence Studies Center, Research School of Pacific Studies, Australian National University, 1988.

Shearing. Clifford. "Reinventing Policing: Policing as Governance." In *Policing Change, Changing Police: International Perspectives,* ed. Otwin Merenin. New York: Garland, 1996.

———. "The Relation Between Public and Private Policing." In *Modern Policing,* ed. Michael Tonry and Norvil Morris. Chicago: University of Chicago Press, 1992.

Shestack, Jerome J. *The Case of the Disappeared: In Foreign Countries, "Missing Persons" are the Nightmare Victims of State Terrorism.* New York: American Bar Association Press, 1980.

Sidel, John T. "Coercion, Capital, and the Post-Colonial State: Bossism in the Postwar Philippines." Ph.D. diss., Cornell University, 1995.

Siegel, James T. *A New Criminal Type in Jakarta: Counter-Revolution Today.* Durham, N.C.: Duke University Press, 1998.

Sklar, Holly. *Washington's War on Nicaragua.* Boston: South End Press, 1988.

Skowronek, Stephen. *Building a New American State: The Expansion of National Administrative Capacities, 1877–1920.* Cambridge University Press, 1982.

Sluka, Jeffrey, ed. *Death Squad: The Anthropology of State Terror.* Philadelphia: University of Pennsylvania Press, 1999.

Smith, George Ivan. *Ghosts of Kampala.* New York: St. Martin's Press, 1980.

Snitch, Thomas H. "Terrorism and Political Assassinations: A Transnational Assessment 1968–1980." *Annals of the American Academy of Political and Social Sciences* 463 (September 1982): 54–66.

Soeharto. *Otobiografi: Pikiran, Ucapan dan Tindakan Saya.* Jakarta: Citra Lamtoro Gung Persada, 1988.

Solomon, Joel A. *Implausible Deniability: State Responsibility for Rural Violence in Mexico.* New York: Human Rights Watch, 1997.

———. *Institutional Violence: Civil Patrols in Guatemala 1993–1994.* Washington: Robert F. Kennedy Memorial Center for Human Rights, 1994.

Somoza, Anastacio. *El verdadero Sandino, o el Calvario de las Segovias.* Managua: Tip. Robelo, 1936.

Sono, Themba. *State Terrorism and Liberation Movements: The Case of South Africa.* Pretoria: Centre for Development Analysis, 1993.

Southall, Aidan. "Social Disorganization in Uganda: Before, During and After Amin." *Journal of Modern African Studies* 18, no. 4 (December 1980): 627–56.

Stanley, William. *The Protection Racket State: Elite Politics, Military Extortion, and Civil War in El Salvador.* Philadelphia: Temple University Press, 1996.

Stern, Howard. "The *Organisation Consul.*" *Journal of Modern History* 35, no. 1 (March 1963): 20–32.

Stern, Howard N. "Political Crime and Justice in the Weimar Republic." Ph.D. diss., Johns Hopkins University, 1966.

Stockwell, John. *Praetorian Guard: The U.S. Role in the New World Order.* Boston: South End Press, 1991.

Stohl, Michael. "Demystifying Terrorism: The Myths and Realities of Contemporary Political Terrorism." In *The Politics of Terrorism*, 3rd ed., ed. Michael Stohl, 1–27. New York: Marcel Dekker, 1988.

———. "The Superpowers and International Terrorism." In *Government Violence and Repression*, ed. Michael Stohl and George A. Lopez, 207–34. Westport, Conn.: Greenwood Press, 1986.

Stohl, Michael, and George A. Lopez. *The State as Terrorist: The Dynamics of Governmental Violence and Repression*. Westport, Conn.: Greenwood Press, 1984.

———. *Terrible Beyond Endurance? The Foreign Policy of State Terrorism*. New York: Geenwood Press, 1988.

———, eds. *Government Violence and Repression: An Agenda for Research*. Westport, Conn.: Greenwood Press, 1986.

Streek, Barry, ed. *Death Squads Continued—The Mad Hatter's Tea Party?* Tamboerskloof; Cape Town: South African Pressclips, 1990.

Streytler, Nico. "Policing Political Opponents: Death Squads and Cop Culture." In *Towards Justice? Crime and State Control in South Africa*, ed. Desirée Hannson and Dirk vanZyl Smit. Cape Town: Oxford University Press, 1990.

Taussig, Michael. *The Nervous System*. London: Routledge, 1992.

Terrorism and the Violence of the State. Working Papers in European Criminology, 1. Hamburg: European Group for the Study of Deviance and Social Control, 1979.

Terrorismo de estado: 692 responsables: programa de documentacion, estudios y publicaciones. Buenos Aires: El Centro 1986.

Theweleit, Klaus. *Male Fantasies*. Trans. Erica Carter, Stephen Conway, and Chris Turner. 2 vols. Minneapolis: University of Minnesota Press, 1989.

Thiele, Leslie Paul. *Thinking Politics: Perspectives in Ancient, Modern, and Postmodern Political Theory*. Chatham, N.J.: Chatham House Publishers, 1997.

Thoolen, Hans, ed. *Indonesia and the Rule of Law: Twenty Years of "New Order" Government*. London: Frances Pinter, 1987.

Tilly, Charles. *Coercion, Capital, and European States, AD 990–1990*. London: Basil Blackwell, 1990.

———. "War Making and State Making as Organized Crime." In *Bringing the State Back In*, ed. Peter Evans et al., 169–91. New York: Cambridge University Press, 1985.

Titley, Brian. *Dark Age: The Political Odyssey of Emperor Bokassa*. Montreal: McGill–Queen's University Press, 1997.

Tobler, Hans Werner, and Peter Waldmann, eds. *Staatliche und Parastaatliche Gewalt in Lateinamerika*. Frankfurt a. M.: Vervuert Verlag, 1991.

Tooley, T. Hunt. *National Identity and Weimar Germany. Upper Silesia and the Eastern Border, 1918–1922.* Lincoln: University of Nebraska Press, 1997.

Trelease, Allen W. *White Terror: The Klu Klux Klan, Conspiracy and Southern Reconstruction.* New York: Harper & Row, 1971.

Truth and Reconciliation Commission. *Truth and Reconciliation Commission of South Africa Report.* 5 vols. Cape Town: Juta, 1998.

Tulchin, Joseph S., ed., with Gary Bland. *Is There a Transition to Democracy in El Salvador?* Boulder, Colo.: Lynne Rienner, 1992.

Uekert, Brenda K. *Rivers of Blood: A Comparative Study of Government Massacres.* Westport, Conn.: Praeger, 1995.

United Nations. *The United Nations and El Salvador 1990–1995.* Blue Book Series, vol. 4. New York: United Nations, Department of Public Information, 1995.

———. *Final Report of the U.N. Commission of Experts Established Pursuant to Security Council Resolution 780 (1992).* New York: United Nations, 1994.

United States Department of State. *The United States and Nicaragua: A Survey of Relations from 1909–1932.* Washington, D.C.: Government Printing Office, 1932.

Uzoigwe, G.N., ed. *Uganda: The Dilemma of Nationhood.* New York: NOK Publishers International, 1982.

Van Bruinessen, Martin. "Turkey's Death Squads." *Middle East Report* 26 no. 2 (April-June 1996): 20–23.

Vanden, Harry E. "Terrorism, Law, and State Policy in Central America: The Eighties." *New Political Science* 18/19 (Fall/Winter 1990).

Van den Muijzenberg, Otto D. "Political Mobilization and Violence in Central Luzon." *Modern Asian Studies* 7, no. 4 (1973): 691–705.

Van der Kroef, Justus M. "'Petrus': Patterns of Prophylactic Murder in Indonesia." *Asian Survey* 25, no. 7 (July 1985): 745–59.

———. "The Philippine Vigilantes: Devotion and Disarray." *Contemporary Southeast Asia* 10, no. 2 (September 1988): 163–81.

———. "The Philippines: Day of the Vigilantes," *Asian Survey* 28, no. 6 (June 1988): 631–49.

———. "Terrorism by Authority: the Case of the Death Squads of Indonesia and the Philippines." *Current Research on Peace and Violence* 10, no. 4 (1987): 143–58.

Van Rooyen, Johann. *Hard Right: The New White Power in South Africa.* London: I.B.Tauris, 1994.

Verbitsky, Horacio. *The Flight: Confessions of an Argentine Dirty Warrior.* New York: The New Press, 1996.

Vujačić, Veljko. Communism and Nationalism in Russia and Serbia. Ph.D. diss., University of California at Berkeley, 1995.

Wade, Wyn Craig. *The Fiery Cross: The Ku Klux Klan in America.* New York: Simon & Schuster, 1987.

Waite, Robert G.L. *Vanguard of Nazism: The Free Corps Movement in Postwar Germany, 1918–1923.* Reprint. Cambridge, Mass.: Harvard University Press, 1970.

Watts, Meredith W. *Xenophobia in United Germany: Generations, Modernization, and Ideology.* New York: St. Martin's Press, 1997.

Wehler, Hans-Ulrich. *Modernisierungstheorie und Geschichte.* Göttingen: Vandenhoeck & Ruprecht, 1975.

Werz, Nicholas. "Die ideologische Wurzeln der 'Doktrin der nationalen Sicherheit' in Lateinamerika." In *Staatliche und Parastaatliche Gewalt in Lateinamerika,* ed. Hans Werner Tobler and Peter Waldmann. Frankfurt a. M.: Vervuert Verlag, 1991.

Weschler, L., "A Miracle, a Universe II." *New Yorker,* 1 June 1987, 227.

White, Stephen K. *Political Theory and Postmodernism.* Cambridge: Cambridge University Press, 1991.

Whitfield, Teresa. *Paying the Price: Ignacio Ellacuría and the Murdered Jesuits of El Salvador.* Philadelphia: Temple University Press, 1995.

Williams, Paul, and Norman Cigar. *War Crimes and Individual Responsibility: A Prima Facie Case for the Indictment of Slobodan Milosevic.* Washington, D.C.: Balkan Institute, 1996.

Williams, Philip J., and Knut Walter. *Militarization and Demilitarization in El Salvador's Transition to Democracy.* Pittsburgh: University of Pittsburgh Press, 1997.

Winter, Gordon. *Inside BOSS: South Africa's Secret Police. An Ex-Spy's Dramatic and Shocking Expose.* Harmondsworth, U.K.: Penguin, 1981.

Witness for Peace. *What We Have Seen and Heard: The Effect of Contra Attacks Against Nicaragua.* Washington, D.C., 1985.

Wolpin, Miles D. *State Terrorism and Death Squads in the New World Order.* Peace Research Reviews XII, no. 3. Dundas, Canada: Peace Research Institute, 1992.

———. "State Terrorism and Death Squads in the New World Order." In *The Culture of Violence,* ed. Kumar Rupesinghe and Marcial Rubio C., 198–236. Tokyo: United Nations University Press, 1994.

Woodward, Susan. *Balkan Tragedy: Chaos and Dissolution After the Cold War.* Washington, D.C.: Brookings, 1995.

Wünderich, Volker. *Sandino, una biografía política.* Managua: Nueva Nicaragua, 1995.

Zarnow, Gottfried [Ewald Moritz]. *Gefesselte Justiz—Politische Bilder aus deutscher Gegenwart.* 2nd ed. Munich: J. F. Lehmann, 1930.

ABOUT THE CONTRIBUTORS

CYNTHIA J. ARNSON is Assistant Director of the Woodrow Wilson Center's Latin American Program. She is editor of *Comparative Peace Processes in Latin America* (Woodrow Wilson Center Press and Stanford University Press, 1999), and author of *Crossroads: Congress, the President, and Central America, 1976–1993* (Penn State Press, 1993), as well as numerous articles on Central America, Colombia, and U.S. policy in Latin America. Previously, she was Associate Director of Human Rights Watch/Americas, and, as a consultant, coauthored several of Americas Watch's earliest reports on El Salvador. She was Assistant Professor of international relations at the American University's School of International Service and served as a senior foreign policy aide in the House of Representatives during the Carter and Reagan administrations. She has a Ph.D. from the Johns Hopkins University School of Advanced International Studies

ARTHUR D. BRENNER is Assistant Professor of History at Siena College in Loudonville, N.Y., where he teaches modern world, European, and German history. He received his Ph.D. in Modern European History from Columbia University in 1993. His book, *"One-Man Party": The Weimar Pacifist and Professor Emil J. Gumbel*, will be published in the series Studies in Central European Histories by Humanities Press. He also edited the microfilm of *The Emil J. Gumbel Collection: Political Papers of an Anti-Nazi Scholar in Weimar and Exile, 1914–1966* (University Publications of America, 1990).

BRUCE B. CAMPBELL teaches German Studies and History at the College of William and Mary. He earned a Ph.D. from the University of Wisconsin–Madison and has studied in Freiburg, Hamburg, and Berlin. He focuses on Germany in the twentieth century, and on the Weimar Republic in particular. His research specialties include paramilitarism, National Socialism (particularly through biography), the German youth movement, the German far right, and the political use of culture. His publications include *The SA Generals and the Rise of Nazism* (University of Kentucky Press, 1998) and articles on the SA and the German youth movement. He is currently writing a biography of Gerhard Rossbach, a paramilitary and cultural figure in Weimar Germany, and a political and cultural history of amateur radio in Germany and the United States.

ROBERT CRIBB teaches Southeast Asian History at the University of Queensland in Brisbane, Australia. He writes on modern Indonesian history, especially on the place of violence in the political process. His publications include *Gangsters and Revolutionaries: The Jakarta People's Militia and the Indonesian Revolution, 1945–1949* (1991), *Modern Indonesia: a History Since 1945* (with Colin Brown, 1995), and (ed.) *The Indonesian Killings of 1965–1966: Studies from Java and Bali* (1990). He was director of the Nordic Institute of Asian Studies in Copenhagen 1997–99 and has taught at universities in Australia and the Netherlands.

PATRICIA GOSSMAN is a Public Policy Scholar at the Woodrow Wilson Center on a research grant funded by the U.S. Institute of Peace. She was Senior Researcher at Human Rights Watch, an independent human rights organization, where she did field research on human rights in Afghanistan, Bangladesh, India, Nepal, Pakistan, and Sri Lanka. She received her Ph.D. in South Asian studies from the University of Chicago in 1995. Her doctoral study of communal violence in pre-partition India, *Riots and Victims,* was published by Westview Press in 1999. In 1996 she received a fellowship from the John D. and Catherine T. MacArthur Foundation for research on obstacles to restoring civil society in Kashmir. She is currently completing a book on the study.

KEITH GOTTSCHALK teaches Political Studies at the University of the Western Cape, South Africa. He is a member of the African Association of Political Science and the South African Political Studies Association. He is the author of more than two dozen scholarly publications, including "Restructuring the Colonial State: Pretoria's Strategy in Namibia," in G. Toetemeyer et al., eds., *Namibia in Perspective* (Windhoek, 1987), and "The Political Economy of Health Care in Colonial Namibia 1915–1961," *Social Science and Medicine* 26 (1988), and is a regular contributor to *African Contemporary Record.* His creative publications include over 100 published poems, including a collection, *Emergency Poems.*

EVA-LOTTA HEDMAN is a Lecturer in the School of Politics and the Deputy Director of the Insitute for Asia-Pacific Studies at the University of Nottingham. Having published several articles on the politics of civil society and social movements in Southeast Asia, she recently completed a work on civil-military relations in the Philippines (Routledge, forthcoming).

MARTHA K. HUGGINS, Roger Thayer Stone Professor of Sociology at Union College in Schenectady, New York, has conducted research and published several books and numerous articles on crime, the police, and extralegal violence in Brazil over the past 24 years. Her most recent book, *Political Policing: The United States and Latin America* (Duke University Press, 1998), was awarded the 1999 Michael Hindeling Prize of the American Society of Criminology for the best book in criminology. Huggins is writing a book on torturers and murderers from Brazil's military period (with Mika Haritos-Fatouros and Philip Zimbardo).

EDWARD KANNYO earned his Ph.D. in Political Science from Yale University. He has taught and written widely about African politics and human rights issues. He has worked with international human rights organizations and the United Nations on issues of human rights promotion and protection. He is coauthor of *Presidents and Foreign Policy* (State University of New York Press, 1997). He is currently Adjunct Professor of African History at the Rochester Institute of Technology.

JAMES RON is Assistant Professor of Sociology at Johns Hopkins University in Baltimore, Md. He earned his Ph.D. in sociology from the University of California at Berkeley in 1999. He has worked extensively for Human Rights Watch, investigating abuses in Israel, Palestine, Nigeria, Turkey, and Kosovo, as well as for the International Committee of the Red Cross and CARE International. He is the author of three lengthy reports on Israeli and Turkish human rights abuses, and is now working on a book comparing Serbian and Israeli methods of repression. His most recent article on state violence appeared in *International Organization*.

MICHAEL J. SCHROEDER received his Ph.D. in History in 1993 from the University of Michigan. His article "Horse Thieves to Rebels to Dogs: Political Gang Violence and the State in the Western Segovias, Nicaragua, 1926–1934" (*Journal of Latin American Studies* 28, May 1996) was awarded Honorable Mention for the 1997 Conference on Latin American History Prize. Currently completing a book manuscript, "Tragedy, Redemption, Power: The Sandino Rebellion in Las Segovias and Nicaragua, 1926–1934," he is Assistant Professor of History at Eastern Michigan University.

INDEX